Media Law

This book is part of the Peter Lang Media and Communication list.
Every volume is peer reviewed and meets
the highest quality standards for content and production.

PETER LANG
New York • Bern • Berlin
Brussels • Vienna • Oxford • Warsaw

Ashley Messenger

Media Law

A Practical Guide
(Revised Edition)

PETER LANG
New York • Bern • Berlin
Brussels • Vienna • Oxford • Warsaw

Library of Congress Cataloging-in-Publication Data

Names: Messenger, Ashley G., author.
Title: Media law: a practical guide / Ashley Messenger.
Description: Revised edition. | New York: Peter Lang, 2019.
Includes indexes.
Identifiers: LCCN 2019007946 | ISBN 978-1-4331-6798-0 (paperback: alk. paper)
ISBN 978-1-4331-6799-7 (ebook pdf) | ISBN 978-1-4331-6800-0 (epub)
ISBN 978-1-4331-6801-7 (mobi)
Subjects: LCSH: Mass media—Law and legislation—United States.
Classification: LCC KF2805 .M47 2019 | DDC 343.7309/9—dc23
LC record available at https://lccn.loc.gov/2019007946
DOI 10.3726/b15502

Bibliographic information published by **Die Deutsche Nationalbibliothek**.
Die Deutsche Nationalbibliothek lists this publication in the "Deutsche
Nationalbibliografie"; detailed bibliographic data are available
on the Internet at http://dnb.d-nb.de/.

The first edition of this book, *A Practical Guide to Media Law* (2014),
was published by Pearson Education, Inc.

The paper in this book meets the guidelines for permanence and durability
of the Committee on Production Guidelines for Book Longevity
of the Council of Library Resources.

© 2019 Peter Lang Publishing, Inc., New York
29 Broadway, 18th floor, New York, NY 10006
www.peterlang.com

Printed in the United States of America

May this book serve well its readers and the interests of Truth

Table of Contents

List of Tables and Figures xvii

Preface. xix

Acknowledgements xxi

PART I

INTRODUCTORY MATERIAL

1 Court Systems, Citation, and Procedure 3

   The Two Court Systems 3

      In Which System Should a Case Be Filed? 5

   The Two Kinds of Cases 6

   How to Find "Law" and Understand Citation Systems. 7

      Constitutions 8

      Statutes 8

      Regulations 8

      Executive Orders 8

      Cases 8

   Why Does All This Information Matter? 10

   Practical Conclusions 11

2 First Amendment–Theory and Practice 12

   The First Amendment and the Scope of Its Coverage 12

   Why the U.S. Started With a Presumption of Freedom 14

   Theories of the First Amendment 15

First Amendment Doctrine. 16

First Amendment Rights 19

Practical Effects 20

Practical Conclusions 21

PART II

WHAT CAN YOU BE SUED FOR? (AND ARE THERE RELATED CRIMINAL CHARGES?)

3   Libel: The Risk of Criticism, Insults, and Trash Talk 25

Elements. 26

Is the Statement Defamatory? 27

What Kind of Statements Are Defamatory? 27

Statements Can Be Obviously Defamatory or Not Obviously So 28

Defamation by Omission 28

Headlines and Captions 29

Is the Statement False? 30

What Constitutes a "False" Statement? 30

The Burden of Proof 31

The Exception: True Statements As a Basis for Libel in Massachusetts. 31

Is There a Factual Assertion? 32

What Kind of Statements Are Typically Protected? 32

Jokes 32

Rhetoric and Hyperbole. 33

Insults and Other Poorly Defined Terms 33

Aesthetic Judgments and Reviews. 34

Speculation 34

Conclusions 34

When Might "Opinion" Not Be Protected? 35

Liar Libel and the #MeToo Movement. 38

Does the Statement Identify a Valid Plaintiff? 38

Who Is a Valid Plaintiff? 39

Ways a Person Can Be Identified by a Statement. 39

Was the Statement Published? 40

Did the Defendant Act With the Requisite Level of Fault?. 41

What Is Negligence? 43

What Exactly Constitutes Actual Malice? 44

Which Standard Applies to Whom? 45

Did the Plaintiff Suffer Damages? 47

How Do the Elements Work Together? 48

Defenses. 51

The "Libel-Proof" Plaintiff. 51

Statute of Limitations 51

Absolute Privilege for Statements Made in the Official Course of Government Business 52

Consent. 52
Fair & Accurate Report Privilege 52
Neutral Reportage 53
Wire Service Defense. 55
Common Interest Privilege 56
Anti-SLAPP Statutes 56
Retraction Statutes and Other Statutory Defenses 57
The SPEECH Act 57
Related Claims 57
False Light 57
Intentional Infliction of Emotional Distress (IIED) 58
Criminal Libel 59
Additional Practical Considerations for Journalists 60
Ethical Considerations. 60
The Risk of Hoaxes 60
Corrections, Clarifications, and Retractions. 61
How Long Should I Keep My Notes? 62
Prior Restraints 62
Practical Conclusions 63
4   Privacy: Publishing Private, Embarrassing, or Sensitive Information 65
Publication of Private Facts. 66
Is the Information Private?. 67
To Whom Was the Information Disclosed? 69
Was the Disclosure "Highly Offensive to a Reasonable Person"?. 70
Was the Information Newsworthy or of Legitimate Public Concern?. 70
Does the Information Concern or Derive From the Kind of Thing That Is Typically "News"?. . . 70
Is the Person Involved a Celebrity or Otherwise Noteworthy?. 71
Is It the Person Who Is Newsworthy or the Topic That Is Newsworthy? 71
Is There a Sufficient Nexus Between the Private Information Disclosed and the
Newsworthiness of the Person or Event at Issue?. 72
What Happens When a Person Voluntarily Reveals Facts About Themselves
That Involve Others?. 73
What Is Not Newsworthy? 75
Are There Any Additional Defenses? 75
The Overlap of Ethical and Legal Issues When Posting "Private" Information Online 76
Trade Secrets: A Version of "Privacy" for Businesses 77
Practical Conclusions 78
5   Publicity: Using Someone's Name or Likeness. 80
What Is the Right of Publicity?. 80
What Does It Mean to "Appropriate" Someone's Name or Likeness? 81
What Constitutes a "Commercial Purpose"?. 83
Is the Right of Publicity Descendible?. 88

    Are There Any Defenses to Publicity Claims? 89

    Practical Conclusions 89

6   Copyright: Issues With Creating Content or Using Other People's Content 91

    Types of Intellectual Property 91

    Principles of Copyright Law 93

        What Is Copyrightable (And What Is Not Copyrightable)? 93

        How Does One Obtain a Copyright? 96

        What Does a Copyright Protect and for How Long? 97

        If a Copyright Holder Sues for Infringement, What Do They Need to Prove? 99

        Under What Conditions Can Someone Use Copyrighted Material? 99

            License 100

            Alternative License 101

            Fair Use 102

            Other Exceptions 108

        Are There Any Defenses to Copyright Infringement Claims? 108

        Is It Copyright Infringement to Link or Embed Material Online? 108

        What Are the Consequences of Copyright Infringement? 109

        What Is the Relationship of Copyright Law to "Moral Rights" and Plagiarism? 110

            Moral Rights 110

            Plagiarism 110

            Do I Have to Credit the Creator of a Work If I Use It? 110

    The "Hot News" Doctrine 111

    Practical Conclusions 111

7   Trademarks: The Use of Product Names and Logos 113

    Trademarks 113

        What Are the Requirements for a Trademark? 114

            Is the Mark Already Taken? 114

            Is the Mark Sufficiently Distinctive? 115

            The Controversy Around Immoral and Scandalous Marks 116

        How Long Will Protection Last? 117

        What Is Infringement? 117

    What Is Dilution? 119

    What Is Cybersquatting? 120

    Practical Conclusions 121

8   Use of Photos, Illustrations, and Other Images 123

    Is the Use of the Photo Legally and Ethically Proper? 123

        Libel or False Light 124

            Intentional Distortion 124

            Juxtaposition 125

            Conceptual but Not Factual Match 125

            Accidental Mismatch 126

        Privacy 127

Are There Special Considerations When Pictures Feature Children? 129

Right of Publicity 129

IIED 130

Do You Have the Rights Required to Use the Photo? 131

Per Use License 131

Agency Photos. 131

Publicity Photos. 132

Online Photos 132

Fair Use 132

Can I Use This Clip? 135

Who Should Be Contacted If Permission Is Required? 135

Can You Be Prosecuted or Fined? 136

Sexual Images of Children 137

Classified Images 137

Images of Stamps and Currency. 137

Regulation of Image-editing Software 137

Practical Conclusions 138

9   Use of Music. 139

Different Kinds of Rights in Music. 140

Getting the Right License for the Use. 141

Fair Use 144

Other Provisions Related to the Use of Music Online. 146

Practical Options for Using Music 147

Practical Conclusions 147

10 Negligence Claims Against the Media: Content That May Result in Personal Injury 149

What Is Negligence? 150

How Does Negligence Apply to Copycats? 150

How Does Negligence Apply to Encouragement and Advice? 151

How Does Negligence Apply to Incorrect, Incomplete, or Otherwise Harmful Information? 152

How Does Negligence Apply to Other Media-Related Harm? 153

Practical Conclusions 154

PART III

HOW DOES ONE GET INFORMATION TO PUBLISH?

11 Is There a Right of Access to Information, Places, or Events? 157

General Rules With Respect to Whether You Have a Right of Access to Information 158

Private Materials 158

Federal Agencies 159

What Does FOIA Cover? 159

Making a FOIA Request. 160

Will the Requester Obtain the Requested Documents? 161

What Can You Do If the Government Ignores or Denies Your Request? 166

Sunshine Act of 1976 166

Federal Legislature 167

State Laws 168

Judicial Branch 169

    Access to Criminal Proceedings 170

    Access to Civil Proceedings 172

    Access to Juvenile Proceedings 172

    Access to Military Proceedings 172

    Access to Alternative Dispute Resolution (ADR) 173

    Access to Court Records and Electronic Court Records 173

    Access to Discovery Documents 174

    Pretrial Publicity and Gag Orders 174

    Use of Cameras and Other Technology in Courtrooms 176

    Social Media Use in the Courtroom 177

    Access to Juror Names and Identities 177

    Access to Jurors (Prohibitions on Juror Contact) 178

    How Does the Press Challenge a Restrictive Order? 179

Specific Laws That Might Affect Your Ability to Access Particular Types of Information 179

  The Privacy Act of 1974 179

  The Family Educational Rights and Privacy Act 180

  The Driver's Privacy Protection Act 180

  The Health Insurance Portability and Accountability Act 181

Rules That Govern Access to Places and Events 181

  Is There a Right of Access to News Scenes? 181

  Is There a Right of Access to Press Conferences? 182

  Is There a Right of Access to Government Social Media Accounts? 183

  Is There a Right of Access to Prisons? 184

  Is There an Enforceable Right to Take Photographs or Use Video Cameras in Public

  Places or at Public Meetings or Events? 184

Practical Conclusions 185

12 Can One Be Sued or Prosecuted for Gathering News? 187

Going on Property (Trespass) 188

Misrepresenting Oneself 189

Audio Recordings and Eavesdropping 189

Taking Photos/Video 191

  Intrusion Into Seclusion 191

  Failure to Obey Reasonable Orders by Police and Security 192

  Violation of Criminal Prohibitions on Taking Photos and Video of Certain Federal

  Facilities Relating to National Security 194

Using Hidden Cameras or Microphones 194

  Ag-Gag Laws: Does the First Amendment Protect Clandestine Investigations

  of the Agricultural Industry? 195

Accessing Emails, Voicemails, or Secure Electronic Systems; or Using Passwords, Badges,

or Other Security Materials 196

Scraping, Bots, and Other Technology-based Newsgathering 197

Looking Through or Taking Someone's Belongings. 197

Violating Ordinary Criminal Laws. 198

Getting Access to Subjects or Sources 198

Making Promises of Confidentiality 199

Practical Conclusions 199

PART IV

HOW DOES THE GOVERNMENT REGULATE OR INTERFERE WITH SPEECH?

13 Efforts to Subpoena or Search Journalists 203

Is There a "Reporters Privilege"? 203

Is There an Applicable Shield Law? 205

Is There Protection Based on Common Law? 206

Are There Procedural Rules That Might Apply? 208

What Happens If There Is No Applicable Privilege? 208

Practical Ways to Protect Sources. 209

Search Warrants Against Journalists 210

Practical Conclusions 211

14 Punishing or Restricting Protests and Other Public Speech 212

Will the First Amendment Protect Dissemination of "Dangerous" Ideas or Beliefs? 212

Where or How Can Ideas Be Disseminated? 214

Public Forums 215

Time/Place/Manner (TPM) Restrictions 216

The Internet as a Public Forum 218

Can Particular Methods of Expression Be Prohibited? 219

Profanity, Fighting Words, and Other Offensive Speech. 219

Symbolic Speech 220

Practical Conclusions 221

15 Punishing or Restricting Sensitive or Offensive Topics. 222

Publication or Possession of Classified Information or Matters That Affect National Security. 223

Attempts to Stop Publication. 223

Criminal Prosecution. 224

Spying on the Media 227

Hate Speech 227

Can the Government Punish Hate Speech? 228

Can Private Entities Punish Someone for Hate Speech? 232

Can a Speaker Be Civilly Liable in a Lawsuit Based on Hate Speech? 232

Sexual Content 233

Obscenity and Indecency. 233

Child Pornography 236

Regulation of "Revenge Porn" 236

Civil Lawsuits 237

Violent Content 237

Threats 238

Can Emoji Be a Threat? 240

Lies. 241

Practical Conclusions 242

16 Regulating Political Speech, Elections, and Campaigns 244

The Constitutionality of Campaign Laws 244

Anonymity. 247

Right of Reply Laws 247

False Statement Laws 248

Practical Conclusions 250

17 Regulating Advertisements/Promotions/Marketing 252

Issues to Consider for Advertising Goods and Services 252

Government Regulation 253

False or Misleading Statements 255

Regulation of Endorsements and "Influencers" 256

Other Issues Relating to the Content of the Ad 256

Issues for Those Who Accept Advertising 257

Liability for False or Harmful Advertising 257

Liability for Discriminatory Housing Ads 257

Refusal of Ads 258

Ethical Issues With Native Advertising. 259

Lotteries, Contests, Prizes, and Other Promotional Activities 259

Practical Conclusions 261

18 Television and Radio—FCC Regulation 263

What Is the FCC and What Does It Do? 263

What Kinds of Entities Are Subject to FCC Regulation? 264

What Kinds of Regulations Can the FCC Enforce? 265

Indecency 266

Profanity 266

The Fairness Doctrine and Right of Reply 266

Political Elections 267

Children's Programming 267

Other Advertising Regulations. 268

Other Content Regulations 268

Emergency Alert Tones 269

Complaints Regarding Broadcast Content. 269

What Are the Issues Pertaining to Public Broadcasting? 270

Political Opinions 271

Editorial Discretion 271

Sponsorship. 271

Can the FCC Regulate the Internet?. 271

Practical Conclusions 273

19 Special Classes of Speakers. 274

Students. 274

Government Employees 277

Speakers Whose Speech Is Government Funded. 278

Practical Conclusions 280

PART V

WHAT PRACTICAL ISSUES ARE RELATED TO MEDIA LAW?

20 How the Internet Has Affected Publishing and the Law 283

Terms of Service. 284

Privacy Policies. 285

The GDPR (General Data Protection Regulation) 286

Gathering Information From Children. 287

Immunity From Claims. 288

Speaking Anonymously 291

International Aspects of Publishing Online. 293

Foreign Censorship 294

Traditional Torts and Claims. 294

Incitement of Racial or Religious Hatred 295

Protection of Cultural Values 296

Protection of Government Interests 296

Jurisdiction 297

Geo-Filtering and Other Potential Remedies 299

Cyberbullying, Cyberharrassment, and Cyberstalking. 299

Social Media. 300

Frequently Asked Questions About Social Media and the Law. 301

Practical Conclusions 304

21 Practical Issues Related to Media Law 305

Non-legal Consequences/Considerations 305

Business Consequences 306

Death Threats 306

Private Censorship. 307

Assessing Risk. 308

Media Liability Insurance. 308

Journalism Ethics 309

The Relationship Between Legal and Ethical Considerations 309

An Overview of the Principles of Journalism Ethics. 313

The Difference Between Ethics and Self-Censorship 315

Practical Conclusions 315

Case Index. 317

Subject Index 327

Tables and Figures

Table 1.1:	The Two Court Systems	4
Table 1.2:	The Two Kinds of Cases	6
Table 1.3:	Case Citations	9
Table 3.1:	Who Is a Valid Plaintiff?	39
Table 3.2:	Classification of Libel Plaintiffs	46
Table 6.1:	Differences Between Copyright and Trademark Law	92
Table 9.1:	Required Permissions for the Use of Music	144
Table 14.1:	Development of U.S. Supreme Court Opinions on "Dangerous" Speech	213
Table 14.2:	Types of Public Forums	215
Table 16.1:	Developments in Campaign Finance Regulation	245
Table 18.1:	Arguments For and Against Net Neutrality	272
Figure 1.1:	The Federal Circuits	4
Figure 2.1:	Evaluating First Amendment Rights	19
Figure 11.1:	Understanding Whether a Right of Access to Information Exists	158
Figure 21.1:	The Relationship Between Law and Ethics	312

Preface

This book is written from a somewhat unique point of view. I am a practicing media lawyer, in-house with a national news organization, and I also happen to teach media law in journalism school. As an in-house lawyer, I have the opportunity to see how journalists do their jobs and the issues they actually face in their day-to-day workflow. I read court opinions on First Amendment and media law topics, but I am also sensitive to how the principles from those cases need to be applied in real life, to the realities of newsgathering and communication.

This book is intended to help non-lawyers understand the legal issues involved in modern communications and journalism. It is particularly useful for future journalists, who need to be trained in the legal issues that will affect their work; but it is also an excellent guide for anyone who communicates in any capacity: tweeting, Facebooking, commenting, blogging, posting photos, managing public relations, running a website, etc. It's a training manual for the real world of communications.

I initially wrote this book to address some specific challenges I encountered while teaching media law to journalism students (or non-lawyers, generally). The main challenge is that, without a law school background, it can be difficult to understand some of the more subtle aspects of the cases and how to apply them to various factual scenarios. Issue-spotting can be challenging; students can be confused about the difference between civil and criminal principles; and procedural issues tend to create a lot of confusion. Although I have tried to provide students with the information they need, I have found that there is simply not enough time in one semester to teach the necessary background information and also teach the substantive legal principles that make up the body of media law. To overcome the students' lack of legal background, I have found that it is useful to completely reorganize the way the subject is taught. Instead of "thinking like a lawyer," I think like a journalist. In other words, I remove the things that are confusing, like issue-spotting, and supply the context to make legal principles applicable to the things journalists do.

I also divide the subject matter into themes that are easy to grasp: how people get sued, how to gather information, how the government interferes with speech, and other practical issues that are related to media law. I have found this organizational structure helps solve the problem of students getting confused about when certain claims are applicable to a particular factual scenario.

The beginning of each chapter provides a checklist of issues that might arise out of the topic covered; the remainder of the chapter explains the legal theories behind those issues and how they apply to various fact patterns. The book discusses cases to illustrate how the principles have been applied in real-life scenarios; however, the case descriptions are brief because the point is not to provide a full examination of the legal theories underlying the arguments, but to show how the legal principles can produce different outcomes based on different sets of facts. Students can supplement their knowledge by finding the court opinions online and reading them.

The law is not static; it is dynamic. Conversations about law should be equally dynamic, incorporating what is historically significant with the practical realities of the present situation. This book tries to balance all the competing interests in a way that will resonate with users and prompt thoughtful consideration of the kinds of issues that generate legal controversy.

Disclaimer

The purpose of this book is to discuss how legal issues arise in the context of media or communications. It illustrates general legal principles with examples of how courts have decided cases in the past and draws general conclusions about what courts tend to do. However, the book should not be construed as providing legal advice. Any person who is faced with a legal issue should consult their own lawyer for advice specific to their factual situation. One thing this book should demonstrate is that the outcomes of any case will be highly dependent on the specific facts presented and the law of the applicable jurisdiction. Therefore, the general information provided herein should not be interpreted as suggesting that there would be any particular outcome in any particular case. This book is for general informational and educational purposes only. Consult a lawyer if you have specific questions or concerns.

Acknowledgements

I would like to thank many people for their suggestions for this edition of the textbook: John Zucker, Micah Ratner, Adam Marshall, Katie Townsend, Ruth Hochberger, Patrick File, and Carolyn Schurr Levin. Special thanks to Griffin Ferre for research assistance with portions of this edition.

I would also like to thank Pearson Education, Inc. for publishing the first edition of the book, and, of course, Peter Lang Publishing, Inc. for publishing this revised edition.

There are so many people who have offered encouragement and support over the years—too many to list here in full, but I am grateful for them all. Special thanks to Lucy Dalglish, Gregg Leslie, Kyu Youm, George Freeman, Barbara Wall, Len Niehoff, Bruce Brown, Lincoln Bandlow, Charles Glasser, John Watson, Wendell Cochran, Amy Eisman, Chris Johnson, Angie Holan, Terri Minatra, Joyce Slocum, Brian Duffy, Peter Dwoskin, Marty Krall, American University School of Communication, University of Michigan Law School, the professors who have adopted my book, all the reporters and editors with whom I have worked, and my friends and colleagues at NPR for their support and/or opportunities that have been provided to me, without which this book could never have existed.

Thanks to my son, Grayson, for his patience, thoughtfulness, and the suggestion that I reference the copyrightability of dance moves in Fortnite, and to all my friends who help me be my best (you know who you are).

Finally, I am, as always, grateful for my students and interns. I have learned at least as much from them as they have learned from me.

PART I

Introductory Material

CHAPTER 1

Court Systems, Citation, and Procedure

There is some basic background information about the legal system that is necessary to understand the rest of the information in this book. This chapter outlines such material, including:

1. The two court systems used in the U.S. and how they relate to one another

2. The two primary kinds of cases: civil and criminal

3. The different sources of "law" and how to find them

4. The concept of precedent, which is why understanding case law matters

The Two Court Systems

The United States has two court systems: federal and state. These systems are separate but symmetrical. Each system has trial courts, appellate courts (meaning a court to which there is an automatic right of appeal), and a supreme court (meaning the highest level court to which an appeal is possible within the system).

In the federal system, the trial courts are called District Courts. They are organized by state. Some states are their own district, others are divided into multiple districts. So, for example, there is a District Court for the District of New Mexico, which is the federal trial court for the entire state of New Mexico. Virginia has two federal trial courts: the Eastern District of Virginia and the Western District of Virginia, each serving as the federal trial court for a portion of the state. The number of District Courts a state will have will depend on its population.

Table 1.1: The Two Court Systems.

The Federal Court System	The State Court System
U.S. Supreme Court	State supreme court
U.S. Court of Appeals (Circuit Courts)	State appellate court
U.S. District Court	State trial court

Any party who is unhappy with the outcome of a trial has a right of appeal to an appellate court. Each federal appellate court is called a U.S. Court of Appeals, or Circuit Court. The Circuits are numbered: First Circuit, Second Circuit, Third Circuit, etc., up to Eleventh Circuit. There is also a D.C. Circuit. The D.C. Circuit obviously hears appeals from the federal court in D.C., and the numbered circuits each represent a geographic region of the U.S. There is also a Federal Circuit and a U.S. Court of Appeals for the Armed Forces, but those are specialty courts. The federal system also has specialty courts for bankruptcy and tax issues. And, there are federal administrative hearings. For the sake of simplicity, this book focuses on the District and Circuit Courts, because the cases discussed herein have come from those courts.

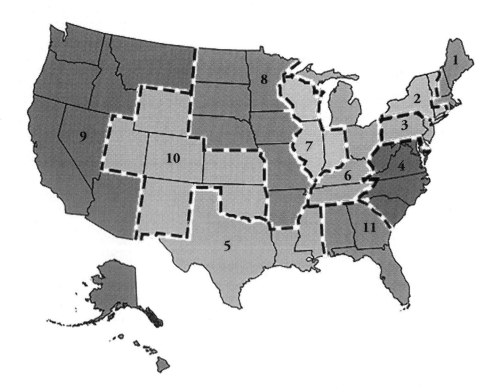

Figure 1.1: The Federal Circuits.

As you can see from the map above, states fall within various Circuits. If a party to a trial in the District of New Mexico wishes to appeal, he must appeal to the Tenth Circuit, because New Mexico is in the Tenth Circuit. Similarly, a party to a trial in the Southern District of New York must appeal to the Second Circuit, because New York is in the Second Circuit.

Once the Circuit Court issues its opinion, a party can try to appeal to the U.S. Supreme Court. A request for an appeal is called a "petition for a writ of certiorari." If the Supreme Court decides to hear the appeal, the Court grants a writ of certiorari to the court of appeals from which the case came. The Supreme Court, though, is not obligated to take a case. It receives, on average, 7000 to 10,000 petitions each year. It chooses which cases it wants, and typically hears fewer than 100 cases per year.

The state court system is similar to the federal court system insofar as each state has trial courts, appellate courts to which there is a right of appeal, and a highest court that has discretion to choose which cases it wants to hear. The main difference is that the names of the courts can vary, and sometimes the names can be confusing. For example, some states call their trial courts "circuit courts," and those who are familiar with the federal system might mistakenly think that refers to a court of appeal. And while most states call their highest court the "Supreme Court" (as in the federal system), New York calls its highest court the "Court of Appeals," which is what most states call the intermediate court. But other than the potential for confusion because of the names, the state system works very much like the federal system.

The two systems run parallel to each other. A case must proceed through one system or the other. You can't file a case in state court and then appeal to a federal court, and vice-versa. The only exception is that if a state's highest court decides a case that involves a constitutional issue, a party may attempt to appeal that decision to the U.S. Supreme Court. An example where that happened is *Heffron v. ISKON*, where a First Amendment case decided by the Minnesota Supreme Court was appealed to the U.S. Supreme Court. (That case is discussed in Chapter 14.)

In Which System Should a Case Be Filed?

The jurisdiction of the federal courts is limited. A case may be filed in federal court only if it is one of the following kinds of cases:

- Prosecution of a federal crime

- The case is based on a federal statute or the Constitution

- The United States itself is a party to the lawsuit

- There is diversity jurisdiction

Diversity jurisdiction means that the parties to the case are from different states. The traditional thought was that a state court might be biased in favor of the party from its own state, but federal courts are thought to be less likely to be biased. Diversity jurisdiction allows a party to choose federal court instead of state court to avoid being treated unfairly in favor of the "hometown" party. However, diversity jurisdiction is permitted only if the amount in controversy exceeds $75,000. There must be enough money at stake to justify the involvement of federal courts.

All other cases can be filed in state court. And, of course, state courts are the appropriate forum for the prosecution of state crimes.

Importantly, constitutional claims are not required to be filed in federal court. They may be filed in state court. In some cases, a state constitution might provide greater protection for speech than the federal constitution, in which case, seeking a resolution in state court might be a superior option. For example, in *Sandals Resorts Int'l Ltd., v. Google, Inc.*, a New York state court acknowledged that New York law extends greater protection to speech in libel cases than the protection granted by the Supreme Court interpreting the federal constitution. Thus, the court extended protection to an email that raised questions about how Sandals Resorts treats Jamaican workers, even if the precedent of the U.S. Supreme Court did not clearly require protection.

When a case is filed, the parties have a certain time period (typically 30 days) to try to move the case from one system to the other, if appropriate. If a case is filed in state court, but diversity jurisdiction exists, the other party can try to "remove" the case to federal court. "Removal" is the name given to this process. If a case is improperly filed in federal court, the case can be "remanded" to state court. Once the time period for removal or remand expires, the case is fixed in either the federal or the state system and cannot be switched from one to the other.

The Two Kinds of Cases

The two primary kinds of cases are civil and criminal. Each type of case has its own procedures and terminology. The following table compares some basic differences between the two types:

Table 1.2: The Two Kinds of Cases.

	Civil	Criminal
Who are the parties?	The "plaintiff" files the lawsuit against the "defendant." If Jeffrey Masson sues *The New Yorker* magazine, then Masson is the plaintiff and the magazine is the defendant, and the case will be styled "*Masson v. The New Yorker Magazine, Inc.*"	The case is brought by the "prosecutor" against a "defendant," although the charging party is usually referred to as the "State" (*e.g.*, *State v. Matthews*) or "People" (*e.g.*, *People v. Flynt*).
What is sought?	In most cases, a plaintiff is suing for money, but in some cases, the remedy is an injunction (for example, an order to stop publishing something) or a declaratory judgment (for example, an order declaring that a certain person holds the copyright to a work).	If a person is found guilty of a crime, he will be sentenced, and the penalty is usually jail time or a fine, although there are other options, such as probation.
What rules apply?	Courts will follow the Rules of Civil Procedure. (There are both state and federal versions, depending on whether the case is in state or federal court.)	Courts will follow the Rules of Criminal Procedure. (There are both state and federal versions, depending on whether the case is in state or federal court.)
What is the burden of proof?	In most cases, a plaintiff must prove the elements of a claim by a "preponderance of the evidence," which essentially means it is more likely than not that the plaintiff's claims are true. However, there are times when a plaintiff must prove something by "clear and convincing evidence," which is a higher standard.	A prosecutor must prove a defendant's guilt "beyond a reasonable doubt." That does not require 100% perfect, fool-proof evidence of guilt. It requires only that there be enough evidence so that reasonable people do not maintain doubts about guilt.
What subject matter is included?	In general, civil claims include torts, contract claims, property disputes, and the like. "Tort" is a legal term that simply means "wrong," and it is used to refer to a wide range of claims that plaintiffs can use to seek recovery when they feel they have been wronged somehow.	When most people think of crimes, they think of things like murder, assault, burglary, and the like. However, there are many kinds of crimes, including petty violations like speeding, jaywalking, or trespassing. There are also numerous content-specific federal laws.

	Civil	Criminal
What kinds of media law issues are included?	This book discusses several torts such as libel, invasion of privacy, right of publicity, and others. Breach of contract and fraud may also be civil claims. Copyright and trademark infringement may also be civil claims.	Many legal concepts that create civil liability can also create criminal liability. Copyright and trademark infringement can be criminal (think of mass pirating of CDs or DVDs, for example). Obscenity laws and child pornography laws are criminal matters. Laws that regulate threats, harassment, profanity, or other kinds of speech may also be criminal matters.

In criminal cases, prosecutors have prosecutorial discretion, which means that they have the option to decide whether to charge someone with a crime and, if so, exactly which crime. For example, a prosecutor might choose to charge someone with manslaughter rather than murder if the prosecutor thinks that the evidence is not clear enough to prove the intent required to obtain a murder conviction. It also means that a prosecutor won't spend the time and money to prosecute everything that might be considered a criminal act. Budgets are limited, so prosecutors sometimes have to choose where to focus their efforts. It may mean that they choose not to pursue pornography that might violate obscenity laws because they prefer to focus on the enforcement of drug laws. That doesn't mean that the pornography isn't obscene or that it deserves First Amendment protection; it simply means that the law isn't being enforced.

In civil cases, the plaintiff chooses whom to sue. If the defendant feels that someone else is at fault, he can seek indemnity from that other party. Contracts sometimes have indemnity clauses, which are agreements that if one party gets sued, the other party will cover the cost of the suit and any damages that must be paid. For example, if a newspaper contracts with a freelancer to write an article, the freelance agreement may have an indemnity clause wherein the freelancer promises to reimburse the newspaper for any costs incurred as a result of a libel claim based on the freelancer's article. Whether the freelancer has the money to actually cover those costs is a separate question, and it may not be practical for the newspaper to bother seeking reimbursement. But the concept of indemnity does arise from time to time.

Similarly, the concept of *respondeat superior* is important to understanding who is potentially liable in a civil case. In short, it means that the employer is responsible for the conduct of its employees. Thus, if a photo editor who works for a website posts someone else's photograph without permission and infringes their copyright, both the photo editor and the website can be sued. The photo editor is directly liable and the website is responsible as *respondeat superior*. In many cases, the plaintiff sues the employer because, presumably, the employer has "deeper pockets" (*i.e.*, more money) than the employee. But the plaintiff has the choice of suing one or the other or both.

How to Find "Law" and Understand Citation Systems

The legal profession is nothing if not organized. There is a coherent system for finding relevant laws or cases, but it does require some explanation.

There are five primary sources of law relevant to media law: constitutions, statutes, regulations, executive orders, and cases.

Constitutions

There is a federal constitution, and each state has its own constitution. All laws must comply with the provisions of the federal constitution; if they do not, they can be "struck down" as unconstitutional. As noted above, states are free to provide expanded protection to citizens, so sometimes a state constitution provides greater protection of certain rights than the federal constitution will. Sometimes, states grant greater protection for free speech than has been granted under the federal constitution. But states also sometimes provide greater protection for other rights, such as privacy rights. California, for example, has a state constitutional right of privacy that is fairly expansive and unlike any right protected by the federal constitution.

Statutes

Federal statutes are the laws that are passed by Congress. They are codified in a book called the United States Code (U.S.C.). A reference to a statute will cite the title and section where the statute can be found. For example, 17 U.S.C. sec. 107 is the citation to the law that describes the "fair use" defense to copyright infringement. It can be found in the U.S. Code in Title 17, section 107. Each state has its own code as well, codifying all state laws. State citations systems tend to be similar to the federal system, although they may have their own quirks.

Regulations

Federal regulations are rules made by federal agencies in order to implement the federal statutes. Examples include the Federal Communications Commission (FCC) regulations on broadcasters or the Federal Trade Commission (FTC) regulations on advertising. Regulations are spelled out in a book called the Code of Federal Regulations (C.F.R.). They follow a citation system similar to the system for statutes. So, for example, the regulation that requires broadcasters who intend to record calls to be used on-air inform callers of the recording can be found at 47 C.F.R. sec. 73.1206 (Title 47, section 73.1206). State agencies may also create regulations, and each state has its own system for publishing them.

Executive Orders

The president (or a governor, in the case of a state) may issue executive orders, which are directives that set forth a procedure, or otherwise declare how an agency within the executive branch shall operate. In recent years, there has been some criticism of these orders by those who believe that the scope of power sought to be exercised is broader than what the executive branch may properly exercise. Executive orders should be based on some preexisting law that the executive branch is tasked to enforce. In any case where one believes the president has exceed his authority in issuing an order, the remedy is to file a lawsuit, just as one would to challenge the constitutionality of a law passed by Congress.

Cases

When a court decides a case (or an issue within a case), the resulting opinion is often published. A case may interpret a statute or the constitution, or judges may create law simply by issuing opinions on a topic. Lawyers and judges refer to the collective body of opinions as case law or common law. So, for example, if a case refers to a "common law right of privacy," it means that, over time, judges have issued opinions that endorse some right of privacy within the bounds set forth by those prior opinions.

The citation system for cases is a little more complicated than for statutes or regulations, but it's not too difficult to catch on. Cases are published in certain books, called "reporters," depending on which court issued the opinion. A case citation will include the name of the case (*e.g.*, *Masson v. The New Yorker Magazine*) and the abbreviation for the reporter. The volume number of the reporter precedes the abbreviation, and the page number where the case can be found follows it. Finally, the citation includes a parenthetical that specifies which court decided the case and the year the opinion was issued. The parenthetical for U.S. Supreme Court cases includes only the year and not the court, because the court is clearly the U.S. Supreme Court.

A reporter is published in volumes 1 to 999. Once 999 volumes are filled, the reporter switches to the second set of volumes. Thus, the Federal Reporter (abbreviated F.) was published up to volume 999. It then switched to Federal Reporter Second (abbreviated F.2d). After volume 999 of F.2d, there was F.3d, and so on.

The following table outlines how federal court decisions are published and cited:

Table 1.3: Case Citations.

	Name of the reporter	Abbreviation of the reporter	Sample case citation
Supreme Court cases	United States Reporter	U.S.	*FCC v. Pacifica Foundation*, 438 U.S. 726 (1978)
Circuit Court cases	Federal Reporter	F. F.2d F.3d, etc.	*Rogers v. Koons*, 960 F.2d 301 (2d Cir. 1992)
District Court cases	Federal Supplement	F. Supp. F. Supp. 2d F. Supp. 3d, etc.	*Doe v. University of Michigan*, 721 F. Supp 852 (E.D. Mich 1989)

Thus, a citation to *Rogers v. Koons*, 960 F.2d 301 (2d Cir. 1992), provides this information:

Rogers sued Koons.
The case was decided by the Second Circuit in 1992.
The case can be found in volume 960 of the Federal Reporter Second at page 301.

Similarly, the citation to *Doe v. University of Michigan*, 721 F. Supp 852 (E.D. Mich 1989) says:

Doe sued the University of Michigan.
The case was decided by the Eastern District of Michigan in 1989.
The case can be found in volume 721 of the Federal Reporter Supplement at page 852.

The U.S. Reporter is the official reporter for Supreme Court cases. There are other reporters that publish Supreme Court opinions, the Supreme Court Reporter (S.Ct.) and Lawyer's Edition (L.Ed.). If you see a reference to those, they are simply alternate versions of citations to Supreme Court cases.

State court opinions follow a similar system, but it is complicated by the fact that the reporters are regional rather than tied to a specific state or court. So, for example, you will see the Northeast Reporter (N.E. or N.E.2d) with cases from many different states. Also, some states have their own reporters, such as the California Reporter (Cal. Rptr.). There are also themed reporters, such as the Media Law Reporter (Media L. Rep.). Despite the wide range of reporter names, the citation format is essentially the same.

In citations to state cases, a reference in a parenthetical to the state alone (*e.g.*, Cal. Minn., or Wisc.) means that the case was decided by the state's highest court. A reference to "App." (*e.g.*, Tex. App.) usually means it was decided by the intermediate appellate court. There are other abbreviations that may apply depending on the unique names or structure of state courts.

Thus, a citation to *McNamara v. Freedom Newspapers*, 802 S.W.2d 901 (Tex. App. 1991) provides this information:

McNamara sued Freedom Newspapers.
The case was decided by the Texas Court of Appeals in 1991.
The case can be found in volume 802 of the Southwest Second Reporter at page 901.

Similarly, a citation to *Shulman v. Group W. Productions*, 955 P.2d 469 (Cal. 1998) says:

Shulman sued Group W. Productions.
The case was decided by the California Supreme Court in 1998.
The case can be found in volume 955 of the Pacific Second Reporter at page 469.

Most reported state cases are from appellate courts. State trial courts do not typically report their cases. Nevertheless, you may sometimes see a reference to a lower-level court decision with a citation to the case number, the court, and the date of the ruling (*e.g.*, *Mayhew v. Dunn*, No. 580-11-07 Wmcv, Windham (VT) Superior Court (Howard J., March 18, 2008)).

One caveat is worth noting: although all courts style the case name as "plaintiff v. defendant" at the trial court level, some courts might have switched the names of parties in appellate cases. Some courts keep the names in the same order, but some courts may, on appeal, style the case as "appellant v. respondent." The appellant is the party who files the appeal—it could be either the plaintiff or the defendant, depending on the outcome of the trial court case. The respondent is the other party. Thus, it may be possible to come across a case where the defendant's name is first. For example, in *New York Times Co. v. Sullivan*, Sullivan was the plaintiff who sued the *New York Times*. However, it was the *New York Times* that appealed to the U.S. Supreme Court.

Most cases can be found by searching online or through a digital data service like Lexis or Westlaw. The nice thing is that, regardless of whether you are looking for the cases in books or digital databases, the citations remain the same. If you search electronically for "960 F.2d 301," you will still get the opinion in *Rogers v. Koons*.

Why Does All This Information Matter?

One of the most important concepts for understanding law is the notion of precedent. Precedent (also called "authority") is a rule that has been established by a court in a prior case that can be referred to for guidance in deciding later cases.

For example, the Supreme Court decided in *New York Times Co. v. Sullivan* that public officials may not recover damages for libel unless they can prove that a statement was made with "actual malice," such as when a speaker knows the statement is false. If another public official sues for libel, the rule established in *Sullivan*—that the public official must prove that the statement was made with actual malice in order to prevail—is precedent that will guide the court that has to decide the new case.

There are two kinds of precedent: mandatory authority and persuasive authority. In order to know which is which, you need to understand how the federal and state court systems work, how cases are published, and how to read a citation.

Mandatory authority is the precedent that a court is obligated to follow. All courts are obligated to follow the decisions of the U.S. Supreme Court. But otherwise, courts are only obligated to follow courts above them. Courts in California are obligated to follow the decisions of the California Supreme Court, but courts in Nevada or Utah are not. A state trial court will also have to follow the decisions of the state's intermediate appellate courts. Similarly, in the federal system, District Courts must follow the decisions of the Circuit Court of the Circuit in which the District Court is located.

Persuasive authority is all other precedent. It is something courts may consider, but they are not obligated to follow it. For example, if a court in Kansas is considering a privacy case, and a similar case had previously been decided in Texas, the Kansas court can consider the ruling of the Texas court. If it finds the reasoning to be persuasive, it can adopt the same rule. But the Kansas court is also free to reject that reasoning and establish its own rule.

The term *stare decisis* refers to the notion that judges are generally expected to adhere to precedent. If judges follow the reasoning and the application of legal principles in the same manner as the courts before them, then there will be a certain predictability and consistency in the law. To honor this principle judges do, for the most part, adhere to precedent. If changes are made in the interpretation of a principle, judges tend to make the changes slowly and incrementally. It is rare for a court to declare a prior principle invalid and establish an entirely different rule; however, it does happen on occasion. Other than the process of appeal and the recognition of the value of *stare decisis*, there is nothing that forces a court to adhere to precedent.

It is useful to know what authority is mandatory and what authority is persuasive when trying to determine the law that might be applicable to your own conduct. If you are thinking about publishing an article that raises privacy issues, it would be useful to know how privacy claims are likely to be evaluated in your jurisdiction, which means knowing what the mandatory authority says, in addition to seeing whether there is any persuasive authority on point.

Practical Conclusions

- State and federal courts serve the same function in society. Where the case is heard usually has more to do with the choices of the parties than anything else (although certain kinds of cases are more likely, or sometimes required, to be filed in one court or the other). Once a case is established within either the state or the federal system, it will rise up through that system only, from trial court, to any potential appeal, to the highest court in that system.

- Civil and criminal proceedings are different in many ways: procedure, burden of proof, and potential penalties. What they have in common is the use of the courts as a "truth-finding" system that is supposed to result in a fair adjudication of the issues.

- The concept of precedent is very important. Prior case decisions provide guidance about what is considered legal or illegal, protected or unprotected, in each jurisdiction. The law may vary substantially from state to state, and one must know how to find the law for a particular jurisdiction.

CHAPTER 2

The First Amendment—Theory and Practice

A ny book on media law will be replete with references to the First Amendment. Courts have granted the media—as well as individual speakers—certain rights or protection based on First Amendment principles. But that fact alone probably doesn't mean much without understanding what the First Amendment is and why the rights and protections it provides are defined the way they are. This chapter will discuss:

1. What the First Amendment is and the scope of its coverage

2. Why the United States began with a presumption of freedom rather than regulation

3. What theories underlie First Amendment protection and how they shape the scope of its application

4. The legal doctrines that have arisen from those theories

5. The practical effects of how the First Amendment is applied

The First Amendment and the Scope of Its Coverage

The First Amendment is part of the U.S. Constitution, the first of several amendments in the Bill of Rights. It reads:

Congress shall make no law respecting an establishment of religion, or prohibiting the free exercise thereof; or abridging the freedom of speech, or of the press; or the right of the people peaceably to assemble, and to petition the Government for a redress of grievances.

Any sentence with an abundance of commas and semicolons will inevitably be subject to multiple interpretations, and the First Amendment is no different. There are disputes, for example, about whether "speech" and "press" are the same right or a different right; whether "press" simply refers to written speech; or whether there is a distinction between press as an industry and press as a technology. One might also argue about whether all of these rights are simply different variations on the notion of freedom of conscience and the expression thereof, and that they should be broadly interpreted to effectuate such freedom, or whether they are intended to be specific forms of freedoms that apply only to limited circumstances.

In any event, one thing is clear: as part of the Constitution, the First Amendment applies to what is called "state action." It restricts government power; it does not restrict private parties.

The Constitution outlines the powers of government, and the Bill of Rights was attached to set forth specific limits on those powers. The First Amendment is, foremost, a limit on what the government may do.

With that in mind, consider the subject matter in this book. It covers rights of access and the newsgathering process; civil torts, such as libel and privacy; government regulation and prosecution; and various forms of public or private censorship. The First Amendment applies to some of these things, but not others. Even when it applies, there are varying degrees of protection.

The most obvious and relevant applications are to government regulation or punishment. When the government attempts to restrict speech, force speech, or impose criminal sanctions for speech, such efforts are classically within the scope of what the First Amendment is designed to prevent: government censorship or compulsion. The Founders were concerned about both. England had required publishers to be licensed. The king could punish those whose speech was offensive by revoking printing licenses or imposing criminal penalties. The Founders did not want the U.S. government to have that kind of power. They also believed that being forced to speak—to pledge allegiance to a particular religion, theory, belief, nation, or law was an unacceptable imposition. Thus, the courts have generally recognized that the First Amendment applies to a wide range of government actions that either restrict or compel speech.

There are many references in this book to media law issues that involve government regulation or punishment, such as regulation of commercial speech (advertisements), obscenity laws, prosecutions for threats, and many more. The potential application of the First Amendment should be obvious in such cases—although, in fairness, it must be admitted that the Supreme Court has not always provided robust protection. In cases involving student speech or government-funded speech, for example, the Supreme Court has been more willing to tolerate restrictions.

But if the First Amendment applies to state action, then why does it apply in lawsuits when a private party is suing another private party, such as in libel or privacy cases? In those cases, the private parties are using the courts to resolve their dispute and enforce a judgment, and they are relying on the laws of the State to do so. Thus, the government is still involved. The government, via the judiciary, has enforcement power over civil claims, and thus, courts have found First Amendment principles apply when the courts adjudicate these kinds of lawsuits.

The trickier question may be why First Amendment protections are sometimes applied to access rights and newsgathering issues, and other times they are not. The Supreme Court has, from time to time, acknowledged that there is some First Amendment interest in newsgathering derived from the reference to freedom of the press. But the free press provision is poorly defined and inconsistently applied. There are a few conclusions that can be drawn from court decisions.

First, there is some protection for newsgathering, but the scope of that right is often balanced against other interests. In recording cases, for example, the courts may grant some First Amendment protection, but they will also grant some deference to state laws that are intended to protect privacy. The newsgathering interest will not always prevail.

Second, courts have been reluctant to grant special rights to the press. There are numerous decisions that have declined to extend special rights or protection to the professional "press." Journalists may be liable, for example, if they trespass, breach a contract, or engage in criminal activity, just as any other citizen would be liable. The general sentiment is that the press has whatever rights the public may have, and journalists must adhere to generally applicable laws. The Court has been reluctant to say that a law is unconstitutional when applied to "journalists" but constitutional for everyone else. The one possible exception to that rule is the potential protection for journalists from abusive subpoenas, but in most cases, that protection is provided by statute rather than being derived from constitutional principle (see Chapter 13).

Third, even if the press doesn't have special rights, it may have an enforceable right of access to places or information in limited cases when the press acts as a surrogate for the public. For example, courts have said that the press has a right of access to attend court proceedings so that the press can inform the public about what happened. It wouldn't be realistic for every member of the public to attend the proceeding in person. Thus, the right of the press in such cases is actually a right of the public, which just happens to be manifested via the press. (This principle is explained more fully in Chapter 11.)

Finally, the First Amendment does not apply at all to private action. Private companies, private schools, private employers, and your mom all may censor you, and such censorship is entirely outside the scope of the First Amendment. There is no government action, and thus, there are no First Amendment protections. Now, one might object to such censorship as a matter of principle or ethics, or there might be a statute that prohibits a particular form of censorship—for example, certain labor laws prohibit certain forms of censorship by employers about labor issues. Nevertheless, there are no enforceable First Amendment rights in such cases with respect to private persons or entities.

Why the U.S. Started With a Presumption of Freedom

The right of free speech in modern America is broad. It can be difficult to imagine how restrictive the rules were in 17th-century Europe. For the most part, governments determined who was allowed to print books or newspapers, could restrict what was published, and punished those who spoke in any way offensive to the government. Criminal libel charges could be brought against those who criticized officials.

In 1644, John Milton wrote *Aeropagitica*, an argument in favor of freedom of speech and press. In particular, he criticized the English licensing system. At the time, authors were required to get permission of the government prior to publishing anything. Milton argued that books and the ideas contained therein should not be restricted prior to publication. On the contrary, the ideas should be fully considered and then refuted if necessary. He also argued that the government should not control what is considered "truth." True and false ideas should be allowed to "grapple," with the expectation that genuine truth will prevail.

Aeropagitica failed insofar as England did not abandon its licensing system until close to 1700. But it succeeded insofar as it influenced others to think about what freedom of the press means.

Several Enlightenment-era thinkers began to propose a notion that men should be treated as equals and that they should be free to have thoughts, beliefs, or ideas that were different from others. Truly, this was a shocking proposal at the time. John Locke is often cited as one of the leading thinkers of the time whose theories on liberty and freedom greatly influenced those who wrote the U.S. Constitution. Other thinkers, such as David Hume and Jean Jacques Rousseau, refined theories that reflect the prevailing thoughts of the time and are often credited as important influences on the founding fathers. Some of their most important and influential ideas involved notions of equality among men, the idea of a social contract, and a form of skepticism that called into question official claims of truth.

The drafting of the First Amendment was the culmination of such thinking, writing, and challenging government power. One event that is often cited as a turning point in thought about freedoms of speech and press is the trial of John Peter Zenger.

Zenger was the publisher of the *New York Weekly Journal*. In his publication, he criticized William Cosby, then-governor of New York. In 1734, he was arrested and criminally charged with libel. (As noted in Chapter 3 on libel, libel used to be more commonly pursued as a criminal prosecution; that is no longer true in the U.S. Most libel cases are now civil claims.)

Back then, libel law was very different than it is now. The government only needed to prove that the libelous statements were published. Whether they were true or not was entirely irrelevant. Zenger's attorney argued to the jury that the law was wrong; that men should be free to publish truths about government officials, even if they are unflattering; and that the jury should find Zenger not guilty in spite of the letter of the law. The jury returned with a not guilty verdict.

In 1769, William Blackstone, an influential English judge, published a book stating that freedom of the press should mean that no prior restraints are imposed on speech. Although men may be punished for their speech, governments should not restrict the speech first. This was less than 100 years after the nation had abandoned its restrictive licensing rules.

Shortly thereafter, as America's founders drafted the First Amendment, the notion that Congress "shall make no law … abridging the freedom of speech, or of the press," was fairly well-accepted—so much so that some delegates at the Constitutional Convention thought that a Bill of Rights was unnecessary; *of course* the government shouldn't restrict speech or press. But as history has proved, governments will exert power unless checked by some external force, even if that "force" is the power of a principle based on Enlightenment-era philosophy.

Theories of the First Amendment

There are many, many arguments made in favor of freedom of speech or press in various cases. But there are a few theories that are commonly used to justify interpretations of how the law should be applied.

Perhaps the most famous theory underlying First Amendment protection is the notion of a marketplace of ideas. This theory asserts that ideas should be aired freely and that this will allow the public to compare competing ideas. The presumption is that truth will prevail. This theory is most famously stated in Justice Holmes's dissent in *Abrams v. U.S.*, in which he said, "the best test of truth is the power of the thought to get itself accepted in the competition of the market."

The marketplace of ideas theory has been criticized on several grounds. First, many protest that there is often no objective truth, and thus a model based on the triumph of a truth is inherently flawed. Second, many argue that marketplace models are dangerous because powerful interest groups will have a better chance to promote their ideas and have them adopted, regardless of their inherent truth. Third, there are those who believe that this model fails to account for the harm that can be caused by false ideas.

Nevertheless, the marketplace theory is well entrenched in American jurisprudence. The Supreme Court often references the importance of allowing ideas to compete and objects to the censorship of speech merely because the speech is unpopular, offensive, or disfavored, allowing ideas to compete freely, even if they are weak.

Another influential theory was proposed by Alexander Meiklejohn, an early-20th century philosopher known for his advocacy of free speech. He is most well known for his argument that freedom of speech naturally derives from principles of self-government. To self-govern, the people need access to information, facts, opinions, and ideas. Absent this kind of information, people can't make informed choices.

The self-government theory has been criticized because it allows for some kinds of restrictions. If speech is justified only for the purpose of self-government, then speech could be censored if it is unrelated to self-government. Speech that is frivolous or unimportant, such as celebrity gossip, gets no support from Meiklejohn's theory. Also, Meiklejohn emphasized the needs of society as a whole over the needs of the individual. Some speech restrictions, particularly restrictions on campaign finance, rely on such arguments—that the needs of the nation as a whole override individual freedoms.

The concept of individual freedom is the third theory that supports freedom of speech. Many commentators have argued that people need to express themselves. Self-fulfillment and individual freedom are important principles on their own that need no further justification and that support broad protections for free speech.

The main criticism of the individual freedom theory is that there are always other interests that compete with individual freedom. While individual freedom is admittedly important, it is not necessarily more important than other interests. However, courts often do reference the importance of freedom, which is why content-based regulations on speech are often struck down as unconstitutional absent compelling interests that could outweigh freedom.

Contemporary scholars have raised other arguments to support freedom of speech. First Amendment protections can help prevent abuses by those in power. They also facilitate interpersonal communication and understanding. There are many other arguments or justifications for free speech that can be raised in various cases, and the theories listed herein are by no means an exclusive or exhaustive list.

Theories of the First Amendment are used to argue in favor of particular tests that courts can use to evaluate cases that implicate freedoms of speech and press. But no one theory is applicable in all circumstances. The justification for supporting free speech in one case may not apply at all in other cases. Or a theory might indicate that speech should be protected in one instance but not another. The mishmash of theories used has resulted in various doctrines that try to balance all the competing interests.

First Amendment Doctrine

As if there weren't enough debate about First Amendment theory, there is also an abundance of debate over First Amendment doctrine. "Doctrine" is a set of principles used to sort out issues and guide courts in making decisions. Thus, while First Amendment theory explains the reasons why we support freedom of speech in general, First Amendment doctrine explains how we will decide whether a particular instance of speech should be protected or not. Scholars—and even Supreme Court Justices—do not agree on the tests and principles that should guide decision-making in cases involving free speech or press.

First Amendment doctrine has evolved over time. At one point in American history, advertising received no First Amendment protection, any sexual content could be banned, and anti-government speech could be punished if it had a "bad tendency" to cause harm. Now, advertising receives some presumptive protection and can be regulated only in narrow circumstances, spelled out in a four-part test; sexual content may be banned only if it is deemed to be "obscenity," as defined in a three-part test; and speech usually may be punished only if it is likely to imminently incite violence. And the doctrines continue to evolve. Some argue that advertising should receive even greater protection, that the restrictions on sexual content in broadcast media are outdated and no longer justified, and that speech should be punishable in numerous circumstances where it offends or causes psychological harm.

To understand why the rules are the way they are, it is helpful to grasp a few overarching principles. First, courts have placed different kinds of speech into various categories and declared that some categories are unprotected, while other categories receive varying degrees of protection. Categories of unprotected speech include obscenity, fraud, and incitements to violence. But the analysis is not so simple as to simply declare speech to be in one of those categories. There are tests the courts use to determine when speech constitutes obscenity, fraud, or incitement. Nevertheless, if speech falls into an "unprotected" category, no further analysis is needed.

One of the great debates in the last few years has been whether there should be categories of unprotected speech other than those already established. For example, many have argued that violence should be a category of unprotected speech. Others would like to see hate speech be classified as unprotected. Nevertheless, the Supreme Court has so far been unwilling to add new categories of unprotected speech.

But even when speech falls into a "protected" category, there are still times when the speech can be punished or banned. The Supreme Court has established various tests that are used to evaluate laws that regulate various categories of speech. Regulations of commercial speech, for example, are evaluated using the *Central Hudson* test. Cases involving symbolic speech often refer to the *O'Brien* test. In libel cases, the Court has established the "actual malice" standard as a constitutional safeguard. There are many, many tests the courts use in different circumstances, and much of this book is an outline of the tests applicable in particular situations to determine whether the First Amendment protects the speech at issue or whether the speech may be punished or regulated.

Another important principle is that there are varying levels of scrutiny applied in different kinds of cases. One may see references to "strict scrutiny" or "intermediate scrutiny." These phrases refer both to the relative importance given to the speech at issue and to the presumption of protection the speech may receive. In cases where strict scrutiny is applied, the speech is presumed to be of great importance and the First Amendment is likely to protect it unless the government can meet a very high burden, showing that there is a "compelling government interest" and that the regulation is narrowly tailored to limit the least amount of speech necessary to fulfill the interest. In cases where intermediate scrutiny is applied, the speech is considered somewhat important, but the courts will consider other factors. The government will need to prove only an "important," but not "compelling," interest.

A third principle is that courts must preserve due process, which means that there are certain substantive and procedural considerations that must be applied when evaluating the constitutionality of a law. Laws must not be vague, overbroad, or viewpoint-discriminatory, nor may they be applied in an arbitrary or capricious manner.

A vague law is one that is poorly written, such that a reasonable person cannot determine what the law prohibits from its plain language. For example, a law that prohibits "offensive" speech is vague, because it is not clear what is prohibited. The concept of offensiveness is too subjective to provide clear guidance.

An overbroad law is poorly written in another way: It applies to more things than necessary. For example, if the government wanted to ensure that children did not have access to online pornography, it might consider a law that mandated a block on websites that use the word "breast." But such a law would be unconstitutionally overbroad because it would block all sites discussing breast cancer as well as any sites containing pornography.

A law or regulation can be struck down as unconstitutional either "on its face" or "as applied." A "facial challenge" to a law means that the plain language of the law is so clearly unconstitutional that it cannot stand. For example, in *U.S. v. Alvarez*, the Supreme Court invalidated the Stolen Valor Act, a law that punished false statements about having earned a military honor, because the Court found that falsity on its own was an insufficient basis for a law that bans speech.

A law can be deemed unconstitutional as applied if it has been enforced in a way that improperly infringes on a person's First Amendment rights. For example, in *Texas v. Johnson*, the Supreme Court found a flag burning law to be unconstitutional as applied to a protester who burned the flag for expressive purposes.

Government regulations are also supposed to be viewpoint neutral, meaning that they are not supposed to punish speech depending on one's stance toward an issue. This is different from being "content-neutral," a term that refers to laws that do not depend on the content of one's speech. For example, a law that regulates speech about abortion is content-based and not content-neutral, but it can nevertheless be viewpoint neutral if it takes no position with respect to the speaker being pro-life or pro-choice. A law that bans pro-choice speech about abortion is neither content-neutral nor viewpoint neutral.

Finally, it is important to note that government regulations are supposed to be applied fairly to all persons, and not applied in an arbitrary or discriminatory manner. Laws that give too much discretion to public officials may be unconstitutional. For example, in *City of Lakewood v. Plain Dealer Pub. Co.*, the Supreme Court struck down an ordinance requiring newspaper publishers to get a license to put news racks on public sidewalks; the Court found that the law gave too much discretion to public officials in granting or denying an application. In the United States, media companies—and all disseminators of information—must comply with generally applicable laws, including business licenses or taxes. But speakers should not be subject to any discriminatory taxes or other laws that differentiate based on content. Thus, in *Ark. Writers Project v. Ragland*, the Supreme Court struck down a tax on "general interest" magazines, finding that the tax was discriminatory because it was not applied to other kinds of magazines.

There are many other tests and principles that may be applied in various circumstances. This book is intended to be a practical guide for non-lawyers to understand what kinds of speech or conduct the courts have protected or not, rather than an exhaustive study of theories or doctrines that could be used when First Amendment interests are present. Thus, while there will be references to some of the more esoteric aspects of constitutional analysis, the focus will be on what non-lawyers need to know to make informed decisions.

First Amendment Rights

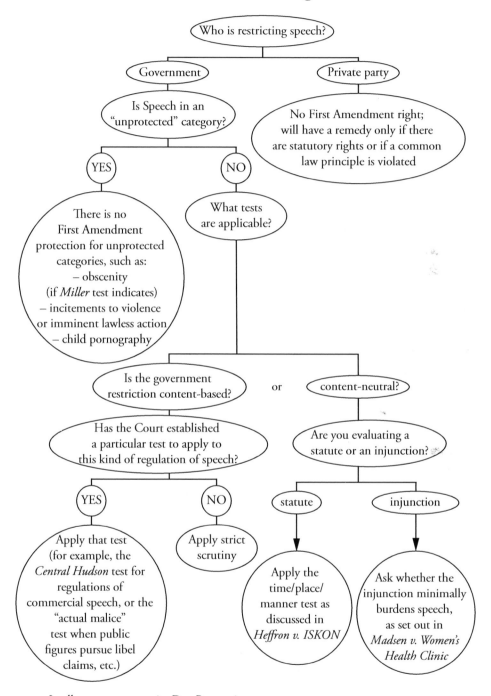

In all cases, you can raise Due Process issues:
     – Is the law vague?
     – Is the law overbroad?
     – Did the government meet its burden of proof?
     – Was the law applied in an arbitrary or discriminatory manner?
A law may be challenged "on its face" or "as applied."

Figure 2.1: Evaluating First Amendment Rights.

Practical Effects

It's important to remember that the First Amendment is not self-executing. There is no First Amendment Fairy who will remedy a government intrusion with a flick of her wand. It usually requires litigation to remedy a First Amendment violation, and it can sometimes be difficult to determine whether there is a First Amendment violation at all.

Moreover, determinations are subject to the discretion of judges and justices. Although there is a right to at least one appeal, at some point there will be a final appeal, and the losing party may feel as if First Amendment principles were not properly applied. People can and do disagree about what the First Amendment should or should not protect. It is important to try to understand the guidance provided by courts in their opinions to evaluate what kind of similar actions might or might not be protected or prohibited.

This is what lawyers do. Lawyers study cases to try to understand how best to guide a client.

Sometimes, a client will call a lawyer and ask whether a planned action is "ok" from a legal perspective. It is difficult to declare with certainty that something is "ok," because there is always some risk that the client will be sued, even if there is no legitimate legal claim. And, in some cases, there is bona fide legal risk, but the risk is well justified and a client may very well choose to take the risk, regardless of potential consequence. There are times when a statement or an action might not be guaranteed protection under current law, and yet it is still the right thing to do from an ethical perspective. In short, lawyers cannot guarantee that there are no risks, but they can help their clients figure out which risks are worth taking.

Lawyers look at precedent. What have previous court decisions said and how closely analogous are the fact and analysis of that prior case to the situation the client is facing now? Lawyers will figure out which cases are analogous and likely to be controlling precedent, and which cases are distinguishable because the factual scenarios are so different. They will engage in a careful analysis of the facts and how they match up to prior case law. There must be a mix of rational analysis of what fits preexisting principles as well as an intuitive sense of what seems unwarranted. Then, a lawyer can offer some guidance about what the best course of action might be.

It should be emphasized that lawyers guess. No one I know can see the future. But lawyers make educated guesses based on substantial experience and knowledge of case law. Non-lawyers can educate themselves, too, so they can engage in thoughtful and well-informed discussions about what kinds of risks might be worth taking.

In other instances, a client is facing a problem that has already occurred. Someone has published or done something that has created a threat, claim, or government action of some sort. In these cases the lawyer does more or less the same thing in the sense that the lawyer will examine precedent and try to analyze how the law applies to the facts at issue. But the lawyer will be trying to develop the best arguments possible to represent the client's interests and use these arguments to negotiate a resolution or, if necessary, present these arguments to a court.

Lawyers will make their best arguments on behalf of clients in the hopes of persuading a court to rule in their favor. But courts have substantial leeway to adopt their own tests and reasoning, and they may make decisions that seem unfounded or unfair in a given case. Nevertheless, court opinions bind the parties to that case and inform future potential litigants of what may be deemed acceptable or unacceptable.

The information in this book is simply an organized way of looking at the kinds of controversies that have arisen in the past, what courts have decided, what kinds of things seem to be squarely protected, and what kinds of ambiguities may still exist in the law. It's impossible to know or predict how future cases may turn out, but arming oneself with knowledge of the past certainly helps one to be aware of the kinds of things that might create problems in the future and require legal guidance. If, in a particular case, one feels that the law should be more expansive, there is no prohibition on taking the risk of acting broadly and hoping for a favorable outcome. There are times when one must stick up for principle, even if one may lose. But it's better to take such risks knowingly. The First Amendment is a grand idea, but it is not an impenetrable shield from consequence.

Practical Conclusions

- The First Amendment only applies to "state action." Any government regulation of speech or press or use of the courts to enforce penalties on speech or press activity should give rise to First Amendment considerations. However, there are no "First Amendment rights" if you are censored by private parties, such as your employer, websites, or your mom.

- There are very few categories of speech that are unprotected. Speech that is deemed "obscene" under the *Miller* test, incitements to violence, fraud, and child pornography will receive no protection whatsoever.

- For other kinds of speech, there are tests or factors that the courts use to balance the competing interests. Laws may also be struck down as unconstitutional if they are vague, overbroad, or are applied in an arbitrary or discriminatory manner.

- It can be difficult to predict in advance what will create liability. Some speech is clearly protected and other speech is clearly not protected, but a lot of it falls somewhere in the gray area. Understanding the relevant case law helps to make informed decisions about what risks one may be willing to take.

PART II

What Can You Be Sued For? (And Are There Related Criminal Charges?)

CHAPTER 3

Libel

The Risk of Criticism, Insults, and Trash Talk

It is common for a speaker to want to convey information or express opinions that will reflect poorly on someone else, insult others, or seem unfairly mean. These kinds of comments can range from accusations of wrongdoing to ordinary criticism to trash talk to gratuitously cruel outbursts or can arise in the ordinary course of reporting on controversial matters.

The most common legal issue that will arise in such situations is libel. This chapter will discuss how libel claims are evaluated in the U.S.

A speaker risks being sued any time he communicates something that would harm someone's reputation. Libel suits have been filed, for example, when radio hosts called a reality television contestant a "skank," or when Senator John Murtha said that marines killed civilians in Afghanistan. Such statements may seem perfectly ordinary. They are the kinds of things people say all the time. Yet the people who are the subject of the statements may feel as if they need to vindicate their reputations, resulting in libel lawsuits.

Even though it is difficult for most plaintiffs to win libel suits (neither of the two previously mentioned lawsuits were successful), defending a libel suit can be extremely expensive and time-consuming. Thus, it's best to avoid libel claims where possible.

Courts have established rules that try to balance the interest of the plaintiff in protecting his good reputation with the defendant's interest in free expression or the free flow of information. Obviously, the principles of free speech are in conflict with a person's claim to a good reputation, because to protect a person's reputation, it would be necessary to restrict anyone else from speaking ill of him. Thus, First Amendment protection is sometimes extended to allegedly libelous statements. But even though the Supreme Court has established some constitutional protection for some kinds of speech, libel is a matter of state law, and every state has quirks in its interpretation of the law. A lawsuit can have very different outcomes depending on what state it is filed in and how broadly that state protects certain kinds of speech.

Rather than explain the intricacies of each state's law, this chapter will provide a general overview of the types of considerations that courts evaluate in libel cases. This chapter will first discuss the elements of a libel claim. A plaintiff has the burden of proving ALL of the elements in order to win a lawsuit. The chapter will then discuss possible defenses. Even if a plaintiff can prove all the elements of the claim, a defendant can prevail if there is an applicable defense. The chapter then explains some related torts and practical considerations related to libel claims.

As a preliminary matter, some terms should be defined: libel, slander, and defamation. People sometimes use the terms interchangeably, because they all refer to harming someone's reputation. In fact, one element a plaintiff would have to prove in a lawsuit is that the statement at issue is defamatory, meaning that the statement is capable of being interpreted in a way that would harm the subject's reputation. Some states use the term "defamation" as a catch-all term to describe any legal claim based on injury to reputation. However, the concepts of libel and slander are more technical. Libel traditionally referred to claims based on written defamatory statements and slander referred to claims based on spoken defamatory statements. Most states have eliminated any significant distinctions in the way the two claims are treated, although there may be some minor distinctions in a particular state's law, particularly with respect to the way damages are calculated. For the sake of simplicity, this chapter will refer to all claims as libel, regardless of whether they are based on written or spoken communications.

Elements

As mentioned above, libel is a state law claim. Each state has its own rules and the rules vary, so it is important to know the laws of the state where the claim is filed. Even if a case is filed in federal court due to diversity jurisdiction, the court will follow the libel law of the appropriate state. There is no federal libel statute.

Generally, to win a libel claim, all of the elements must be decided in favor of the plaintiff. That means a plaintiff cannot win unless ALL of the following can be proven:

1. The statement is defamatory.

2. The statement is false.

3. The statement is a factual assertion (as opposed to an opinion or joke).

4. The statement is about a valid plaintiff, who is identifiable.

5. The statement is published.

6. The defendant acted with the requisite level of fault.

7. The plaintiff suffered damages.

Each element will be explained separately, and then examples will show how they work together.

Is the Statement Defamatory?

WHAT KIND OF STATEMENTS ARE DEFAMATORY?

A defamatory statement is a statement that reflects poorly on a person's reputation, morality or integrity. Certain types of statements have traditionally been considered defamatory, such as statements that impute the commission of a crime or tend to injure someone in his occupation. In *Walker v. Kiousos*, for example, a court found that accusing a police officer of using profanity and making threats during a traffic stop is the kind of statement that "tends to injure plaintiff in his occupation," and therefore can be "defamatory." However, any kind of statement that would harm someone's reputation can be deemed defamatory, such as calling someone a prostitute, suggesting excessive alcohol use, or otherwise imputing negative behavior to the plaintiff. Actress/Comedienne Carol Burnett once prevailed in a libel lawsuit based on the following blurb:

> In a Washington restaurant, a boisterous Carol Burnett had a loud argument with another diner, Henry Kissinger. Then she traipsed around the place offering everyone a bite of her dessert. But Carol really raised eyebrows when she accidentally knocked a glass of wine over one diner and started giggling instead of apologizing. The guy wasn't amused and "accidentally" spilled a glass of water over Carol's dress.

In *Burnett v. National Enquirer*, the court found that the defamatory nature of the statement was "abundantly clear," because it suggested that Burnett's actions "were the result of some objectionable state of inebriation." While such accusations may seem mild compared to hard-hitting reports of corruption or crime, they nevertheless can be construed as defamatory.

Changing norms, however, may change what is deemed defamatory. It used to be defamatory to suggest that a white person was a person of color. This is no longer an acceptable argument for defamation. Although the misidentification of a person, whether by race or otherwise, is an error that warrants correction as an ethical matter, misidentification by race is not the kind of error that warrants a libel claim, as the courts have acknowledged that there is nothing inherent in being of any particular race that should lower one's esteem in the community.

It also used to be defamatory to suggest that someone was gay. However, there have been several recent cases holding that it is no longer defamatory to call someone gay. In *Stern v. Cosby*, for example, a court rejected such a libel claim because gays are no longer viewed as "contemptible and disgraceful." Such reasoning by the courts seems to be expanding, although there is no guarantee that courts in every state would agree. The case law in some states still holds that it is defamatory to make accusations of homosexuality, and there is no guarantee that those courts will adopt the logic of *Stern*.

A court has also found that it is "arguably not" defamatory to say that a married couple has made a sex tape. In *Spears v. US Weekly LLC*, pop singer Britney Spears sued US Weekly for saying that she and her then-husband Kevin Federline made a sex tape. The court found that she could not likely sustain a libel claim, given contemporary standards of what would be defamatory. The court took into consideration the fact that Spears has performed in sexually suggestive ways, spoken openly about sex, and profited from her sexual persona, thereby making it unlikely that she would be defamed by a statement that she had made a sex tape with Federline.

Thus, court are not willing to say that a statement is defamatory simply because the plaintiff is subjectively offended by the statement. The statement must be likely to harm a person's reputation given contemporary social standards.

STATEMENTS CAN BE OBVIOUSLY DEFAMATORY OR NOT OBVIOUSLY SO

A statement can be obviously harmful to one's reputation, such as saying that someone committed a crime. This is called libel per se.

There is another kind of statement called libel per quod. This involves a statement that is not obviously harmful. An example of a non-obvious defamatory statement would be to say that a particular man—let's call him John Smith—is dating a particular woman—let's call her Jane Doe. There is nothing obviously reputation-destroying about the sentence that John Smith is dating Jane Doe. It becomes harmful only if the audience knows that either John or Jane is married—to someone else. In that case, the sentence becomes an accusation of adultery rather than mere idle gossip, and it enters the realm of defamatory statements.

Watching out for obviously defamatory statements is easy because the potential harm is clear. Some types of statements that are libel per se include accusing someone of being a criminal or engaging in illegal activity, incompetent for his/her occupation, promiscuous or engaging in adultery, a child molester or sexual deviant, corrupt with respect to business practices, insane or mentally ill, or an alcoholic or drug abuser. It is also libel per se to suggest that a company sells defective business products or that a person has a "loathsome disease." A "loathsome disease" is one that is both contagious and socially repugnant. Sexually transmitted diseases and leprosy are common examples; but cancer, for example, does not qualify, as it is not contagious.

One must be more careful, however, about libel per quod. If a person sees John and Jane together without knowing that one is married and simply assumes (incorrectly) that they are dating, the person will be making a false, defamatory statement if he reports his assumption as a fact. Publishing a false, defamatory factual assertion about specifically named individuals is several steps down the road to a successful libel claim. This is why it is imperative not to make assumptions and to verify facts before publishing.

DEFAMATION BY OMISSION

The defamatory "statement may occur by omission if there is some false implication as a result of a crucial omission. In *Memphis Publishing Co. v. Nichols*, a libel claim was based on the following article:

Woman Hurt By Gunshot

Mrs. Ruth A. Nichols, 164 Eastview, was treated at St. Joseph Hospital for a bullet wound in her arm after a shooting at her home, police said. A 40-year-old woman was held by police in connection with the shooting with a .22 rifle. Police said a shot was also fired at the suspect's husband. Officers said the incident took place Thursday night after the suspect arrived at the Nichols home and found her husband there with Mrs. Nichols. Witnesses said the suspect first fired a shot at her husband and then at Mrs. Nichols, striking her in the arm, police reported. No charges had been placed.

The article omitted the fact that several other people were present at the time of the shooting, leaving the false impression that the wife had caught her husband having an affair with that other woman. In defending the libel suit brought by Mrs. Nichols, the newspaper argued that each statement in the article was technically true, regardless of what anyone might conclude as a result. However, the court found that the overall thrust of the article falsely suggested that there was an adulterous affair, thereby harming Mrs. Nichols's reputation.

It is important to note, however, that libel-by-implication cases, as they are called, can be challenging for plaintiffs. Courts are not willing to impose liability simply because a speaker fails to mention every possible fact or detail. In one case, Bill Janklow, then-Governor of South Dakota sued a magazine that published the following:

> Along the way, Banks made a dangerous enemy—William Janklow. Their feud started in 1974, when Banks brought charges against Janklow in a tribal court for assault. A 15-year-old Indian girl who babysat for Janklow's children had claimed that he raped her in 1969. Federal officials found insufficient evidence to prosecute, but Banks persuaded the Rosebud Sioux chiefs to reopen the case under tribal law. Janklow, who was running for election as state attorney general at the time, refused to appear for the trial. But the tribal court found "probable cause" to believe the charges and barred Janklow from practicing law on the reservation. Eight months later Janklow—who had won his election despite the messy publicity—was prosecuting Banks. And his case—based on the 1973 Custer riot—was successful. Found guilty of riot and assault without intent to kill, Banks jumped bail before sentencing.

Janklow argued that he was defamed because the paragraph suggested that he prosecuted Banks in revenge for Banks prosecuting Janklow. In truth, however, the prosecution of Banks had begun before that. (It should also be noted that the rape charges against Janklow were later proved to be false.) Nevertheless, in *Janklow v. Newsweek*, the court found that the article was protected by the First Amendment. Even though it would have been "fairer to Janklow and more informative to the reader" if the chronology of events were clearer, the court felt that the article overall expressed opinion about the feud between the two men, and it would have been inappropriate for the court to interfere with editorial decisions about how to express that opinion.

To avoid libel-by-implication, some editors will specifically counter any potentially false implications that obviously arise from a story: *e.g.*, "she did not intentionally harm the victim" or "he has not been implicated in criminal activity." In other instances, editors attempt to provide more context for the statement. In any event, the important factor to the courts is not whether the speaker intended any particular implication, but whether the natural implication of the story is an accurate reflection of the facts.

HEADLINES AND CAPTIONS

It is worth mentioning that a libel suit can be based solely on a defamatory headline or caption. Kato Kaelin, who was a witness in the infamous O. J. Simpson murder trial, sued the *National Enquirer* over a cover headline that read "Cops Think Kato Did It." If a reader actually bothered to open the tabloid and read the article, it would become clear that "It" refers to perjury; the police accused Kaelin of lying during his testimony. But in *Kaelin v. Globe Comm. Corp.*, the court found that the headline could be defamatory because the average reader would see it and think that it meant that the police suspected Kaelin of committing murder.

Kaelin is not unique; misleading headlines and captions often serve as the basis for libel claims. Actress Ashley Olsen sued the *National Enquirer* over a cover that referred to a "drug scandal" and showed a picture of her looking squinty-eyed and haggard; the article inside was about her then-boyfriend who allegedly had drug-related issues. There was no statement that Olsen had used drugs, even though that was the clear implication left by the cover. Similarly, actress Katie Holmes sued *Star* magazine over a cover that read "Addiction Nightmare—Katie Drug Shocker!" The article, if one were to read it, explained that the Scientology counseling sessions Katie attended were "like" a drug. The magazine apologized and said it "did not intend to suggest that Katie Holmes was a drug addict." Both the Olsen and Holmes cases settled. Ethically, headline writers should strive to create copy that accurately represents the story that follows and avoid sensational or misleading headlines. Legally, headlines that stand alone (especially those on a tabloid cover) and leave a false, defamatory impression could lead to liability.

Is the Statement False?

Even if a statement is defamatory, there is usually no valid libel claim unless the statement is also false (or, perhaps, if there is a false implication).

WHAT CONSTITUTES A "FALSE" STATEMENT?

Obviously, statements will be false if the speaker intentionally lies, fabricates material, omits material facts, or otherwise phrases statements in such a way as to deliberately create a false impression. A statement can also be false when a speaker incorrectly assumes facts (as in the example given above of John and Jane dating). However, the greatest danger comes from an ordinary fact about life: we are not omniscient. A speaker won't always know when a statement is false. Sometimes, a person has every reason to believe a statement is true but, nevertheless, it happens to be false.

It is important to remember that sometimes sources lie. Even if sources don't lie outright, they often have an agenda of their own that might skew their perspective. Or, they might lack information themselves, meaning that the information they provide is incomplete or wrong. One should not assume that information from sources is true. It can be hard to detect misinformation, especially if a source deliberately hides relevant information or is trying to promote a specific agenda. But good ethical practices, such as corroborating details with multiple sources, can help prevent libel suits because such practices help weed out false information. Unfortunately, those methods are not foolproof, but at least they help minimize risk. One should always look for contradictory or supplemental information to be as informed as possible. Some news organizations have a "two source" rule (information must be obtained from two distinct sources) in order to minimize the risk of inadvertently making false statements.

Most jurisdictions recognize the concept of "substantial truth." The substantial truth doctrine holds that statements need not be technically correct as long as the gist of the statement is true. For example, if a man kills four people, but a newspaper falsely reports that he killed five people, the court will probably find the statement to be "substantially true," and thus not a basis for a libel claim. The "sting" of the report—the part that harms his reputation—is that he killed multiple people, and that aspect of the report is true. The technical falsity that the number of victims is four rather than five does not affect the sting, and therefore, the killer shouldn't be able to win libel damages on such a technicality.

Along the same lines, it is not considered false to modify a source's quote, for example, to correct a grammatical error, as long as the change does not substantially change the meaning of the quote. However, in *Masson v. New Yorker Magazine, Inc.*, the Supreme Court ruled that changing or fabricating quotes may be the basis of a libel claim if it results in a "gross distortion."

THE BURDEN OF PROOF

Usually, the plaintiff has the burden of proving that the allegedly defamatory statement is false. In *Philadelphia Newspapers v. Hepps*, the Supreme Court established this rule as a matter of constitutional principle. The burden of proof can be an important factor, because it can be very difficult to prove that a statement is true. The source of the information might disappear or be uncooperative or change his story, leaving a defendant with no witness to help him at trial. Thus, to preserve maximum protection for speech, the Court determined that the burden of proving falsity should be on the plaintiff rather than forcing the defendant to prove the truth of the statement in question.

However, there may be an exception if the allegedly libelous statement involves a private person (as opposed to a public official or public figure) and is not of public concern. Matters of public concern, however, can be difficult to define. The general principle is that the subject matter must be something that a significant number of people care about or that would affect the lives of a significant number of people. Admittedly, this is a poorly defined concept, but the courts use it nevertheless. If a court deems the subject matter of a communication to be of private concern, as opposed to public concern, then the defendant may have the burden of proving the statement is true in order to fend off liability.

Also, even though the plaintiff usually has the burden of proving the statement is false, juries sometimes ignore that fact. It has been reported, for example, that the jury in a libel lawsuit brought by a Mobil Oil executive against the *Washington Post* found in favor of the plaintiff because the *Post's* story didn't "prove" that the executive had engaged in nepotism.[1] The *Post* shouldn't have had to prove the story was true. The executive needed to prove it was false. Nevertheless, juries are often sympathetic to plaintiffs, and they may sometimes ignore the principle that the plaintiff bears the burden of proving falsity.

THE EXCEPTION: TRUE STATEMENTS AS A BASIS FOR LIBEL IN MASSACHUSETTS

The requirement of falsity is a general rule, and there's a good argument to be made that it should be a constitutional requirement in all cases. But there is at least one exception under state law. Massachusetts apparently will permit a libel claim based on a true statement in cases involving private individuals and matters of private concern.

This rule was affirmed in a case called *Noonan v. Staples*. The case involved an employee who was fired from Staples for violating the company's travel and expense policies. He admitted that he often "pre- populated" his expense reports and submitted expense reports with incorrect entries. After he was fired, an Executive Vice-President sent an email to all the employees in Staples's North American Division saying that Noonan's employment had been terminated because he was "not in compliance with our [travel and expenses] policies." The email also reminded employees that they must comply with company policy. Noonan sued for libel based on a state statute from 1902 allows a true statement to be the basis of a libel claim if the statement is made with "actual malice." The First Circuit, interpreting Massachusetts law, found that actual malice in the 1902 law meant "ill will." This interpretation of actual malice must be distinguished from the constitutional concept of actual malice established in *New York Times Co. v. Sullivan*, which means "knowledge of falsity," and is discussed in more detail in the section later in this chapter on the level of fault required in libel cases.

The ruling in *Noonan* appears to be limited to situations in the state of Massachusetts where the subject of the statement is a private person and the statement involves a matter of private concern. Nevertheless, this is a notable exception to the general principle that statements must be false.

Is There a Factual Assertion?

This factor is one of the most important and also one of the most difficult. The basic principle is that a libel claim should be based on a factual assertion as opposed to on an opinion, a joke, rhetoric, or hyperbole, which are usually granted First Amendment protection. In other words, to have a libel claim, the statement at issue must be something that a person could reasonably believe states actual fact. To make this determination, courts look at the overall context and tone of the statement, not simply the technical syntax of the sentence.

But the distinction between a "factual assertion" and an "opinion" is fuzzy, and many courts have acknowledged the difficulty distinguishing the two. In *Levin v. McPhee*, the Second Circuit noted, "[c]ategorizing a defendant's statements as either fact or opinion … is often not an easy task. As one commenter has noted, 'No area of modern libel law can be murkier than the cavernous depths of this inquiry.'"

To make matters more complicated, sometimes courts consider this factor as an element of the plaintiff's claim, and sometimes the notion of opinion is treated as a defense the defendant can raise. But regardless of how the issue is raised procedurally, the basic principle remains the same: The First Amendment should protect expressions of opinion or other similar kinds of speech that cannot reasonably be interpreted as stating actual facts.

In an effort to establish some clarity, this section will first address the kinds of speech that are typically granted First Amendment protection, and then it will discuss the more complicated precedent to illustrate how difficult and murky the analysis can be.

WHAT KIND OF STATEMENTS ARE TYPICALLY PROTECTED?

Jokes

In general, humor, no matter how lame or offensive, cannot be the basis for a libel claim, unless the joke appears to assert a fact. There are numerous cases that illustrate this principle, and perhaps the best way to convey the point is simply to consider the wide range of jokes that have been protected.

The most famous is probably *Hustler v. Falwell*, the Supreme Court case concerning Hustler magazine's ad parody suggesting that Televangelist Jerry Falwell had lost his virginity to his own mother in an outhouse. The parody was modeled after actual Campari ads that included interviews with various celebrities about their "first time," referring to the first time they sampled Campari, but playing on the sexual double entendre of the term "first time." In small print at the bottom of the page, the *Hustler* parody contained the disclaimer, "ad parody—not to be taken seriously."

At trial, the jury found the *Hustler* ad parody could not "reasonably be understood as describing actual facts about [Falwell] or actual events in which [he] participated," and the Supreme Court agreed, finding that the parody could not be the basis of a libel claim.

Similarly, in *Knievel v. ESPN*, the court found that stuntman Evel Knievel had no claim based on a photo caption humorously referring to him as a "pimp"; in *Yeagle v. Collegiate Times*, the court found that a student newspaper that inadvertently used the phrase "Director of Butt Licking" as a photo caption was not liable because the caption "cannot reasonably be understood as stating an actual fact"; in *Polygram Records v. Superior Court*, the court found that a winery owner could not sue based on Robin Williams's comedy routine about "black wines"; in *New Times, Inc. v. Isaaks*, the court found that a satirical editorial mocking a judge's ruling was not actionable; and in *San Francisco Bay Guardian v. Superior Court*, the court rejected a landlord's attempt to sue over a fake "letter to the editor" in a special parody issue of the newspaper. What all of these cases—and many more—have in common is that they all involve statements that are clearly jokes and not to be taken seriously. The courts protect these because they are not "factual assertions" upon which a libel claim can be based.

However, libel cases have been permitted in some circumstances where the speech at issue was intended to be humorous, but the courts nevertheless found that the statement could be interpreted as a factual assertion. In *Martin v. Municipal Pub.*, the court allowed a "mummer" to sue based on a humorous caption underneath a photo of him. The Mummers Parade is held each year on New Year's Day in Philadelphia. It is an unusually elaborate parade involving costumes, dance routines, sets, music, and comedy. One of the most notable features is that it often involves very large, burly men dancing down the street in frilly dresses. It is quite a sight. Many people, both participants and spectators, are often drunk.

Given that background, *Philadelphia Magazine* published a photo of one such "mummer" with the caption "A New Year's tribute here to all the ostriches who gave their tails to make the world free for closet transvestites from South Philly to get themselves stinking drunk. Have a nice year." Although the magazine argued that the statement was satirical, the court allowed the plaintiff to go forward with his claim, finding that the statement could be construed to say defamatory things about the man. While that case may be a bit of an outlier, it does illustrate the point that if it is not clear to an audience that a statement is a joke, the courts are more willing to allow a case to go forward.

Rhetoric and Hyperbole

The Supreme Court has consistently ruled that libel claims are meritless where the statement at issue cannot reasonably be construed to state actual facts, and this is particularly true where the statement is rhetoric or hyperbole that is clearly not meant to be taken literally. For example, in *Greenbelt Cooperative Publishing Assn., Inc. v. Bresler*, the Court ruled that the use of the word "blackmail" to describe a proposed deal between the city council and a citizen was clearly hyperbole and should receive First Amendment protection. Similarly, in *Letter Carriers v. Austin*, the Court overturned a libel verdict based on the use of the word "traitor" because the word was clearly used in a hyperbolic context in the midst of a labor dispute. It is therefore fairly well established that the First Amendment will protect speech if the words are used hyperbolically to express an idea and are not meant to be interpreted literally.

Insults and Other Poorly Defined Terms

Courts have generally been unwilling to impose liability on vague insults, such as calling someone a "jerk," "loser," or "creep." What, exactly, does it take to be a "jerk"? No one can define it. These terms don't have specific criteria that can be proven true or false, and thus, even though an audience will understand that the subject of the statement is not held in high esteem by the speaker, the statement cannot be the basis of a libel claim because it doesn't convey *facts*. The terms clearly reflect an opinion of the speaker.

In *Seelig vs. Infinity Broadcasting*, for example, a radio host referred to a contestant on the reality television show *Who Wants to Marry a Multimillionaire* as a "skank." The contestant sued for libel, but the court found that the term "skank" lacked a precise definition that could be proven true or false and thus her claim was dismissed. Specifically, the court said, "The word skank is a derogatory slang term of recent vintage that has no generally recognized meaning." It may indicate that the speaker disapproves of the subject, but it is "devoid of any factual content." The court also noted that the plaintiff failed to provide any dictionary definition of the term, further indicating that the word had no verifiable meaning.

Thus, terms like "loser," "skank," or "creep," that have no verifiable meaning, are usually protected, unless there is some other statement or context that creates an implication of false facts.

Aesthetic Judgments and Reviews

Reviews of books, movies, restaurants, etc., are generally protected as opinion, as long as harsh statements are backed up with valid examples or the statement is clearly hyperbolic. For example, in *Havalunch v. Mazza*, the court protected a restaurant review that said one needed to bring a "can of Raid" to eat there; and in *Moldea v. New York Times*, the court protected a book review accusing a writer of "sloppy journalism," because that opinion was supported with examples from the book. Courts are equally likely to protect statements that reflect aesthetic value judgments, such as referring to someone or something as "ugly" or "disgusting."

Speculation

Courts are usually willing to distinguish factual assertions from speculation. For example, in *Madison v. Frazier*, the court found that the statement "maybe he planned to run for some sort of political office or was trying to obtain a politically connected employment opportunity" was non-actionable "opinion." The court said it was obvious that the author "wondered" about the person's motives, but did not go so far as to state as fact that the person was motivated by political concerns. The courts tend to protect statements that are clearly theoretical or speculative.

Conclusions

Courts have been willing to protect statements that are clearly conclusions, as long as the speaker provides all the facts on which the conclusions are based. For example, in *Riley v. Harr*, the court protected a book about some controversial litigation that gave mixed information supporting each side of the case and allowed readers to draw their own conclusions. Even though the author may have had a viewpoint about the case, the court found that drawing a conclusion when one provides all the relevant facts is a form of opinion. What is difficult, however, is determining when adequate facts have been provided.

The kind of conclusion that should be protected is one where the facts are known to speaker and audience alike, and it is clear that the speaker has no additional, inside knowledge that gives his opinion or conclusion more weight. For example, after 9/11, the U.S. invaded Iraq. Several individuals wrote that "Bush lied" about whether Iraq had weapons of mass destruction (WMDs). There were certain established facts:

1. People within the Bush administration represented to the public that Iraq had WMDs; and

2. As of the date of this writing, no WMDs have been found in Iraq.

Given those facts, there were three logically possible conclusions one could have drawn:

1. That Bush lied (*i.e.*, intentionally misrepresented facts) when he said that Iraq has WMDs;

2. That Bush was simply incorrect (he genuinely believed that Iraq had WMDs, but was wrong); or

3. That Iraq did have WMDs, but they have not yet been discovered.

Any of those three conclusions are logically valid, and it is unlikely that the American public will ever know with certainty which is true. But some people will say that Bush lied, meaning that they believe the correct conclusion is the first. No one would plausibly believe that the speaker has any special information that makes his conclusion more significant than anyone else's. The audience should understand that the speaker is drawing one specific conclusion from the publicly known facts. But, in order to warrant protection as a conclusion, the facts leading up to the conclusion have to be fairly described or well known.

Being able to distinguish facts from opinions is crucial to understanding libel law. Asserting false facts would not be protected, but opinions are not "false" in the same sense that facts are. Some opinions may be more justifiable than others. Nevertheless, the courts do not punish people for having stupid opinions. The only question is whether the statement is properly conveyed as an opinion.

When Might "Opinion" Not Be Protected?
It should be clear from the foregoing that it's not the words used that matter—it's the context and interpretation of how they are used. Nevertheless, it can be difficult to discern when a statement will be interpreted as a factual assertion or as some form of protected speech. The "skank" cases present an interesting contrast.

In *Seelig vs. Infinity Broadcasting*, noted above, radio personalities referred to Seelig (who appeared on the television show *Who Wants to Marry a Multimillionaire?*) as a "skank." She sued for libel. The court ruled that, in context, the term "skank" did not convey any specific meaning and could not be the basis for a libel claim.

Cohen v. Google, Inc., involved the blog, "Skanks of New York," which identified a particular model as a "skank." The blog also referred to her as "whoring" and posted sexually suggesting photos of her. The court allowed her libel claim to go forward, finding that the statements were not clearly and opinion and may be taken to suggest actual facts about the manner in which she conducts her sex life.

Thus, it's not the word itself ("skank," in these cases), but the context in which the word is presented that matters. Many common words could have a specific defamatory meaning or a broad, hyperbolic meaning, depending on context. Words like bankrupt, traitor, liar, pervert, and thief fall into this category. The court will look at the context to see whether the term should be interpreted in the literal sense or the hyperbolic sense.

The Supreme Court has addressed the issue of when opinion should be protected only once, and it was a difficult, complex case. In *Milkovich v. Lorain Journal Co.*, the Court considered whether to allow liability for a sports column that said that high school wrestling coach Michael Milkovich "lied."

The case arose after a fight broke out at a wrestling match, and Coach Milkovich's team was placed on probation and deemed ineligible for the state tournament. A subsequent hearing overturned those punishments. In response, a local sports columnist wrote an editorial with the heading "Maple beat the law with the 'big lie.'" The column said:

> When a person takes on a job in a school, whether it be as teacher, coach, administrator or even maintenance worker, it is well to remember that his primary job is that of educator. There is scarcely a person concerned with school who doesn't leave his mark in some way on the young people who pass his way—many are the lessons taken away from school by students which weren't learned from a lesson plan or out of a book. They come from personal experiences with and observations of their superiors and peers, from watching actions and reactions. Such a lesson was learned (or relearned) yesterday by the student body of Maple Heights High School, and by anyone who attended the Maple-Mentor wrestling meet of last Feb. 8. A lesson which, sadly, in the view of the events of the past year, is well they learned early. It is simply this: If you get in a jam, lie your way out. If you're successful enough, and powerful enough, and can sound sincere enough, you stand an excellent chance of making the lie stand up, regardless of what really happened. The teachers responsible were mainly head Maple wrestling coach, Mike Milkovich, and former superintendent of schools H. Donald Scott. Last winter they were faced with a difficult situation. Milkovich's ranting from the side of the mat and egging the crowd on against the meet official and the opposing team backfired during a meet with [Mentor] and resulted in first the Maple Heights team, then many of the partisan crowd attacking the Mentor squad in a brawl which sent four Mentor wrestlers to the hospital. Naturally, when Mentor protested to the governing body of high school sports … the two men were called on the carpet to account for the incident. But they declined to walk into the hearing and face up to their responsibilities as one would hope a coach of Milkovich's accomplishments and reputation would do, and one would certainly expect from a man with the responsible position of superintendent of schools. Instead they chose to come to the hearing and misrepresent the things that happened … attempting not only to convince the board of their own innocence, but, incredibly, shift the blame of the affair to Mentor. I was among the 2000-plus witnesses of the meet … and I also attended the hearing … so I was in a unique position of being the only non-involved party to observe both the meet itself and the Milkovich-Scott version presented to the board. … "I can say that some of the stories told to the judge sounded pretty darned unfamiliar," said Dr. Harold Meyer, commissioner of the OHSAA, who attended the hearing. "It certainly sounded different from what they told us." Nevertheless, the judge bought their story, and ruled in their favor. Anyone who attended the meet, whether he be from Maple Heights, Mentor, or impartial observer, knows in his heart that Milkovich and Scott lied at the hearing after each having given his solemn oath to tell the truth. But they got away with it. Is that the kind of lesson we want our young people learning from their high school administrators and coaches? I think not.

Both Milkovich and Scott sued for libel. The Ohio Supreme Court found that the lawsuits were meritless, following the four-part test set forth in *Ollman v. Evans*, which, at the time, had been the most influential court ruling on the topic of distinguishing factual assertions from opinions. The court considered (1) the specific language used, (2) whether the statement was verifiable, (3) the general context of the statement, and (4) the broader context in which the statement appeared.

The court determined that the context of the statements was clearly an editorial, and a sports page was "a traditional haven for cajoling, invective, and hyperbole." Thus the court felt that a reader would interpret the article as a whole as opinion.

The U.S. Supreme Court, however, took the case and said that First Amendment principles did not "create a wholesale defamation exemption for anything that might be labeled 'opinion.'" In fact, the Court took a rather dim view of "opinion":

If a speaker says, "In my opinion John Jones is a liar," he implies a knowledge of facts which lead to the conclusion that Jones told an untruth. Even if the speaker states the facts upon which he bases his opinion, if those facts are either incorrect or incomplete, or if his assessment of them is erroneous, the statement may still imply a false assertion of fact. Simply couching such statements in terms of opinion does not dispel these implications; and the statement, "In my opinion Jones is a liar," can cause as much damage to reputation as the statement, "Jones is a liar." As Judge Friendly aptly stated: "[It] would be destructive of the law of libel if a writer could escape liability for accusations of [defamatory conduct] simply by using, explicitly or implicitly, the words 'I think.'"

The Court also rejected the notion that the statements could be opinion in context. It drew a distinction between statements like, "In my opinion Mayor Jones is a liar," which implied facts, and "In my opinion, Mayor Jones shows his abysmal ignorance by accepting the teachings of Marx and Lenin," which "would not be actionable." The Court concluded that the column implied that Coach Milkovich had perjured himself at the hearing, which would be a factual assertion rather than "loose, figurative, or hyperbolic language."

The difficulty with *Milkovich* is that the term "liar" can be interpreted as either a factual assertion or an opinion, depending on context. The Court concluded that a jury could find that the columnist implied that he *did* have particular knowledge as to whether Milkovich lied (unlike the example given above where someone claims that "Bush lied," and they have no special knowledge of the facts). It may have been possible to express the idea that Milkovich lied in a manner that would be interpreted as an "opinion," if the tone or context had been different.

The lesson drawn by many courts from *Milkovich* is not that opinions cannot be protected, but that where there is ambiguity about whether the statement is a factual assertion or opinion, the courts should err on the side of finding the statement to be a factual assertion if the statement seems to imply particular knowledge of unstated facts. Many courts, however, still employ a test examining the context of the statement to determine whether it is a factual assertion or opinion. Courts will often consider:

- The language of the statement itself

- Whether the speaker is in a position to know the facts

- The context in which the statement appears

- Whether the terms have figurative, hyperbolic, ambiguous or slang meanings

- The reasonable expectations of the audience

- Whether the statement is capable of being objectively characterized as true or false

- The broader social context, including references to pop culture or any customs or conventions which might signal to readers or listeners that what is being read or heard is likely to be opinion

- The use of phrases such as "appeared to be," "might well be," "could well happen," or "should be" that signal presumptions or predictions rather than factual assertions.

At this point, it should be clear that the issue of what purports to be a factual assertion and what is an opinion is difficult and complex. Determinations are very fact-specific and depend on the exact words used, the overall context of the statement, and the degree to which the court thinks the statement relies on unspoken assumptions. It is therefore in a speaker's best interest to be extraordinarily careful to distinguish between what is a factual assertion and what is speculation, conclusion, humor, or hyperbole. If it is ambiguous, there is a higher risk of liability.

Liar Libel and the #MeToo Movement

In the years since *Milkovich*, lower courts have interpreted the Court's holding to mean that accusations of "lying" are actionable when the speaker implies knowledge of the underlying facts and that a specific falsehood had been made. In some cases, the courts have found that accusations of "lying" are "rhetorical hyperbole" or some other form of protected opinion. The outcome depends on the context in which the statement was made.

The issue of "liar" libel has become a hot topic, because of the slew of lawsuits arising from #metoo claims. Sometimes the men who are accused of sexual misconduct sue their accusers for libel based on the allegation of misconduct itself. But sometimes, the accusers sue the alleged perpetrators for suggesting that the accusers are lying. The courts have come to different conclusions about whether such claims are actionable. For example, some of the women who accused Bill Cosby of rape have sued him and his attorney for libel for suggesting that their claims were false. In *McKee v. Cosby*, the First Circuit concluded that the statements at issue (admonishing the newspaper for its decision to publish the allegations against Cosby without investigating McKee's credibility) were non-actionable opinion. The First Circuit also ruled that McKee was a limited purpose public figure because she voluntarily thrust herself into the middle of public controversy when she told her story to the newspaper. Similarly, in *Hill v. Cosby*, the Third Circuit found that statements suggesting that journalists should fact check the accusers claims and comparing the situation to the discredited report about rapes at the University of Virginia were opinion and "no reasonable recipient could read [the statements] as implying the existence of undisclosed defamatory facts." However, in *Green v. Cosby*, the court found that blanket statements that the accusations were "discredited" and "unsubstantiated" were actionable because none of the statements disclosed sufficient facts to qualify as opinions. The Court was not persuaded that the statements were merely rhetorical hyperbole. And in *Dickinson v. Cosby*, the court found the statements that Dickinson's accusations were "false and outlandish" and her story was "fabricated" and "an outrageous defamatory lie" were actionable. The statements failed to disclose sufficient facts to render them "opinion based on fully disclosed, nonactionable facts." These cases suggest that the outcomes will be dependent on how carefully the denials of misconduct are crafted and whether they are consistent with principles governing statements of opinion. Context matters!

Does the Statement Identify a Valid Plaintiff?

Libel claims cannot be filed by random citizens simply because they dislike a story. The person who is defamed can sue, but other people cannot sue on their behalf. For example, if you think a story about a politician is defamatory, you cannot file a lawsuit arguing that the politician has been defamed; the politician would have to sue on his own behalf, if he wished. The person who sues must be recognized by the courts as a valid plaintiff.

In most cases, the plaintiff can be any person who is identified in any way by the statement. Corporations count as "persons," so companies can sue just as individuals may sue.

There are limitations, however. Courts do not recognize libel claims on behalf of people who are deceased. The theory is that once a person dies, they no longer have a protectable interest in their reputation. Courts also do not recognize claims on behalf of government agencies. Individual government officials may sue if they are defamed, but an agency itself may not.

The United States does not usually recognize "group libel," meaning that one cannot defame a large group, such as a race, religion, gender, ethnicity or other large group. However, libel claims are permitted when the group defamed is a small, identifiable group and the statement applies to "all" or "most," not merely "one of," the group members. Thus, a court in *Fawcett Publications v. Morris* determined that football players could sue when the entire football team was accused of using amphetamine nasal spray; and in *Lins v. Evening News Ass'n*, two local union leaders were allowed to sue for libel when statements were made about "local union leadership" (there were seven leaders in total). However, claims are not permitted when the group is too large. In *Granger v. Time, Inc.*, *Time* magazine stated that arson had become common in Butte, Montana. Business owners whose buildings had burned were not allowed to sue for libel, because there were over 200 burned buildings and no person could reasonably identify that the plaintiffs were accused of arson. Similarly, in *Gales v. CBS Broadcasting*, a 60 Minutes segment about large jury verdicts in Mississippi did not defame juror plaintiffs because it did not specifically reference those 6 jurors; statements were about county jurors in general, and the group of jurors was so large that no one could reasonably infer that the statements referred to those specific jurors.

The following table summarizes who can be considered a valid plaintiff in libel cases:

Table 3.1: Who Is a Valid Plaintiff?

Valid plaintiff	Not a valid plaintiff
Any person identified in any way by the statement	Someone other than the person named who sues on their behalf (except parents or guardians on behalf of minors)
Specific government officials named in a story	Government agencies
Corporations	Deceased individuals
Members of a small group if "all" or "most" members of the group are implicated	Members of a large group or members of any group if only "some" or "a few" members are implicated

WAYS A PERSON CAN BE IDENTIFIED BY A STATEMENT

A person can be identified for the purposes of libel law in various ways: directly, indirectly, in fiction, or by error. Direct identification occurs when the person is specifically named. This is the most straightforward way that someone would have a libel claim. Indirect identification occurs when the story describes a person or circumstances with sufficient detail so others can determine to whom the speaker is referring. For example, if a story describes a woman dressed in red at the scene of the accident, and there is only one woman dressed in red at that time, the person could be identified even though the story did not use her name. In one case, a paper reported on a teen runaway who was killed, and the report referred to her parents who abused her. The teen was named, but her parents were not. Nevertheless, they were identified because a reader could figure out who they were based on the name of the teen.

Libel claims can be brought based on fictional characters if there are circumstances that would lead a reasonable person to think that the character is based on a real person. The classic example is *Bindrim v. Mitchell*, where a fictional book about "nude encounter marathon" therapy sessions was similar to the therapy sessions of the real Dr. Bindrim, and he prevailed in a libel claim. Dr. Bindrim was well-known for his unusual therapy method, and thus it was not difficult for the court to conclude that the story referenced him. However, not all claims of fictional identification are successful. For example, in *Carter-Clark v. Random House, Inc.*, the court dismissed a claim brought by a librarian who claimed she was referenced in the book *Primary Colors*. The court found that she could not show the book referred to her because the description of the librarian in the book was sufficiently vague and could have referred to any one of many librarians. Similarly, in *Pring v. Penthouse*, the court found that a reference to Miss Wyoming in a fictional story about a contestant in the Miss America pageant did not refer to the plaintiff, who happened to be Miss Wyoming one year. The character in the story had a different name and there was no indication what year the story was supposed to be. Thus, she was not identified by the story.

In sum, there must be some strong connection between the character and the real person in order to state a claim for libel by fiction. Courts must balance real-life identification against fictional expression, which shouldn't be unnecessarily chilled. To be safe, when writing fiction, writers should consider how the expression comes across. Is it a genuine fantasy, or does it seem like veiled libel? Authors sometimes label works as "fan fiction" or "satire" if there is any question.

Finally, errors are a surprisingly common way for a person to be identified for the purposes of libel. A person may be accidentally identified when a statement refers to a person with a similar or the same name, confuses victim and criminal, or misspells a name, resulting in confusion about who did what. A classic example is *Little Rock Newspapers, Inc. v. Fitzhugh*. In that case, an article described the upcoming prosecution of Eugene Fitzhugh, who had been indicted in connection with the Whitewater scandal. However, the accompanying photograph, captioned "Fitzhugh," was a photo of J. Michael Fitzhugh, a different person. He sued for libel and won.

Was the Statement Published?

For the purposes of a libel claim, "publishing" means revealing the information to any third party (anyone other than the person defamed). It does not require publication in mass media, although publication in mass media is definitely publishing.

In general, publishers and broadcasters are liable for republishing defamatory statements made by others. The fact that a source made the statement is NOT a defense to the element of publication. (It might help with other defenses, such as determining fault, but it is not a defense to the element of publication.) Repeating a statement carries the same consequence as originating the statement. This is called the "republication rule."

Let me repeat that because it is counterintuitive to what many people expect: Under the republication rule if someone tells you something defamatory and you repeat that statement, then YOU may be liable for that statement because you republished it. Even if you did not originate the statement, you can be liable for transmitting it. In short, you are responsible for what you publish, even if you got the information from someone else. That doesn't mean that there are no other defenses available. However, the statement will be deemed to be published by you.

There is one narrow exception to the republication rule. Section 230 of the Communications Decency Act contains a provision that exempts internet service providers from liability for content posted by third parties. Thus, if a commenter posts a defamatory statement on a website, the commenter may be liable, but the website probably won't be liable.

The CDA (discussed more fully in Chapter 20) makes a distinction between "service providers" and "content providers." The "content provider" is the person who creates the content, and he is always liable for the content he creates. The "service provider" is the person or entity that operates a website or service that is open to third party users. Service providers are not liable for content generated by the third parties that use their service or site.

Section 230 has created some interesting scenarios for modern libel law. As a practical matter, section 230 often means that a plaintiff must sue the person who originated the statement if the libel occurred online. However, the person who originated the statement often has no assets. If the case has no merit, the defendant may simply lack the resources to defend themselves. But even if the plaintiff has a legitimate case, the defendant may have no assets from which to pay any judgment. In neither case is justice done.

Did the Defendant Act With the Requisite Level of Fault?

Historically, a person who published a false, defamatory factual assertion about someone would be liable for libel. The primary ways to avoid liability were to show that one of those conditions did not apply—that the statement was true (as opposed to false), that it was not defamatory, or that it was "fair comment" (as opposed to a factual assertion). But, in general, if a person made a statement that happened to be false—even if he had good reason to believe it was true—the speaker would be liable. The legal standard for fault was "strict liability," meaning that the person was liable if the set conditions were met (*i.e.*, if a defamatory false statement was made).

That changed with the U.S. Supreme Court's decision in *New York Times Co. v. Sullivan*. L. B. Sullivan was an elected official in Montgomery, Alabama, who oversaw the city's police department. A political advertisement ran in the *New York Times* that criticized the conduct of the police officers who treated civil rights demonstrators badly. Sullivan sued for libel, arguing that it defamed him in his role overseeing police conduct.

The Court recognized that there needed to be some First Amendment protection for statements that criticize elected officials, even if the statements happen to be false, because factual errors are inevitable. It is simply not possible to know all the facts all the time, and it would harm political discourse to self-censor out of fear of liability if the statement turned out to be false. Thus, the Court ruled that elected officials such as Sullivan cannot prevail in a libel action unless they can prove that the defendant acted with "actual malice," defined as "knowledge of falsity or reckless disregard of the truth." Such a rule should leave room for citizens to discuss the conduct of officials without unreasonable fear of liability if a statement (unknowingly) happens to be incorrect.

The principle underlying the *Sullivan* decision—that the plaintiff's interest in protecting his reputation must be balanced against First Amendment interests—led to a flurry of cases attempting to sort out what level of constitutional protection should be granted to different kinds of statements about different kinds of people. In *Curtis Publishing Co. v. Butts*, the court considered a libel claim brought by Coach Wally Butts of the University of Georgia. A paper alleged that he had conspired with Coach "Bear" Bryant of the University of Alabama to fix a football game between the two schools. College football at those schools is wildly popular and the question of whether a game was fixed would have been of great public concern. The two coaches were well-known, but neither qualified as a "public official." The Court determined that the same principles that supported constitutional protection in *Sullivan* required some level of protection in *Butts*, and it therefore ruled that the *Sullivan* standard should apply to criticism of public figures as well as public officials.

In *Gertz v. Robert Welch, Inc.*, however, the Court made it clear that the actual malice standard need not be used in every case. It established a rule that the level of fault required could vary depending on the status of the plaintiff.

The *Gertz* case arose from a murder. A Chicago policeman (Nuccio) shot and killed a boy (Nelson), and Nuccio was convicted of second-degree murder. The Nelson family hired Elmer Gertz, a reputable attorney, to represent them in a lawsuit against Nuccio.

For nearly a decade, the magazine *American Opinion*, a publication of the John Birch Society, had been warning of a "nationwide conspiracy to discredit local law enforcement agencies and create in their stead a national police force capable of supporting a Communist dictatorship." Consistent with that message, the magazine published an article on the murder trial of Officer Nuccio, "FRAME-UP: Richard Nuccio And The War On Police." The article alleged that the testimony at Nuccio's trial was false and that his prosecution was part of the supposed Communist campaign against the police. Gertz attended the coroner's inquest and filed a lawsuit on behalf of the Nelson family, but he otherwise played no role in the criminal proceeding, nor did he speak out on the subject. Nevertheless, the article portrayed Gertz as an architect of the "frame-up." The article made numerous false allegations about Gertz. It stated that:

- The police file on Gertz took "a big, Irish cop to lift." (Gertz actually had no criminal record.)

- Gertz had been an official of the "Marxist League for Industrial Democracy, originally known as the Intercollegiate Socialist Society, which has advocated the violent seizure of our government." (He had never been a member of either group.)

- He was a "Leninist" and a "Communist-fronter." (There was no apparent basis for these statements.)

- He had been an officer of the National Lawyers Guild, described as a Communist organization that "probably did more than any other outfit to plan the Communist attack on the Chicago police during the 1968 Democratic Convention." (Gertz had been an officer of the National Lawyers Guild, but there was no evidence that he or that organization had taken any part in planning the 1968 demonstrations in Chicago.)

The magazine also published a photograph of Gertz with the caption, "Elmer Gertz of Red Guild harasses Nuccio."

It was clear that the magazine had published false defamatory statements about Gertz, but the Court acknowledged that the strict liability standard was too harsh. The Court again noted that errors are inevitable, and found that "a rule of strict liability that compels a publisher or broadcaster to guarantee the accuracy of his factual assertions may lead to intolerable self-censorship. Allowing the media to avoid liability only by proving the truth of all injurious statements does not accord adequate protection to First Amendment liberties." On the other hand, the Court was concerned that reputational interests of ordinary people would not be adequately protected if the actual malice standard were applied in all cases. If it were, publishers might feel free to make any accusation, no matter how unjustified, as long as they don't *know* it's false, and such a standard would leave ordinary people vulnerable to outrageous claims.

In considering whether the actual malice standard should be applied to public figures as well as private figures, the Court noted a couple factors that justified different treatment for different kinds of plaintiffs. First, public officials and public figures typically have access to media and other effective channels of communication that allow them to counteract false statements. Private persons typically did not have such access. There is, however, some dispute now about whether the internet and social media are eroding that distinction. It will be interesting to see whether libel law changes as social media develops and ordinary citizens have the ability to self-publish rebuttals to allegedly defamatory statements, in many cases in the same forum as the original statement and in real-time. But at the time *Gertz* was decided, the distinction was more valid.

Second, the Court said there is a "compelling normative consideration underlying the distinction between public and private defamation plaintiffs." Those who seek office are subject to public scrutiny on any topic relevant to their fitness for office, including "dishonesty, malfeasance, or improper motivation, even though these characteristics may also affect the official's private character." Public figures endure similar scrutiny. Private figures, however, have not voluntarily exposed themselves to such scrutiny. If a person has not sought influence, then they are more deserving of protection.

The court therefore decided that there should be some middle ground for private figures. It held that "[s]tates may define for themselves the appropriate standard of liability," as long as they don't impose strict liability. As a result, many states have applied a "negligence" standard, holding publishers liable if they fail to act with reasonable care.

Thus, there are two standards of fault in libel cases, "actual malice" and "negligence," and the standard used depends on who the plaintiff is.

WHAT IS NEGLIGENCE?

Negligence means failure to act with "reasonable care." In *McCall v. Courier-Journal*, the court said that the negligence standard asks a court to consider "what a reasonably prudent person would or would not have done under the same or similar circumstances." This is not a difficult standard from which to find fault. The negligence standard favors the plaintiff because it is usually easy to argue that it would have been "reasonably prudent" for the defendant to have taken additional steps to verify the truth of the statement. If a journalist has failed to adhere to basic principles of journalism ethics, it may be more likely that a court will find their behavior to be negligent, because they have failed to act as journalists are expected to act.

WHAT EXACTLY CONSTITUTES ACTUAL MALICE?

Actual malice is defined as "knowledge of falsity or reckless disregard of the truth." Actual malice is usually difficult to prove, so this standard tends to favor the defendant and protect expression, even if the speaker was wrong. However, there are cases where the courts have found that actual malice existed, so the application of that standard should not be viewed as a free pass to say anything, no matter how absurd.

There is a fine line between failing to investigate thoroughly (negligence) and purposely avoiding the truth (actual malice). Reliance on a single source, for example, might be negligent, but in *Saenz v. Playboy Enterprises, Inc.*, the court ruled that in the absence of "strong indicators of probable falsity or unreliability," reliance on a single source does not constitute actual malice. On the other hand, in *Harte Hanks v. Connaughton*, the U.S. Supreme Court ruled that the purposeful failure to interview a person with an opposing viewpoint can be evidence of actual malice. If it appears that the reporter is trying to "build a case" and is intentionally avoiding any information that would be contrary to the point he is trying to make, such an approach may be viewed as evidence of actual malice.

In *St. Amant v. Thompson*, St. Amant had repeated allegedly defamatory statements about Thompson, and the question before the Supreme Court was what it meant to speak with "reckless disregard" for the truth. The Court determined that it is not necessary for the speaker to act like a "reasonably prudent" man. The Court applied a subjective, rather, than objective standard: did the speaker actually entertain doubts about the truth? The Court concluded that a speaker acts with "reckless disregard" if he did actually entertain serious doubts about the truth of the statement. However, the Court also acknowledged that there may be situations in which there are glaringly obvious reasons to doubt the truth of the statement, and in such cases, a speaker may act with reckless disregard by republishing it, regardless of any protestations of innocence. For example, the Court suggested that, although reliance on a single source is not necessarily evidence of actual malice on its own, reliance on a single source could constitute actual malice if there were obvious reasons to doubt the source.

Courts have found actual malice in both circumstances—when there are subjective doubts about the truth of a statement, and also when the facts indicate that there are obvious reasons that anyone should doubt the truth of the statement.

As an example of the former, consider *Kaelin v. Globe Comm. Corp.*, the case where a tabloid used the headline, "Cops Think Kato Did It." The editor testified that he knew that people would think "It" referred to murder, even though it referred to committing perjury. The court found that such awareness of the likelihood that readers would misunderstand the headline was evidence of actual malice.

In an example of the latter, a dean at the University of Virginia successfully sued Rolling Stone magazine over a story entitled "A Rape on Campus." The story initially described an incident in which a woman named "Jackie" was raped at a fraternity. The story also stated that the dean tried to persuade "Jackie" not to pursue her case and failed to respond when told about other alleged rapes at the fraternity. Shortly after the story was published, people began to question some of the facts described, and within a matter of months, the story was retracted, and it became clear that there were numerous inconsistencies between "Jackie's" version of events and other known facts. The reporter had relied heavily on "Jackie" and did not attempt to corroborate some of her claims; if she had, she would easily have found some of the inconsistencies. The jury found that the reporter had acted with actual malice by intentionally failing to investigate some of "Jackie's" claims and believed that the reporter knew it would destroy the story if they turned out not to be true.

Courts have also decided that actual malice could be found in cases where there is outright fabrication or distortion. For example, in *Cantrell v. Forest City Publishing Co.*, the Court determined that actual malice could be found where a reporter allegedly fabricated an interview and exaggerated facts. Similarly, the court allowed a claim to proceed in *Schiavone Construction Co. v. Time, Inc.* In that case, the magazine published a story that quoted an FBI memo. The original memo said that the FBI was investigating whether there was a connection between a construction company and organized crime, but that no link had been found. The story quoted the first part—that the FBI was investigating a connection—but left out the second part—that no link had been found. The court found that such an omission could be interpreted as actual malice. And, in *Goldwater v. Ginzburg*, the court found there could be actual malice where a magazine distorted expert comments to give a false impression about the psychological state of presidential candidate Barry Goldwater. The magazine had asked psychologists whether certain behaviors indicated mental illness. It then linked those behaviors to Goldwater, but did so in such a way as to suggest that the psychologists were referencing Goldwater personally rather than responding to abstract, impersonal questions.

What can be learned from these cases? Actual malice will almost definitely be found if a reporter or speaker knowingly makes things up or intentionally distorts the facts. Actual malice may be found if a reporter or speaker has an agenda and willfully ignores evidence, facts, sources, or statements that are adverse to the position he/she wishes to advocate AND if this is presented as objective fact rather than opinion. An editorial that is obviously biased will likely be protected as an opinion, as long as the requirements for opinion reporting are met. But a report that purports to be straight news might be found to have been published with actual malice if the reporter is purposefully pursuing an agenda, ignoring relevant facts, or intentionally failing to verify information that could easily have been verified. Finally, actual malice might be found if there are significant reasons to doubt the truth of a statement, but the statement is published anyway. Although courts do give reporters significant leeway to publish important allegations without proving they are true, they are also quite reluctant to protect the publication of allegations when the reporter has crossed the line into recklessness.

WHICH STANDARD APPLIES TO WHOM?

To evaluate the "fault" element of a libel claim, a court will classify the plaintiff into one of five categories and then apply the level of fault applicable to that type of plaintiff. It should be noted that states differ on the exact terminology used and criteria used when classifying a plaintiff, so this chart may represent a bit of an oversimplification. But, for the sake of simplicity, and because this book will not address all the complexities among all state laws, this chart outlines the basic considerations courts use to decide which standard of fault applies to various plaintiffs.

Three of the five categories are obvious from Supreme Court decisions: public officials, public figures, and private figures. The other two categories, limited-purpose public figures and involuntary limited-purpose public figures, are based on some *dicta* from *Gertz*:

Hypothetically, it may be possible for someone to become a public figure through no purposeful action of his own, but the instances of truly involuntary public figures must be exceedingly rare. For the most part those who attain this status have assumed roles of especial prominence in the affairs of society. Some occupy positions of such persuasive power and influence that they are deemed public figures for all purposes. More commonly, those classed as public figures have thrust themselves to the forefront of particular public controversies in order to influence the resolution of the issues involved. In either event, they invite attention and comment.

Courts have since made distinctions between public figures in general, those who seek prominence in limited contexts, and those who are involuntarily thrust into the spotlight. Courts also make a distinction between those with media access and those without, reasoning that you need to give more legal remedy to those without media access. Those who have media access can counteract any libelous statements with their own statements, suffer less damage, and need less protection. One of the problems that arises in libel cases is how to classify a plaintiff and how that class of plaintiff should be treated. States differ on how they treat plaintiffs, but the following table shows how courts generally approach the issue.

Table 3.2: Classification of Libel Plaintiffs.

Type of Plaintiff	Description	Applicable standard of fault
Public official	A government employee who has or appears to have "substantial responsibility for or control over the conduct of government affairs." This does not include every government employee, but it is broader than just the top officials.	Always actual malice
Public figure	People who have achieved pervasive fame or notoriety; people who are "intimately involved with the resolution of important public questions or, by reason of their fame, shape events in areas of concern to society at large."	Always actual malice
Limited purpose public figure (LPPF)	People who inject themselves into public debate on a certain topic. One of the main factors the courts consider is whether the person has access to the press. Have they given a press conference? Could they obtain press coverage if they chose to speak out?	Actual malice if the statement involves the subject for which they have sought attention. Otherwise, they are treated like private persons.
Involuntary limited purpose public figure	Those who become notorious unwillingly. Often criminals, crime victims, or those embroiled in a scandal, as long as they do not speak out or engage in a course of conduct that invites attention.	Some states treat them like LPPFs, other states treat them like private persons, so it depends on state law.
Private figure	Everyone else. Ordinary people.	In most cases, states only require proof of "negligence." However, some states apply "actual malice" if the statement involves a matter of public concern. The *Gertz* case says that states have latitude to provide a remedy for plaintiffs, as long as the standard is not "strict liability."

It can be extremely difficult to determine to which category a potential plaintiff would belong. People or entities that become the subject of news coverage are not always "public figures." In *Hutchinson v. Proxmire*, for example, the Supreme Court held that a scientist that received government funds and was awarded the satirical "Golden Fleece Award" for wasteful government spending was not a public figure.

An interesting question is whether corporations are public or private figures. The answer generally depends on state law. In general, large publicly traded companies that offer goods or services to the public will be considered public figures, but some businesses have been deemed private figures. States may consider factors such as the size of the business; whether it is a large corporation or simply the incorporation of a single individual; whether the business offers goods or services to the public in general, or whether it has a specialized, targeted clientele; and whether it is well-known in the community.

Another open question is whether bloggers or those with an active social media presence would be considered public figures. Commentators have debated whether internet use could make someone a public figure, even if for a limited purpose, and the case law has been mixed. Compare, for example, the court's conclusion in *Tipton v. Warshavsky*, holding that the plaintiff was a limited purpose public figure (LPPF) "because he voluntarily involved himself in public life by inviting attention and comment" by posting information online, with the conclusion in *Nehls v. Hillsdale Coll.*, holding that the plaintiff was not a limited purpose public figure because he was neither engaged in a public controversy nor did he assume a prominent position in a controversy simply by posting his story on a website. These cases represent very different approaches to and understandings of the internet, and this aspect of case law will surely develop more over the next several years.

There are some cases where the categorization of the plaintiff is obvious, but in many cases, it is debatable. The parties will look at the facts of the plaintiff's situation and the relevant precedent; the defendant will try to argue that the plaintiff qualifies as some form of public figure and the plaintiff will try to show he is a private person. The court will have to decide based on how the jurisdiction's law applies to the facts.

Did the Plaintiff Suffer Damages?

Normally, if a person files a lawsuit seeking monetary compensation, they must prove that they have suffered some loss, usually a financial loss, that can be compensated. So, for example, if a person is in a car accident and incurs medical expenses, the injured person can "prove" his loss by admitting into evidence his medical bills. The compensation a jury awards for the loss incurred is called "actual damages."

In libel cases, however, the "damage" is to reputation, something that is difficult to quantify. If a person loses his or her job as a result of a libelous statement, it might be easy to calculate loss based on the lost salary. But in most cases, the harm is incalculable, and a jury has little basis for establishing the amount of compensation that should be paid. Juries, therefore, have to exercise some discretion is awarding "actual damages," which may include any out-of-pocket loss as well as compensation for the harm to reputation. Nevertheless, the plaintiff would be required to present some evidence, such as testimony about how the statements have caused people to think less of him, to provide the jury some basis for making a determination about what the loss is worth.

Courts will sometimes allow "punitive damages," as well. Punitive damages are intended to punish the defendant for his bad behavior, unlike actual damages, which are intended to compensate the plaintiff for his loss. Punitive damages can be awarded in additional to actual damages in cases where the defendant has acted badly.

The Supreme Court, however, has put some limits on punitive damages in libel cases. In *Gertz*, the court noted that even if there is an interest in compensating people for injury to reputation, there is a competing First Amendment interest in ensuring that speakers are not punished excessively if mistakes are made. Thus, the Court ruled that punitive damages cannot be awarded unless the plaintiff proves that the statement was made with actual malice, meaning that the defendant knew the statement was false or recklessly disregarded the truth. Only then has a defendant acted badly enough to justify the imposition of punitive damages on top of actual damages.

The Court also applied this rule to "presumed damages," which are an oddity of libel law. In some states, plaintiffs were not required to prove that they suffered any actual loss in cases of libel *per se*. The courts figured that damages could be presumed—that if someone made an obviously defamatory statement, then a jury could presume that harm occurred, and the plaintiff needn't introduce evidence to show that there was actual harm. But, for the same reason the Court limited punitive damages to cases of actual malice, the Court also limited presumed damages to cases where actual malice was proved. Otherwise, plaintiffs must present evidence of actual damages.

The Supreme Court later backed off a bit on its strong protections against punitive and presumed damages in *Dun & Bradstreet v. Greenmoss Builders*. In that case, the Court ruled that such protections apply only if the speech is a matter of public concern. If the speech is purely about matters of private concern, then the First Amendment does not require such protection. *Dun & Bradstreet* involved libel allegations arising from a credit report, and the court did not require the plaintiff to prove actual malice.

There is one case that illustrates the danger of suing when no actual damage is caused by a defamatory statement. In *Franklin Prescriptions Inc. v. New York Times*, the jury found that the *New York Times* had defamed a business but no damages were awarded because no actual harm occurred. The article was about the dangers of buying pharmaceuticals on the Web. It was illustrated with a picture of Franklin's website next to box telling consumers to beware of sites that don't include addresses or phone numbers. Franklin's site had both. Although Franklin felt it was defamatory to be connected to disreputable websites, there seemed to be no practical effect on business. In fact, the evidence showed that Franklin actually increased business after the article was published. Thus, even though the jury found that Franklin was defamed, no damages were awarded.

How Do the Elements Work Together?

Consider the following facts: Kitty Kelley wrote a book entitled, *The Family: The Real Story of the Bush Dynasty*. In it, she cited an unnamed source who said that George W. Bush (who at the time of publication was the President of the United States) had snorted cocaine at Camp David when his father, George H. W. Bush, was President. If George W. Bush had wanted to sue Kitty Kelley for libel, he would have had to prove the following:

1. The statement is defamatory.

   It is. Saying that someone snorted cocaine is both an allegation of illegal activity and the kind of thing that would lower one's esteem in the community.

2. The statement is false.

   The reader would have no way to know whether it is false, but for the purpose of this example, let's suppose it is.

3. The statement is a "factual assertion."

   It is. It is not hyperbole, a joke, speculation or some other kind of protected speech. The book alleges that it is actual fact.

4. The statement is about a valid plaintiff.

   It would be. Bush is still alive, is directly named, and has standing to bring a claim.

5. The statement was published.

   Clearly, it was. The fact that a source told Kelley the statement is irrelevant to this element. She included it in her book and may therefore be liable for it.

6. The speaker acted with the requisite level of fault.

   Because Bush was President, he would have been a public official, so he would have to prove that Kelley made the statement with actual malice, meaning she knew it was false or acted with reckless disregard of the truth. Assuming that Kelley would testify credibly that she had no reason to doubt the veracity of the statement and there is no obvious reason why the statement should be doubted, it is unlikely that a court would find that she acted with actual malice.

7. Damages were incurred.

   Bush would need to present some evidence of actual damages. But he could not collect punitive damages absent a showing of actual malice.

Looking at the elements together, it seems unlikely that President Bush would have been able to prevail in a lawsuit. Although the statement is a defamatory, false, factual assertion that was published and presumably caused damages, it is unlikely that the author acted with actual malice, and therefore Bush would not prevail. He would prevail only if there were evidence that Kelley made up the allegation or if there was some other evidence of actual malice.

Suppose, however, that the same allegation of snorting cocaine were made about some ordinary person. So, hypothetically, suppose Lana is waiting for her friend Vickie to get out of work so they can check out a band at a local club. Lana posts a status update on Facebook that tags Vickie says, "Vickie is snorting coke in a ladies room again, so we're going to be late for the show." Considering the elements again, you might get a different outcome if Vickie sued Lana. Vickie would have to prove:

1. The statement is defamatory.

   It is.

2. The statement is false.

    Again, let's suppose it is.

3. The statement is a "factual assertion."

    This is a more interesting case. The question would be whether Lana meant it as a joke or not, and whether it would be obvious if she did. If she meant it literally, this element would be met. But even if she meant it as a joke, this element may be met because it's not clear from the statement or its context that the statement is a joke. On its face, the statement appears to assert actual facts. A court could find that an ordinary reader would interpret the statement to assert facts, regardless of what Lana intended.

4. The statement is about a valid plaintiff.

    It would be. Vickie is alive, she is named and tagged, and she would have standing to sue.

5. The statement was published.

    It was. Publishing on Facebook counts. But note that Vickie can't successfully sue Facebook, because section 230 of the Communications Decency Act would provide immunity to the service provider. Her only remedy is to sue Lana, who posted the statement.

6. The speaker acted with the requisite level of fault.

    Vickie is a private figure, and her behavior is not a matter of public concern. Therefore, the standard of fault could be negligence. Was Lana negligent in asserting that Vickie was snorting cocaine? Assuming Lana was not in the ladies room and made no effort to investigate what Vickie was doing, and considering the immense harm that could follow an allegation like that, most juries probably would conclude that making the statement was negligent. Moreover, if Lana simply made it up—whether to be mean or funny—then she would have acted with actual malice and would certainly be liable.

7. Damages were incurred.

    Vickie would have to show damages, which probably wouldn't be difficult, or she may be able to presume damages because the statement is libel *per se*.

Thus, Vickie has an excellent chance of winning her case against Lana—although there is a practical question as to whether she would be able to collect any money from her. But, the important point is that liability will turn on how the particular facts of a case relate to the elements. Understanding how those elements might be applied in various cases is important to knowing when there might be liability or how to avoid it.

There is one other important aspect of understanding how the elements work together, and that is understanding that the first three elements must involve the same statement. In other words, the statement at issue must be a defamatory, false, factual assertion. In the examples given above, the statements about snorting cocaine are factual assertions, clearly defamatory, and could potentially be false. However, there are circumstances when a story contains defamatory statements and it also contains false factual assertions, but none of the factual assertions are defamatory and none of the defamatory statements are false factual assertions. In such cases, there would probably be no valid libel claim. For example, suppose an article claims that a particular lawyer is an unfit mother. It notes that she works long hours and is constantly on the phone. The statements that she works long hours and is constantly on the phone may be factual assertions, but they are not defamatory. The suggestion that she is an unfit mother is defamatory, but it might not be a factual assertion if it is merely a conclusion based on the opinion of the speaker that mothers should not work a lot. Most courts would probably not find such an article to make a "defamatory, false factual assertion," as long as it was clear that the conclusion was based on the facts given and not on any unstated facts. Thus, when evaluating a statement, is it important to learn how to interrelate those first three factors.

Defenses

In addition to the elements discussed above, there are some affirmative defenses that can be raised to protect defendants from liability. The defenses, however, are not applicable in all cases, and available defenses are not consistent from state to state. This section will discuss some of the defenses that might be available in some cases.

The "Libel-Proof" Plaintiff

A plaintiff is libel-proof if his reputation is already so bad that he can't be defamed further. This doctrine is accepted in a few jurisdictions in limited circumstances. It is a disfavored defense (and rejected in D.C.) because "it rests upon the assumption that one's reputation is a monolith, which stands or falls in its entirety." However, some courts have used it in cases where the false accusation refers to the type of conduct for which the person already has a bad reputation. For example, in *Cerasani v. Sony*, John Cerasani sued over the 1997 film *Donnie Brasco* because it portrayed him as a violent mobster. Cerasani has pled guilty to racketeering, conspiracy to rob a bank, and possession of illegal drugs with intent to distribute. He has also been indicted for extortion and securities fraud in connection with mob activities. The court found that his reputation could not suffer further harm, even if he did not engage in the beatings and murder portrayed in the film. Similar outcomes were obtained in *Lamb v. Rizzo*, finding that a convicted murderer and kidnapper is libel-proof and cannot sue reporter who falsely wrote that he had also been convicted of rape (he had been accused but not convicted of rape); and *Guccione v. Hustler Magazine*, finding that the publisher of a pornographic magazine is libel-proof with respect to allegations of adultery. His reputation for adultery was already so bad that a false allegation of adultery would no longer harm it.

Statute of Limitations

All civil claims have a statute of limitations, which means that a plaintiff must file a lawsuit within a certain time period. Statutes of limitations for libel vary from state to state; they range from six months to three years. So, for example, if the statute of limitations in D.C. is one year, a plaintiff has one year from the date the defamatory statement is published to file a lawsuit in D.C. If a plaintiff files a claim after that date, the case can be dismissed on this basis alone. There might be circumstances that would allow the statute of limitations to run from a later date, but those are rare and very technical and not discussed in detail here, but you should know the possibility exists.

The longest statutes of limitations among states allow a claim to be brought within three years of publication. The states that have such long statutes often find themselves being used by plaintiffs who are "forum-shopping," meaning that they are looking for a jurisdiction where the statute still permits them to file a claim, or perhaps where the state law is favorable to their case. However, many courts will dismiss cases in which it seems that a plaintiff is merely forum-shopping and there is no substantive connection to the jurisdiction. For example, in 2004, U.S. District Judge Bruce Black in New Mexico dismissed a lawsuit, *Condit v. USA Today*, filed by Carolyn Condit, in which Condit claimed that she was libeled by an article in *USA Today* discussing the disappearance of Chandra Levy. The paper had repeated the *National Enquirer's* allegations that Condit had confronted Levy over the phone concerning the allegations that Levy was having an affair with Condit's husband. Judge Black ruled that there was no evidence that the paper had been distributed in New Mexico and that the only apparent reason for filing the case there was to take advantage of the long statute of limitations. Thus, while there is a risk of being sued in a far-away place by a forum-shopper, one can always argue that one shouldn't be sued there if there is no legitimate connection to the forum.

Absolute Privilege for Statements Made in the Official Course of Government Business

This privilege, recognized in *Barr v. Matteo*, protects government officials acting in an official capacity from libel claims for the simply policy reason that government functions could essentially be shut down if officials had to perpetually defend libel claims with people unhappy with what was said about them.

This privilege is usually applied to statements made in court, too. A witness in a court case, for example, may testify in a way that hurts someone's reputation, but the witness can't then be sued for libel. If the witness had lied under oath, however, there is no exemption from perjury, so he can be charged with perjury, even if he can't be sued for libel. However, the interpretation of this privilege is based on common law and may vary by state.

Consent

Consent can apply as a defense any time a person knowingly and validly waives the right to sue, such as when a person signs a contract or a release that includes such a waiver.

This defense may seem weird: Who would agree to let defamatory statements be made about them? Alas, one need only look to modern reality television to get an idea. In many cases, companies that produce reality television shows have contestants or participants sign a release waiving any right to sue for libel, invasion of privacy or other related claims. These releases can be binding and valid.

Fair & Accurate Report Privilege

This is one of the most important defenses in libel law. It generally permits people to repeat statements that were made in court, at hearings, during legislative sessions, or from other official government reports without being liable for defamatory content. The privilege applies if you fairly and accurately describe the government report or hearing and properly attribute the statement to the source.

This defense becomes particularly important when reporting on alleged crimes. Accusing someone of criminal activity would be defamatory *per se*, and if the accused is not a public figure of some sort and the actual malice standard does not apply, then a false accusation of crime might constitute libel.

This is particularly important because not every suspect or person accused of a crime is actually guilty. The best defense in these types of cases is often the fair report privilege.

The theory behind the fair report privilege is that it is important to inform the public about or to be able to discuss what the government does, and part of what the government does is make allegations. The statements are protected because what is important about them is not whether the allegations are true or false, but simply the fact that the allegations were made.

There have been a lot of libel suits filed by those who were at some point suspects or investigated by the government for being potentially associated with a crime: Richard Jewell, Gary Condit, the Ramsey family, and Steven Hatfill are a few examples. And libel suits are becoming more common in terrorism investigations, as people are "linked" to terrorist groups and sue. It is therefore important when reporting on allegations of criminal or terrorist activity to attribute the statements properly to a government source and to describe the allegations fairly and accurately. In doing so, it is also important to be precise when using terms in criminal cases and investigations. Being arrested is not the same as being charged; being charged is not the same as being convicted. Reporters strive to use the correct terminology to preserve the use of the fair report privilege—and also because, ethically, it is important to be accurate.

The trickier question in these cases is what qualifies as an official report. The interpretation of the fair report privilege is a matter of state law, and each state's definition of what is protected differs. Some states limit this defense to established press, others have no limits on who may use the defense. Some states limit the defense to statements contained in written government reports, others cover spoken statements by government officials. Some states limit fair report privilege to descriptions of court proceedings or police records; other states apply the privilege to any government record. Thus, the scope of the defense will depend on state law.

One must also consider whether fair report privilege protects those who repeat statements by foreign governments. In some cases, the privilege has been applied, but in other cases, it has not. In cases where courts have refused to apply the fair report privilege to foreign reports, it is usually because the governments at issue are not viewed as particularly reliable or truthful, and thus, according to those courts, allegations in their reports are not worthy of repetition.

Neutral Reportage

The concept of "reportage" is the idea that one should be able to report what someone said simply because there is value in knowing that it was said, regardless of whether it is true or not. For example, if a foreign government accused someone of a crime, the allegation might be completely false. However, even if the government were lying, it would be worth knowing that the accusation had been made. It might not convey useful information about the accused, but it would convey something useful about that government; namely, that it lied.

This concept—that sometimes the important thing about a statement is not its truth but the fact of its existence—led to the adoption of a defense called "neutral reportage." It was established by the Second Circuit in *Edwards v. National Audubon Society*.

In *Edwards*, the editor of the National Audubon Society's publication *American Birds* wrote that scientists who advocated the use of DDT were "paid to lie." Specifically, he said, "[a]ny time you hear a "scientist" say the opposite [of the position that DDT is harmful], you are in the presence of someone who is being paid to lie, or is parroting something he knows little about." The editor testified that he never intended to portray anyone in particular as a liar; he merely expressed his belief that many supporters of DDT use were spokesmen for the pesticide industry. The *New York Times* published an article about the controversy and repeated the editor's allegations. The article also named certain scientists that the editor thought were spokesmen for the pesticide industry. The court instructed the jury that the plaintiffs were public figures, but the *Times* could be liable under *Sullivan's* actual malice test if the writer had serious doubts about the truth of the allegations, even if he were accurately describing the allegations, and the jury found the paper liable.

The Second Circuit reversed, finding that the First Amendment required protection of the paper:

> At stake in this case is a fundamental principle. Succinctly stated, when a responsible, prominent organization … makes serious charges against a public figure, the First Amendment protects the accurate and disinterested reporting of those charges, regardless of the reporter's private views regarding their validity. What is newsworthy about such accusations is that they were made. … The public interest in being fully informed about controversies that often rage around sensitive issues demands that the press be afforded the freedom to report such charges without assuming responsibility for them.

Some courts have since adopted this neutral reportage privilege in one form or another in an effort to make a distinction between false facts disseminated for the purpose of intentional distortion and false facts disseminated for some other "useful" purpose, such as to inform the public about important controversies. In virtually all of these cases, the courts recognize that the important fact is that the statement was made, not whether the statement is true.

It should be noted that a couple of courts have adopted essentially the same principle but given it a different name. For example, in *Global Relief Foundation v. The New York Times Co.*, the court extended protection to news reports stating that an Islamic charity was "suspected" by the federal government of having terrorist ties; however, it did so based on the concept of "substantial truth," discussed in the section on falsity above. The court reasoned that whether the charity *actually* had ties to terrorists was irrelevant. It was true that the government *suspected* them, regardless. The logic is similar to that of the neutral reportage defense: it is the existence of the suspicion that is important, even if the underlying allegation is false. However, this interpretation of substantial truth is not widespread, and, like neutral reportage, cannot be relied upon in every state to provide a defense.

Not all courts have adopted the neutral reportage privilege or any similar defense, and it has led to some unfortunate results. A case that highlights the problem well is *Norton v. Glenn*. The facts of *Norton* are bizarre: a local newspaper published an article that detailed heated exchanges that occurred among members of the local town council. One councilman, William T. Glenn, Sr. ("Glenn"), made outrageous statements about Council President James B. Norton III ("Norton") and Mayor Alan M. Wolfe ("Wolfe"). Glenn had claimed that Norton and Wolfe were homosexuals; that Glenn had observed Norton involved in a homosexual act; that Norton and Wolfe were "queers and child molesters;" and that Norton had made homosexual advances toward Glenn. Glenn had declared that he had a duty to make the public aware of this information as Norton and Wolfe had "access to children. …" The newspaper also published Norton's response to the charges: "If Mr. Glenn has made comments as bizarre as that, then I feel very sad for him, and I hope he can get the help he needs."

The paper argued that the neutral reportage privilege should be applied to protect the statement. However, the court noted that the U.S. Supreme Court has never adopted the concept, relying instead on the "actual malice" standard to protect First Amendment interests. The court acknowledged the "visceral appeal" of neutral reportage, but felt that its role was not to "champion what we perceive to be good public policy." Thus, the court rejected the neutral reportage privilege and applied the actual malice test, which did nothing to help the newspaper.

A concurring opinion in *Norton* noted that the lack of constitutional protection for cases such as this, where a known falsity was nevertheless useful, was highly problematic:

> I am concerned also with the practical difficulties the press will encounter in trying to walk the very fine line between accurately reporting public governance-related comments such as these, while avoiding liability for doing so. Absent a privilege, the newspaper may be forced to sanitize the report or resort to vagaries—highly subjective changes which inevitably will operate to mislead the public as to the seriousness or rashness of the accusations. Moreover, by forcing newspapers to recharacterize what actually occurred, the absence of a privilege essentially requires the substitution of editorial opinion for accurate transcription. Such a transformation of the actual event inevitably alters its context and content. In addition to being inaccurate, news reports altered for fear of litigation would be of far lesser value to the general public in learning of and passing upon the appropriateness of the public behavior of their elected officials. Such a stilted reporting regime would contravene the United States Supreme Court's seminal statement that "debate on public issues should be uninhibited, robust, and wide-open, and … may well include vehement, caustic, and sometimes unpleasantly sharp attacks on government and public officials."

The reporting of Glenn's statements served an important purpose that one might expect to be protected by the First Amendment: it conveyed information about the behavior and judgment of a public official. While the statement at issue was superficially about Norton, the statement actually conveyed information about Glenn. Reporting his statements helped the public understand what transpired at the city council meeting, and conveyed useful information about Glenn's mindset and behavior. Surely, voters would want to know about his outrageous outburst. Although his statements were most likely false, what matters is that they were made, aside from their truth or falsity. But under current libel law, there isn't a constitutional privilege to publish this kind of false statement. The lack of an adequate, consistently-applied defense in these kinds of cases is a problem for which the Supreme Court has yet to provide a solution.

Wire Service Defense

Some jurisdictions allow for a "wire service defense," which essentially provides immunity to those that merely republish news from a "reputable news agency" without editing content, as long as the publication had no reason to doubt the truth of the report. Such a defense makes sense from a policy perspective; the reason smaller news outlets subscribe to a wire service is precisely because they lack the resources to gather all the news on their own. If they had the resources to ensure the validity of the report, they could have gathered the news on their own in the first place. Any potential plaintiff may still sue the wire service itself for libel, so there is little harm in excluding these other defendants from liability.

Common Interest Privilege

The common interest privilege is available in some states to protect people who inadvertently make false defamatory statements in some context where people share some legitimate interest in communicating information. As a practical matter, the most common scenario where this arises is giving job references.

For example, in *Noel v. River Hills Wilsons, Inc.*, a court dismissed a libel lawsuit based on a faulty job reference because of the common interest privilege. In that case, a potential employer sought a reference from a past employer. The former employer confused the employee with someone else and, because of the confusion, falsely stated that he had been terminated for "loss prevention issues."

Thinking back to the elements of a libel claim, the plaintiff would theoretically have a good case: the statement is a defamatory false factual assertion (falsely accusing him of stealing); it is unambiguously about him; it was published (because it was conveyed to a third party, even if not in mass media); because the plaintiff is a private person, the standard of fault would be negligence, and the speaker was negligent in misidentifying the employee; and the statement caused damages (the lost opportunity for a new job). He could prove all of the elements of a claim. But because of the common interest privilege, the case was dismissed.

The policy behind this privilege is that there are certain kinds of situations where, as a society, we should want people to feel they can convey information freely, and we do not want them to remain silent out of fear that they will be liable if they make a mistake. Job references are one of those situations. If employers had to fear that they could be sued if they made a mistake, like in *Noel*, no one would ever be willing to give a reference. The common interest privilege provides some leeway in such cases.

Anti-SLAPP Statutes

A "strategic lawsuit against public participation" (SLAPP) is a lawsuit that is filed to intimidate, silence or harass someone for their speech. It usually involves a case where someone is criticizing the actions or business of someone else, and the criticisms are valid opinions. However, the person or business who is the subject of criticism files a suit in an effort to halt the criticism. A classic example is *Melius v. Keiffer*, where bar owners sued local residents who spoke out in opposition to the expansion of the bar. The court dismissed the case, finding that the suit would have the effect of infringing on the defendant's First Amendment rights to speak on matters of public concern, and the plaintiffs were unable to meet the procedural burden required by the state's anti-SLAPP statute.

Anti-SLAPP laws don't provide an additional defense or privilege to libel claims as much as they provide a procedure for quicker dismissal of a claim. Rather than spend hundreds of thousands of dollars to defend oneself through the discovery process and a trial, anti-SLAPP laws provide an expedited means of letting the court determine whether the speech at issue is most likely to be protected as opinion or under some other defense.

Not all states have anti-SLAPP statutes. Even among those that do, the requirements for dismissal will depend on the specific requirements of the statute in that state, which vary. Moreover, many federal courts have ruled that state anti-SLAPP laws apply only to cases filed in state courts and do not apply in federal courts. A federal anti-SLAPP law has been introduced multiple times in the legislature, but has not yet passed. Thus, any reliance on an anti-SLAPP statute as a defense will be highly contingent on where a case is filed and whether there is an applicable statute.

Retraction Statutes and Other Statutory Defenses

There might be other defenses available to a defendant, depending on state law. For example, some states have retraction statutes, which require plaintiffs to request a retraction before filing suit. Failure to seek a retraction may result in restrictions on monetary damages.

For example, California Civil Code § 48a says:

> In any action for damages for the publication of a libel in a newspaper, or of a slander by radio broadcast, plaintiff shall recover no more than special damages unless a correction be demanded and not be published or broadcast, as hereinafter provided. Plaintiff shall serve upon the publisher, at the place of publication or broadcaster at the place of broadcast, a written notice specifying the statements claimed to be libelous and demanding that the same be corrected. Said notice and demand must be served within 20 days after knowledge of the publication or broadcast of the statements claimed to be libelous. "Special damages" are all damages which plaintiff alleges and proves that [s]he has suffered in respect to h[er] property, business, trade, profession or occupation, including such amounts of money as the plaintiff alleges and proves [s]he has expended as a result of the alleged libel, and no other.

Requests for retraction should be seriously considered. A publisher will have to weigh the risk of being found liable and the potential for higher damages if they are. Although the retraction statute might not bar a claim completely, it is far preferable to pay less in damages if liability is imposed.

The SPEECH Act

Because it is difficult to win a libel suit in the United States (especially for public figures), some plaintiffs have filed lawsuits against U.S. defendants in England, Canada or other countries where the libel laws are more plaintiff-friendly. This is called "libel tourism." Congress passed a law called the Securing the Protection of our Enduring and Established Constitutional Heritage (SPEECH) Act that targets the problem of libel tourism and prohibits U.S. courts from enforcing foreign libel judgments that couldn't have been obtained in U.S. courts. It was signed into law by President Obama on August 10, 2010.

The SPEECH Act is a great step toward preserving the First Amendment rights of Americans in light of the conflicting libel laws around the world. However, it does not prevent a person from being found civilly or criminally liable in another country. (The question of international liability is addressed more fully in Chapter 20.) It also does not guarantee protection from liability for other kinds of claims, like invasion of privacy or copyright infringement.

Related Claims

False Light

False light has historically been considered a privacy claim, but it straddles the concepts of privacy and libel, and the claim is usually raised in circumstances where libel claims are raised. In fact, the claims are so similar that some states will require a plaintiff to choose to sue for either false light or for libel, but not both. And some states—Colorado, Massachusetts, Minnesota, Missouri, New York, North Carolina, Ohio, Texas, Virginia, and Wisconsin—do not recognize false light as a claim at all.

Most states that recognize false light claims use some version of these elements: (1) the widespread dissemination (2) of highly offensive (3) false material (4) about the plaintiff (5) with fault. Those elements are very similar to the elements of libel, although there are two notable differences. First, the dissemination must be widespread, as opposed to a libel case where the material is "published" if only one other person receives it. Thus, libel is the only claim available if the false information is disseminated to only a few people. Second, in false light cases, the information need not be "defamatory," meaning that it needn't harm one's reputation. It need only be "highly offensive." Thus, a plaintiff might choose to bring a false light claim if the statement is awful, but not awful enough for libel. For example, in *Solano v. Playgirl, Inc.*, the actor Jose Solano, Jr. brought a false light claim for a headline that suggested he might be featured nude in the magazine (he wasn't). A suggestion of nudity might not be sufficiently "defamatory" to support a libel claim, but it may be "offensive" enough for false light.

Intentional Infliction of Emotional Distress (IIED)

IIED is an odd tort. The theory behind it is that some conduct is so outrageous that the courts need some means of providing a remedy to those who are harmed by conduct of this kind. But the formal definition of IIED isn't particularly helpful in clarifying what, exactly, subjects a person to liability.

The tort is applicable when conduct is "so outrageous in character and so extreme in degree as to go beyond all possible bounds of decency, and to be regarded as atrocious and utterly intolerable in a civilized community." The plaintiff will be required to prove that the defendant engaged in "extreme and outrageous conduct" that caused severe emotional distress. It is the definition of "extreme and outrageous conduct" that is the issue in most cases. When the "extreme and outrageous conduct" at issue is speech, plaintiffs are rarely successful.

The most famous case on this topic is *Hustler Magazine v. Falwell*, where Televangelist Jerry Falwell sued *Hustler* magazine for an ad parody that mocked Falwell, suggesting he had lost his virginity to his own mother in an outhouse. While the ad was vile, the Supreme Court determined that, as a public figure, Falwell was subject to criticism, even if the criticism was distasteful and cruel. With that in mind, the Court ruled that a public figure may not recover for IIED unless he proves that the plaintiff made a false statement of fact made with actual malice.

If that requirement sounds very much like libel, it is (except for the "defamatory" requirement—but then, people don't sue over nice statements). Falwell had also sued for libel, but didn't win that claim either because the parody was clearly a joke and not an assertion that anyone would take seriously. It is therefore very difficult for a public figure to win an IIED claim, and they might as well just sue for libel. IIED cannot be used to create liability in lieu of libel if a libel claim wouldn't exist.

Private persons also have a slim chance of recovery for IIED for speech that reflects a matter of public concern, even if the speech might otherwise seem like "extreme and outrageous conduct." This issue was addressed by the Supreme Court in *Snyder v. Phelps. Snyder* involved protests by the Westboro Baptist Church at the funerals of deceased military personnel and others who have been killed in high-profile incidents. The church would regularly protest these funerals holding signs with messages like

"God hates fags" and "You're going to hell." The church members believe that military personnel and others die because God is angry with the U.S. for its tolerance of homosexuality, and their protests are designed to draw attention to their beliefs. The plaintiff was the father of a marine whose funeral was protested by the church. The church members were over 1000 feet away from the actual funeral, so they were neither seen nor heard by the family, although the family became aware of the protest when they saw the television coverage later that day. The church also posted a statement on its website saying that the Snyder parents had turned their son against God and raised him to worship the devil. The father sued the church and its members for IIED, arguing that protesting a funeral constitutes extreme and outrageous conduct.

The Supreme Court ruled that the church's activities were protected by the First Amendment and the father could not recover on any of his claims. The court found that the church's speech was on a matter of public concern, namely the political and moral conduct of the United States. The fact that they protested Snyder's funeral was incidental—they would have protested any funeral of any military or high-profile death. Because the speech was on a matter of public concern, it receives the highest level of First Amendment protection, and there is no basis in that particular case for denying First Amendment protection. The Court noted that the "outrageousness" standard of the IIED tort is too vague to be applied fairly, and there was a danger that a jury would find liability to punish the church simply for having disfavored views. The Court also noted that such protests can potentially be regulated by legitimate content-neutral regulations, but there was no such regulation in effect at the time of the protest for the Court to consider. (The use of content-neutral regulations to control these kinds of protests is discussed in Chapter 14.)

Justice Samuel Alito was the lone dissenter, arguing that the First Amendment should not bar recovery, equating the church's protest to an assault, and suggesting that the protesters could have chosen any other street in the country, or any other event or outlet to promote their views—that it was unnecessary to use Snyder's funeral as their venue.

The Court's opinion did not address the issue of whether a private person may use the IIED tort to sue for statements that are solely on private matters, and Justice Stephen Breyer wrote a concurring opinion that suggests that the majority opinion should be read narrowly, affirming the applicability of the IIED tort in other circumstances. The tort has therefore not been struck down completely, but its use is certainly limited in cases involving speech.

Criminal Libel

Historically, libel was mostly a criminal matter. Governments were concerned with criticism of government officials, and thus they prosecuted people who spoke out against them. But criminal libel cases have mostly disappeared in the United States. Libel cases are now usually civil claims, although a few notable criminal cases have arisen.

An important aspect of criminal libel is that any criminal libel statute must require proof of actual malice to be valid. In *Ivey v. Alabama*, the conviction of Garfield Ivey was overturned precisely because the state statute lacked such a requirement, even though actual malice potentially could have been proved. Ivey was accused of paying a former prostitute to claim, knowing that it was false, that a candidate for lieutenant governor was her client and had physically abused her. An appellate court ruled that, as a matter of constitutional principle to preserve freedom of speech, proof of actual malice must be required in a criminal libel case. The court specifically stated that its opinion "cannot and should not be viewed as vindication of Ivey's version of the evidence." However, the court recognized, on principle, that First Amendment protections must be extended in criminal libel cases. Thus, while criminal libel cases are rare, speakers are entitled to the highest degree of constitutional protection.

Additional Practical Considerations for Journalists

Ethical Considerations

Most of the time, adherence to principles of journalism ethics will help reporters avoid libel claims. Do not take what sources say as absolute truth; check your assumptions; attempt to verify facts and corroborate them from all possible sources; give subjects of stories a fair opportunity to comment on allegations. However, there are occasions when information simply cannot be verified and you cannot know for sure whether an allegation is true. You may believe it is true, or it may be likely to be true, and you may not have any reason to believe it is false, but you must also acknowledge that you do not know for sure whether it is true or false. In such cases, it is worth considering whether the allegation should be published (at least, at the moment, until more information can be obtained). If it involves a public figure, you may have a very strong legal defense if you are sued, assuming you did not act with actual malice. But that begs the question of whether the allegation *should* be published. Just because you can doesn't mean you should. One must consider whether the allegation is important enough to risk the harm of it being false. If the allegation is that a Congressman is embezzling money or sexually harassing interns, then, yes, perhaps the allegation is important. If the allegation is that a public figure is cheating on his or her partner, one must consider whether that would truly affect a matter of public concern.

A case study for consideration: in 2005, *Newsweek* reported that an American interrogator at Guantanamo Bay had flushed a copy of the Koran down the toilet. Violent protests broke out in several Muslim countries as a result, and at least 16 people were killed. *Newsweek* later retracted the claim, and it was reported that *Newsweek* had been given the information by one anonymous source and had not verified it further. One one hand, one could argue that *Newsweek* had an obligation to inform the public about what was happening at Guantanamo Bay. On the other hand, one could argue that it was irresponsible to publish such an inflammatory charge based solely on an anonymous source. There are often not easy answers to these dilemmas, particularly where there are valid competing interests. Reporters need to have thoughtful discussions with editors in such circumstances. It is important to note that *Newsweek* would not have libeled anyone in the story (unless it named the interrogator, which it didn't). But avoiding libel claims is not the sole consideration. The question from an ethical perspective is not whether there is a legal defense to publish the story; it is whether it should be reported at all under the circumstances. Ethical considerations are equally as important as legal ones when choosing what to publish.

The Risk of Hoaxes

People have been known to try to hoax the media. Sometimes hoaxes are nothing more than silly pranks. Sometimes they are the result of concerted efforts to mislead the media. Regardless, journalists must be aware that sometimes "sources" are fakes (as noted above, sometimes sources lie!). It is important to try to verify claims, because ethically it is the right thing to do, legally it helps prevent libel claims, and it prevents the media from being embarrassed by those who are trying to hoax them.

In one recent incident, a woman approached the *Washington Post*, claiming that she had been impregnated as a teenager by Roy Moore, who was then a candidate for U.S. Senate from Alabama. The *Post* attempted to verify her claims, but was unable to corroborate them. The *Post* then reported that they saw the woman walking into the offices of Project Veritas, and organization that, as the *Post* described, "sets up undercover 'stings' that involve using false cover stories and covert video recordings meant to expose what the group says is media bias." The *Post* never published her allegations as if they were factual, but it did publish a story about their belief that the organization was trying to hoax them. That story also noted that someone was making phone calls in Alabama claiming to be a *Post* reporter and seeking women "willing to make damaging remarks" about Moore. The *Post* noted that such calls were not authentic. Sometimes people falsely claim to be a journalist, but those kinds of hoaxes are hard to remedy, in part because it is difficult to know they occurred unless someone reports them, and in part because there might not be a legal remedy, as lying can actually have First Amendment protection unless it rises to the level of libel or fraud (see chapter 15 for more information about constitutional protection for lying).

Corrections, Clarifications, and Retractions

If a story is published, but it is later discovered that the story is incorrect in some way, it is important, ethically, to correct the story. It may also be necessary to correct it from a legal perspective. However, the exact nature of the correction will depend on the nature of the mistake.

If there is a factual error—which can be minor or significant, anything ranging from the misspelling of a name to an inaccurate description of events—then the story should have a "correction," which means that the story will be edited to fix the mistake and an editor's note will signal that changes were made. If the story is basically accurate but one realizes it could be misinterpreted, an editor may wish to issue a "clarification," which may include editing the story to be clearer or specifically disclaiming the potential misinterpretation. If the story turns out to be so fundamentally flawed that it cannot be corrected without essentially rewriting the entire story, then it should be "retracted," which typically means the story is removed and replaced with an editor's note explaining the retraction.

In all these situations, it is ethically appropriate to post some kind of note with the online version of the story explaining what happened, but it is important not to repeat the error in the note. For example, if a story reported, "John Smith murdered five people," but actually, it was *Joe* Smith who was the murder, the text of the story should be changed to say, "Joe Smith murdered five people," and the editor's note should say, "A previous version of this story incorrectly stated the name of the murderer." If the story was published on television or radio, companies will often make time for a correction on the air and also make a correction on the company's website.

If the error in the story has libel implications, then one should definitely consult with a lawyer before posting any kind of correction or retraction, because the way the correction/retraction is handled could have significant legal consequences. Making a mistake in the retraction could be disastrous; there have been cases where courts have found that a poorly written retraction could support a finding of actual malice. Conversely, many courts tend to find that publishing a correction promptly upon notice of an error indicates that the publication genuinely did not know of the error and did not act with actual malice.

How Long Should I Keep My Notes?

Some reporters like to keep all their notes from every story they have ever worked on forever. Other reporters get tremendous joy from dumping all their notes into the trash once a story is completed and published. Whether you, personally, tend to be a hoarder or a purger, it is worth considering that having access to one's notes, tapes, interviews, background research, and other materials can be a vitally important part of defending a libel lawsuit. Even if you generally prefer not to keep old records, it might be worth saving materials related to particularly risky stories for some time period. The statute of limitations for libel claims in most states is one year, and the longest statute of limitations for libel or related claims like false light or IIED is around 4 years. A reporter can choose whether to keep records forever, for a 4-year period (particularly if one works for a national organization that could be sued in any state), or for the time period covered by the statute of limitations in one's home state. Some companies have policies that set forth the time periods for which their reporters should keep records, but others don't. Having those records can help defend a lawsuit and show that the reporter did not act negligently or with actual malice. In any event, if you have saved the records, do not discard or destroy them once you are on notice that you are being sued! That is called "spoliation of evidence," and can result in sanctions by the court.

Prior Restraints

Prior restraints are disfavored under U.S. law. If someone is going to publish something potentially libelous, it is unlikely that the courts will try to stop them from doing so. Instead, the remedy is for the defamed person to sue after the fact. However, in recent years, courts have been more willing to consider injunctions against speech in certain limited circumstances. Prior restraints are presumptively unconstitutional, and therefore anyone seeking an injunction against speech has a very high burden of proving that the restriction would serve a compelling interest and is very narrowly tailored so as not to restrict legitimate expression. But some courts do not want to say that prior restraints can never be issued. In libel cases in particular, the rule is generally that it is not appropriate to stop someone from saying something that might be libelous, but any aggrieved party can sue for libel and receive damages afterwards. But what happens when a person continues to make the same libelous statement over and over? What happens if the speaker has no money and the plaintiff can never recoup a judgment? What happens when the speaker has access to a wide audience because of the internet and insists on using that platform to unjustly harm another person? The reality is that a hostile speaker who insists on spreading false statements and has no money to lose may continue to spread falsities and the plaintiff would have no recourse.

Several courts have found that injunctions might be appropriate if (1) the speaker insists on repeating the same statement that a court has already adjudicated to be libelous; (2) the speaker is judgment-proof [which means they don't have enough money to pay the damages awarded to the plaintiff]; and (3) the injunction is limited to the statement that has been adjudicated to be libelous and does not otherwise restrict expression. In such cases, there is no other remedy available to redress the harm to the plaintiff, although the injunctions must be very narrow. For example, in *Balboa Island Village Inn, Inc. v. Lemen*, the court found that a narrow injunction preventing the speaker from repeating specific libelous accusations about a local bar was constitutional. These kinds of injunctions are more common in cases involving hostile divorces or other kinds of bitter, ongoing feuds where the accusations are persistent, severe, and, notably, *false*.

Other courts, though, have found that even such narrow injunctions can be unconstitutional. The First Circuit, for example, ruled in *Sindi v. El-Moslimany* that permanent injunctions of libelous statements fail to account for the fact that libel is highly contextual. What might be libelous in one context might not be libelous in another context. In *Sindi*, the injunction prevented the speaker from saying that Sindi "is an academic and scientific fraud." At trial, the court has found that the speaker made that statement in a context that conveyed a factual assertion and was made with actual malice. However, the First Circuit noted that there could be situations in the future where the utterance of those words would be appropriate; for example, if such claims were true in the future, if the speaker wanted to apologize for using such a phrase, or if the speaker were trying to explain what he was prohibited from saying. Thus, the injunction was overbroad because it failed to account for context.

The U.S. Supreme Court has taken only one case on this topic, *Tory v. Cochran*, but it was never resolved. The case involved a long-standing feud between lawyer Johnnie Cochran and a disgruntled client. The trial court ordered the client to stop speaking publicly about Cochran, and he appealed all the way to the U.S. Supreme Court. Unfortunately, Cochran died before the Court decided the case. Thus, the Court ruled on a technicality—that the injunction "lost its underlying rationale" in light of Cochran's death—and never ruled on the issue of whether a permanent injunction would be valid. It is still unclear whether the Supreme Court would consider it constitutional to impose an injunction on a speaker who continually insists on making false, defamatory statements. The question is under what conditions such orders would be constitutional? The issue has not yet been fully resolved.

Practical Conclusions

- Being sued for libel is a common risk arising from criticism, allegations of wrongdoing, insults, and trash talk—any statement that harms a person's reputation.

- It is very difficult for a plaintiff to win a libel claim. They have the burden of proving several elements of the claim, plus, there are additional defenses a defendant can use to escape liability.

- One of the most difficult things about libel cases is that the defendant often will not know whether the statement is false until after publication. It's hard to have perfect information! Sources can be wrong, and sometimes they lie. Don't assume what people tell you is true. Try to verify information and corroborate facts with other sources. When there is conflicting evidence about what happened, keep an open mind. The fact that you are repeating what someone else told you does not, in itself, protect you from liability.

- Even though the actual malice standard gives a lot of protection to the media, it is not an absolute defense. Actual malice may be found if a speaker fabricates or distorts facts; where what purports to be an objective news report actually promotes an agenda and willfully ignores evidence, facts, sources or statements that are adverse to the position stated; and where the speaker has significant reasons to doubt the truth of a statement, but publishes the statement anyway. Most importantly, don't make stuff up!

- Think about who you are referencing in a negative light. A private person is far more likely to have a claim than a public figure.

- It can be hard to guess in advance who will be deemed a public or private figure. One traditional factor has been "access to the media," but it is unclear how the internet will affect the court's interpretation of these categories. Is blogging or posting on Facebook or tweeting enough to make a person a limited purpose pubic figure? There is not yet a consistent body of law on this topic. Figuring out the plaintiff's status can be the most difficult aspect of a libel claim, and the determination is likely to be very fact-specific.

- Be clear about what is fact and what is opinion. Make sure the context is clear when you are joking, speculating, or being hyperbolic. If you are drawing conclusions, be sure to lay out the basis for your conclusion and be clear about your thought process.

- If you are relying on a government report or conveying what happened in a government proceedings, be sure to describe the event accurately, giving attention to all "sides" or interpretations, and attribute the information to the report or proceeding, to maximize your protection under Fair Report Privilege.

- The most risky statements are unproven allegations against "private" persons and the repetition of a false fact about a public figure, even if the existence of the false fact is an important fact in itself (such as in *Norton v. Glenn*).

- Be conscientious about making corrections when appropriate, but get a lawyer involved if there are potential libel implications from the error.

Note

1   Rod Smolla, Suing the Press: Libel, Media and Power (Oxford University Press 1986) at 188–189 (referencing *Tavoulareas v. Washington Post*, 567 F. Supp. 651 (D.D.C. 1983)).

CHAPTER 4

Privacy

Publishing Private, Embarrassing, or Sensitive Information

The term "privacy" is used often in a wide variety of contexts, and it can mean different things in different contexts. There are five distinct concepts for which the term "privacy" is often used:

1. Constitutional privacy. The Fourth Amendment explicitly grants protection against unwarranted governmental search and seizure. This is a right granted to citizens vis-à-vis the government, meaning that it bars the government (as opposed to private parties) from intruding into a citizen's home. There is no federal constitutional right to privacy to protect individuals from other individuals or the press. If a person has an enforceable legal right of privacy against another person, it will likely derive from one of the privacy torts, mentioned below. Some state constitutions offer a right of privacy, but each state interprets this right according to their own courts, and so the right is not necessarily the same in all states. Generally, any constitutional right of privacy protects against state government intrusion.

2. Presumed constitutional privacy, as established by the U.S. Supreme Court. The Court has extended protection against governmental intrusion into private matters in cases such as *Roe v. Wade* (abortion), *Griswald v. Connecticut* (birth control), and *Lawrence v. Texas* (consensual sexual activity). These protections are not explicitly spelled out in the Constitution, but have been recognized as a natural extension of what the concept of privacy should mean with respect to government power. Again, these principles apply only with respect to government action, and not to the actions or rules of private parties.

3. Privacy torts. These claims give one person or group the ability to sue another person or group for perceived invasions of privacy. If a news organization is going to be sued based on privacy concerns, the claims will likely be one of the privacy torts.

4. Statutory privacy. Both government and private entities collect massive volumes of information about people, and the release or use of this data might, in some circumstances, create privacy concerns. Thus, there are laws that regulate the disclosure or non-disclosure of records. For example, the Freedom of Information Act (FOIA) exemptions 6 and 7(C) are based on a concept of privacy, the Family Educational Rights and Privacy Act (FERPA) regulates the disclosure of educational records, and the Health Insurance Portability and Accountability Act (HIPAA) regulates the disclosure of health records. The perceived need for data privacy laws is a hot topic, and Congress is considering several laws that would regulate the rights of citizens with respect to how data about them is collected and used. Such laws already exist in Europe, although the only federal law in the United States that governs such material now is the Children's Online Privacy Protection Act (COPPA). FOIA, FERPA, and HIPAA are discussed in Chapter 11, and COPPA is discussed in Chapter 20.

5. Personal notions of privacy. People use the term privacy subjectively to refer to those things that they wish not to discuss or expose publicly. It's not a legal concept, just the idea that people should mind their own business. Whether a person's subjective notion of privacy is actually enforceable will depend on whether any of the concepts of privacy listed above apply to the situation.

This book does not discuss either explicit or presumed constitutional privacy, as it is outside the scope of media law. The privacy torts are what are important to media, as they may form the basis for lawsuits against the press.

The privacy torts were derived from ideas proposed by Louis Brandeis and Samuel Warren in an 1890 *Harvard Law Review* article. The two prominent men argued that newsgatherers and photographers were invading the private life of well-known persons and that people should have a "right to be let alone." The "right" proposed by Warren and Brandeis has never fully come to being in the United States, in large part because such a right would obviously conflict with First Amendment principles, including newsgathering and the dissemination of information. States have acknowledged that privacy interests may exist, but the torts are limited in deference to First Amendment principles.

This chapter will focus on one important privacy tort: publication of private facts. This claim is exactly what it sounds like: the plaintiff is suing the defendant because he believes that the defendant has improperly published private information. It also briefly mentions the concept of trade secrets, which is a claim that allows businesses to sue for the publication of "sensitive" information.

Publication of Private Facts

Many states permit a person to bring a claim for publication of private facts; it is a state law tort, and thus the exact requirements of the tort may vary by state. Some states, including Nebraska, New York, North Carolina, and Virginia, have not recognized this tort at all. Nevertheless, most jurisdictions allow such claims and take into consideration in some form the following factors:

1. Whether the information is "private"

2. To whom was the information disclosed

3. Whether the disclosure was "highly offensive to a reasonable person"

4. Whether the information is newsworthy

5. Whether there are any additional defenses that might apply

Is the Information Private?

There is no specific definition of "private" information, but the courts generally consider information to be private if (1) it is the kind of information that most people would try to keep private, and (2) the person at issue actually did try to keep it private. The kinds of information that courts may consider private include:

- Health or medical information

- Grades or related educational information

- Nudity, sex tapes, or information about sexual activity or sexual orientation (including being gay, lesbian, or transgender)

- Drug or alcohol abuse

- Financial information

- An address or phone number that is not publicly available

- Other sensitive or embarrassing information

However, information may not be private if:

- It is a matter of public record

- The information was previously disclosed

- It occurred in a public place with no expectation of privacy

The question of whether something is a matter of public record is usually easy to resolve. Information found in court records or government reports will not be protected as private. In fact, regardless of the tenets of state law, the Supreme Court has twice ruled that there is a First Amendment privilege to publish lawfully acquired information from public records, absent a state interest "of the highest order." In both *Cox Bct. Corp. v. Cohn* and *Florida Star v. BJF*, the Supreme Court dismissed privacy lawsuits filed because a rape victim's name was disclosed in media reports. In both cases, there were applicable state laws that prohibited the disclosure of the name of a rape victim, and in both cases the reporter obtained the information legally from public records (a court record and a sheriff's report, respectively). In both cases, the court found that the reporter had a First Amendment privilege to publish the information, relying in large part on the fact that the information came from public records. As an ethical matter, many news organizations will not publish the name of a rape victim, but that choice is based on ethical considerations, not a legal mandate.

Along the same lines, events that occur on public streets, at events open to the public, or other places where there is no reasonable expectation of privacy will not be "private." In *Heath v. Playboy Enter. Inc.*, for example, the court found that the publication of a photo taken in front of a courthouse did not give rise to a privacy claim.

Also, information that is disclosed to a broad segment of the public will be deemed not private. In *Sipple v. Chronicle Publishing Co.*, the court found that the fact that plaintiff was gay was not "private" information because he was active in the San Francisco gay community. Even though he kept his sexual orientation secret in his hometown, there was a broad segment of the public that was aware of the information.

Nevertheless, there are limits on what is deemed public, as illustrated by *Huskey v. National Broadcasting Co.* In *Huskey*, NBC filmed inside a prison to report on conditions there. In the course of newsgathering, NBC filmed Huskey, who was in the prison's "exercise cage." He told NBC he did not want to be filmed, but footage was taken nevertheless.

NBC attempted to have the case dismissed for two reasons: first, that the information was not "private" because Huskey's conviction and imprisonment were a matter of public record; and second, that Huskey was in a place with no expectation of privacy because others could see him in the exercise area. The court, however, disagreed on both points. First, the court found that even if the fact of Huskey's imprisonment were public record, it did not follow that he has completely lost all privacy rights while in prison. Second, the court found that the fact that others can see you does not mean there is no expectation of privacy from an expanded intrusion. "Persons are exposed to family members and invited guests in their own homes, but that does not mean they have opened the doors to television cameras." Whether the exercise area was a place where a prisoner could reasonably expect privacy was not a clear-cut decision, and thus, the court refused to dismiss the case and ruled that it would be up to a jury to determine whether Huskey's privacy was invaded. What's important to draw from that case is that there are some places where a person might be exposed to a limited group of other people, but that does not mean that they would lack a privacy claim if material were published more broadly.

A similar analysis is employed in cases where the information at issue was previously disclosed. Courts have ruled that a fact is not private if it had been previously disclosed, but there are also cases that say that a prior disclosure to family or close friends does not mean that a person has waived their privacy rights entirely. If someone else discloses the fact to a much larger audience, a claim may still exist. For example, in *Multimedia WMAZ, Inc. v. Kubach*, a man with AIDS brought a claim against a television station that had promised to digitize his face and voice if he would appear on a program about AIDS. The station failed to adequately conceal his identity and he was recognizable on television. When the man sued for publication of private facts, the station argued that the fact he had AIDS was not private because he had previously disclosed the fact to family, close friends, his doctor, and members of his AIDS support group. However, the court found that the limited disclosure to a small group of people who had legitimate reasons to know the fact did not bar him from bringing a claim when the news media broadcast the fact to the public at large. Information need not be completely secret to be "private."

In fact, courts have allowed privacy claims to go forward even when the information was voluntarily disclosed to a reporter. In *Virgil v. Time, Inc.*, a man who was interviewed by *Sports Illustrated* for an article about body surfing disclosed a lot of information about himself to the reporter. When he realized that the magazine intended to publish some of the more embarrassing details, he said he did not consent to publication. The magazine published the information anyway, and he sued. The court noted that there is a difference between telling one person and telling a broad audience. Even if the one person told is a reporter, an individual may still have a protectable privacy interest if they do not consent to broad disclosure:

> Talking freely to a member of the press … is not then in itself making public. Such communication can be said to anticipate that what is said will be made public since making public is the function of the press, and accordingly such communication can be construed as a consent to publicize. Thus if publicity results it can be said to have been consented to. However, if consent is withdrawn prior to the act of publicizing, the consequent publicity is without consent.

Similarly, in *Hawkins v. Multimedia Inc.*, the court allowed a teenager who spoke to a reporter about what it was like to be a teen father to sue for publication of private facts because the teen did not understand that the reporter planned to publish his name in the story.

Reporters must therefore beware of situations where subjects disclose information without realizing it is intended for publication. As an ethical matter, reporters should be clear about what is on the record and may be published, and such a practice helps from a legal standpoint as well.

Once information is exposed to the public, though, it is no longer "private." A plaintiff may be able to sue the person who made the initial disclosure, but others who repeat the information might not be liable.

It should also go without saying that the private information must be about someone who can be identified in order for that person to bring a claim. There are cases holding that there is no valid claim where the person is not actually identified in the publication. But even if the person is not named, there may be a claim if there is enough information for the audience to figure out who is referenced.

To Whom Was the Information Disclosed?

Most jurisdictions require a plaintiff to show that the disclosure of private information was public or widespread. Unlike libel cases where the defamatory material is published if it is disseminated to only one other person, privacy claims require "publicity," meaning that the information is given to the public, or at least a large segment of the public. Most courts will therefore dismiss claims where the information was disclosed to a small group. But information published on the internet, in print, broadcast, or otherwise use any form of mass media can certainly be a basis for liability.

Some states, however, do not require widespread disclosure and will permit claims based on disclosure to a small group. Even in jurisdictions that require a public disclosure, a segmented group can suffice. In *Miller v. Motorola, Inc.*, for example, the court found that the disclosure of an employee's health problems to a group of coworkers was sufficient to state a claim for publication of private facts. Thus, disclosure within a church, workplace, or neighborhood—even if it is not to the public at large—may constitute a public disclosure under state law.

Was the Disclosure "Highly Offensive to a Reasonable Person"?

A claim will not be permitted unless the disclosure was "highly offensive," but the test is whether the disclosure would be offensive to a person of "reasonable sensibilities," not whether it was subjectively offensive to the plaintiff. In many cases, if the information is genuinely private, then its disclosure will be deemed "highly offensive." Most reasonable people would be offended by the widespread disclosure of information about their medical conditions, sexuality, and other traditionally private matters. But courts have found that some disclosures are not offensive, either where a plaintiff is unusually sensitive or where the disclosure is reasonable in context. For example, in *Johnson v. Harcourt Brace Jovanovich*, a court found that it was not offensive to disclose that man who found $240,000 returned it to the rightful owner. In *Challen v. Town & Country Charge*, a court found that it was reasonable for a debt collector to send one letter about the plaintiff's debt to plaintiff's employer. Many such cases have arisen out of debt collection efforts, and courts will usually rule that sending a letter to family members or employers in an effort to reach a debtor is not highly offensive. But cases of this nature are relatively rare, and most of the time, the disclosure of information, if it is deemed "private," is also likely to be deemed highly offensive.

Was the Information Newsworthy or of Legitimate Public Concern?

All states take into consideration the newsworthiness of the information. The traditional common law privacy tort included as an element a requirement that the plaintiff prove that the information was not "of legitimate public concern." Courts have also acknowledged that, as a matter of First Amendment principle, there should be a privilege to publish private information when there is a legitimate public interest in that information. This defense is considered separate from the element of the claim (that the information is "not of legitimate public concern"), but as a practical matter, they end up meaning the same thing. Whether a court considers the issue of legitimate public interest as an element of the claim or as a defense has made little difference in the outcomes of cases.

The question, then, is how to define "newsworthy." There is no widely accepted definition, but there are some general principles that can be drawn from the case law. The following factors are the kinds of things courts consider when making a determination of whether something is newsworthy.

DOES THE INFORMATION CONCERN OR DERIVE FROM THE KIND OF THING THAT IS TYPICALLY "NEWS"?

There are certain topics or events that are inherently newsworthy: crimes, accidents, fires, acts of public officials, charitable events, sporting events, entertainment, and other events—these are things that are typically in the news and matters of public concern. Thus, even the most embarrassing, offensive information can be published without liability if it demonstrates criminal activity or otherwise falls within the scope of newsworthy information. In *Cinel v. Connick*, for example, a court found that the publication of a video showing a Catholic priest engaging in sexual activity with an alleged minor was of legitimate public concern. There is little that could be more horrifying or embarrassing than that, and yet the newsworthiness of the video outweighed the privacy concerns.

In many cases, the events at issue are open or accessible to the public, a factor that further negates claims of privacy. In *McNamara v. Freedom Newspapers*, for example, a soccer player sued a newspaper that published a photo in which the player's genitalia was visible. The photo had been taken at a game, and the newspaper hadn't noticed the offending content until the paper was published and distributed. But despite the embarrassment and private nature of the content, the court ruled that the player had no privacy claim because the photo accurately depicted a public, newsworthy event. Similarly, in *Shulman v. Group W. Productions*, a court ruled that a woman who had been severely injured in car accident could not recover for publication of private facts arising from news reports of her rescue because the car accident occurred on a public street, was publicly visible, and was newsworthy.

IS THE PERSON INVOLVED A CELEBRITY OR OTHERWISE NOTEWORTHY?

Courts tend to find information about celebrities and public figures to be newsworthy, in part because of the substantial public interest in their activities, and in part because public figures tend to seek publicity and therefore subject themselves to a certain amount of "public gaze." It is important to note, however, that celebrities may nevertheless maintain some privacy rights. When a sex tape of musician Bret Michaels and actress/model Pamela Anderson Lee surfaced, they sued to prevent its disclosure online. In *Michaels v. Internet Entertainment Group, Inc.*, the court noted that the fact that the sex tape existed and the fact that litigation ensued were both newsworthy facts that could be reported, but the tape itself depicting intimate activities was not newsworthy. Thus, the fact that someone is a celebrity does not guarantee that all material is newsworthy, but a lot of information about them will be.

Information about public officials is also likely to be newsworthy. In *Municipality of Anchorage v. Anchorage Daily News*, for example, a court found that the disclosure of a public official's performance evaluation was newsworthy. Public officials are subject to higher levels of scrutiny precisely because they are supposed to serve the public, so any material that relates to the performance of their public duties should be newsworthy. Nevertheless, like celebrities, they may maintain a privacy interest with respect to other materials.

One question the courts have faced is whether a person who has achieved notoriety at some point in life may remain newsworthy even if he is no longer in the public eye—especially if the person intentionally avoids publicity. The courts have, for the most part, found that the passage of time does not diminish the newsworthiness of the individual, as long as the subsequent publications relate to the reason for which they initially became known. *Sidis v. F-R Publishing Corp.*, for example, involved a "Where Are They Now?" article about a former child prodigy. He had become famous for giving lectures in mathematics at Harvard University when he was only 11 years old, but he had since dropped out of the public eye. The court found that the material about his adult life was newsworthy, as there was an interest in knowing what had happened to this former star.

IS IT THE PERSON WHO IS NEWSWORTHY OR THE TOPIC THAT IS NEWSWORTHY?

An important conflict in this area is whether the person identified in the story is newsworthy, as opposed to whether the topic of the story is newsworthy.

A classic example is *Barber v. Time, Inc.* In that case, *Time* magazine published a story about a rare eating disorder and used information about a woman who suffered from the disorder. The question was whether the information was "newsworthy," and the court ruled that the disease was newsworthy, but her identity was not.

A more difficult case is *M.G. v. Time Warner*. *Sports Illustrated* published a story about Little League players whose coach turned out to be a child molester and had molested some of the children on the team. The court found that the intrusiveness of the disclosure (identifying the children) greatly outweighed its relevance to the matter of public concern (the problem of child-molesting coaches), and therefore allowed their claim to go forward.

Barber and *M. G.* were cases where the stories at issue did not involve breaking news, but rather were general interest stories about a type of problem, and the identities of the people involved was collateral to the discussion of the problem (that people can get a rare eating disorder, or that children's sport's coaches might be child molesters). In many such cases, courts have been inclined to rule that the person's identity is not newsworthy. The anecdotes about specific people may be useful from a storytelling perspective to illustrate certain points or evoke empathy, but journalists should nevertheless obtain consent from the persons featured to minimize the risk of being sued for invasion of privacy. (It may also be important to obtain consent from an ethical perspective—to show sensitivity to the subjects of the story who are dealing with difficult matters.)

However, even in general interest stories, a person can become newsworthy if they present a risk to the public due to their behavior. For example, in *Veilleux v. NBC, Inc.*, the court considered whether it was newsworthy to disclose that a particular long-haul trucker had failed a drug test. The plaintiff argued that the topic of drug use among interstate truckers was of legitimate public concern, but the identity of any individual trucker was not. But the court disagreed, finding that it was newsworthy to disclose that he failed a drug test, particularly in light of his claims that he did not use drugs and was a safe driver. Similarly, in *Gilbert v. Medical Econ. Co.*, the court found that an anesthesiologist had no privacy claim when an article disclosed her psychiatric and martial problems because they plausibly contributed to claims of alleged medical malpractice against her and were therefore newsworthy. In both cases, the person involved was not merely an example of some issue—they arguably presented a risk to the public themselves (unlike the plaintiffs in *Barber* and *M. G.*, who were victims rather than perpetrators), thereby becoming newsworthy.

It is important to make the distinction between the newsworthiness of a topic and the newsworthiness of an individual. If the person would not be newsworthy on their own, there is a risk that a court will find that information about them is not newsworthy absent some adequate nexus to a newsworthy topic or event, which leads to the next question.

IS THERE A SUFFICIENT NEXUS BETWEEN THE PRIVATE INFORMATION DISCLOSED AND THE NEWSWORTHINESS OF THE PERSON OR EVENT AT ISSUE?

There are many cases involving some event that is clearly newsworthy, and the identities of the persons involved are clearly newsworthy, but some additional private information is revealed—and then the court must determine whether the additional information is adequately connected to the event.

A classic example is *Sipple v. Chronicle Publishing Co.*, where Sipple saved President Ford from an assassination attempt. The event is newsworthy, as is his identity. But the newspaper also discovered and disclosed that Sipple was gay. Sipple argued that saving the president was newsworthy but his sexuality was not. The court found the detail was newsworthy because it contradicted negative stereotypes about gay men, and also because there was speculation that Ford delayed thanking him due to his homosexuality.

Similarly, in *Nobles v. Cartwright*, a woman who worked for public official accused him of sexual harassment. She was promised that details of her report would remain confidential, including information about her extramarital affair with him, but the details were later published. She sued, arguing that the specific details disclosed were not newsworthy. The court acknowledged that even public officials are entitled to some degree of privacy, so the real question is whether there is an adequate nexus between the newsworthy event (harassment allegations) and the private details that were published. The court stated that sexual information, even about public officials, is usually not of legitimate public concern, but concluded that in this case it was because the specific details were relevant to whether harassment occurred, and the allegations of harassment and the administration's handling of them were clearly newsworthy.

Nevertheless, courts are not willing to find that all details related to newsworthy events are equally newsworthy. For example, in *Diaz v. Oakland Tribune*, the court was asked to determine whether it was newsworthy that the first female student body president at a college was transgender. The court refused to find that it was newsworthy as a matter of law because there was nothing about the fact of being transgender that reflected on her ability to do her job as student body president.

California has established a three-part test for evaluating newsworthiness: (1) the social value of the facts published, (2) the depth of intrusion into private affairs, and (3) the extent to which the party voluntarily acceded to a position of public notoriety. In *Diaz*, the court determined that there was little value to the disclosure of the fact, it was highly intrusive, and even though Diaz had voluntarily sought the position of student body president, it was a rather limited public role that did not warrant such an intrusion into her private life.

Similarly, in *Green v. Chicago Tribune Co.*, the court questioned whether a mother's statements made in a private hospital room to her deceased son killed by gang violence were adequately connected to general concern about gang violence to be newsworthy. Even if the topic of gang violence and the identity of the boy killed were newsworthy, it was up to a jury to determine whether the mother's statements were adequately related to overcome her privacy rights. The court also noted that the fact that reporters overheard her statements did not mean they were not private. Citing *Virgil v. Time*, as well as the fact that the mother told the reporters she did not want to make a statement, the court concluded that the question was whether the statement was intended to be disclosed or not.

There must therefore be an adequate connection between the detail disclosed and the newsworthy material. This issue becomes more complicated when the detail is disclosed not by third-party reporters, but by a person actually involved in the event, which leads to the next issue.

WHAT HAPPENS WHEN A PERSON VOLUNTARILY REVEALS FACTS ABOUT THEMSELVES THAT INVOLVE OTHERS?

Courts have noted that there is a problem inherent in autobiographical accounts. If a person reveals private information about their own life, it may implicate the rights of others who are involved. The speaker's First Amendment right to talk about themselves conflicts with the other person's privacy rights. This issue has been addressed in a few cases.

Susanna Kaysen, an author who had achieved some notoriety for her book *Girl, Interrupted*, wrote another book entitled *The Camera My Mother Gave Me*. In it, she described a period of her life where she suffered significant vaginal pain and struggled to find a correct diagnosis of the problem. The book also conveyed intimate details of a relationship with a boyfriend during that time, suggesting that he was sexually aggressive despite her physical discomfort and suggesting at one point that he may have crossed the line in attempting to coerce her into non-consensual sex. Friends, family, and business associates of her former boyfriend determined that the boyfriend described in the book was him, even though she did not use his name and changed details, such as his occupation and where he was from, and thus he sued her for violating his privacy.

In *Bonome v. Kaysen*, the court noted that there was a conflict between Kaysen's right to disclose information about herself and Bonome's right to maintain privacy. The court also noted that "courts have held that where an autobiographical account related to a matter of legitimate public interest reveals private information concerning a third party, the disclosure is protected so long as there is a sufficient nexus between the private details and the issue of public concern." In this case, the court concluded that the issue of when physical intimacy crosses the line to non- consensual sex was a matter of legitimate public concern, and Kaysen's disclosure of her own personal experience was relevant to that issue. "Because the First Amendment protects Kaysen's ability to contribute *her own* personal experiences to the public discourse on important and legitimate issues of public concern, disclosing Bonome's involvement in those experiences is a necessary incident thereto." The court also looked favorably upon the fact that she at least attempted to hide his identity by not using his name and changing facts about him. Even though his identity may have been apparent to close friends and associates, it was not disclosed to the public at large.

A similar issue arose in *Anonsen v. Donahue*, where a woman disclosed on a television talk show that her husband had raped their daughter, who later gave birth to a son who had been raised as the woman's own. Clearly, such a revelation implicates the privacy interests of the other people involved. Nevertheless, the court found that there were only two questions relevant to the issue of whether the First Amendment protected the disclosure: (1) was the topic of rape and incest of legitimate public concern, and (2) was her disclosure of her own identity protected by the First Amendment? Looking at similar previous cases, the court said:

> We tread on dangerous ground deciding exactly what matters are sufficiently relevant to a subject of legitimate public interest to be privileged. First Amendment values could obviously be threatened by the uncertainty such decisions could create for writers and publishers. Only in cases of flagrant breach of privacy which has not been waived or obvious exploitation of public curiosity where no legitimate public interest exists should a court substitute its judgment for that of the publisher.

Thus, the court found that the disclosure was protected by the First Amendment.

Not all courts, however, have found every disclosure to be adequately newsworthy and protected by the First Amendment. In *Winstead v. Sweeney*, for example, the Michigan Court of Appeals reversed the lower court's dismissal of a case, finding that a jury should decide whether the disclosures at issue were adequately newsworthy to justify First Amendment protection. The case involved a story on "unique" love relationships. The newspaper solicited readers to tell them about unusual relationships, and a man responded, telling the reporter about his relationship with his ex-wife. He revealed, among other things, that his ex-wife had several abortions and engaged in partner-swapping. The newspaper did not use the last names of the people involved, but according to the plaintiff, people immediately identified her as the ex-wife named in the story. The court was reluctant to declare that the facts disclosed were inherently protected, finding "although it is without question that the subject of the article (unique love relationships) constitutes a newsworthy topic … the facts revealed about plaintiff are not so clearly newsworthy." Moreover, the court questioned the notion that the media had an absolute First Amendment privilege to publish these facts on the basis that the man should have a right to tell his story. The court distinguished a case that protected disclosures in an autobiography, noting that while a person may have a privilege to tell their own story, granting an absolute privilege to the media to disclose such facts would render privacy interests null. The court concluded that the press' privilege must be limited to information that is legitimately newsworthy and implied that these kinds of personal facts are not.

WHAT IS NOT NEWSWORTHY?

As much as commentators like to say that the newsworthiness exception has swallowed the tort, there are cases that result in plaintiff victories, like the *Winstead* case mentioned above. Courts are not always willing to concede that every story published by a news organization is of legitimate public concern.

Buller v. Pulitzer Publishing Co., is another example. The case arose out of a newspaper report about a professional psychic. The reporter went to see the psychic without mentioning she was a reporter, sought her services, and then published an article portraying the psychic as a fraud, or at least as a joke. The court considered the elements of a privacy claim and found that the woman's psychic abilities and the nature of her consultation with clients was private, and the disclosure was offensive because she was depicted as doing her work in an unprofessional manner. But most importantly, the court found that her consultations with clients were not of legitimate public concern. Unless she was accused of a crime, or predicted world disaster, or otherwise made some newsworthy claim, there was nothing obviously newsworthy about her work. On the contrary, her work was highly personal—attempting to predict future events in the lives of individual clients. The court decided:

> This is far removed from the traumas and disasters which catapult private people into the public eye, or of crimes and law enforcement with which the public is validly concerned. Buller's practice is clearly dissimilar to any of the matters which courts have determined to be within the public interest.

Speakers must therefore be careful to distinguish what is merely interesting from what is of "legitimate public concern," as the courts have defined it, and to obtain consent from individuals to publish private information about them if it fails the newsworthiness test.

Are There Any Additional Defenses?

There are some additional defenses that apply to privacy claims, such as the statute of limitations and consent.

Just as in libel cases, the statute of limitations will vary by state, so it is important to check the law of the relevant state. In any event, claims must be filed within a certain time period to be valid.

With respect to consent, reporters will sometimes ask interview subjects to sign a release when the information to be disclosed is obviously private and offensive, and it most often occurs when the information to be disclosed is about children. But there are legitimate questions about who can consent on behalf of a child. In *Foretich v. Lifetime Cable*, the mother of a girl consented to have her daughter featured in a documentary about abused children. The film showed the daughter using dolls in a therapy session with her mother to demonstrate how her father had allegedly sexually abused her. The allegations were part of a hotly contested custody dispute. A guardian ad litem was later appointed for the girl and was permitted to file a suit on behalf of the daughter despite the prior consent.

Also, consent may be limited to a particular context. A release that permits a private photo or information to be used in one context may not authorize use in other media. For example, in *McCabe v. Village Voice*, Inc., the court found that the fact that plaintiff had given consent to publish a photo of her in a book did not mean that a newspaper had consent to publish the photo. Any permission must be specific to the use in question.

Consent can be implied, as noted in *Virgil*, and it doesn't need to be in writing, but if there are any concerns about needing to prove consent later, it is maybe worthwhile to obtain a release specifying the exact use of the material.

The Overlap of Ethical and Legal Issues When Posting "Private" Information Online

There have been several incidents in which private information or images have been disclosed online, and such disclosures have prompted a discussion about what should or should not be disclosed, either legally or ethically.

In one rather notorious case, a website known as Gawker published an article claiming that a Condé Nast executive had arranged to meet a gay escort. The executive never actually met the escort, and there were questions about whether the escort had attempted to blackmail the executive. The story resulted in a backlash against Gawker, which eventually took down the post.

Most of the criticism of Gawker was based on ethical considerations. Critics felt that it was abhorrent to out someone who was not in a public role and was not a hypocrite about gay rights. Gawker had taken the position that the man was the CFO of a major media company—and married to a woman— and therefore, there was sufficient reason to hold him accountable.

From a legal perspective, applying the factors for publication of private facts, the information was widely published, private, and disclosure would be highly offensive to a reasonable person. The question is whether it is "newsworthy" or of legitimate public concern. In this case, obviously from the commentary, many people felt that it was *not* of legitimate public concern, but there was never a lawsuit, and therefore we don't know what a court would have ruled.

Gawker had outed several other people, too, including a wealthy executive who later got his revenge on Gawker by funding a lawsuit that eventually put the site out of business.

That case arose when Gawker published clips of a sex tape featuring Hulk Hogan (real name: Terry Bollea), and Bollea sued for invasion of privacy, arguing that the sex tape was not a mater of public concern. The trial judge in *Bollea v. Gawker* refused to rule that the publication was newsworthy as a matter of law (meaning that no reasonable person could dispute it), and thus the case went to a jury. The jury found that Gawker invaded Bollea's privacy and awarded him $140 million.

Nevertheless, there are arguments that the use of the clips should have been deemed newsworthy, at least from a legal perspective. Bollea, in his public persona as Hulk Hogan, boasted about his sexual exploits, and the Gawker story included commentary arguing that what one sees in the video is not necessarily what one might expect based on his persona. Gawker did not appeal the jury verdict, because it was unable to post an adequate bond, but it's possible that, if the appeal had gone forward, the appellate court could have determined that the material was newsworthy; the state court of appeals had previously refused to issue an injunction against the story because it could possibly be deemed newsworthy, although the court did not make a final ruling on that issue. As a result of the lawsuit, Gawker was forced to declare bankruptcy, and its assets were auctioned to another media company. The reporter who wrote the post also had his assets seized. The case has been a cautionary tale on many levels. As a matter of journalistic ethics, it is an excellent case study for discussing what grounds should be required to publish matter of such a personal nature.

In general, images of nudity or sex tapes are going to be considered "private" and are probably not newsworthy in themselves unless the image itself is necessary to prove a point. That said, most people are opposed to the disclosure of nudity without consent. Courts in both *Michaels v. Internet Entertainment Group* and *Toffoloni v. Hustler* found that the disclosure of sex tapes and nude images, respectively, were not newsworthy. More recently, a model was banned from a gym after she posted an image on Snapchat of another gym-goer in the shower, criticizing her body. Even though that incident did not result in a lawsuit, the backlash against the model was severe. People tend to be ethically opposed to the indiscriminate publication of those kinds of private images, especially if the only justification is to make snarky and cruel commentary.

On the other end of the spectrum, many people have supported the disclosure of sensitive information when it reveals misconduct or could bring perpetrators to justice. For example, a video was posted online of young men in Steubenville, Ohio, sexually assaulting an unconscious young woman at a party. While such a video is equally as embarrassing as the celebrity sex tapes, the justification for publishing it—bringing the perpetrators to justice—is markedly different. Two of the young men were eventually convicted of juvenile offenses as a result of the incident. Some, though, have argued that the video should have been given to authorities but not posted online. Others have speculated that without the public pressure of making the video public, the authorities might not have taken action. In any event, there are still legal, ethical, and social issues to be resolved around the issue of what kinds of content should be posted online in light of potential privacy considerations.

Trade Secrets: A Version of "Privacy" for Businesses?

The Supreme Court has said that businesses don't have "privacy" rights. However, they do have an interest in keeping secrets. That interest is protected by the concept of trade secrets.

A trade secret is something that is generally not known to the public and gives a business a competitive advantage. The formula for Coca-Cola would be a classic example of a trade secret.

Most trade secret lawsuits involve companies suing competitors or former employees who act improperly. There is very little case law interpreting how trade secret laws would apply if a journalist or commenter were to disclose trade secrets, but there are a few relevant cases.

One of the most well-known litigants in this field is Apple Computer. In February of 2000, an online poster known as "worker bee" disclosed information about several upcoming Apple products, including the iBooks and PowerMac G4. A court ordered Yahoo to turn over documents to reveal the identity of "worker bee." Worker bee turned out to be a former temporary employee who had signed a confidentiality agreement. The case eventually settled, so there is no clear ruling as to whether worker bee would have been liable, but the existence of the confidentiality agreement makes the situation different from the typical journalistic disclosure.

A few years later, Apple again tried to seek the identity of people posting information online about upcoming products (this time involving a project codenamed "Asteroid," related to Apple's GarageBand program). The court in that case, *O'Grady v. Superior Court*, decided that the identities of the posters were protected from disclosure under the state shield law and the Stored Communications Act. In the course of making its decision, the court noted First Amendment issues can be raised when trade secrets are disclosed. The court determined that the fact that something was labeled a "trade secret" by the company was not, in itself, determinative. If the information were truly "newsworthy," then there may be some First Amendment protection for the disclosure. Because the court was only considering the issue of whether the identities should be disclosed and not whether there would ultimately be liability for violating trade secret laws, it is still not entirely clear how that principle would be applied in future cases.

In another instance, Gizmodo, a technology website, obtained a prototype iPhone 4 and wrote a review of it that included pictures and a breakdown of the phone's parts. Several commentators argued that the website should have been liable for disclosing trade secrets. The case received a lot of attention, and the person who sold the phone to Gizmodo was criminally prosecuted, but Apple chose not to sue Gizmodo in that case.

In general, it is fair to say that disclosing information about research, development and other non-public information is potentially fair game for trade secrets lawsuits. There should be some First Amendment protection for disclosing genuinely newsworthy information, but the case law on this subject is sparse and gives little guidance. The disclosure of information that is truly competitive and serves no legitimate news purpose might not be protected. It is therefore worthwhile to consider the risk of being sued for disclosing trade secrets whenever one publishes information that a company probably intended to keep secret. There are potential criminal penalties, as well.

It is also worth noting that companies will sometimes ask journalists to sign nondisclosure agreements (NDAs) as a condition to obtaining access to some event or information. NDAs are binding contracts, so they may impose enforceable prohibitions on the disclosure of information, regardless of newsworthiness. Agreeing to an NDA raises issues of journalism ethics; typically journalists would not want to agree not to publish newsworthy information. Nevertheless, NDAs may be appropriate in limited circumstances or for limited time periods. It is common, for example, for a reviewer to receive an advance copy of a book or film for the purpose of writing a review on the condition that the details about the book or film won't be released until a certain date. A reviewer must always consider the ethics of such an arrangement, but in many instances involving entertainment rather than news investigations, such agreements are practical and innocuous.

Practical Conclusions

- Certain kinds of information are more likely to create claims: medical or financial information, embarrassing or sensitive information involving children, information about drug or alcohol abuse, addictions or other embarrassing vices, and nudity or sexual information.

- There is probably no privacy interest if the information is in a public record, occurs in public, or is already publicly known or available, although there may be some dispute about what that means in certain cases.

- The most important consideration is "newsworthiness."

- The fact that a source tells you something doesn't mean you have the right to publish it. Reporters should be very clear with sources about what they plan to publish to avoid situations where a source thinks they are revealing something in confidence and later sue for invasion of privacy.

- There should be no problem publishing information about ordinary "breaking news," such as accidents, sporting events, emergencies, and the like.

- Information about public figures is typically newsworthy, although there may be limits. You might not get to see celebrity sex tapes just because they involve celebrities.

- The most risky scenario involves publishing information about private persons simply to illustrate a concept or issue. Distinguish between the newsworthiness of the *topic* and the newsworthiness of a *person*. If the topic is newsworthy but the person is not, it is more likely you will need their permission to disclose sensitive information if it is not already public. Also, just because something is interesting doesn't mean the courts will protect it as newsworthy.

- Signed releases can be a great way to protect oneself from privacy claims, but the release should be very specific about how the information will be used.

- Even though companies don't have privacy rights, they are permitted to bring claims for disclosure of trade secrets, and the courts have not fully addressed how the First Amendment interests of journalists would be balanced against a company's trade secret rights.

CHAPTER 5

Publicity

Using Someone's Name or Likeness

Whenever the name or likeness of a person—whether a celebrity or otherwise—is used, one must consider whether the use infringes the person's right of publicity. The tricky problem with publicity laws is that they vary substantially from state to state. Whether a use is protected or not may depend on nothing more than the jurisdiction in which the lawsuit is filed. This chapter will go over some of the issues to take into consideration to evaluate publicity claims or to avoid a suit in the first place.

What Is the Right of Publicity?

The right of publicity is the right to control the use of one's identity in commercial contexts. State laws typically prohibit "the appropriation of the name or likeness of another for commercial purposes without consent." This is one of the most confusing and complex areas of law, and states are not consistent in how they handle it.

Initially, there were two different but similar tort claims based on using someone's name or likeness: "right of publicity" and "misappropriation of name or likeness." Both torts hinge on the notion that a person uses another person's name or likeness for a commercial purpose without consent. Traditionally, the difference between the claims was that misappropriation focused on the harm done to a person's privacy right—the right not to be exposed to the public—and the right of publicity focused on the harm done to a person's right to make money from the use of their likeness—more of an economic harm than a personal harm. Thus, one could argue that celebrities don't have misappropriation claims because they are already "exposed" to the public, but ordinary people don't have publicity claims because their image has no obvious economic value. Over time, however, the two claims have been conflated. But one philosophical question continues to perplex the courts: what right are we trying to protect—is it privacy or economic harm? Both? Does it matter? Some of the confusing results in the case law derive from this question. For the purpose of this chapter, I will refer to all claims as "publicity" claims, but some states might refer to the tort as "misappropriation of likeness." In some states, these torts may be embodied in a statute; in other states, the claim is a matter of common law. The Supreme Court has addressed the issue of publicity rights only once, and it was such a unique and unusual case that it provides little guidance to those trying to determine when the use of a person's name or likeness will be protected by the First Amendment and when liability may be imposed. To make matters worse, states are inconsistent in their application of the basic principles, so there are outcomes in some cases that seem as if they are in direct conflict with outcomes in other cases.

In many instances, the law is intended to avoid false implications of endorsement. For example, if a company sells footballs and uses a picture of New England Patriots quarterback Tom Brady on their product advertisements, consumers might wrongly get the impression that Brady endorses this particular brand of football. Brady has an interest in protecting himself from being associated with a product that he does not endorse, and consumers have an interest in not being misled about whether Brady endorses the product. Publicity laws protect both interests by providing a remedy to the person whose likeness was used without consent. Even in cases that don't involve celebrities, publicity laws protect people from being associated with products without their consent.

Second, the law acknowledges that names and likenesses are valuable things that can be licensed, much like intellectual property rights. Regardless of whether a use implies endorsement or not, the use of a person's name or likeness may warrant compensation.

Finally, the courts acknowledge that there is a competing interest in preserving First Amendment principles that would be hindered if people could not ever use the name or likeness of another person without consent. There must be some protection for people to express thoughts, ideas, and historical facts that involve others, and thus the cases generally try to strike some balance between protecting publicity rights on one hand and preserving First Amendment rights on the other. But, as the case law will show, the balance is not always struck consistently or correctly.

What Does It Mean to "Appropriate" Someone's Name or Likeness?

Appropriating someone's name is fairly straightforward in most cases: it simply requires the use of the person's name. The person does not have to be famous. It is a common myth that only celebrities have publicity rights—probably because most cases are brought by celebrities—but no state imposes such a limitation. Any person can have a publicity claim if their name or likeness is used without consent.

The question, though, is how specific the use must be. In *Abdul-Jabbar v. General Motors Corp.*, a court found that a famous basketball player could go forward with a claim when a company used his birth name (which he later changed) in an advertisement. One of the more interesting cases, which was settled and therefore never resolved in court, involved actress Lindsay Lohan, who sued E-Trade over an advertisement that featured babies and referred to a "milkaholic" named "Lindsay." Lohan claimed that the ad referred to her because it used the name "Lindsay" and because she had been publicly known as an alcoholic. E-Trade claimed that it has randomly chosen the name Lindsay and it did not reference her at all; nevertheless, the case was settled, so there is no case law to clarify whether the reference to "Lindsay" would have been enough to impose liability.

Courts have found that a person's likeness can be appropriated in a wide range of ways, including the use of pictures, look-alikes, sound-alikes, cartoons, nicknames, catchphrases, and even robots. The best way to illustrate the scope of potential appropriation is to consider the variety of ways in which courts have found appropriation of likeness:

- In *Onassis v. Christian Dior-New York, Inc.*, a court said Jackie Onassis had a valid claim against Christian Dior for their use of a look-alike in a fashion advertisement. The court said the look-alike may legitimately appear at parties or events or in TV or films, but the use in advertising violated Onassis' publicity rights.

- In *Midler v. Ford Motor Co.* and *Waits v. Frito-Lay, Inc.*, Bette Midler and Tom Waits, singers with very distinctive voices, were successful in bringing publicity claims against advertisers who used sound-alike singers in their ads, leaving the audience with the false impression that the famous singers were involved in the production.

- In *Hirsch v. SC Johnson & Son, Inc.*, a court found that a company violated a football star's right of publicity by using his nickname "Crazylegs" as the name of a women's shaving gel.

- In *Carson v. Here's Johnny Portable Toilets Inc.*, Johnny Carson prevailed in a case against a company called Here's Johnny Portable Toilets, because the name obviously referenced his famous catchphrase, "Here's Johnny." Also, the company sold a toilet called the "World's Foremost Commodian." Clever, but the court found it violated the rights of the "World's Foremost Comedian."

- In *Motschenbacher v. R. J. Reynolds Tobacco*, the court found that a race car driver had legitimate publicity claim when an ad used an image of his car, even though the driver was not visible. The car was so closely linked with the driver, it invoked his "image."

- In *White v. Samsung Elec. Am. Inc.*, the court found that Wheel of Fortune spokesmodel Vanna White was identified when an ad featured a robot with blond wig and evening gown in front of a *Wheel of Fortune* set, reasoning that the audience would think of White when the saw the ad.

The *White* case was quite controversial and raised a question that has never quite been fully resolved: is "reminding" an audience of a person enough to "appropriate" their likeness? Judge Kozinski, who was well-known for his strong support of First Amendment rights, wrote a scathing dissent when the court refused to rehear the case, pointing out the many flaws with the majority decision. He particularly emphasized the serious problem with barring "reminders" of people:

> I can't see how giving White the power to keep others from evoking her image in the public's mind can be squared with the First Amendment. Where does White get this right to control our thoughts? The majority's creation goes way beyond the protection given a trademark or a copyrighted work, or a person's name or likeness. All those things control one particular way of expressing an idea, one way of

referring to an object or a person. But not allowing any means of reminding people of someone? That's a speech restriction unparalleled in First Amendment law.

An important factor was that the robot looked nothing like White. In fact, as Judge Kozinski noted, that was precisely the point—that it wasn't her:

> The ad that spawned this litigation starred a robot dressed in a wig, gown and jewelry reminiscent of Vanna White's hair and dress; the robot was posed next to a Wheel-of-Fortune-like game board. ... The caption read "Longest-running game show 2012 A.D." The gag here, I take it, was that Samsung would still be around when White had been replaced by a robot. ... The ad just wouldn't have been funny had it depicted White or someone who resembled her—the whole joke was that the game show host(ess) was a robot, not a real person. No one seeing the ad could have thought this was supposed to be White in 2012.

Kozinski predicted that giving people such an expansive right to control anything that reminds people of them would interfere with copyright law and prevent commentary on popular works:

> It's impossible to parody a movie or a TV show without at the same time "evok[ing]" the "identit[ies]" of the actors. You can't have a mock Star Wars without a mock Luke Skywalker, Han Solo, and Princess Leia, which in turn means a mock Mark Hamill, Harrison Ford, and Carrie Fisher. ... The public's right to make a fair use parody and the copyright owner's right to license a derivative work are useless if the parodist is held hostage by every actor whose "identity" he might need to "appropriate."

Kozinski's prediction turned out to be accurate. The conflict between copyright exploitation and the right of publicity was raised in *Wendt v. Host Int'l*. That case was filed by George Wendt and John Ratzenberger, actors in *Cheers*, a popular television show that centered around people at a bar in Boston. A company attempted to create *Cheers*-themed bars with robots that sat at the end of the bar, like the characters Norm (played by Wendt) and Cliff (played by Ratzenberger). Paramount Studios owned the copyright in the show, which included the copyright in the characters. As a matter of copyright law, Paramount had the right to license the use the characters and create the *Cheers*-themed bars. But the court ruled that even though Paramount owned the rights to the characters, the actors owned the rights to their images. If the robots at the bar evoked the likenesses of Wendt and Ratzenberger, then they were entitled to protection of their publicity rights. Kozinski was right: Paramount could be "held hostage" by the actors who happened to play the characters that had been created by the copyright holder.

Because the exact parameters of "appropriation" are still evolving, it is wise to consider whether a use may evoke the idea of a person, and if so, consider whether the use will be considered "commercial" or not.

What Constitutes a "Commercial Purpose"?

The main issue in publicity cases is distinguishing between "commercial uses," and expressive uses that are considered newsworthy or otherwise deserving of some First Amendment protection.

Advertisements have almost always been considered commercial purposes. *White v. Samsung Elec. Am., Inc.*, illustrates the point. Vanna White was permitted to recover damages when Samsung ran an ad that featured a robot wearing a blond wig and evening gown in front of a *Wheel of Fortune* set.

Once the court determined that White's likeness had been appropriated by the use of the robot, the question of whether the use was commercial was easy to decide. Advertisements are the classic form of commercial use, and a person who is identified in one will almost certainly have a valid claim. Basketball player Michael Jordan, for example, won a case against a grocery store that ran a congratulatory advertisement praising Jordan for his exemplary career in a commemorative issue of *Sports Illustrated*. In *Jordan v. Jewell Food Stores, Inc.*, the Seventh Circuit acknowledged that the congratulatory message was, on its face, speech that would ordinarily be considered expressive and not commercial; however, the context of the speech was "image advertising." Even though the message did not overtly propose a commercial transaction, the reference to Jordan was nevertheless in an advertisement that contained the store's logo and which might help the brand by association. Therefore, the court found the use to be "commercial."

The question that has not yet been clearly decided is whether there could be situations where the use of a person's name or likeness in an ad is nevertheless protected by the First Amendment because the use involves serious commentary that warrants protection. Consider an ad run by Gov PX, a data service company. It featured a picture of Saddam Hussein, with the caption, "History has shown what happens when one source controls all the information." An Iraqi diplomat argued that the ad violated Hussein's right of publicity. The ad was changed to depict Stalin instead.

If there had been a lawsuit, would the court have found the company liable? The example highlights the conflict presented in publicity cases. On one hand, the person featured in the advertisement should have some right to control the use of his image and to avoid any false implication of endorsement. On the other hand, the advertisement was making a point, engaging in legitimate commentary that would have been protected by the First Amendment if it had been presented in any other format. Moreover, it is highly unlikely that any consumer would be fooled into believing that Hussein endorsed either the commentary about him or the product. Whether First Amendment protection might ever be extended to commentary about a person contained within an advertisement is an open question.

There are not many cases addressing the issue. Most of the time, when presented with a case involving an advertisement, courts do not exempt the advertiser from liability on First Amendment grounds. One notable exception is *New York Magazine, Inc. v. Metropolitan Transportation Authority*. The facts of that case were undisputed: *New York Magazine* entered into an agreement with MTA (the New York City public transit system) to run advertisements on the side of city buses. One of the ads featured the magazine's logo and the line, "Possibly the only good thing in New York Rudy hasn't taken credit for." Then-Mayor Rudy Giuliani's office called the MTA and asked that the ad be removed because it violated his right of publicity. The magazine sought an injunction to prevent the city from interfering with its First Amendment rights.

The court ultimately did not rule on either the question of whether the speech was commercial or whether Rudy Giuliani's publicity rights had been violated. Instead, it ruled on procedural grounds that prior restraints are abhorrent, regardless of whether the speech at issue is commercial or political, and therefore the MTA should not bar the magazine's advertisement. But in doing so, the court noted that the First Amendment should play an important role in the analysis of whether the speech is protected:

> This case aptly demonstrates that where there are both commercial and political elements present in speech, even the determination whether speech is commercial or not may be fraught with ambiguity

and should not be vested in an agency such as MTA. While the Advertisement served to promote the sales of a magazine, it just as clearly criticized the most prominent member of the City's government on an issue relevant to his performance of office, subtly calling into question whether the Mayor is actually responsible for the successes of the City for which he claims credit. While we accord somewhat lowered scrutiny to government restrictions on the right to propose commercial transactions, … protecting the right to express skeptical attitudes toward the government ranks among the First Amendment's most important functions.

Thus, the court declined to find that the ad was overtly commercial and seemed to reinforce the principle that the question should be whether the expression at issue is what the First Amendment was designed to protect.

The use of a person's likeness on merchandise—items such as posters, mugs, t-shirts, and the like—is also likely to be considered a commercial use, unless there is some significant expressive purpose involved. For example, in *Brinkley v. Casablancas*, the court found that posters of Christie Brinkley violated her right of publicity because they were not expressive, but rather, they were created for the sole purpose of capitalizing on her fame. Similarly, in *Martin Luther King Jr. Center For Social Change v. American Heritage Products*, a court found that mugs featuring the image of Dr. Martin Luther King, Jr. violated his right of publicity. But in *Paulsen v. Personality Posters, Inc.*, the court found that "campaign" posters of a comedian who had joked that he was running for President did not violate his publicity rights because his commentary on elections—whether serious or joking—were newsworthy.

One of the most controversial but well-known cases on this subject is *Comedy III Productions, Inc. v. Gary Saderup, Inc.* That case involved t-shirts that were created by an artist named Gary Saderup. He sold shirts that replicated his own charcoal drawing image of the Three Stooges. Like in *Wendt*, there was a conflict between Saderup's right to exploit his copyright in his own drawing and his First Amendment rights to express himself, and the Stooges' right to control the use of their likeness. The court decided that a "transformative use" test should be employed in publicity cases to determine when the use of a person's image warrants First Amendment protection. In short, to be protected, the use of the image must have some creative elements that makes the use more than merely a replication of the person's image.

Interestingly, the court referred to Andy Warhol's paintings of celebrities and suggested that they would be "transformative" because they critiqued celebrity culture. But the court failed to adequately explain what, exactly, distinguished Warhol's images from Saderup's images, such that Warhol's could be protected as a "critique" and Saderup's would not. The court said, "[t]hrough distortion and the careful manipulation of context, Warhol was able to convey a message that went beyond the commercial exploitation of celebrity images and became a form of ironic social comment on the dehumanization of celebrity itself." Saderup's images, according to the court, were "literal, conventional depictions" of the Three Stooges. It could be argued that the court simply prefers the message of the Pop Art movement to the message of Realism and discounted the value of Saderup's creative expression as a result. Or, it may be that Warhol's fame entitled him to a presumption that his art expressed ideas about fame, whereas Saderup's lack of similar status results in the assumption that his motives could have been nothing more than crass commercialism. In any event, the case provides inadequate guidance for those who seek clarity with respect to what would be a protected form of expression.

Nevertheless, products that are truly expressive are likely to be protected, even if the companies that created them are otherwise commercial. One of the first cases to address this issue was *Rogers v.*

Grimaldi. Actress Ginger Rogers had filed a lawsuit, claiming that the film *Ginger & Fred* violated her publicity rights. The court in that case determined that creative works should be protected by the First Amendment unless the use of the likeness is "wholly unrelated" to the work or is "simply a disguised commercial advertisement for the sale of goods or services." Courts also tend to protect the dissemination of factual information, even if there is some commercial component to the dissemination. For example, Anheuser-Busch, a beer company, distributed a film about Hispanic recipients of the Congressional Medal of Honor. One of the men featured in the film sued, but in *Benavidez v. Anheuser-Busch, Inc.*, the court found that the documentary was a protected use, even though it was shown in the company's "beer hospitality centers." The case is consistent with the principle that the use of basic facts about a person tends to be protected, even if the facts involve people's names. Thus, in *Vinci v. American Can Co.*, a court found that Olympic wrestlers whose pictures were on Dixie cups featuring Olympic athletes with notes about their records could not prevail on publicity claim because records and images were historical facts. Similarly, in *Major League Baseball Advanced Media v. C.B.C. Distribution and Marketing, Inc.*, a court found that the First Amendment protects the use of baseball players' names and statistics in a fantasy baseball league.

Even though companies or people that create artistic works (movies, books, music, art, etc.) may make a profit from selling those works, those uses are usually considered "artistic" rather than "commercial" and are granted First Amendment protection. For example, noted golfer Tiger Woods sued an artist who had made an artistic print that featured Woods. Entitled, "The Masters of Augusta," the print was an original work that portrayed Woods in front of the famous Augusta clubhouse after he won the Masters Tournament. In *ETW Corp. v. Jireh Publishing Inc.*, the court found that the work was a legitimate artistic work worthy of First Amendment protection, and it did not violate Woods's right of publicity. Courts came to similar conclusions in *Sarver v. Chartier*, denying a claim brought by an Army sergeant portrayed in the film *The Hurt Locker*; *Dora v. Frontline Video, Inc.*, protecting a movie that used footage of a famous surfer; *Joplin Enterprises v. Allen*, protecting a play about the life of Janis Joplin; and *Winter v. DC Comics*, protecting a comic book featuring characters Johnny and Edgar Autumn from a claim by Johnny and Edgar Winter. For the same reasons, parodies are usually granted First Amendment protection as long as they are not in actual product advertisements. Thus, in *Cardtoons, L.C. v. Major League Baseball Players Ass'n.*, the court found that baseball card parodies did not infringe baseball players' right of publicity.

Not all courts, however, have been favorable toward artistic uses. In *Parks v. LaFace Records*, Rosa Parks sued the band Outkast for using her name as a title to a song. The trial court dismissed the case, finding that Outkast's use was an artistic use and did not violate Parks's publicity rights. But on appeal, the court reversed dismissal and sent the case back to the lower court to determine whether there was a sufficient relationship between Parks and the song to justify use of Parks's name. Similarly, in *Doe v. TCI Cablevision*, a court allowed hockey player Tony Twist to pursue a claim over a comic book that featured a character named Tony Twistelli. There was little doubt that the comic book character was an homage to Tony Twist, but there were also expressive elements to the use of Twist's identity. In both *Parks* and *Doe*, the plaintiffs were offended by the use of their name, and the courts were surprisingly willing to allow the claims to move forward despite the fact that artistic uses are usually given First Amendment protection. Also, the Ninth Circuit has been particularly hostile towards video game makers, finding in three cases that people depicted in video games may have valid publicity claims for the use of their likenesses. In *Keller v. Electronic Arts*, the court found that former college athletes may bring publicity claims against the maker of *NCAA Football* (a series of games that features actual players and teams), and in *Davis v. Electronic Arts*, the court found that former NFL players could move forward with publicity claims against the maker of *Madden NFL* (a series of games that also features actual players and teams). In each case, the court rejected the notion that the games were expressive and represented historical facts, circumstances that usually defeat publicity claims. Instead, the court ruled that the games were not "transformative," because they accurately recreated the players' characteristics, and therefore the use of their likenesses was "commercial." Similarly, in *No Doubt v. Activision Publishing, Inc.*, the court found that accurately recreating the likeness of the members of the band No Doubt in the video game *Band Hero* was not "transformative." The band members had actually licensed the use of their likenesses to the game maker, but then they claimed that the video game exceeded the scope of the license, because it allowed users to make the characters do unrealistic things, like sing in other voices or sing songs by other artists. The game maker argued that such changes were precisely what was transformative, but the court disagreed, focusing instead on the faithful recreation of the band members image. These cases illustrate well the risk associated with publicity rights in contexts in which courts might feel that the people represented should have been consulted or compensated.

On the other end of the spectrum, courts almost always deny publicity claims arising out of news uses. Obviously, it would be impossible to report unfavorable news if you needed permission of the person mentioned, so news and editorial uses are usually protected as long as the material is newsworthy. In practice, cases tend to arise when there is a question about whether the editorial content has some commercial aspect, but courts have nevertheless protected a wide range of uses. For example, in *Montana v. San Jose Mercury News, Inc.*, when the San Jose Mercury News reproduced some of its Superbowl coverage as a poster, the court found it to be a legitimate editorial use and denied Joe Montana's right of publicity claim. Similarly, in *Hoffman v. Capital Cities/ABC*, a court rejected the claims of actor Dustin Hoffman, who starred in the 1982 film *Tootsie*, when he sued over a magazine spread that altered famous movie images, imagining what fashions the characters would wear from the Spring 1997 collections. The spread included the famous image of Hoffman standing in front of an American flag in a red sequined gown, but altered it to show him in a more elegant, spaghetti-strapped, cream-colored, silk gown. Hoffman felt that this implied his endorsement of the designer, but the court rejected his publicity claim. And finally, in *Stewart v. Rolling Stone LLC*, Rolling Stone magazine was sued by several indie bands because the magazine had placed an article about them within an advertising gatefold, but the court found that the placement of the story did not constitute a "commercial purpose." The magazine's content was traditional editorial content, and thus the bands had no right of publicity claim.

The definition of newsworthiness may be broad but some states have drawn some limits. In *Toffoloni v. LFP Publishing Group, LLC (d.b.a. Hustler Magazine)*, the court ruled that nude photos of Nancy Benoit (who was killed by her husband, pro wrestler Chris Benoit) taken at least 20 years prior were not newsworthy, and therefore their use was not protected. The photos accompanied an article about Nancy's life, including information about her early career when she posed nude. Nevertheless, the court found that Nancy's right of publicity was implicated and the photos were not newsworthy.

The court said that those who are drawn into public controversies, such as crime victims, may be subject to some scrutiny related to the drama at hand, but they retain rights in the remainder of their life. The nude photos had no relation to the murder:

> These private, nude photographs were not incident to a newsworthy article; rather, the brief biography was incident to the photographs. Additionally, these photographs were neither related in time nor concept to the current incident of public interest. We hold that these photographs do not qualify for the newsworthiness exception to the right of publicity.

Courts have also failed to protect news uses when the use creates a false implication. In *Cher v. Forum Int'l Ltd.* and *Eastwood v. National Enquirer*, Cher and Clint Eastwood, respectively, sued tabloids that falsely implied that the celebrities gave the magazines an exclusive interview. In both cases, the courts allowed the publicity claims to go forward. The question of whether there is an implied endorsement will affect the issue of whether the content is truly editorial or whether it is commercial. Similarly, in *Downing v. Abercrombie & Fitch*, a surfer sued over the use of his image in *Abercrombie & Fitch Quarterly*, a publication that is primarily a marketing tool but contains editorial content. The court found that the possibility of an implied endorsement of the brand raised sufficient questions to deny a First Amendment defense.

Finally, a publicity claim may exist for editorial uses that completely appropriate the commercial value of someone's performance. As noted above, the Supreme Court has taken a right of publicity case only once. The case, *Zacchini v. ScrippsHoward Bct. Co.*, involved a "human cannonball" who appeared at a county fair. A local television station filmed his act and showed the entire performance—which lasted 15 seconds—on the news. The court found that the broadcast of the entire act "poses a substantial threat to the economic value of that performance."

The *Zacchini* case has provided little guidance for interpreting other cases, as the facts of *Zacchini* are unusual. Nevertheless, the case highlights the precise conflict in publicity cases: where is the line between a person's right to exploit the economic value of their likeness and the right of others to convey thoughts or information about that person? It is a question still in the process of being clarified.

Is the Right of Publicity Descendible?

"Descendibility" is the ability to pass on a right to one's heirs when one dies. Libel claims are not descendible, and most states do not permit privacy claims to be brought by heirs. However, the right of publicity is descendible in several states either by case law or by statute. For example, California enacted the Celebrity Rights Act, which allows heirs of deceased celebrities to profit from the name of likeness of the deceased for 70 years after death.

Descendibility rules are controversial because they give the families of the deceased tremendous power to control and profit from what other people do. Even if it is fair to allow a person to control the use of their image while they are alive, there are legitimate questions about whether heirs should retain that same level of control. Moreover, because the law is inconsistent across states, it is difficult to predict whether the use of a deceased person's image will result in liability.

A person might be liable if they can be sued in a jurisdiction like Tennessee (where descendibility is allowed), but not if they are sued in New York (where publicity rights are not descendible). But since one can't predict where a suit will be filed, that risk may lead to self-censorship, even in jurisdictions where descendibility is not permitted.

Are There Any Defenses to Publicity Claims?

Aside from arguing that the First Amendment should provide protection, the best defense in most cases would be to have consent. A signed release permitting the use of a person's name or likeness should protect the user from claims. A trickier question is whether there can be implied consent in places where photos are taken or shows are being filmed. Courts have differed on whether it is sufficient to give notice that filming or photography is taking place. Compare, for example, *Greenstein v. The Greif Co.* with *Nieves v. HBO*. Both cases involved reality television shows that filmed in public places. In *Greenstein*, a judge dismissed a man's publicity claim for his appearance on *Gene Simmons's Family Jewels*. The judge ruled that consent need not be in writing and people in the area were advised that filming was taking place. Thus his consent to appear on the show could be implied. In *Nieves*, however, the judge refused to dismiss a publicity claim brought by a woman who was filmed standing on a street corner in the reality show *Family Bonds*. Thus, one should not assume that one is free from claims merely by posting a notice. If one wants certainty, then it is preferable to obtain a signed release.

The other defense that may be available in some cases is the concept of "incidental use." The idea of incidental use is exemplified by *Namath v. Sports Illustrated*. That case involved ads for *Sports Illustrated* magazine. The ads showed images of the magazine itself. Joe Namath, being a famous quarterback, was featured in some of editorial content within the magazine. Thus, his image appeared in the ads insofar as his image was in the magazine and the magazine was in the ads. The court ruled that this was an incidental use. The appearance of Namath in the ads was incidental to his appearance in the magazine. Allowing such incidental use makes sense because it would otherwise be very difficult for producers of editorial content to show what their product contains.

Practical Conclusions

- Whenever the use of a person's name or likeness might be a commercial use, you have to think about publicity rights.

- Ads are almost always considered commercial uses. You typically need someone's permission to use their name or likeness in an ad or to promote a product or service.

- Merchandise (like T-shirts, posters, mugs, *etc.*) are often considered commercial uses and require permission from the person featured, except in rare circumstances where the product serves as some form of commentary in itself.

- Artistic works, like songs, plays, books, movies and the like, are usually not considered commercial uses, although there are some cases to the contrary.

- News reporting is almost never a commercial use. There are a couple cases to the contrary involving instances of a false implied endorsement, and of course, the rare and unique *Zacchini* case. The use of a performer's entire routine may create liability.

- Publicity rights might arise any time a commercial use invokes the idea of a person, including nicknames, slogans, sounds, objects associated with the person, and even robots similarly situated, so you're not off the hook just because you don't use the person's exact name or picture.

- Copyright holders that wish to exploit their works must consider whether their use implicates the publicity rights of any actor or celebrity that has an association with the work.

- The best defense against publicity claims is a signed release!

CHAPTER 6

Copyright

Issues With Creating Content or Using Other People's Content

There is one significant problem that arises from the use of any content (whether it's text or images) from another source, and that is the fact that copyright law most likely protects the content, and the owner may have a copyright claim if it is used. Or, if you are the creator of content, then you may be able to use copyright law to protect your content from other people's unauthorized use.

People who work in media consider copyright to be a delicate subject because they want both the protection from unwarranted use of their work as well as the right to use the work of others in reporting and creating new material. There is very much a "do unto others" mentality when it comes to copyright issues. It is therefore important to learn the scope of the law so that one's conduct matches one's expectations.

Unfortunately, there are a lot of myths about copyright law and "fair use," or the conditions under which people can use copyrighted material without consent. This chapter will address what the law covers and discuss what kinds of uses are likely to be protected, and which ones are not. This chapter will address:

1. The difference between different types of intellectual property (to clarify exactly what kind of scenarios are covered);

2. Whether a use would violate copyright law; and

3. Whether a use would create liability under the "hot news" doctrine.

Types of Intellectual Property

It is important to use the correct terminology when discussing the different kinds of intellectual property rights a person might have. People often use the terms copyright, patent, and trademark interchangeably, but they mean very different things. Copyrights protect creative works such as music, movies, books, articles, and all other expressive arts. Trademarks protect things that denote a brand, such as business names, logos, distinctive colors, designs, or sounds. Classic examples are the Nike "swoosh," the red soles of Christian Louboutin shoes, or the name "Pepsi." Patents protect systems, processes, and inventions.

The practice of patent law usually requires knowledge in scientific fields such as biology, chemistry, engineering, or pharmacology, and for the most part, patent law has little to do with media law. In recent years, however, there have been several lawsuits against media companies, bloggers, podcasters, and other communicators for patent infringement, so it is worth a short discussion of what patent law covers and why it might affect the ordinary communicator.

Patent law covers scientific or technological systems or processes. A person can create a new technology and get a patent on it. The purpose of patent law is much like the purpose of copyright law: to encourage creativity and provide an economic incentive to those who invent new things.

As new technologies are created, the inventors seek a patent on their creation. However, patents don't simply restrict competitors from making similar technology. A patent holder can sue someone who simply uses the technology.

For example, the person who claims to hold the patent in the technology underlying podcasting has sued podcasters, demanding a license fee for the use of the technology. The podcasters aren't competing with the patent holder, they are simply using the technology that is readily available via computers and the internet. Nevertheless, the use of the technology can, arguably, be a basis for liability, and most defendants simply settle these cases because it is too expensive to litigate.

Some people feel that such claims are an abuse of patent law and have called for reform. Most patent claims are against large companies, but some litigants have pursued individual users. Until the issue is more fully resolved, it is important to be aware that the convenience of modern technology brings with it the risk of patent infringement claims, simply for the use of technology in modern communications.

Both copyright and trademark law are relevant to media law, but they cover different aspects of one's work. The following table shows the differences between copyright and trademark concepts:

Table 6.1: Differences Between Copyright and Trademark Law.

	Copyright	Trademark
What does it protect?	Original creative works	Business logos and marks
Where is the constitutional authority?	Copyright clause	Commerce clause
What is the governing law?	Copyright Act 17 U.S.C. 101 et seq.	Lanham Act 15 U.S.C. 1051 et seq.
What is the test for infringement?	Substantial similarity, plus access to the original work	Whether there is a likelihood of confusion about origin or sponsorship
What defenses account for the First Amendment interest in expression?	Fair use (a 4-factor balancing test)	The expression makes clear that there is no likelihood of confusion
What is the justification for the law?	To encourage creativity by securing the ability to profit from one's work	To facilitate economic transactions by ensuring that consumers know the source of goods and services

Trademark law is discussed in Chapter 7, and copyright law is discussed below.

Principles of Copyright Law

Copyright is an extremely complex subject. The basis of the law is the Copyright Act, and there are many statutory provisions that govern our understanding of copyright law. However, there are also many cases that interpret how copyright law should be applied to various scenarios that arise and to new technologies that are created. With that in mind, this chapter will address the following issues:

1. What is copyrightable (and what is not copyrightable)?

2. How does one obtain a copyright?

3. What does a copyright protect and for how long?

4. If a copyright holder sues for infringement, what do they need to prove?

5. Under what conditions can someone use copyrighted material?

6. Are there any defenses to copyright infringement claims?

7. Is it copyright infringement to link or embed material online?

8. What are the consequences of copyright infringement?

9. What is the relationship of copyright law to moral rights and plagiarism?

What Is Copyrightable (And What Is Not Copyrightable)?

Copyright law protects "original works of authorship fixed in any tangible medium of expression." The basic criteria for any work to be copyrighted are that it be "original" and "fixed."

A work is original if it was independently created by the author and has some minimum degree of creativity. How much creativity is required? The Supreme Court addressed this question in *Feist Publications, Inc. v. Rural Tel. Serv. Co.* In that case, a company that published a phone book sued another phone book company for copying their book. The court held that a phone book was not copyrightable because it was merely a compilation of facts and not sufficiently original. It doesn't take much creativity to list names in alphabetical order. But an arrangement of facts can be copyrightable if it is done in a creative manner. News stories, for example, are usually copyrightable, because the reporter uses some degree of creativity in how he chooses to arrange and present the information.

Works do not have to be unique to be original. For example, two people might each photograph the same object and the photos might look similar, but since they were independently created, they each qualify as original and each is copyrightable. However, infringement may occur if someone directly copied one of the photos. It is not the object or idea represented by the photo that is protected by copyright law—it is the effort and creativity that went into making it.

A work is fixed if it exists in some stable form that allows it to be perceived or reproduced. A musical work, for example, can be fixed either by making a recording of the music, or by writing the notes on paper so that another musician can play it. Otherwise, simply playing music would be too transitory to be fixed and would not be copyrightable.

Given the minimal requirements, copyright law covers a wide range of works. The copyright statute specifically lists literary, musical, dramatic, pantomime, choreographic, pictorial, graphic, sculptural, architectural, motion picture, audiovisual, and audio works. Thus, almost any article, story, text, photo, drawing, image, video, or other material you might want to use could be potentially copyrighted. However, there are a few things that are not copyrightable:

1. Ideas: Copyright law protects the expression of an idea, but not the idea itself. Romantic comedies, for example, all seem to have pretty much the same plot: boy meets girl, misunderstanding occurs, they somehow get back together and live happily ever after. The general idea that underlies rom-coms is not copyrightable. But a specific film, such as *Bridget Jones's Diary*, would be copyrightable.

2. Facts: Facts cannot be copyrighted. The fact that the Declaration of Independence was signed on July 4, 1776 can be used by anyone without permission. However, if a person writes a specific account of the signing of the Declaration of Independence, that work is copyrightable, even though the facts contained therein are not.

3. Names and short phrases: Names, titles, and other short phrases do not qualify for copyright protection; however, they may be protected under trademark or unfair competition laws. Thus, Donald Trump could not copyright the phrase "you're fired!" but he may trademark it to the extent he used it in commerce (such as in the television show *The Apprentice*). He cannot copyright his name, but he can trademark his name, for example, for use in "Trump Tower."

4. Federal government works: Federal government works are not copyrightable. Congress specifically exempted federal government works from copyright protection. Thus, you can make copies of congressional reports, Supreme Court cases, advisory opinions of federal agencies, such as the FCC or SEC, and a wide variety of other federal materials. However, there are a few limitations to consider.

First, a federal government work is defined as a work created by an officer or employee of the federal government in the course of performing his or her duties. By definition, that means that certain works are still copyrightable even though they might seem like federal works. For example, if a senator writes a book, it may be considered outside the scope if his official duties and therefore may still be copyrightable. Or, if the First Lady writes a book, it may be copyrightable because, officially, she is neither an officer nor an employee of the government. Also, the U.S. Copyright Office has stated that certain works are not federal works and may be copyrightable:

• Works by the U.S. Post Office are copyrightable. (Yes, that means stamps.)

• Works by the governments of D.C. and Puerto Rico are copyrightable.

• Works by the United Nations or Organization of American States are copyrightable.

- Works by state, local and foreign governments are copyrightable, except for court decisions, laws, administrative regulations, official orders, and other such materials.

Some states have declared that their works are not copyrightable except for limited exceptions, and other states do copyright their works, so it may be necessary to research the law of a particular state if you plan to use a state or local government work.

Second, a person must make their own copy of a federal work and not copy other people's copies. For example, Westlaw is a company that publishes court opinions. They cannot claim rights in the opinions themselves, but they can copyright their own versions of the opinions, which include particular formatting and summaries they add to the opinions called "key cites." Thus, a photocopy a Westlaw version of a court opinion might violate Westlaw's copyright, even though the original opinion is not copyrightable.

Finally, works that have copyright protection and that are transferred to the federal government do not lose copyright protection. For example, if the Smithsonian Institution is given a painting by a famous artist, the painting may still be copyrighted, even though it is in the possession of the government.

Even if a type of work is theoretically copyrightable, there are some minimum standards that must be met to qualify for copyright protection. The lawsuits alleging copyright infringement in dance moves illustrate this point.

Fortnite is a popular video game in which players can make their avatars do certain dance moves (called "emotes"). The emotes are pre-programmed and based on dance moves from popular culture. Some famous performers have sued Fortnite, claiming that Fortnite has used their signature dance moves without permission. These suits raise an interesting question about whether one can copyright a dance move.

Federal copyright law does, in fact, allow for copyrights in choreography if the choreography is "fixed." The U.S. Copyright Office describes the fixation requirement as revealing "the movements in sufficient detail to permit the work to be performed in a consistent and uniform manner." This could be accomplished by making a video of the choreography or describing the moves in writing.

However, copyright protection is not extended to "common" moves, "social" dances, or simple routines. The U.S. Copyright Office guidelines say that one may not copyright gestures such as spelling out words with one's body, yoga postures, victory dances in sporting events, specific types of "steps" (such as the grapevine or the hustle), folk dances, square dances, or very short routines with only a few movements.

A rapper, 2 Milly, is among the performers who have sued Fortnite, alleging that he created the "Milly Rock" dance, which was "fixed" by being performed in a YouTube video. Fortnite later created an emote which was a recreation of the Milly Rock dance, but it consists of only a couple moves which are repeated over and over. Similarly, the actor Alfonso Ribeiro claimed that Fortnite used his dance "the Carlton," and the Backpack Kid claimed that Fortnite stole his move "the Floss." In all of these cases, the moves at issue are short and simple, even if they are quite distinctive. Thus, while choreography in general can be protected, courts will have to determine whether the routines at issue are too short to be protected. For all kinds of works, the U.S. Copyright Office establishes guidelines for when a work meets the requirements for copyrightability.

How Does One Obtain a Copyright?

A work is copyrighted immediately upon creation. There are no other requirements. However, a creator should consider adding a notice and registering the work with the copyright office.

Notice (*e.g.*, "Copyright 2019 Ashley Messenger") is useful because it lets other people know whom to contact for permission to use the work. Also, if you sue someone for copyright infringement and your work contains a notice, it is much harder for the infringer to argue that they acted in good faith.

Part of the copyright statute, 17 U.S.C. sec. 411(a), says that registration with the Copyright Office is a requirement to sue for damages in federal courts. One need not register to have a copyright, only to enforce the copyright, to the extent that means suing for monetary damages. However, in *Reed Elsevier, Inc. v. Muchnick*, the Supreme Court ruled that failure to register a work does not deprive federal courts of jurisdiction over a copyright infringement case. Thus, the defendant can seek dismissal of a case on the basis that the plaintiff failed to register the work, but if the defendant forgets or doesn't realize there is no registration, the case can proceed. Also, in *DRK Photo v. Houghton Mifflin Harcourt Pub. Co.*, a court ruled that a copyright holder can seek an injunction against the use of a photo, regardless of whether it was registered. Thus, registration is not required, but does provide an added level of protection. Creators usually register the work if there is any commercial value worthy of protection. The Copyright Office is part of the Library of Congress, and registration forms are available online at www.copyright.gov.

Typically, the copyright is owned by whoever created the work. This may be an individual, but it may also be two or more people, or it may be a corporation or other organization.

A "joint copyright" is when multiple people create something together, and they will jointly own the copyright. (For example, several people who write a song together or two companies that collaborate on making a video will be deemed to have joint copyright unless they agree otherwise.) If it is a joint work, any creator can exploit the work in any way, as long as they pay shares of any income derived to the other creator(s). Joint copyright can sometimes create conflicts when one person wants to sell rights and the other doesn't. Joint creators therefore sometimes write contracts agreeing that any license must be approved by all creators. Otherwise, one creator cannot stop another from "selling out"—he would only be entitled to a share of the profits from doing so.

A "work for hire" is a work created in the course of employment and will be owned by the employer. Thus, the *New York Times* would own the copyright in articles written by its employees. It wouldn't own the rights to articles written by freelancers, unless it specifically asks the freelancers to assign all rights in the articles to it in a freelance contract.

Absent a contract spelling out the transfer of rights, it can be tricky to determine what is a work for hire in cases where contractors are used. In *CCNV v. Reid*, the Supreme Court had to decide whether an artist that was hired by a non-profit group to make a sculpture owned the copyright, or whether it was a work for hire. The Court applied general principles of employment law, and using a highly fact-specific analysis, found that the artist was not an employee. Nevertheless, the Court also found that it was possible that the sculpture might be considered a "joint work." The complexity of that case illustrates why it is preferable for parties who are not in a typical employer-employee relationship to agree in advance to a contract spelling out who will own the copyright in the work and what rights each party will have.

It is important for content creators to understand these principles. Anyone who takes a photo, writes a song, prepares text, or otherwise creates a work will own the copyright, unless it was done in the course of employment or rights were transferred. Keep this in mind when reading contracts because the contract will spell out whether the creator retains rights or transfers them in whole or in part. This is particularly important online. Terms of service for any websites operate as contracts and will generally contain a provision concerning the copyright in material posted. Users sometimes inadvertently give away rights. Some sites require users to transfer some copyright rights to them; others merely ask for the rights to display the work. Others might ask for broader rights, including a right to reproduce, sublicense, or transfer the work. It is important to understand what the terms allow and the consequences thereof.

What Does a Copyright Protect and for How Long?

A copyright is a limited monopoly that grants the copyright holder an exclusive right to do five things:

1. Reproduce the copyrighted work: This right is exactly what it sounds like—the copyright holder has the exclusive right to control making copies. When commentators refer to the challenges that technology has created for copyright law, they are usually referring to the fact that technology has made it easier to copy works. It is now easy to cut and paste vast amounts of text, rip images from a website, or make copies of songs or movies. It is therefore important to realize that just because it can be done, doesn't mean the law allows it.

2. Prepare derivative works: A "derivative work" is a second work that is based on some preexisting work. Typical examples include a translation, a movie version of a book, a fictionalized version of a true story, an abridged version of a book, a reproduction of an original artwork, prequels, sequels, revisions, or any other adaptation of a work.

3. Distribute by sale, transfer, rental, lease, or lending: Copyright holders can control whether or how a work is distributed, but one important limitation is the "first sale doctrine," which provides that a copyright holder's right to control an individual copy terminates after the first sale of that copy. Thus, a person who buys a book or a cd can resell it or give it away; companies like Netflix can buy and then rent out videos or DVDs; and stores can include used items among their merchandise. None of these transactions require a royalty to the copyright holder. The only exception is that sound recordings cannot be rented (although libraries are exempt from that restriction).

4. Perform the work in public: Copyright holders are entitled to control the public performance of works, whether it is a play, a movie, a song, or other protected work. Having people over to your house to watch a movie, for example, is not a "public performance," but showing the movie in a theatre would require consent of the copyright holder. Usually, public performance requires a royalty or payment of some kind; royalties for the public performance of music, which includes simply having music playing in the background at a venue, are discussed more thoroughly in Chapter 9 on use of music.

5. Display the work: This right gives a copyright holder control over public display; for example, whether a work is posted on a website, or whether a painting or sculpture is on display. The

public display right has been one of the rights at issue in lawsuits over the use of thumbnail images on the internet. In theory, a copyright holder should be entitled to control where the work appears, although none of these rights are absolute insofar as "fair use" is permitted, as discussed in more detail below.

These rights can be sold or transferred in whole or in part. The agreements to let someone use or control copyrighted material are often called "licensing" agreements, discussed below.

Copyright law also protects against contributory infringement, which is providing the means to let others infringe copyrights. For example, in *Sony Corp. of America v. Universal City Studios*, television companies argued (unsuccessfully) that Sony was a contributory infringer because it provided video recorders that let people tape copyrighted television shows. A similar argument was used more successfully by record companies to shut down music file-sharing websites as contributory infringers. In *A&M Records v. Napster*, a court found that file-sharing site Napster could be a contributory infringer because it allowed direct copying of music and did not provide "space-shifting" the way VCRs provide time-shifting. Then, in *MGM Studios v. Grokster*, the Supreme Court ruled that there can be liability when there is evidence that the site encourages infringement. Given the widespread concern with avoiding technology that allows infringement, federal law now makes it illegal to make or sell software that breaks encryption codes or otherwise permits users to circumvent copy protection.

With respect to how long copyright lasts, the law has changed over the years. The first American copyright statute was passed in 1790. It protected works for 14 years, plus another 14 years if the request was renewed. Term limits were expanded by the 1909 Copyright Act, then again by the 1976 Copyright Act. Most recently, terms were extended by the Copyright Term Extension Act of 1998. The rule now is that copyright lasts for the life of the author plus 70 years. For a work for hire, an anonymous work, or a pseudonymous work, the term lasts either 95 years from first publication or 120 years from creation, whichever comes first. Once copyright expires, the work goes into the "public domain."

The concept of public domain is important. Public domain is a technical term that simply means that a work is no longer under copyright protection, either because the time period for protection expired or because the author intentionally waived or was not entitled to protection. A common misperception is that anything that is publicly accessible is public domain, but that is not what the term means. Works found on the internet, for example, may be freely available for people to read or see, but they may nevertheless be protected by copyright, meaning that they cannot be copied, reused or otherwise exploited without permission or a defense. To reiterate, the fact that a work is publicly accessible does not mean that it is in the public domain.

Works created prior to 1923 are now, with a few exceptions, in the public domain. There was, for a long time, a dispute over the song "Happy Birthday." It is believed to have been written in the late 1800s, but not copyrighted until 1935. Warner/Chappell Music claimed that it had rights to the song and that it was still under copyright protection. However, in 2013, a company sued to obtain a declaratory judgment that "Happy Birthday" was actually in the public domain. The case eventually settled, and as part of the settlement agreement, Warner/Chappell agreed that the song would be deemed public domain.

Works created as of 1978 are not yet in the public domain, unless the author has intentionally waived copyright. For works created between 1923 and 1978, the rules vary depending on several factors, including whether there was notice or registration, because copyright terms and requirements have changed over time. If there is any uncertainty, it is best to consult a lawyer to determine whether copyright protection is still in effect for such works.

The continued extension of copyright laws was challenged in *Eldred v. Ashcroft*. The argument against expanding copyright terms is that copyright is supposed to be a limited monopoly that gives authors some right to control works for a certain time period in order to recoup economic benefit from their work; but, at some point, the copyright is supposed to expire so that the work can pass into the public domain and be used freely. The argument in favor of expanding copyright is that creators should be able to maximize the economic advantage from their work. In *Eldred*, the Supreme Court ruled that the extension of copyright terms was "rational" (the constitutional test for economic regulations) and within Congressional authority. It therefore upheld the constitutionality of the time extension. The question, of course, is how far Congress can go in extending copyright protection before it is no longer rational, or whether there will be sufficient political pressure on Congress to scale back copyright protection. The Supreme Court also ruled, in *Golan v. Holder*, that foreign works that had been in the public domain could receive copyright protection, so it is important to carefully scrutinize rights of foreign works.

If a Copyright Holder Sues for Infringement, What Do They Need to Prove?

If a copyright holder thinks infringement has occurred, they will need to prove two things: (1) that the infringing work is substantially similar to their copyrighted work, and (2) the defendant had access to the copyrighted work.

Showing that the work is substantially similar is usually easy. In cases of direct copies, it is clearly the same. In the case of similar works, the question is often how similar the works are. Do the two works simply express the same ideas or discuss the same basic facts (in which case, there is no infringement, as ideas and facts are not protected), or are there protectable elements that are copies in the second work, such as the use of characters, specific language or other copyrightable similarities? It is useful to think of a continuum of similarity, with vague ideas being on one end, and exact similarity being on the other. The closer the use is to the vague ideas end of the spectrum, the less likely a court will find it to be an infringement; but the more similarities or the more important the significant similarities are, the more likely a court will find it to be an infringement.

The plaintiff must also prove that the defendant had access to the original work because, as noted above, copyright law does not require works to be unique. Two people can create similar works, such as each taking a photo of the same item, and neither is an infringement as long as each was created individually without copying the other. The plaintiff will have to show that the similar work was not created simply by coincidence.

Under What Conditions Can Someone Use Copyrighted Material?

In general, you can use material created by another if any one of the following apply:

1. It is not copyrightable (see above).

2. Copyright has expired (see above).

3. The user gets permission or a license.

4. The use of the work is permitted under Creative Commons or similar alternative to copyright law.

5. The use qualifies as a fair use.

6. Some other exception or defense applies.

LICENSE

Getting permission from a copyright holder to use a work is one way to ensure that the use of a work will not be an infringement. There are certain things to consider in obtaining permission.

First, the user must determine who the copyright holder is. It may be an individual, a group, a corporation, or some other entity, and it is possible that the rights have been transferred, either in whole or in part. It is important to ensure that the person granting permission actually has the authority to grant it.

Once one finds the copyright holder, the parties must negotiate the terms of the agreement. Common terms include:

a. Rights: What rights are requested? Will the material be disseminated in print, or online, or used in a video, or as part of a television show, or all of these? If it will be used in print, how many copies will be made? Can the user sell, syndicate, or sublicense the use? The agreement should spell out all the ways the material can be used.

b. Cost: How much will the copyright holder charge for the use of the material? They are free to demand payment or give permission without payment. The cost will probably depend on the scope of the rights sought.

c. Territory: Materials used online are available internationally, but in some cases, rights can be granted for use in a limited area (such as for print materials or public performance).

d. Duration: Is there a time limit on the permission? Sometimes, copyright holders will grant permission for a particular time period, say, to publish content online for 30 days or one year. After that, permission expires, and the user is no longer free to use the material. To use the work forever, the license must grant perpetual rights.

e. Exclusivity: Are rights granted to only one person, or can other people use the work as well? Exclusive rights cost substantially more than non-exclusive rights.

f. Indemnity: Will the user or the copyright holder take legal responsibility for any damages caused by the use of material? For example, the copyright holder may want the user to indemnify him/her if he/she gets sued because the material was used in a libelous way. Conversely, a user may want the copyright holder to indemnify him/her if the purported rights holder doesn't actually hold the rights to the image, or if he/she violated a law in creating the content.

g. The work and the parties: This may be obvious, but an agreement must include a description of who the Licensor is (who owns the copyright), who the Licensee is (who is allowed to use it), and what the Licensed Work is (the material to be used).

h. Governing law and jurisdiction: Parties sometimes decide in advance that a certain state's law or courts will govern any disputes that might arise out of the agreement or the use of the material. It is not necessary to do this, but it is a common term in contracts. Some people like to know in advance which state law will apply or, if a lawsuit is filed, in which courts they can be sued.

Finally, any agreement should be in writing. The terms listed above should be in the license agreement, and other terms may be included too, depending on the interests of the parties. License agreements should be clear on all terms because ambiguities may lead to lawsuits. For example, in *New York Times Co. v. Tasini*, freelancers sued the *New York Times* because of an ambiguity in the freelance agreements. The freelancers had been paid a license fee for print publication of their works, but the agreement did not specifically permit any other uses. The newspaper later sent the content to electronic databases such as Lexis Nexis. The freelancers argued that they were entitled to an additional fee for use in electronic databases, because it is a separate use that was not specifically authorized. The Supreme Court agreed with the freelancers. Now, licenses usually pay a fee for use in all formats to avoid the *Tasini* problem. Nevertheless, it is possible that a user might use material in some way that is not spelled out in the contract, and there may be a legal issue if the agreement does not grant clear consent to use material in such a manner.

ALTERNATIVE LICENSE

A creator is not obligated to copyright his or her work. He or she may declare the work to be in the public domain and allow anyone to use it freely, or he/she may provide some alternative license with particular terms and conditions. Two popular ways to declare one's work to be public domain or to license alternatively are through the Creative Commons system or the GNU Free License. If a work is covered by one of these license systems, then a user does not need permission to use the work as long as he/she complies with the terms of the license.

Creative Commons allows creators to tag their works with the following conditions:

Attribution (BY): Any work tagged "BY" may be used as long as the user credits the creator in whatever manner the creator requests.

Share-Alike (SA): Any work tagged "SA" allows any user to use it freely; however, the user must make any work derived from the original work freely available to others, too. It is important to understand what this means; namely, someone who uses a work tagged SA cannot claim copyright in the work that incorporates it. The user must make the work available on an SA basis as well.

Non-commercial (NC): Any work tagged "NC" may be used by any person but only for non-commercial purposes. There is some dispute about what qualifies for a non-commercial use, so it is important to consider whether a use might be considered commercial before using these works.

No Derivative Works (ND): Any work tagged "ND" may be used freely as long as the work is used on its own, without modification. It may not be used to make derivative works and may not be modified in any significant way (although in the case of photos, it may be permissible to size it within reasonable limits).

Creators can mix-and-match the tags to create whatever terms they wish. A work tagged "BY-SA-NC," for example, can be used by anyone who is doing something non-commercial, as long as the user credits the creator and makes the subsequent work freely available to others as well. Creative Commons licenses also require that a user link back to the terms of the license.

There is another alternative license called the GNU Free Documentation License. It is a bit more complicated, but it is similar to the Creative Commons BY-SA license. A person may use the material for any use (commercial or noncommercial, modified or not), but the material must remain free to anyone else and credit must be given to the creator with a particular notice provision.

FAIR USE

The copyright statute, at 17 U.S.C. sec. 107, allows for fair use of a work for purposes such as "criticism, comment, news reporting, teaching (including multiple copies for classroom use), scholarship, or research." However, those purposes are not exclusive. To determine whether a use is fair, a court would use the four-part test in the copyright statute. The four factors to be balanced are:

1. The purpose and character of the use, including whether such use is of a commercial nature or is for non-profit educational purposes. In *Campbell v. Acuff Rose Music, Inc.*, the Supreme Court has made it clear that this factor—whether the use is not-for-profit or educational—is not the sole determinative factor. Any use can be fair if it is adequately "transformative," meaning that the use adds something to the original in such a way as to make the new use distinct. This is often done by adding comment or criticism or by incorporating the original work as merely a small example in a larger work that illustrates some other point (as is often the case with teaching or scholarship).

2. The nature of the original copyrighted work. This factor requires the courts to consider a couple things. First, was the original work published or not? Unpublished works are generally entitled to greater protection than published works simply because copyright law grants the creator to control first publication. Second, was the work primarily factual or fictional/creative? Facts cannot be copyrighted, but creative elements can be.

3. The amount and substantiality of the portion used in relation to the original copyrighted work as a whole. In general, the more of the original work that is used, the more likely a court will find it to be an infringement, but there is no fixed amount that is fair or not. It is a common myth that someone can safely sample 10 seconds or less from an audio recording, or that one can copy 3 paragraphs or less from a book. Such guidelines might be adopted in certain

workplaces to simplify the decision-making process, but the law does not actually contain such provisions. Small amounts can still constitute an infringement, and the use of a whole work can still be fair, depending on the other factors involved.

4. The effect of the use upon the potential market for or value of the copyrighted work. This factor is quite influential because it goes to the heart of the policy underlying copyright law: Is the use competitive with the original in such a way as to interfere with the copyright holder's ability to profit from his work? Uses that supplant the original in the marketplace are unlikely to be fair.

No single factor is determinative; the four factors must each be considered and balanced against each other. Some people think that the lack of strict guidance is problematic because it leaves courts with too much discretion to decide what is fair, but others believe that strict rules would not be able to account for the wide range of ways in which works can be fairly used. Thus, it is important to look at how the courts have interpreted the fair use factors in the past to get an idea of which uses are considered fair and which are not. A review of the case law shows that the two most important factors seem to be the degree to which the use is transformative and the degree to which the works compete in the marketplace. These determinations are often closely related because truly transformative works will serve some new purpose entirely and therefore will not compete with or detract from the value of the original.

Generally, a use is a fair use if you are commenting directly upon the other work. A perfect example is a book review. A book review that quotes a couple of paragraphs to illustrate a point about the author's writing style will be a fair use. The quotes are used for the purpose of commentary, it's a small amount, and it doesn't compete with or detract from the original (assuming the reviewer doesn't use the most important part of the book). The direct commentary on the original work is "transformative," or, one might say, it "adds value." It is not simply a copy of the original, nor does is compete with the market for the whole book.

One of the most common mistakes people make is to assume that it is ok to copy something entirely if the person works for a non-profit or is acting without profit motive, or if the intent is to educate people about some issue. It is not necessarily a fair use to do this. If the use competes with the original, it may still be an infringement. So, suppose someone takes an article from a magazine's website and posts it on a message board with the intent of educating the public about the topic. If someone else searches for the article, both the original magazine site and the message board post will show up in search results. The magazine wants people to click on their original version because they make money by selling ad space on their website next to these articles. If viewers click on the message board site instead of the magazine site, the copy has taken viewers away from the magazine and harmed the market value of their work. That may not have been the intent of the copier, but it is the practical reality of the situation, and copyright law is supposed to help protect the economic incentives for creating works, and thus the magazine may request that the person remove the copy, or alternately, sue for infringement. Instead of copying the whole article, the user could link to the original, directing viewers to the magazine's site, thereby serving both the interest of the reader in finding the article and the magazine in preserving its ability to profit from its work. It would be reasonable to quote a small portion of the original or briefly describe it to give other readers an idea of the topic or nature of the story (just like in the book review example above), but it would be preferable from a copyright holder's standpoint to link to the whole article rather than copy it wholesale. In general, copying an entire work will not be fair use unless it is truly necessary for the transformative purpose, but such instances are rare. One of the earliest cases involving re-posting articles on the internet was *Los Angeles Times v. Free Republic*. The issue in that case was whether it is fair use to repost entire newspaper articles on internet bulletin boards so that readers can comment on them. The defendant argued that the purpose of reposting was for "commentary," which is one of the classic purposes of fair use, but the court found it was not fair use, in large part because the entire article was copied. Using a small quote would probably be acceptable, as would a link, but wholesale copying will require some significant transformative use to qualify as fair use. Similarly, in *BMG Music v. Gonzalez*, the court found that it was not fair use to download a whole song from a file-sharing service. Thus, while many people have argued that the internet is somehow different and special because it allows for easy copying and sharing of information, the courts have not been willing to invalidate copyright protections. Just because it's easy doesn't mean it's legal.

A use might be a fair use if it is a parody of the original; however, not all parodies are protected. It is a common misperception that parodies are protected simply because they are parodies; that is not true. There have been many cases in which parodies were not protected. The courts still balance all four factors of the fair use test. Thus, a parody may not be protected if it fails to be transformative (which usually means that it's not clear that it's a parody), if too much of the original is used, or if it harms the market for the original work.

The most common flaw in parody cases is that the parody fails to comment on the work used. A classic example is *Dr. Seuss Enter. v. Penguin Books*, involving a book that parodied the O. J. Simpson trial by writing about it in the style of *The Cat in the Hat*. The owner of *The Cat in The Hat's* copyright sued, and the court ruled that the parody was not protected because, even though the parody constituted comment or criticism of the trial, it did not provide any comment or criticism with respect to the book. There was no reason to use *The Cat in the Hat* as opposed to any other format. In order to have a use protected as a parody, the parody has to be *of the work used*, not of some other thing.

Courts have also been reluctant to protect parodies that are in bad taste. For example in *Walt Disney Prods. v. Air Pirates*, the court stated that a parody of Disney characters doing drugs and having sex was an infringement because the parodist used too much of the original work. However, it is hard to see how a parody of Disney characters could be accomplished without drawing the whole character. The court's reasoning seems like a cover for the fact that the court simply disliked the message at issue. Similarly, in *MCA, Inc. v. Wilson*, the court's assertion that the parody "Cunnilingus Champion of Company C" competed with the original song "Boogie Woogie Bugle Boy of Company B" is completely laughable. These songs could not possibly substitute for one another in the marketplace. Even if the music were identical, the lyrics distinguish one song as wholesome entertainment and the other as serving an entirely different market. In *Campbell*, which was decided after the aforementioned cases, the Supreme Court expressly said that whether a parody is in bad taste should not be a factor, so perhaps it will not be a consideration in future court decisions.

In both parody and non-parody cases, a court may deny a fair use defense if the use competes with the original work or is a use that would typically be licensed. A classic example is found in *Harper &*

Row Pub. v. Nation Enter., where a magazine published an excerpt from a forthcoming book by President Ford. *Time* magazine had bought the exclusive rights to publish an excerpt from the book, but someone leaked a portion of the manuscript to *The Nation*, and *The Nation* scooped *Time* by publishing the details describing Ford's pardon of President Nixon. The Supreme Court found that it was not fair use for several reasons, but primarily because of the effect on the economic value of the work. The Court noted that control over first publication is a valuable right that has economic value and can be a factor in publicity and marketing. Furthermore, the use had an actual effect on the market value of the work because *Time* canceled its agreement due to the scoop, thereby depriving the publisher of the exclusive license fee. *The Nation* published the heart of the book, the part most of interest to the public, taking away potential readers who otherwise might have bought the book. *The Nation* argued that the use should be protected because it was "news," but the Court noted that there was little public benefit in circumventing the publisher's choice of date and medium. The information was about to be released, and there was no legitimate reason to preempt publication. It served only the magazine's interest in getting the scoop.

The same issue was raised in *HarperCollins Publishers LLC v. Gawker Media LLC*. Gawker published on its website excerpts of Sarah Palin's forthcoming book. After Palin complained about the posting, Gawker claimed it was fair use and posted a taunt telling Palin to "take a moment to familiarize yourself with the law." The court found it was not fair use and ordered Gawker to take the excerpts down. Lesson: If you are going to be snarky, you had better be right.

It should be noted that excerpts of unpublished books tend to get heightened protection from courts because they are unpublished works. Courts tend to give more protection to unpublished works than published ones, and if the amount used is significant, then it would be very difficult to claim fair use.

Courts have been equally unwilling to declare that "sequels," "prequels," and other extensions on original works are fair use. For example, when Fredrik Colting wrote the book *60 Years Later*, a "sequel" to *Catcher in the Rye*, J. D. Salinger sued to prevent the publication of the book, arguing that it infringed his copyright in *Catcher in the Rye*. *60 Years Later* featured a character named Mr. C., who was an elderly version of Holden Caulfield and behaved much like the original character. In *Salinger v. Colting*, the court ruled that there was nothing transformative about the sequel, no commentary on the original that warranted protection. The author simply took the character from the first book and continued his story, violating the author's control over the work. It was therefore not a fair use.

This theme—that the copyright holder can decide for himself exactly how the work should be used—consistently appears in fair use cases. Consider *Clean Flicks of Colorado, LLC v. Soderbergh*, the lawsuit brought by several movie directors and studios against companies that make "clean" versions of movies by editing out sex, violence, profanity and other offensive content. The court ruled that the new versions were not transformative because they did not add anything new to the original. The court also relied heavily on the fourth factor: the effect on the market value of the original. The defendants argued that the studios were actually benefiting because they were selling more copies of the movies (the companies had customers give them a purchased copy of the DVD, and the company would clean up that DVD; they were not separately selling copies of the movies). However, the court relied heavily on the desire of the copyright holder to control the content of what is sold. If the copyright holder chooses not to sell to the segment of the market that wants "clean" versions, that choice is part of their rights.

If they choose, they may sell clean versions themselves. Thus, the court determined that the "clean" versions were not a fair use.

News uses are mentioned in the fair use statute as a potential fair use, but it is important to note that not all news uses have been protected. The question is what is used and why. Facts are not copyrightable, so there is no infringement when news organizations report facts they got from other sources, although there is still a question as to whether that might constitute a form of unfair competition in certain cases, as discussed in the section below on "hot news," or it might constitute plagiarism if proper credit is not given. It is not fair use, however, to copy another news organization's exact wording or footage, because those expressions are copyrightable. In *LANS v. KCAL*, for example, the court found it was not fair use when KCAL copied LANS' footage of the Reginald Denny beating during the 1992 Los Angeles riots. There was nothing transformative about the use, a significant amount was used, and they could have sought permission to license the footage. Similarly, in *Murphy v. Millennium Radio Group, LLC*, the court said, "[n]ews organizations are not free to use any and all copyrighted works without the permission of the creator simply because they wish to report on the same events a work depicts." And in *Monge v. Maya Magazines, Inc.*, the court found that the use of celebrity photos in a news story was not fair use, citing several cases holding that news reporting does not get a blanket exemption from copyright law. The lesson to be drawn is that the fact that something is newsworthy does not inherently make another use of it fair.

Two cases that illustrate the difficulty of applying fair use to news arise from broadcast obituaries of famous actors. In *Video-Cinema Films, Inc. v. CNN*, the court considered whether it was fair to use short clips from the film *The Story of G. I. Joe* in an obituary for Robert Mitchum. Mitchum had appeared in the film, and the clips used totaled less than 1% of the movie. The court found that the use was fair because such a small portion was used and because the use did not lessen the value of the film. However, the court in *Roy Export Co. Estab. Of Vaduz v. CBS*, found that the use of clips from Charlie Chaplin's films was not fair use when CBS prepared an obituary broadcast. The facts in that case are more complex than in the *Mitchum* case. First, CBS was not starting from scratch. NBC had previously, with permission, made a montage honoring Chaplin for use in the Academy Awards show several years earlier. CBS obtained NBC's montage and modified it. Also, CBS knew that Roy Export (the company that held the rights to Chaplin's films) was making a competing biographical film. In discussions between the two companies, Roy Export had refused to give CBS permission to use clips to make their own biography, and CBS had refused to license Roy Export's version. Although the court did not provide an extensive fair use analysis, it seems that the competitive nature of the materials was an important factor in the court's determination that the use was not fair. Also, the amount used was substantial. The broadcast showed famous scenes from six different films, each of which was significant on its own. This case illustrates well the principle that not all news uses are protected; a use should still strive to be transformative, short, and non-competitive to be protected.

Incidental uses, however, are usually protected as fair use. For example, in *Italian Book Corp. v. ABC*, a news clip of a parade happened to include a band playing a copyrighted song. The court ruled that the use of the song was a fair use because the song was incidental to the primary point of the clip, which was to show what was in the parade. Also, the news clip did not compete with the market for the song. Thus, news organizations are generally not burdened with paying royalties every time a news event happens to include music. The intentional use of a song, however, might create different issues. The court will still consider whether the use is transformative, short and non-competitive.

Of course, uses on the internet have generated many lawsuits, and one of the most controversial questions has been whether the conduct of Google and other search engines falls within the parameters of fair use. In *Field v. Google*, a court found that caches and archives are fair use; in *Perfect 10, Inc. v. Google Inc.*, a court found that the use of thumbnail images in searches was fair use; and in *Authors Guild v. Google, Inc.*, the Second Circuit ruled that Google's Library Project, in which Google made digital copies of books that the public can search and review snippets, was fair use. However, fair use is an American legal principle and not necessarily recognized overseas. In 2006, a Belgian Court ruled that Google News' use of newspapers and images was copyright infringement, and Google later settled those claims. Similarly, Agence France-Press sued Google over its use of headlines on Google News, but that case settled too.

Procedurally, fair use is a defense to copyright claims, meaning that if a person is sued for copyright infringement, he can argue that the use is "fair use," and if the court agrees, then he would not be liable for infringement. However, in *Lenz v. Universal Music Corp.*, the Ninth Circuit stated that potential plaintiffs have some obligation to take "fair use" into consideration before they seek a takedown on online "infringements." The facts of the case may seem laughably mundane. Ms. Lenz posted a 29 second video on YouTube of her young children dancing in her kitchen to the song "Let's Go Crazy" by Prince. Universal Music Group had employees whose job was to scan YouTube for unauthorized uses of music to which the company controlled the publishing rights. (The concept of publishing rights is explained further in Chapter 9 on music.) Lenz's video was identified as infringing, she received a takedown notification, and her video was removed. After getting legal counsel and filing two counter-notifications, her video was restored. She then sued Universal Music Group, alleging that they misrepresented facts and abused the takedown provision of the Digital Millennium Copyright Act, section 512. The primary dispute between the parties was whether Lenz's use of the music was "authorized by law." Lenz argued that the Copyright Act authorizes the fair use of copyrighted material, and therefore her use was "authorized" even if she lacked specific permission to use it. Universal argued that, because fair use is a defense to an infringement claim, it merely *excuses* misconduct rather than *authorizes* it. The court ultimately agreed with Lenz, distinguishing between defenses that are labeled as such due to how they are raised procedurally from defenses that are considered excuses from misconduct. The court found that fair use happens to be a defense from a procedural standpoint, but it is a *right*, not an excuse. Thus, the court found that a potential plaintiff must consider fair use before sending a takedown notification under the DMCA for allegedly infringing content online. In fact, the court went a step further and stated, "if a copyright holder ignores or neglects our unequivocal holding that it must consider fair use before sending a takedown notification, it is liable for damages under sec. 512(f)." Copyright holders should therefore consider whether a use is fair before reflexively seeking takedown of any use of their material.

Last but not least, it should be noted that, aside from the issue of whether a use might be a fair use, FCC regulations prohibit any broadcaster from retransmitting any other broadcast content without consent. This rule was designed to prohibit various kinds of unfair competition between different broadcasters, and the rule is still in effect. It has nothing to do with copyright law, but is an additional regulation that must be met in the broadcasting industry. Thus, even if a use might qualify as a fair use, the FCC rule overrides copyright principles and will require the user to get consent if the user is a broadcaster and the original work was a broadcast work.

OTHER EXCEPTIONS

The Copyright Act does contain some other exceptions that permit a person to use a copyrighted work without consent. Most of these involve statutory licenses for musical works. Such licenses are discussed in Chapter 9 on use of music. There are also special exceptions for libraries.

Are There Any Defenses to Copyright Infringement Claims?

The main defenses to copyright infringement are the kinds of legitimate uses discussed above. Fair use is probably the most commonly used defense. Sometimes, a defendant will argue that his use is covered by a license or that there is implied consent to use the work (such as when material is made embeddable by the copyright holder). In rare instances, a defendant can prevail by showing that the plaintiff does not actually hold a valid copyright in the original work.

The other important defense is the "safe harbor" provision of the Digital Millennium Copyright Act of 1998 (DMCA), found at 17 U.S.C. sec 512. The DMCA provides a defense to "Internet Service Providers" if they follow certain notice and takedown procedures for alleged copyright infringement by third parties who post on their sites. This gives some protection to websites if third parties post infringing material on their sites, similar to the way section 230 of the Communications Decency Act provides protection to Internet Service Providers (ISPs) from liability for material posted by third parties. The person who posted the infringing material may still be liable, but the ISP will not be if the safe harbor provisions are followed.

In short, the law requires ISPs to provide the name and contact information for an agent to whom notice of alleged infringements can be sent. A copyright holder may then send notice that he/she has a "good faith belief" that the posted material is an infringement. The ISP must remove the material and notify the poster of the removal. The person who posted the material may provide a counter-notice if they believe the material does not infringe someone else's copyrighted material. The copyright holder then has 14 days to file a lawsuit in federal court. Otherwise, the ISP must repost the material.

The DMCA notice and takedown provisions have generated some controversy for several reasons, but the most practical concern is that it creates a game of chicken between a copyright holder and poster in cases where there is genuine dispute. Either party can end up being liable for damages if they are wrong. The ISP, however, will be protected, as long as it follows the procedures set forth in the statute.

Is It Copyright Infringement to Link or Embed Material Online?

Links alone generally do not create copyright issues in the United States, and links are often a copyright holder's preferred mechanism for others to draw attention to their work. However, in *Live Nation Motor Sports Inc. v. Davis*, a court held that a link can create copyright problems if it essentially involves stealing content by deep-linking in a deceptive way. There is also an unresolved issue as to whether "framing" (dividing a web page into sections, some of which allow a user to see content from other sites) constitutes copyright infringement. Until these issues are resolved, users should be aware that their legality is in question.

Embedding is a particular type of linking where an item from one site appears on another site. For example, if one "embeds" a YouTube video onto a web page, a user can see the video from the web page and play it without leaving the page; however, the video is still being served from YouTube's servers. It is not technically "copied" onto the other site, but it is "displayed," which still invokes copyright rights. In *Perfect 10*, the court had created what lawyers now call the "server test." The court ruled that embedding an image does not violate the display right of the copyright holder of the image because the image is still served from the original server. If the copyright holder has made the image embeddable, users should be allowed to use that link to display the image. However, one must be careful if the embedded material was posted by someone other than the original copyright holder. In *Goldman v. Breitbart News Network, LLC*, a judge ruled that various media outlets had violated Justin Goldman's copyright in a photograph by embedding tweets that contained the photograph. The people who had tweeted Goldman's photo did not have permission to make the photograph available, and the court found that the copyright holder had therefore not authorized the public display of the image. Moreover, the court rejected the "server test," finding that there was nothing in the Copyright Act that justified it. The judge found that the display right is based on any mechanism that allows the display of the image. While the server test may prevent liability with respect to the issue of actually making a copy of the image, the display right is not contingent of the location of the image. There are not many court opinions addressing the issue of whether embedding can be copyright infringement, but given the decision in the *Goldman* case, users may want to ensure that, if they embed material, the material was posted by the rights holder who can properly authorize the use of the embedding functionality (in which case, there may be an implied license to use it). Otherwise, it is possible that the original copyright holder could bring a claim for infringement.

It should be noted that linking could potentially create legal issues in other countries. The European Union is currently considering a revised Copyright Directive that is intended to make copyright law more consistent with modern usage of content online. Article 11 of that Directive would require companies to pay a "link tax." This provision was intended to force big platforms, like Facebook or Google, to pay news organizations for using snippets of their stories. Some people see this as a good thing, because it would direct money back to journalism organizations, which have lost money as digital media has expended. However, there are many questions about how this provision would work in practice. News organizations frequently quote from other news stories; would that now require payment? And how would the payment mechanism work or be enforced?

Moreover, individual nations have attempted to pass similar provisions, and the result has not been what advocates had hoped. In Germany, news organizations opted to give Google the right to use snippets without payment. In Spain, where the law did not allow the news organizations to opt-out of payment, Google News simply shut down. While it is not clear yet whether this Directive will be adopted, it is worth noting that other countries make take different approaches with respect to linking and other copyright issues.

What Are the Consequences of Copyright Infringement?

A person who is found liable for infringement can be subject to several penalties, including:

1. Actual damages (the copyright holder's lost profits)

2. Disgorgement of profits (the money the defendant made)

3. Statutory damages ($500–$100,000 per infringement, based upon the judge's discretion and depending on whether the infringement was willful or accidental)

4. Injunction (an order to stop infringing)

5. Criminal prosecution (punishment may include fines or jail)

What Is the Relationship of Copyright Law to "Moral Rights" and Plagiarism?

Moral rights and plagiarism are two issues that are often confused with copyright, but they are distinct.

MORAL RIGHTS

Moral rights are similar to copyright protection, but go beyond what copyright protects. These rights are European in origin and are generally protected in Europe. The two main rights are (1) the right of attribution (to have your works identified as your works) and (2) the right to integrity (the prevention of destruction or distortion of an artistic work).

The United States does not generally protect moral rights, except for what is covered by the Visual Artists Rights Act, which was passed in 1990. It protects the right of attribution and the right to prevent intentional distortion or mutilation of art works, but it applies only to limited edition visual art and terminates upon the death of the artist.

PLAGIARISM

While copyright infringement and plagiarism can theoretically overlap, they are separate issues. Copyright is a legal issue involving the use of material, and plagiarism is an ethical issue involving proper credit.

For example, if a student quotes a paragraph from a book for a paper he is writing, and he fails to note the source of the material, he has engaged in plagiarism (taking another's material without properly crediting it), but not copyright infringement (because it would probably be a fair use).

If one cuts-and-pastes an entire article from the *New York Times* and posts it on a blog, noting that the article came from the *New York Times*, one has infringed the *Times's* copyright (because it is probably not a fair use), but has not plagiarized (because the origin was properly credited).

However, if someone took that article and tried to pass it off as his own material, then he would have both infringed the copyright and plagiarized. That person could be sued for copyright infringement, but cannot be sued for plagiarism; one can only be embarrassed or discredited for that.

DO I HAVE TO CREDIT THE CREATOR OF A WORK IF I USE IT?

As an ethical matter, you should always credit the creator of a work, regardless of whether it is used with permission or per fair use or any other reason. If you have licensed the work, you may be required to credit the creator as called for in the agreement. If you are displaying a work of visual art, then you may have an obligation to credit the artist, and failure to do so may create a claim under the Visual

Artists Rights Act. Please note: it is a myth that simply giving credit to the copyright holder is enough to protect oneself from liability for infringement.

The "Hot News" Doctrine

The hot news doctrine is a historical quirk with a vague relation to copyright law. It has been used to protect facts in limited circumstances, even though facts would not be protected under copyright law. It is more akin to unfair competition laws than intellectual property laws.

The principle was established in *International News Service v. Associated Press*, as a matter of common law. The ruling is based in the idea that it is unfair competition for the International News Service (INS) to copy facts from Associated Press (AP) articles and rewrite them to distribute to its own clients without incurring the same expense that AP incurs in creating the original news articles. The decision was based on the "sweat of the brow" theory. According to this theory it is the labor and expense involved in collecting the facts (rather than the facts themselves) that is valuable and protectable.

As digital media expanded, some creators wanted to use the hot news doctrine to prevent aggregators from using material without paying for it. They argued that content creators need an economic incentive to continue to produce quality journalism and other interesting content. If the facts underlying material can be immediately copied by others with no effort, then the economic incentive to create content is diminished, if not killed.

A plaintiff probably won't have a hot news claim unless there is an investment of time, money or effort to gather the facts and the defendant is free-riding on that investment. In *NBA v. Motorola, Inc.*, the court ruled that the NBA did not have a hot news claim against Motorola when Motorola provided a sports scores service on its pagers. Even if the NBA had a competing service that provided sports scores, Motorola could have its own service because it gathered its facts (the scores) with its own expense of money and effort. It did not free-ride on the NBA's service, which, the court noted, could create a claim.

Also, there is a bit of a technical dispute about whether copyright law preempts the hot news doctrine if the material taken is a copyrightable work rather than merely a compilation of facts. Compare, for example, *X17, Inc. v. Lavanderia*, where the court allowed the hot news doctrine to be used in a case involving photographs, which are copyrightable, with *Barclays Capital, Inc. v. TheFlyOnTheWall. com*, where the court ruled that federal copyright law preempted the hot news doctrine because a copyrightable work was at issue. Preemption means that a particular law controls the situation. In this case, it means that if the work is copyrightable, then a plaintiff's only remedy is whatever would be available under copyright law, and the hot news doctrine can't be applied. Courts have tended to find that copyright law preempts the hot news doctrine when copyrightable content (something more than mere facts) is at issue.

Practical Conclusions

- You don't have to formally copyright any works you create, although filing with the Copyright Office can be helpful if you want to sue to enforce your copyright.

- Most creative works are probably under copyright. The main exceptions are federal government works and works older than 1923.

- The concept of "public domain" means that the copyright term has expired. IT DOES NOT MEAN "PUBLICLY AVAILABLE ON THE INTERNET."

- To use someone else's work—which includes even seemingly mundane things like cutting and pasting something off the internet or making a CD of songs—you probably either need permission of the copyright holder, or your use has to be fair use.

- If you get permission, try to get it in writing, and include terms like cost (if any), duration, and the exact uses permitted.

- "Fair use" is determined using a 4-part balancing test, factoring in:

1. The nature of the use, including whether it is commercial, noncommercial, whether there is commentary or criticism of the original, and whether the use is transformative;

2. The nature of the original work, including whether it was published or unpublished, factual or fictional;

3. The amount used; and

4. The effect on the market value of the original.

- In general, a use will have to be transformative to be fair. Copies made for personal use that have no effect on market value will probably be fair, too. Small amounts of content used in news reporting or other descriptive works are probably fair if they illustrate the point the speaker is trying to make.

- However, the case law seems to indicate that you can't just take copyrighted material and put it in news. Being a news report, on its own, is not enough to make a use fair.

- Moral rights, plagiarism, and "hot news" are concepts somewhat related to copyright law but different and should be distinguished.

CHAPTER 7

Trademarks

The Use of Product Names and Logos

In most instances, a person who merely references a company, product, or slogan will not face any liability for that use, but there are times when the use of a name, logo, or design will create legal issues.

Trademark law protects business names, logos, slogans, and other identifying characteristics. Thus, it is important to understand what would constitute infringement or dilution. Also, anyone who establishes a business or website may want to establish a trademark for themselves. Media companies and writers will sometimes seek trademarks for company names, product names, titles of regular features, columns, shows, and other editorial products that are distinctive.

Another potential issue is cybersquatting. Cybersquatting laws apply to certain uses of trademarks in URLs.

Because of the potential for such issues to arise, this chapter will discuss:

1. Trademark issues, including how a mark is established and how long protection lasts

2. What is dilution?

3. What is cybersquatting?

Trademarks

As defined by federal law, a trademark is "any word, name, symbol, or device, or any combination thereof adopted and used by a manufacturer or merchant to identify his goods and distinguish them from those manufactured or sold by others." A trademark can be the name of a company (Nike,

Coca-Cola) the name of a product (Air Jordan, Coke), or the symbol that represents it (the swoosh, the red-and-white stylized letters that spell "Coca-Cola"). There may also be distinctive sounds, phrases, designs, or colors that constitute a trademark. For businesses that offer services rather than material goods, there are "service marks," which are conceptually the same thing as trademarks, except that they denote services rather than goods. As discussed in the chapter on copyright, names, words, and short phrases cannot be copyrighted, but they can be trademarked, so things like band names (U2) or catch phrases ("You're fired!") can theoretically be trademarked.

The purpose of trademark law is to help consumers figure out which products come from which producers. When you see a brand's name or logo, you should be able to rely on that brand being of the quality you expect. One of the primary goals of trademark law is to prevent "passing off," which is when a seller represents falsely that his products are from another's company (for example, when street vendors sell fake Rolexes or fake Kate Spade purses). Even if you know the fakes are fake, it is still a form of trademark infringement. Companies are entitled to have products with their name on it be their own.

A registered mark will often be denoted by "R" in a circle. Unregistered trademarks are sometimes identified with a superscript "TM," and service marks with a superscript "SM." These notices are not required, however, so any name, mark, design or device that represents a product or service may be protected even without a notice.

What Are the Requirements for a Trademark?

Some trademark protection occurs automatically upon any legitimate use of the mark in commerce. In other words, once a person or business sells a product or service with a particular name on it, they are entitled to some protection, assuming their use is not an infringement itself. Filing with the federal U.S. Patent and Trademark Office (USPTO) is not required.

However, to get all the benefits of federal trademark protection, including presumptive ownership of the mark and the right to sue in federal court, trademarks must be filed with the USPTO, which can be done at www.uspto.gov.

A trademark filed with the USPTO should be accepted and granted protection if the mark is not already taken and it is sufficiently distinctive or has acquired "secondary meaning."

IS THE MARK ALREADY TAKEN?

Prior to adopting a trademark, a potential applicant should search the USPTO database to see whether someone else is using the same or a similar mark. The search is available via the USPTO website and is very easy to use. One can search for key words and phrases to see whether a similar mark already exists, and if so, for what kind of product or service. It is possible for different companies to use the same or similar name for different kinds of products. For example, the name "Dove" is used to identify both soap, sold by Unilever, and chocolate, produced by Mars. Consumers are not confused about the source of each product or whether one company endorses the other simply because they have the same name. If a similar name shows up in the search, a business would have to decide whether the use is competitive or whether it still wants to adopt the mark regardless of the use of the name by another company.

Even if the USPTO search does not indicate that there is already a registered mark for a particular name or phrase, a potential trademark user might consider doing a basic online search to see whether or how the name/phrase is used. There are sometimes surprising results. It may be that a competing business already uses the name, even without registering it. Or, it may be that the name or phrase has a negative use or connotation of which the business was unaware and with which the business would not want to be associated.

IS THE MARK SUFFICIENTLY DISTINCTIVE?

A mark must be sufficiently distinctive to qualify as a trademark. It might be a common word or symbol that is arbitrarily applied to the goods or services at issue (for example, "Tide" applied to laundry detergent, or "Dove" applied to soap or chocolate), or it might be a word coined expressly to be a trademark ("Cheerios" or "Pepsi").

When names or phrases are merely descriptive of the good or service they represent, a purported trademark holder will have to show that the name or phrase has developed "secondary meaning," which means that consumers associate the good or service with the particular source. A classic example is the name "Raisin Bran." Both Post and Kellogg's make a cereal consisting of bran flakes and raisins. Because the name is merely descriptive, either company would have to prove it has acquired secondary meaning to obtain a trademark in the name, but neither has done so; thus, you can buy Post Raisin Bran or Kellogg's Raisin Bran, with the manufacturer's name rather than the product name being the protectable element that allows consumers to identify the source of the product.

Another example is the phrase "Best of," usually used in the context of editorial content such as "Best of Boston," or "Best of Dallas." Village Voice Media, a company that had owned several weekly newspapers around the country, sought a trademark in the phrase "Best of" and sued Time Out, one of its competitors in New York, for publishing a "Best of New York" issue. The case settled before any court opinion on the merits was issued, but numerous commentators pointed out that Village Voice Media would have a difficult time winning the case, as it would have to prove secondary meaning—that consumers associate "Best of" issues with Village Voice as opposed to other publishers—a difficult task in a world where virtually every paper, magazine, and blog publishes a "best of" list of some sort.

The one thing companies want to avoid is having their trademark become a generic term, because a trademark loses protection if it becomes generic. This has happened several times in the past, for example with the terms "refrigerator" and "aspirin." Thus, companies will sometimes send cease and desist letters when they see their trademarks being used generically. The makers of Xerox, Kleenex, and Bubble Wrap are particularly vigilant because the terms are often used, improperly, in a generic sense, rather than referring to copying, facial tissues, and protective packaging material, respectively. As a matter of journalism ethics, reporters should make an effort not to use brand names generically. The challenge is often that the speaker is unaware that the term is a registered trademark, precisely because the term is often used generically. Nevertheless, once one becomes aware that a term is a registered mark, it would be appropriate to correct or clarify any online or archived versions of a story so that it is clear whether one is referring to a general category of a product or a specific brand.

Sometimes litigants will try to argue that a mark is generic, although this argument is not always successful. For example, in *San Francisco Arts & Athletics, Inc. v. U.S. Olympic Committee*, the organizers of the "Gay Olympics" argued that "Olympics" was a generic term for a collective of sporting events, but the Court ruled that it was not generic and referred to the official international event known as the Olympics. The Court therefore upheld the injunction against the use of "Gay Olympics."

THE CONTROVERSY AROUND IMMORAL AND SCANDALOUS MARKS

A trademark application should be granted unless it falls into one of the categories set forth in 15 U.S.C. sec. 1052. That section had permitted the USPTO to deny protection to a mark that "[c]onsists of or comprises immoral, deceptive, or scandalous matter; or matter which may disparage or falsely suggest a connection with persons, living or dead, institutions, beliefs, or national symbols, or bring them into contempt, or disrepute. ..."

For many years, the USPTO would not accept "immoral" or "scandalous" marks. For example, the actor Damon Wayans attempted to trademark the term "nigga," but his application was rejected by the USPTO because they believed it could not be used in a manner that would not be offensive. Keon Rhodan, a South Carolina entrepreneur, had previously attempted to trademark "Nigga Clothing," but his attempt was rejected, as well. Nevertheless, he continued to sell shirts with the phrase on it. The fact that a trademark had been rejected did not mean it couldn't be used. On the contrary, it means that anyone could use it, and no one can claim exclusive ownership for commercial purposes. Similarly, in a 2014 case, *In re Geller & Spencer*, the government denied protection to the proposed mark, "Stop the Islamization of America," on the grounds that it would be offensive to Muslims.

The USPTO, however, had not rejected all potentially inflammatory marks. For example, the government initially accepted the application for the Washington Redskins mark, which was under protection until it was cancelled in June 18, 2014, following several lawsuits challenging that mark, arguing that the term is offensive. Other registered marks that appeared in the USPTO database included "Dykes on Bikes," "Uppity Negro," "Whores from Hell," "36 Chain Gang Rich Nigga$," and "slutjuice."

The question, then, is when would a mark be too offensive? It is difficult to see a principled distinction between the marks listed above that had been permitted and those that had been denied.

The Supreme Court finally addressed this issue in 2017 in a case entitled *Matal v. Tam*. Simon Tam was the lead singer of a band called The Slants. He attempted to trademark the name, but his application was rejected on the grounds that the name is offensive to Asians. Tam himself is Asian-American, and he said that his goal was to "reclaim" the term and use it in a positive manner. He sued the government, arguing that the USPTO rule was unconstitutional.

The Supreme Court ruled in Tam's favor, but the justices had different opinions about why he should win. The Court's opinion, written by Justice Alito, noted first that trademarks are private speech, not government speech. The government had attempted to defend its rule by arguing that trademarks are a form of government speech and therefore it had broad discretion to control it. (See chapter 19, which discusses government speech, for more information about such restrictions.) The Court rejected that argument, reasoning that if the government could transform the speech of individuals or companies into government speech merely by affixing a "seal of approval" (or acknowledgment, which is what trademark law does), then the government could abuse that process to silence a wide range of speech and silence dissenting viewpoints. Justices Alito, Roberts, Thomas, and Breyer then reasoned that the USPTO rule was unconstitutional because it couldn't even meet the low level of scrutiny given to "commercial" speech as defined by *Central Hudson* (see chapter 17 for a discussion of that case/doctrine). In short, those justices found that the rule was not "narrowly tailored" to meet any stated objective.

Justices Kennedy, Kagan, Ginsberg, and Sotomayor reasoned that the rule was unconstitutional because it constituted viewpoint discrimination, and the government should not be permitted to select some views over others.

Ultimately, the Court found that the government had not met its burden of justifying its restriction on speech, thereby striking down as unconstitutional that portion of the Lanham Act that restricts offensive marks. Immediately after the decision, people began to file for protection of marks that had previously been denied protection.

How Long Will Protection Last?

Protection lasts until one of the following occur:

1. The mark is no longer used in commerce. This is called "abandonment." A mark is deemed abandoned if it is not used for two years.

2. Registration expires and is not renewed. A mark is initially registered for five years. It can then be renewed every 10 years, and it can be continually renewed as long as it is still in use.

3. The mark is successfully challenged. Competitors and other interested persons can challenge the validity of a mark, and although it is rare, a court can invalidate a trademark or find that someone else has prior use and therefore superior rights to the name.

4. The name becomes generic. As described above, trademark holders try to avoid this, although it does happen.

Absent one of those four scenarios, trademark protection can last indefinitely. There are no mandatory limits on protection.

What Is Infringement?

A mark is not infringed just because it is used. In order to constitute infringement, a use of someone else's mark must create a "likelihood of confusion" in the mind of the ordinary consumer as to the origin or sponsorship of the product. I mentioned Nike and Coca-Cola in paragraphs above, but no reasonable person would be confused into thinking that Nike or Coca-Cola created this book or sponsored my reference to the terms. There is therefore no "likelihood of confusion" created by my reference, and thus, no infringement. In most cases, where a person simply references a trademarked company or product, no one will be confused about origin or sponsorship, and thus, there should be no legal issues with a typical editorial use.

Likelihood of confusion can arise by using an identical mark, a similar mark, or some other use that generates confusion in the mind of an ordinary consumer. Usually, using an identical mark is passing off, although sometimes it simply implies false endorsement. A simple example would be if a blogger, without editorial context, posted the logos of business the blogger supports. It might not be clear to the site's visitors whether the businesses intentionally advertised on the site or otherwise supported the blogger. Free publicity does not compensate the trademark holder if the use suggests a false endorsement.

Exact similarity is not required; the marks need only be similar enough that "an appreciable number of reasonable buyers" are likely to be confused. For example, in *Beer Nuts Inc. v. Clover Club Foods Co.*, the court found that there was potential for confusion between "Beer Nuts" and "Brew Nuts," two products with similar names and similar packaging. However, in *Time Inc. v. Petersen Pub. Co.*, a court found that there was no likelihood of confusion between *Teen* and *Teen People* magazines. The fact that they both had "Teen" in their names was not solely determinative. The magazines had different designs and fonts, and the *People* brand was already well-established as a separate product. Thus, in any case, the outcome will be based on the specific facts of the case.

Parodies and artistic uses have generated some interesting lawsuits, but, for the most part, courts have ruled that these types of uses are protected by the First Amendment, and they do not create confusion in the mind of a consumer because the use is obviously not sponsored by the trademark holder. In *Jordache Enters. v. Hogg Wyld, Ltd.*, for example, a court ruled that a company that sold jeans for plus-size women under the name "Lardashe" did not infringe the trademark of Jordache, because the name was obviously a joke and no reasonable person would be confused. The critical and/or comical nature of a parody lessens the likelihood of confusion. A parody is intended to remind the audience of the original mark, but the result should be comedy, not confusion. However, when the use is not clearly artistic or humorous, there can be a likelihood of confusion. For example, in *Dallas Cowboy Cheerleaders v. Pussycat Cinema*, the court found that there was a likelihood of confusion where "fake" cheerleaders were in a pornographic video; the parody element was not clear, and a viewer might have presumed that the women in the video were actual Dallas Cowboys Cheerleaders.

To the extent that cases arise from editorial uses, they typically involve an allegation of implied endorsement. One example is *Playboy v. Welles*. Terri Welles had been Playmate of the Year in 1981, and she used the phrase "Playmate of the Year 1981" on her website, but she also included a disclaimer saying that her site was not affiliated with *Playboy* magazine and that the marks she used were *Playboy's* registered marks. Nevertheless, *Playboy* sued her for infringement, alleging that the use of the marks implied endorsement. The court ruled in favor of Welles, concluding that the use was merely nominative, truthfully indicating that she had, in fact, been Playmate of the Year in 1981 and referring to her appearance in *Playboy* generally. The court noted that it would be absurd to deny her the right to describe herself with a title that had been applied to her: "There is no other way that Ms. Welles can identify or describe herself and her services without venturing into absurd descriptive phrases. To describe herself as the 'nude model selected by Mr. Hefner's magazine as its number-one prototypical woman for the year 1981' would be impractical as well as ineffectual in identifying Terri Welles to the public." However, the court did remand the case for further consideration of her use of the abbreviation PMOY '81 used repeatedly as background of the site. The court found that the abbreviation was merely a design element and was not being used to describe her in any way, and that kind of use might be an infringement.

Implied endorsement was also at issue in *New Kids on the Block v. News America Pub., Inc. USA Today* and *Star* magazine each conducted a poll using a 900 number service, asking members of the public to call and vote on which member of the band New Kids on the Block was their favorite or the sexiest. Callers were charged for calling the 900 number. *USA Today* eventually published the results of the poll for the public's favorite band member. *Star* magazine never revealed the public's choice for "sexiest" member because of the litigation. The band argued that the use of a 900 number was a commercial enterprise that infringed their trademark, as well as their publicity rights. The publishers argued that they were engaged in newsgathering by polling the public, and thus their conduct was protected by the First Amendment.

The court considered various tests that courts have applied and concluded that the First Amendment "provides immunity to the defendants in this case unless their use of the plaintiff's trademark was wholly unrelated to news gathering and dissemination, misleading as to content, or falsely and explicitly denoted authorship, sponsorship, or endorsement by the New Kids on the Block." The court determined that the publishers were engaged in newsgathering and there was insufficient evidence that they had been misleading or implied endorsement or sponsorship. The court acknowledged that there might be some small risk that certain members of the public would be confused about whether the band endorsed the poll, but that risk was not enough to outweigh the interest in gathering the information, particularly where the use of the trademark was not used in a misleading way that would ordinarily cause confusion. Thus, the court held that the publishers were not liable.

The same logic has been extended to websites and domain names that make use of trademarks in a truthful, nonmisleading manner. *Toyota Motor Sales U.S.A., Inc. v. Tabari*, involved a couple who acted as auto brokers, helping consumers find cars based on an ideal mix of price, features, and location. They specialized in brokering Lexus-brand cars and owned the sites buy-a-lexus.com and buyorleaselexus.com. The trial court had ruled in favor of Toyota, finding that the names suggested endorsement by Lexus, despite the fact that the sites disclaimed any formal relationship and clearly explained that the couple simply acted as brokers. On appeal, the Ninth Circuit found that the site could be protected and remanded the case for further reconsideration. The court stated succinctly, "[t]rademarks are a part of our common language, and we all have some right to use them to communicate in truthful, non-misleading ways."

Thus, the use of a trademark for the purpose of accurately describing a person or entity should not be problematic, as long as the use is not misleading nor falsely implies endorsement.

What Is Dilution?

Federal and state laws protect trademarks when there is "dilution," even if there is no likelihood of confusion. "Dilution" is use of a mark that weakens its identity or harms its reputation. Unlike regular trademark laws, which are designed to protect consumers, dilution is designed to protect the trademark holder.

In 1995, Congress passed the Federal Trademark Dilution Act, which was supposed to protect famous trademarks from any uses that would dilute their distinctiveness even in the absence of any likelihood of confusion. The statute was interpreted by the Supreme Court in *Moseley v. V Secret Catalogue, Inc.* In that case, Victoria's Secret, a company that sells women's lingerie and clothing, sued Victor's Little Secret, a shop that sold adult materials. Victoria's Secret argued that the other name was likely to dilute its mark, but the Court concluded that the federal dilution statute requires proof of actual dilution, not likelihood of dilution. Victoria's Secret did not prove actual dilution, and thus did not prevail.

In response to *Moseley*, Congress passed the Trademark Dilution Revision Act of 2006. The new law expressly stated that a plaintiff need only prove "likelihood of dilution" and can bring a claim based on either (1) tarnishment (a use that harms the mark's reputation), or (2) blurring (weakening a mark's distinctiveness).

Because of the First Amendment concerns with restricting speech that involves famous trademarks, the law contains a few exceptions. News reporting and commentary is expressly exempted, so any reporting should be protected. Parody, satire, and other forms of commentary are also exempted. Other non-commercial uses are exempted, as well. Finally, there is some protection for use of a mark in comparative advertising. Nevertheless, commentators have argued that dilution laws might be used in ways that violate First Amendment rights.

Dilution was one of the claims brought in *Mattel, Inc. v. Walking Mountain Productions*, a case that provides a classic example of how a company might attempt to use intellectual property laws to silence critics—precisely the scenario that concerns First Amendment advocates. In *Mattel*, an artist created a series of works called "Food Chain Barbie." The art involved images of Barbie dolls in bizarre situations, such as baked into enchiladas or placed in a blender. Mattel sued, bringing claims under copyright, trademark, and dilution laws. Because the works were clearly parodical and artistic in nature, the court concluded that there was no infringement because the works were fair use and there was no likelihood of confusion. With respect to dilution, the court said that the First Amendment must protect parodies of this type. Dilution laws apply only to commercial speech, not to criticism or artistic works.

What Is Cybersquatting?

Cybersquatting is the intentional adoption of a trade name on the Internet for an improper purpose, such as extorting a payment from the trademark holder or deceiving the public. Typical examples involve the registration of the name of a famous person or company or related variants in the hopes of selling the domain to that person at an inflated price. Suppose, for example, a politician named Dan Smith were running for president in 2024. A cybersquatter might register the domains DanSmith.com, Smithforpresident.com, or Smith2024.com before Dan Smith himself gets a chance to do so. The cybersquatter hopes to either sell the domains for lots of money, or alternately, it is possible that he plans to run a deceptive website that confuses the public about facts or about the ownership of the site, or both. Another scenario involves "typosquatting," where the cybersquatter registers common misspellings of a domain or other variants. With our hypothetical candidate Dan Smith, a typosquatter might register DanSnith.com, DamSmith.com, or DanSmith.org.

The Anticybersquatting Consumer Protection Act (ACPA), codified at 15 U.S.C. sec. 1125(d), was enacted in 1999 to expressly provide a remedy for these kinds of cases. But even prior to that law, courts noted that it may infringe a trademark to deceptively use a mark online. The courts used the same test that was used in regular infringement cases: Is there a likelihood of confusion as to origin or sponsorship? In *Planned Parenthood v. Bucci*, for example, the court found that Richard Bucci infringed Planned Parenthood's trademark. Bucci registered the domain plannedparenthood.com and created a site with a homepage announcement, "Welcome to the Planned Parenthood Home Page." The site also included material that was critical of abortion. Bucci argued that his used should be protected as a parody, but the court found that his use was an infringement because there was a likelihood of confusion. The "joke" nature of the site was not apparent, and reasonable people could be confused about whether it was actually Planned Parenthood's site.

However, the use of a name or trademark on a website or in a URL can be protected by the First Amendment if the site owner is clear about origin and sponsorship. Sites designed to criticize others have been protected where the source of criticism is obvious. In *Lamparello v. Falwell*, for example, the court ruled in favor of a man who created a site criticizing Reverend Jerry Falwell. Falwell owned the domain falwell.com, but Lamparello created a site a fallwell.com, which might otherwise have been a form of typosquatting if not for the commentary on the site. The site consisted of criticisms of Falwell's stance toward gays and lesbians and included an express disclaimer that it was not affiliated with Jerry Falwell. The court found there was no likelihood of confusion as to sponsorship because even if someone went to the site accidentally, it was immediately obvious that the site was not sponsored by Falwell.

Generally speaking, websites that consist of commentary critical of a person or company and that include disclaimers concerning affiliation will not be considered an infringement because there is no likelihood of confusion. In *Ficker v. Tuohy*, for example, the court ruled that the website robinficker.com was not a violation of the ACPA or the Lanham Act because it was obvious that the site was designed to criticize Robin Ficker, a candidate for federal office, not to mislead the public. The site included a disclaimer stating that it was not affiliated with the Ficker campaign and offered a link to the official campaign site, robinficker2004.com. Similarly, in *Bally Total Fitness Holding Corp. v. Faber*, the court found that a site declaring "Bally Sucks," including commentary critical of Bally, and disclaiming affiliation with the company was not an infringement.

However, not all such cases are favorable to the commenter. The World Intellectual Property Organization (WIPO) offers arbitrations for disputed domain names and issues decisions, much like a court, although they are not part of the U.S. court system. A WIPO panel decision ruled that the domain vivendiuniversalsucks.com was not protected commentary and had to be turned over to Vivendi Universal. Even though most Americans would see the domain name and understand that it was designed to be critical of the company, the panel noted that Vivendi Universal was a French company and not all internet users speak English as their primary language. Many users may not know what "sucks" means, particularly in the pejorative slang usage of the term, and thus, Internet users may be misled about the site's ownership.

The lesson to be drawn from these examples is that any person who registers a domain name for a legitimate purpose such a commentary or criticism should be scrupulous about making both the ownership of the site and the legitimate purpose unambiguously clear to bolster a defense if sued for cybersquatting. But even then, there is no guarantee the commenter will win. A court or WIPO panel may find infringement or order that the domain be turned over if there is any question about whether the registrant had a legitimate purpose or not.

Practical Conclusions

- Trademarks protects names, slogans, images, designs, colors, and other marks that designate goods or services in the marketplace. It helps avoid consumer confusion by letting consumers know who is the origin or sponsor of a good or service.

- Trademarks become effective upon the use of a distinctive mark and last for as long as the person or company uses them in commerce. Registration is helpful but not required.

- The test for trademark infringement is whether there is a "likelihood of confusion" about the origin or sponsorship of a product. Simply mentioning a brand is not trademark infringement.

As long as the user is not attempting to "pass off" products or do anything misleading, there is likely to be some First Amendment protection for the use.

- Dilution is a poorly defined concept, but there is a federal dilution statute that prohibits the use of a mark in such a way as to tarnish the mark or weaken the brand. Unless courts apply the concept of dilution narrowly, the law could pose a threat to free expression.

- Cybersquatting is the intentional adoption of a mark for some improper purpose, such as buying a domain with the name of a well-known brand for the purpose of extorting a large payment. In such cases, the trademark owner is entitled to have the domain transferred to them. However, courts have applied the "likelihood of confusion" test to online uses of marks, just as they have in the bricks-and-mortar world. The use of a trademark in a domain or site name will not be a violation of trademark law as long as there is no likelihood of confusion about origin or sponsorship.

CHAPTER 8

Use of Photos, Illustrations, and Other Images

Photos and other kinds of images have special and complex considerations. This chapter will discuss three issues that may arise when someone wants to use, publish, or post a photo (or other images or illustrations):

1. Is the use of the photo legally and ethically proper? (Could you be sued for the use?)

2. Do you have the rights required to use the photo?

3. Could you be criminally prosecuted or fined for the use?

Is the Use of the Photo Legally and Ethically Proper?

There are several ways that legal and ethical issues can arise from the use of a photo.

First, one should consider the ethical issues. If you are taking a photo for fun, to post on social media, or for personal use, the only ethical issue is to have basic consideration for the people who may be in the photo. It is wise to consider whether you are capturing an image that the subject would feel is "private," even it does not meet the criteria for an invasion of privacy claim. You may want to consider whether a person wants to have their photo taken or for it to be shared on social media. If you are in a country other than the United States, you should be aware that people are far more sensitive to privacy issues and may not want to be photographed.

For news uses, the ethical issues are broader. True photojournalists adhere to ethical principles so that the audience can trust that the image is what it purports to be. First, photojournalists should not "set up" a scene. They should not place people in fake situations in order to manipulate what the image looks like. They are supposed to capture images of reality. Along the same lines, photos should not be edited or modified (for example, removing people or items from an image because they are "in the way" of an otherwise good picture). Photos should be accurately captioned and credited. Like any journalist, a photojournalist shouldn't pay sources, accept gifts, or engage in political activity. They should be aware of their own potential biases and be sensitive to the subjects they cover. (More about journalism ethics can be found in Chapter 21, and the National Press Photographers Association's Code of Ethics can be found at https://nppa.org/code-ethics.) Adhering to good ethical principles will go a long way toward avoiding legal liability; nevertheless, there are potential legal claims that can arise from the use of an otherwise ethically acquired photo:

1. Libel: Is there anything about the photo or the juxtaposition of the photo with a caption or any accompanying text that might constitute libel or false light?

2. Privacy: Is there anything in the photo that would be considered private information?

3. Publicity: Are you using the image for a "commercial" purpose?

4. Intentional Infliction of Emotional Distress (IIED): Is there anything about your use of the image that is outrageous or gratuitously cruel?

Although those four claims are each discussed elsewhere in this book in more detail, this chapter will discuss the way they come up with respect to the use of photos in particular.

Libel or False Light

Libel or false light claims can arise from the use of photos either (1) when there is something inherently false in the photo (for example, if it were intentionally distorted or photoshopped in an unflattering or defamatory way), or (2) through the juxtaposition of captions or text with photos or film that don't match.

INTENTIONAL DISTORTION

There aren't many cases involving the intentional distortion of photos, probably in part because it violates the principles of journalistic ethics to distort photos for journalistic purposes, and probably in part because the technology to realistically change photos has become available to the general public only relatively recently. There is one case, however, that illustrates the point. In *Russell v. Marboro Books, Inc.*, the court allowed model Mary Jane Russell, who was famous in the 1950s for being particularly refined, to sue over the modification of a photo that she thought libeled her.

She had originally posed in a photo that depicted her reading an educational book in bed in an ordinary domestic setting. The photo was supposed to be used to advertise educational books, and the caption on the advertisement would read, "For People Who Take Their Reading Seriously." After that ad ran, a company that sells bed sheets and that had a terrible reputation for creating ads in bad taste, took the original photo and modified it to depict the model reading a vulgar book in the company of an older man.

While modern models might be less sensitive to sexual innuendo, the principle remains the same: If a photo were intentionally distorted to suggest that the person depicted was doing something offensive or defamatory, the person may be entitled to sue for libel or false light.

JUXTAPOSITION

A more common problem is the use of a photo or image that doesn't "match" the accompanying text or a caption. This can happen in two ways: where there is a conceptual but not factual match, or where there is an accidental mismatch.

CONCEPTUAL BUT NOT FACTUAL MATCH

In many cases, a person will be looking for a photo to accompany text and choose a stock photo or a randomly acquired photo. In these cases, the photo was not taken with the intention of matching the text. The photo may match conceptually, meaning there is something about the photo that is conceptually related to the text, but it is not factually related, as it does not depict the exact people or events discussed in the text.

The two following scenarios illustrate the difference:

Scenario #1: you are writing an article about people who have been convicted of DUI and how it affects their ability to get a job later. You interview a man named Tom West, who has been convicted of DUI and who tells you about his problems finding work. He understands you are publishing his name in the story and consents to have his picture taken to accompany the story. You take his photo and publish it along with the article and a caption that reads, "Tom West knows that a DUI can hurt in the job hunt."

Scenario #2: you are writing an article about people who have been convicted of DUI and how it affects their ability to get a job later. To accompany the article, you decide to use a stock photo of people drinking beer. You caption the photo to say, "Getting a DUI can hurt in the job hunt."

In scenario #1, one should have no libel problem because the story is true, Tom consented, and the photo matches the story and makes no false implication. Scenario #2 is riskier because the people depicted in the photo might feel they are libeled by the use of the photo. Because the story and the caption refer to people who get DUIs, they may think there is a false implication that they have gotten a DUI.

Maybe the people in the photo wouldn't sue, and even if they did, they may not prevail. There are too many factors to consider. For example, it might happen to be true that the people depicted happen to have a DUI on their record. Or, the people might not think there is any implication about them simply because they are shown drinking beer. Or, a judge might rule that the caption doesn't imply anything about the people depicted but is merely cautionary. Nevertheless, there is a risk of being sued successfully. It would be better to use a photo that matched the facts. A matching photo could be one of a source, as described in scenario #1, or perhaps a stock photo of a famous person convicted of DUI with an appropriate caption, such as, "Celebrities who get DUIs may still find work, but the rest of us aren't always so lucky."

A mismatched photo was at issue in *Reid v. U.S. News & World Report.* The magazine used a photograph of some black youths at a music festival to illustrate a story about unemployment among black youths. However, it was simply a stock photo, and all the young men shown had jobs. The photo matched the story only in the sense that the story was about black youths and the photo depicted black youths. The court allowed their false light claim to proceed because the juxtaposition of the photo with the story left a false impression that the youths depicted were unemployed. This case illustrates how important it is to make sure the photo matches the story factually. You cannot assume that you have artistic license to select compelling images without regard to the facts; you must also consider how the use of the photo will reflect on the individuals shown.

One common way photo editors try to avoid problems is to caption the photo in such as way to make it clear that the photo depicts something separate from what is described in the text. This tactic can be helpful in many cases, but it is not foolproof. At least one case suggests that adding a disclaimer to a photo can be insufficient if the caption is overwhelmed by a potentially defamatory headline. In *Stanton v. Metro Corp.*, the court allowed a girl to bring a libel suit when a photo of some teens, including her, was used to illustrate an article entitled "The Mating Habits of the Suburban High School Teenager." The girl felt that the use of her picture falsely suggested that she was engaged in the types of sexual activity described in the story. The magazine must have realized the potential for such a false implication because it included a disclaimer that persons pictured were not featured in the story. Just above the byline, which appeared at the bottom of the first page, and just below the main article text, the following disclaimer was printed: "The photos on these pages are from an award-winning five-year project on teen sexuality taken by photojournalist Dan Habib. The individuals pictured are unrelated to the people or events described in this story. The names of the teenagers interviewed for this story have been changed." The trial court had decided that, absent the disclaimer, "a reasonable reader could conclude that the teenage girl depicted in the photograph is sexually active and engages in at least some form of sexual misconduct." Nevertheless, that court concluded that the disclaimer adequately negated the negative connotations about the girl. On appeal, however, the appellate court decided that the trial court had failed to consider how many people might overlook the disclaimer and allowed the girl's claim to go forward.

If there is potential for a defamatory juxtaposition, there is still one defense available: consent. Obtaining a release from the individuals depicted getting their consent to use the photo in that context should be sufficient to ward off any claims. It should be noted, however, that "model releases," the standard forms that photographers obtain from models when they do a photo shoot, are usually *not* sufficient to release users from claims for defamatory juxtaposition. Model releases typically say that the photographer is free to sell the photo with their image, but they usually do not waive claims for defamatory uses by publishers. One would need to read the exact release signed by the model to know for sure—but the point is that a publisher cannot assume that a photo being "model released" means they can use the photo in any way they like.

ACCIDENTAL MISMATCH

An accidental mismatch occurs when you intend to use a person's photo to illustrate a story about him or her, but you simply have the wrong person pictured. A classic example is *Little Rock Newspapers, Inc. v. Fitzhugh*. In that case, an article described the upcoming prosecution of Eugene Fitzhugh, who had been indicted in connection with the Whitewater scandal. However, the accompanying photograph, captioned "Fitzhugh," was a photo of J. Michael Fitzhugh. The error was brought to the paper's attention, and they printed a correction the next day. Nevertheless, J. Michael Fitzhugh sued for libel because his photo had been improperly matched with the story, and the Arkansas Supreme Court upheld a jury verdict in his favor.

Such errors occur with shocking regularity. It is vital to ensure you have a photo of the correct person.

Privacy

Privacy claims might arise if there is anything in the photo or arising from the use of the photo that might be considered private information. Types of things that might be considered private include medical information, alcohol or drug use, sexual activity, financial information, gambling problems, or other embarrassing matters that people typically try to keep secret. A photo that was taken at a doctor's office, an Alcoholics Anonymous meeting, or a weight loss camp would be the type of photo that could reveal private information and might serve as the basis for a privacy claim. Nudity or sexual information are of particular concern, as courts have been willing to grant greater privacy protections in cases involving nude photos or sex tapes.

Determining whether photos might create privacy concerns can be extremely difficult because, in many cases, the question is whether the material is genuinely newsworthy, and newsworthiness appears to be extremely subjective. Three cases demonstrate how courts have treated this issue.

A classic example is *Barber v. Time, Inc.* In that case, *Time* magazine published a story about a rare eating disorder and used a photo of a woman who suffered from the disorder. The photo had been taken against her wishes as she lay in a hospital bed. The question was whether the information was newsworthy, and the court ruled that the disease was newsworthy, but her identity was not. The outcome of *Barber* is not surprising because medical information is typically considered to be private information, and a hospital room would typically be considered a private place. Using a photo of a woman in a hospital bed and revealing her medical condition is precisely the kind of thing we would expect to give rise to a privacy claim. Thus, if one wishes to publish a photo of that nature, it would be wise to get consent from the subject.

While photos taken in private places are of more concern, photos taken in public are often less risky. For example, in *McNamara v. Freedom Newspapers*, the court ruled that a newspaper was not liable for publishing an extremely embarrassing photo of a soccer player. The photo had been taken at a soccer match, which was a public, newsworthy event. No one noticed, until after publication, that the soccer player's genitals were visible in the photo. Genitalia would typically be considered private information, and photos thereof usually shouldn't be published without consent. However, in this case, the court found that the photo accurately depicted a public, newsworthy event and was therefore newsworthy, even though it contained otherwise private information.

However, not every photo taken in public can be used without risk. A photo that was taken in public and is otherwise unobjectionable can still form the basis for a privacy claim if the court feels that the use of the photo is not newsworthy. In *M.G. v. Time Warner*, *Sports Illustrated* published a photo of Little League players with their coach, who turned out to be a child molester and had actually molested some of the children on the team. The photo was simply a standard team photo and not objectionable on its own. However, the court ruled that the use of the photo, in conjunction with the story about the molesting coach, revealed private information about the children depicted and was not newsworthy.

Barber and *M. G.* are cases where the stories are not "breaking news," but rather are general interest stories about a type of problem, and the identities of the people involved is collateral to the discussion of the problem (that people can get a rare eating disorder, or that children's sport's coaches might be child molesters). Courts might be more inclined to rule that the use of a photo is not newsworthy in such cases.

Thus, when deciding whether publishing a photo might require consent of the people depicted, you might consider the following factors:

1. Does the photo reveal any private information (such as medical information, drug use, etc.)?

2. Was the photo taken in a public place or a private place?

3. Does the photo depict breaking news or events occurring contemporaneously with the subject of your story? Or, are you discussing a general matter?

Given the reasoning of the courts in the cases discussed, photos that depict breaking news and are taken in public places should be considered newsworthy and should not require the consent of the persons depicted. However, one might consider obtaining consent or consulting with an attorney if a photo reveals private information, was taken in a private place, or is used to illustrate a general point. This is true regardless of whether the publisher is a professional journalist or a private citizen posting photos online. A professional journalist might wrongly assume that anything s/he chooses to publish would be deemed newsworthy. (The *M. G.* case is evidence that is not necessarily true.) And, as in libel cases, model releases are not a surefire defense if the particular use was outside the scope of the permission. For example, in *McCabe v. Village Voice, Inc.*, the existence of a so-called model release did not bar the plaintiff's claim, because it appeared that the model consented only to the use of the photograph in a book and not for other uses, such as publication in a newspaper.

A private citizen may have even more potential trouble with ordinary communications because she or he is more likely to post photos online that might be considered private. If, for example, Angela hosts a party at her home and Tara gets extremely drunk, and Angela takes embarrassing photos of Tara vomiting in the toilet and posts them online, Tara might argue that the information is private and that it is not newsworthy. There are some factors in that scenario that might weigh in Tara's favor:

•   The incident occurred in a private home, not in public.

•   The photos depict alcohol abuse, which is something extremely embarrassing that courts may be inclined to identify as private.

•   Vomiting is arguably a medical condition, which courts tend to protect as private.

The question will be whether there is something about Tara herself that is important enough to make the photos newsworthy, but if she is simply an ordinary citizen who happens to have engaged in a bit of unfortunate overconsumption, there is a risk that a court would find the photos to depict private information and not to be newsworthy.

ARE THERE SPECIAL CONSIDERATIONS WHEN PICTURES FEATURE CHILDREN?

There is a popular misconception that it is always illegal to take or use pictures of children without the consent of their parents. There is no such law. However, a California law provides criminal penalties for the harassment of the children of celebrities. Specifically, the law prohibits conduct that "seriously alarms, annoys, torments, or terrorizes" a child, including "conduct occurring during the course of any actual or attempted recording of the child's or ward's image or voice, or both, without the express consent of the parent or legal guardian of the child or ward, by following the child's or ward's activities or by lying in wait." The law applies only if the child is harassed "because of" the parent's "employment." In other words, the law is trying to target the paparazzi who follow celebrity children. Media companies and other groups have expressed concern that the law violates First Amendment rights, but the law became effective in January of 2014 and there has not yet been a case challenging the constitutionality of the law or otherwise interpreting it.

Also, any parent can bring a claim on behalf of a child for any claim that a person could otherwise bring. Thus, if you use a photo of a child juxtaposed with a story in such a way as to create a defamatory implication, then there may be a valid libel claim. But the validity of the claim has nothing to do with the fact that the photo was of a child—the claim is based on the particular use. Similarly, taking photos of children playing in a public place to illustrate a story about why playing is good for you should not cause any legal issues. But taking photos of children that may be embarrassing and not public—such as photos of children in a doctor's office—might create privacy issues, and when dealing with children, it is probably wise to be extra sensitive to potential issues, simply because courts have proven to be extra-protective of children.

One thing to note about taking pictures in schools, camps, or other places that claim to have releases signed by parents: Read the permission form to see whether the form actually grants permission to the media. Most forms are written to allow schools, camps, etc., to take children's photos and use them in brochures and advertisements. They do not necessarily allow the media to take photos or use them in news stories. If the release does not specifically mention news use, then it may be wise to contact the parents directly for specific permission to take and use photos for the specific use you have in mind.

Right of Publicity

As discussed more thoroughly in Chapter 5, the issue of publicity rights can arise whenever you use a person's likeness, which would certainly include using a photo or illustration of a person. It is wise to obtain a person's consent if the image is going to be used for a commercial purpose to avoid any claims for violating the subject's "right of publicity." The question is what constitutes a "commercial purpose."

Advertising is definitely a commercial purpose, so it is important to obtain consent from anyone whose image is used in an ad or promotion. One may also be liable for violating someone's right of publicity by using an image of someone who looks like them or an image of something associated with the person. The courts have not yet established any kind of fair use exception or any other exception to this principle, so even if the ad comments on a social issue or makes a joke, there may still be liability for the use.

Putting someone's photo on merchandise, such as posters, mugs, T-shirts and other items may be considered a commercial purpose, unless there is some "transformative use." Artistic uses, such as selling an art photo that happens to have someone's image in it, are usually protected by the First Amendment. News coverage and other editorial material are also usually protected and not considered a "commercial use." That is why you see pictures of people in newspapers, magazines and online all the time, and the publications don't have to get every person's permission (which would be extremely difficult in the case of celebrities or crowds, for example). If the image is used in conjunction with some news coverage or commentary, the use of the image should be ok. However, there have been a few cases where the courts have ruled that news coverage did violate publicity rights, either where there is some kind of falsely implied endorsement or the appropriate of the entire value of a person's work.

In sum, it is important to remember that if one's use of a person's photo could be considered a "commercial use," then permission will be required.

IIED

IIED is one of the most difficult legal issues to evaluate because the legal test for it is incredibly subjective. To win a claim for IIED, a plaintiff must prove that the defendant engaged in "extreme and outrageous" conduct. What does that mean? One court unhelpfully said that it is conduct that causes a person to exclaim, "Outrageous!"

Legitimate uses of photos for the purpose of reporting the news or commenting on matters of public concern is generally not considered IIED. However, there are uses that might create liability. A couple of cases may help illustrate the issue.

Catsouras v. California Hwy Patrol is a highly illustrative case. It involved photos taken after the death of Nikki Catsouras. She was decapitated when the Porche 911 she was driving flipped. Some of the officers who arrived on the scene took photos of her and emailed them to their friends and acquaintances for "shock value." The photos found their way online and some people cruelly emailed the photos to her family with captions such as "Hey Daddy I'm still alive." The court permitted her family to go forward with an IIED claim. The case settled in January of 2012.

Disseminating photos of a decapitated teen is not particularly common, but the same type of principle could apply to any other shocking material. Perhaps the most likely cause of an IIED lawsuit would be the dissemination of nude pictures or sex videos. For example, a woman in Ohio sued her ex-boyfriend for invasion of privacy and intentional infliction of emotional distress for emailing five nude photographs of her to the employees of the company where she worked. The jury found that he intended to humiliate and embarrass her and returned a verdict in her favor.

The dissemination of nude pictures or sex videos by an angry ex-boyfriend or ex-girlfriend is a sufficiently common phenomenon to have been given a name: "revenge porn." Purveyors of revenge porn may be liable for IIED (and/or invasion of privacy)—and states are beginning to pass criminal laws against revenge porn (these are discussed in chapter 15). Ironically, if they are found liable and are required to pay a judgment, they may find themselves in the position of having paychecks garnished to pay the judgment to the ex they were trying to harm.

Do You Have the Rights Required to Use the Photo?

Once you have selected a photo that is appropriate and have captioned it correctly, you need to determine whether you need rights to use the photo.

Photographs, drawings, illustrations, and other visual images are "creative works," which means they are usually copyrightable immediately upon creation. If you took the photo or created the image (independently, without relying on anyone else's work), then you own the rights to the photo/image and can do what you like with it. But if someone else took the photo or created the image, or if you are creating an image from someone else's original work, then the copyright interest of the original creator must be taken into account. Copyright issues are discussed more thoroughly in Chapter 6, but this chapter will discuss some of the issues that are unique to photos and images.

To use a photo taken by someone else, one must either obtain permission or the use must qualify as a fair use. Getting permission can be interesting, though, because photos are often distributed or licensed in unique ways that do not apply to other kinds of material. This section discusses the various considerations applicable to getting rights to use an image.

Per Use License

One thing that is unique about photos is that they are usually licensed on a per use basis. Photographers who try to make their living solely on photography understand that they need to maximize their income. They make more money if they can sell a photo to twenty news outlets than if they sell it to just one outlet. Similarly, if a news outlet publishes a dozen stories on a topic over the course of several months, the photographer will make more money if he can sell rights to use the photo twelve times than if he sells it only once. With that in mind, photographers tend to sell "per use" or "one-time use" rights to their photos. A user must buy the right to use a photo every single time they want to reproduce it. It is possible to buy total rights to use a photo, but it is extremely expensive to do so. Photographers can make more money to sell rights on a per use basis in most cases, and they will insist on doing so. Thus, even if you have obtained the right to use a photo in conjunction with one story, you don't necessarily have the right to re-use the photo if you do a follow-up story six months later.

Agency Photos

Photos are often distributed through photo agencies or subscriber services like the Associated Press. News organizations, in particular, often subscribe to an agency to obtain photos for news uses because they don't have the resources themselves to send a photographer to every event they cover. Agencies obtain photos from a variety of photographers and license the photos on behalf of the photographers. People who want to license the photos are required to agree to certain contractual provisions, which usually impose limitations on how the photos can be used or distributed (having to buy rights per use, as described above, is a common provision). The important thing to know about agency agreements is simply the fact that they are agreements, and a user is obligated to adhere to the terms of the contract, whatever those terms may be. An easy way to get into legal trouble is to violate the contractual terms, whether intentionally or unintentionally. Agreements often regulate the size at which the image can be reproduced, the platforms for distribution, and whether the image can be used in advertising or pro-motional contexts. It is important to read the applicable contract!

Publicity Photos

The job of a publicist is to get publicity for his or her client. In doing so, they often hand out photos of the client to use in conjunction with media coverage. But it is incredibly—and surprisingly—common for publicists (or artists, bands, executives, and other subjects of stories) to hand out photos to which they don't have the rights to convey to the media. The copyright in a photograph is held by the pho-tographer, not the person featured in the picture. Thus, you need permission from the photographer to use the image. Consent from the person featured or their publicist is not sufficient—unless the subject of the photo has properly purchased sublicensable rights to give the image to the media. It is important to check with the photographer, because it is common for people to misunderstand what rights they have to use an image. The media can be sued for copyright infringement for using images that were "handout" photos if the rights aren't properly cleared. Getting consent from the person in the photo is not necessarily adequate!

Online Photos

Many people make photos available online through sites like Flickr, Wikimedia, Facebook, or Twit-ter. The fact that the pictures are available online does not change the fact that they are presumptively copyrighted and one must obtain permission to use them.

Some photographers will intentionally place their photos in the public domain and claim no copy-right, but that is rare. Others will use a Creative Commons designation, which allows them to be used as long as the user adheres to the terms of the applicable license. The only tricky aspect of a Creative Commons license as applied to photos is the No Derivative Works (ND) provision. Such a provision prohibits any modification of the work, which would include photoshopping or cropping.

Some sites, like Flickr and YouTube, allow copyright holders to activate an embed code that allows third parties to embed the content on other websites. There is nothing wrong with embedding material when such codes are provided, as long as the person who posted the image is actually the copyright holder.

Otherwise, one must assume that any photos online are copyrighted and permission must be obtained from the copyright holder, unless the fair use exception applies.

Fair Use

The copyright statute says that fair use applies to purposes such as "criticism, comment, news report-ing, teaching (including multiple copies for classroom use), scholarship, or research." However, those purposes are not exclusive.

To determine whether a use is fair, a court would use the four-part test in the copyright statute. (Fair use is discussed more fully in Chapter 6; this section focuses solely on how fair use has been applied to photos and visual clips.)

In this section, we will discuss the following types of uses, some of which may be fair, and some may not:

1. Use of an image where the image itself if the subject of reporting/commentary

2. Use of an image where the image is related to the reporting/commentary but is not the primary subject

3. Use of images related to breaking news

4. Incidental use

5. Artistic use

Generally, news organizations may claim fair use to use images in news reports and other editorial material if the image itself is the subject of coverage or if the use is incidental. For example, if a culture writer is discussing an art exhibit currently being shown at a local gallery and critiques a particular work, it probably would be a fair use to include a picture of the work along with the article because the article is specifically a critique of the work. In *Leveyfilm, Inc. v. Fox Sports Interactive Media*, LLC, a court found that it was fair use for a blogger who was commenting on a lawsuit that arose from the "Superbowl Shuffle" to use a picture of the cover of the "Superbowl Shuffle" DVD. (For those too young to recall, the Superbowl Shuffle was a rap video made by the 1985 Chicago Bears football team and became a pop culture phenomenon.) The court reasoned that the video was the subject of discussion and using the image to visually show what was at issue was a fair use.

However, it might not be a fair use to use an image simply because it is somehow related to the news coverage. For example, in *Roy Export Co. Estab. of Vaduz v. CBS*, the court ruled that it was not fair use to use a one minute and fifteen second clip of a Charlie Chaplin movie when the station reported on Chaplin's death. In that case, the coverage was about Chaplin himself, not about the movie, so the use of the movie wasn't protected because the movie wasn't truly the subject of news reporting. Along the same lines, if the station had simply wanted to show a photo of Chaplin, it would typically have licensed a photo of him from a photo agency. At least in the print industry, it is well understood that one cannot take any photo of a celebrity and use it without consent merely because one is writing about a celebrity. The image must be licensed from the copyright holder. Similarly, in *Murphy v. Millennium Radio Group LLC*, the court found that the use of a photo on a website not fair use simply because it was used for news reporting. Reporting, in itself, is not "transformative." There must be something special about the reason or manner in which the photo is used to make the use transformative.

In breaking news situations, news organizations often look to online materials, including Facebook photos or other images that appear in social media sites of the persons involved. The fact that a person is suddenly thrust into the public eye does not mean that all pictures of that person are suddenly fair game and may be used in reporting. If one can obtain permission to use a photo, that's great. If one wants to rely on fair use, then the four fair use factors must still be applied. The question will almost always be whether the use is transformative. Is there commentary on the photo itself, or is it being used merely because it is a picture of the person? Again, the case law has indicated that the courts do not consider reporting, in itself, to be transformative. There must be some commentary or other transformative aspect of the use.

Along the same lines, news organizations are generally not permitted to use other people's images of news events without permission. For example, in *LANS v. KCAL-TV*, the court ruled that it was not a fair use to use a 30 second clip of another person's video of the Reginald Denny beating. A news organization (or anyone, for that matter) must take its own footage or get permission to use someone else's footage. It affects the creator's potential for licensing the work at his discretion to take it without permission. Also, in *Video-Cinema Films, Inc. v. Lloyd E. Rigler-Lawrence E. Deutsch Found.*, the court found that a use was not fair because of the impact on licensing. In that case, a nonprofit foundation used an 85 second clip of an opera singer's performance. Three of the fair use factors favored the use: it was an educational use by a nonprofit, the work had already been published, and only a small portion of the work was used. However, the court felt that those factors were outweighed by the potential loss of licensing revenue.

Incidental uses can be a fair use under copyright law. An incidental use occurs when a copyrighted work is "captured" as a result of covering some other event. For example, if a television reporter is covering an event in Times Square, and one of the billboards in Times Square happens to have a copyrighted photo on it, there should be no infringement if the photo/billboard appears in the background when the news broadcasts the footage. The use is incidental. Another example is *Italian Book Corp, v. American Broadcasting Co.*, where the court ruled it was a fair use to film a band playing a copyrighted song while covering a festival on the news.

Artistic uses can be protected as fair use if they are sufficiently transformative. Two cases involving the artist Jeff Koons illustrate this point. In *Blanch v. Koons*, Koons created a collage painting that copied but modified part of a photograph of a woman's legs taken by fashion photographer Andrea Blanch. The court ruled that Koons's use of the original photo was a fair use because Koons's art was a commentary upon popular culture. Blanch's photo had originally appeared in a fashion magazine, and Koons was commenting on "the social and aesthetic consequences of mass media." Also, Koons used only a small part of the original work and mixed it with other images.

However, in *Rogers v. Koons*, the court ruled that Koons's use of a photo was not a fair use. In that case, Koons had created several works in a "Banality" series. One of the works was a sculpture entitled "String of Puppies." Koons had seen a card with a picture of a man and a woman sitting on a bench with several puppies. His sculpture was an exact replica of the picture. Koons argued that he was commenting on "the commonplace," but the court concluded that his work could not be protected as a fair use because a viewer wouldn't necessarily know that there was an original underlying the so-called parody in this case. Although the court didn't use this term, one might say that there was nothing "transformative" about the work.

Thus, to have an image protected as a fair use, there must be something transformative about the use. The best scenario is if the viewer is able to discern how you have taken part of some original and used it to comment upon that original. Ideally, your commentary should be obvious. For example, in *Sedgwick Claims Mgmt Serv. v. Delsman*, a court considered the use of photos of insurance executives that were transformed into images of Nazis. The commentary was fairly obvious to the court, and regardless of whether it was nice or original or even reasonable, the court found that it was "transformative," and thus protectable as a fair use.

Can I Use This Clip?

Communicators often want to use audio or video clips from other sources to help illustrate their stories. Often, people will jump right to the question of whether the use is "fair use," as described above, but actually, that is only one of several considerations. There are four questions to ask before using the clip:

1. Does the particular use create a false implication or any ethical dilemmas?
    Like photos, video and audio clips can be juxtaposed against other elements to create a false impression that could lead to a libel or false light claim. Try to make sue your use doesn't create any false implications. Also ensure that there are no ethical problems with your use and that it wouldn't create any other liability (privacy, publicity, IIED, etc.).

2. Is there an FCC regulation that applies? The rebroadcast rule prohibits a broadcaster from rebroadcasting content from another broadcaster without consent. This applies to you only if (a) you are a television or radio broadcaster, (b) you are using material taken from another television or radio broadcast, and (c) you are using it to rebroadcast over the airwaves. In such cases, you are supposed to get consent from the original broadcaster. Fair use is not an exception to the FCC rule.

3. Is there a contract that governs your use of the clip?
    Sometimes, audio or video clips may come from an agency or other content services. In such cases, your use of the clips might be governed by a contract that you have with the service. You must consult the terms of your contract to ensure that your use is consistent with what is permitted. Clips that are obtained from websites may also be governed by a contract insofar as a site's Terms of Service may operate as a binding contract in some cases. Make sure your use is consistent with what is permitted.

4. Are there any other copyright issues?
    Audio and video clips are probably protected by copyright. Consider whether you have permission or whether the use qualifies as a fair use.

Who Should Be Contacted If Permission Is Required?

Copyrighted works should contain a notice that includes a date and author name (*e.g.*, "Copyright 2019 Ashley Messenger") to let other people know whom to contact for permission to use the work. However, notice is not required, and it is particularly difficult to attach a notice on an individual photo, so there may be occasions when it is difficult to track the copyright holder.

A copyright in a photograph is held by the photographer who took it, unless it is a "work for hire" or he transferred the rights to someone else. Assuming the photographer retained the copyright in the work, you must get permission from the photographer. It is not sufficient, for the purposes of copyright law, to get permission from the person depicted in the photo or from the person who has possession of the photo. For example, if you are writing about the First Lady as a young girl, and one of her relatives provides you with a photo in her possession that was taken by a friend when she was 8 years old, neither the First Lady's permission nor the relative's permission is adequate for the purposes of copyright law. You need the permission of the friend who took the photo because it is the photographer who holds the copyright. Sometimes celebrities are sued for posting photos of themselves on Instagram or other social media sites, because they used pictures taken by professional photographers without consent. Again, just because you are *in* the picture doesn't mean you can *use* the picture. The photographer holds the copyright and can control use of the image. The same is true for images other than photos (such as charts, graphs, or illustrations): the person who created them owns the copyright unless it was made as a work for hire or the artist transferred the copyright.

That said, there may be occasions when it is impossible or unrealistic to track down the photographer/creator. The friend who took the First Lady's photo might not even remember taking it. If you find a napkin with a beautiful design drawn on it at a bar and want to publish it as found art, it may be difficult if not impossible to find the artist. And, as a practical matter, individuals are not supposed to sue in federal court for copyright infringement unless they have registered their works with the government; it is unlikely that the friend or the bar room artist did that. There may be little risk in publishing those works under certain circumstances. Nevertheless, it is theoretically possible that a claim could be made. It is important not to assume that photos or images are fair game just because they don't have a copyright notice on them. Professional photographers—which include not just famous photographers but also photographers who shoot weddings or school photos or other organized events—are familiar with copyright law and may track the use of their photos.

If the work was a work for hire, the copyright may be held by a company or other employer. This is particularly true in the case of media companies that have staff photographers or illustrators.

Finally, a photographer/creator can sell or license the rights in his or her works. With respect to photos, it is common for photographers to license their works through an agency, as noted above. In that case, you may have to get permission through the agency rather than the photographer.

Given all the possible scenarios, how do you tell whom to contact for permission? Start with the copyright notice, if any, and contact the person or company named. If there is no notice, start with the photographer or creator, if known. If you have no way of knowing who the creator is, you can try to search the federal Copyright Office's records, or ask them to perform a search (they will charge you if they do it). You can also ask the person who gave you the image what information they have about the photographer. It is very important to find the right person. Photo tracking software has become very sophisticated, so many photographers use agencies that track their images and make claims on their behalf. It has always been important, ethically, to obtain permission from the copyright holder, but it is even more important, legally, to get permission, as infringements are easier to track and claims increase.

Can You Be Prosecuted or Fined?

There are laws or government regulations that concern the use of photographs or images:

1. Sexual images of children

2. Classified images

3. Images of stamps and currency

4. Regulation of image-editing software

Sexual Images of Children

Child pornography is banned in the U.S. It is illegal to distribute or possess it, and the Court upheld the constitutionality of such laws in *Osborne v. Ohio*. If you use it for any reason, you can be criminal prosecuted. There are no exceptions under current law or court interpretations. In *U.S. v. Matthews*, a journalist who was investigating the proliferation of child pornography on the Internet was convicted of possession of child pornography. He argued that, as an investigative journalist, he should be able to argue that the First Amendment provides some protection for the press to investigate the topic. The court disagreed, meaning that a journalist can be prosecuted for possession of child pornography, even if it is for legitimate news purposes.

However, in *Ashcroft v. Free Speech Coalition*, the Supreme Court ruled that portions of a law banning fake images of children is overbroad. Cartoon drawings, or images of adults posing as minors, for example, may be tasteless, but cannot be prosecuted under the Child Pornography Prevention Act of 1996. Nevertheless, the law may still apply in any circumstance where an actual minor in involved, even if the photo isn't genuine.

Classified Images

Publishing classified photos could be a violation of the Espionage Act and may result in criminal prosecution. One example is *U.S. v. Morison*, where a former government employee was convicted for providing classified photos of Soviet ships to a magazine for whom he went to work. Although he was later pardoned by President Clinton, his prior conviction demonstrates the potential criminal liability for publishing classified photos.

There is great dispute about whether attempts to prosecute a journalist under the Espionage Act or other laws would violate the First Amendment. Many people argue that Morison's conviction was valid only because he had been a government employee rather than a typical journalist. It is unclear whether a journalist who received classified images and then published them would be liable. There is little case law on the subject to provide clear guidance. (The issues with respect to classified material are discussed more fully in Chapter 15.)

Images of Stamps and Currency

The use of images of stamps and currency is regulated to prevent counterfeiting, and in *Regan v. Time, Inc.*, the Supreme Court upheld limitations on the use of images of currency with respect to size and color. In the past, the Treasury Department has provided media organizations with images they can use to educate the public about new bill designs, which explains why you might see a picture of a new $20 bill in the newspaper. Nevertheless, one should check the current regulations before publishing images of stamps or currency.

Regulation of Image-editing Software

Commentators have complained for decades that manipulated images that make women look extraordinarily thin or give them a perfect complexion can cause great harm by creating unrealistic expectations. Some countries have attempted to combat eating disorders and harm to body image by regulating edited images. For example, as of 2017, it is mandatory under French law to label a photo "photographie retouchée" ("retouched photo") if it is used for commercial purposes and has been modified to change a model's figure. (A companion law also requires models working in France to have a doctor certify their health, taking into consideration their Body Mass Index, and an earlier French law made it a punishable offense to advocate anorexia or extreme thinness.) Israel similarly has a law that regulates edited images. Such laws have not yet made their way to the United States, and it is likely that any such law would be challenged as a violation of the First Amendment. But those who work for international publications or on the internet should be aware that such regulations exist (see chapter 20 for more information about potential liability overseas for posting things on the internet).

Practical Conclusions

- There may be civil liability arising out of the use of a photo if:
  - The use of the photo creates some falsity, either by suggesting a false implication or by actually containing an error, that libels someone.
  - The photo contains private information, such as showing a medical condition, nudity, alcohol abuse, or other embarrassing or private information.
  - The photo is used for a commercial purpose.

- Even if a photo illustrates a story nicely, the use of a photo can create libel claims if it is juxtaposed with text in such as way as to create a false implication. Don't use stock photos showing identifiable people in conjunction with negative stories! The same is true for b-roll and stock video. However, liability may be avoided if the person pictured in the photo consents to the use of the image, so it can be important to get consent, and to ensure that there is consent for the particular use at issue.

- There's no law in general against using photos of children, but do give extra consideration if there's anything about the photo or story that might raise privacy concerns; and, of course, completely avoid sexualized images of children.

- In California, photographers should be careful about how or when they take pictures of the children of celebrities.

- Photos are creative works subject to copyright, and the rights are typically held by the photographer. Make sure you get permission from the right person. The person shown in the photo is probably not the right person (although it's possible). If you are relying on fair use, the use should be transformative, which typically means that there is some direct commentary upon the image itself.

CHAPTER 9

Use of Music

Obtaining rights to music was, until recently, of concern only to those in the music and entertainment industries. However, the internet has created great opportunities for multimedia content, and now music can be found everywhere, from self-produced YouTube videos to podcasts to multimedia journalism projects by professional news organizations. It is therefore very important for journalists as well as ordinary citizens to understand the legal issues surrounding the use of music.

Music is copyrightable and is fiercely protected by the industry. Thus, the use of music probably requires some kind of license, even in an editorial or commercial context. Getting rights to use music, though, can be far more complicated than getting rights to other kinds of material because of the quirks in the music industry. There are also several statutory provisions related to the use of music that may govern what is used or how.

This chapter will cover:

1. The different kinds of rights that exist in music and who owns them

2. The different kinds of licenses one needs for different uses

3. What might be considered fair use with respect to use of music

4. Other provisions related to the use of music

5. Practical options available to creators who want to use music in their work

Different Kinds of Rights in Music

There are two kinds of rights that may exist for a musical work: musical composition rights and sound recording rights.

Whoever writes the song (the songwriter) initially holds the copyright in the song and owns what are called "musical composition" rights. This right covers the specific arrangement of the musical notes. If the song has lyrics, the lyrics are also copyrightable, but as a separate work. The songwriter can be an individual, or multiple people can own the rights jointly, or a company can own it if the song was a work for hire. In order to use the song, a person would have to get permission, but not necessarily from the songwriter. In the music industry, it is common for a songwriter to have the rights to use his songs administered through a "publisher." To get permission, one must contact the publisher, and the publisher will pay royalties back to the songwriter.

Sometimes a songwriter writes songs for himself to perform, and sometimes he writes songs for someone else to perform. Regardless of who performs the song, anyone who records the performance would be the owner of the "sound recording" right, which is the right to the actual physical embodiment of the song, often called the "master recording." Sound recording rights are sometimes called "master rights;" those terms refer to the same thing. Typically, the performing artist will have a contract with a record company, and the contract provides that the artist will be "exclusive" to that record label. The record label would arrange to record the performance of the song and the label would own the sound recording rights, which means they have the right to control distribution of that recording, such as by selling CDs or authorizing downloads on iTunes. Record contracts typically prohibit artists from allowing anyone else to record them. There are occasional instances where an artist performs and is recorded by someone else—for example, if a band performs on *Saturday Night Live*, then the television production company is making the recording, and the rights to that sound recording will typically be spelled out in an agreement between the production company and the record label. If a person wants to use a particular sound recording, they will often need to obtain permission from whoever owns those rights.

To illustrate how these rights work, consider the song, "Oh, Pretty Woman," which was written by Roy Orbison and Bill Dees. It was originally recorded by Roy Orbison on Monument Records and released in 1964. In 1982, the band Van Halen did a cover of the song on the album *Diver Down*, which was released by Warner Bros. Records. In 1989, the band 2 Live Crew made a parody of the song on the album *As Clean as They Wanna Be*, released by Luke Records. Orbison & Dees would own the musical composition rights in the song, unless they transferred those rights to someone else. Even though Van Halen covered the song, it was not a new musical composition. Orbison and Dees would still hold the musical composition rights regardless of how many people might cover the song, because that right covers the arrangement of the musical notes—the thing that makes that song recognizable as that song, no matter who performs it. However, there are three different rights holders for the three different sound recordings. Assuming the record labels hold the sound recording rights in each case, Monument Records owns the sound recording rights to the Orbison version, Warner Bros. Records owns the sound recording rights to the Van Halen version, and Luke Records owns the sound recording rights to the 2 Live Crew version. Each version is a different physical embodiment of the musical composition, and thus there are separate sound recording rights for each one.

In most cases, if a person wants to use music, he will have to get permission. Whether one needs permission from the owner of musical composition rights or the sound recording rights, or both, will depend on what one intends to do. The kind of license one needs will depend on how the music is used, and that will dictate from whom permission is required. In many cases, one will have to obtain the right kind of license for both sets of rights. It is often necessary to go to at least two different places to get permission. One will have to get permission from the publishing company that owns the musical composition rights, and then also get permission from the record company for the sound recording rights. In some cases, if there are multiple songwriters or multiple publishers, it might be necessary to go to multiple people to get the necessary musical composition rights. There are, however, a couple quirks in the law that may change the rules, discussed below.

Also, it's important to note that getting permission from the band, a manger, a tour promoter, a publicity person, or anyone else related to a group is often not sufficient. A common scenario is for a new band to go on tour and tell people they can use or post their stuff online for promotional purposes. They want the publicity! But the fact that it's good publicity for them does not mean that the use is legal. Music rights are very complicated, and very often, the band does not own or control the rights to the music. They might, but they might not. One must obtain rights from the correct person or entity.

It is also important to remember that copyright holders are not obligated to grant you permission to use a work. They can deny permission because they think it's not good marketing, they don't approve of your plans, or simply because they don't feel like it. There is no guarantee you will get permission, and you might not be able to use the work legally.

Getting the Right License for the Use

As noted above, you must first decide what you want to do with the music. Then, you can figure out what kind of license you need and from whom you must get permission.

One of the main things a person might want to do is called "public performance." This includes playing the song in public or broadcasting it over the air. It would include singing a song at a concert, whether it is a professional performance or simply a school concert. It also includes playing music in any kind of business, whether it's a restaurant, store, office, or any other kind of facility. In most cases, the person who wants to use the music needs to get permission only from the holder of the musical composition rights. However, most rights holders have arranged with a "performing rights society" (PRS), also known as a "performing rights organization" (PRO), to keep track of public performances and collect money on their behalf. The primary performing rights organizations are ASCAP, BMI, SESAC, and GMR. Most radio stations and businesses have what's called a "blanket license" with each PRO, and that blanket license allows them to use any song for which that PRO has public performance rights. The station or business will pay a certain fee for the blanket license, and then they must keep track of which songs they play and report back to each PRO. The PRO will compile the data they receive about how frequently songs get played and pay their members accordingly.

There is a quirk in the law concerning public performance rights. Traditionally, it was necessary to obtain permission only from the administrator of the musical composition rights; one did not need permission from the owner of the sound recording rights. However, sound recording rights holders became concerned when music was played over the internet; they realized that this technological development could destroy the market for records and CDs, and they therefore lobbied for a change in the law. Congress passed the Digital Performance Right in Sound Recordings Act of 1995 and gave those who hold rights in sound recordings the right to receive royalties on digital performances. Thus, to make the song available on the internet or other digital transmission (such as satellite), one needs a "digital audio transmission license." SoundExchange is the company that provides such a license to digital platforms and pays the royalties to the copyright holders. Thus, if the song is being played via the internet or any other form of digital media, one must pay both the musical composition rights holder (through a PRO) and the sound recording rights holder (through SoundExchange).

The blanket licenses one may obtain through the PROs or through SoundExchange only cover certain types of uses. One of the main restrictions on digital platforms is that the use must be "non-interactive," which at the most basic level means that the user cannot select the song that is played. Also, those licenses do not cover downloads of music. In an effort to bridge the gap between what the blanket licenses cover and what many digital services are actually doing, Congress passed the Music Modernization Act ("MMA") in 2018. The law created a system that will provide a blanket mechanical license for "interactive" streaming of musical works—uses not otherwise covered by other available blanket licenses. The Copyright Royalty Board will set rates using a "willing buyer/willing seller" standard. The MMA also created a collective, whose board mostly consists of songwriters and publishers, to administer these blanket licenses and distribute royalties to the appropriate parties. The collective is supposed to create and maintain a public database that identifies musical works and their owners (along with ownership share information). Such a database would be very helpful to those who are trying to track down rights holders. Finally, the MMA included a provision called the "Classics Act," which extends federal copyright protection to sound recordings made before 1972. Previously, federal copyright law covered only sound recordings fixed after 1972, although there was an argument that such recordings were protected under pre-existing state copyright laws. Some rights holders had filed lawsuits against large digital streaming services, claiming that their use of pre-1972 sound recordings without direct payment of royalties infringed their rights. To help resolve the ambiguity in the law, the MMA officially pre-empted state law and extended federal law to cover such recordings, and it also contained a provision that gave digital platforms the option to pay three years worth of royalties to settle any outstanding legal disputes. The law further clarified that other federal copyright principles, such as fair use, the first sale doctrine, and the provisions of the Digital Millennium Copyright Act apply to pre-1972 recordings as well.

There is one other quirk in the law concerning public performance. Suppose a store or restaurant wants to play a local radio station in the background. The radio station has already paid for the right to broadcast the music, and the airwaves are free to the public, right? Well, it's possible that the facility will have to pay a license fee to play the music. The Fairness in Music Licensing Act of 1998, 17 U.S.C. sec. 110, sets out the conditions for when stores and restaurants have to pay for a public performance license and when they don't. There are multiple factors, including the size of the facility, the number of speakers, or the number and size of televisions for customers to view.

Another common desired use for music is to "synchronize" the music with something else—a video, a voiceover, an advertisement, or some other multimedia project. If one wants to use a song in any audio-visual media, one needs to obtain synchronization rights. Synchronization rights must be obtained from both the holder of the musical composition rights and the holder of the sound recording rights. Then, if the video is going to be played in public or on the internet, one may have to secure the public performance rights as well. Typically, whoever is broadcasting or hosting the audio-visual work must have a license to make it available.

If one wants to make a physical copy of the song, whether on a CD, tape, DVD, flash drive, or some other format, one needs what is called a "mechanical" license. A person making a soundtrack CD, for example, would need a mechanical license for each of the songs featured on the CD. Again, this license would have to be obtained from both kinds of rights holders (the composition and the sound recording).

For either a synchronization license or a mechanical license, the person who wants to use the song must get permission from the publisher of the musical composition and also obtain a master use license, which is permission to use a particular sound recording. In most cases, the record label owns the rights to the recording, although it is possible that someone else does. For example, suppose a band records a song for a CD. The CD is sold, lots of people like the song, and it becomes very popular. The band then goes on tour. A live version of the song is recorded and that live version also becomes popular. A person who wants to use the song in a video may want either the CD version or the live version. They are two different "master recordings." The user will need a master use license from whomever owns the rights to whichever of the two versions he decides to use. It may be the case that the record company owns the rights to both; or, the CD version may be held by the record company, and the live version may be owned by someone else.

If one wants to use lyrics only, lyrics are copyrightable, separate, and apart from the music. One will need permission from whomever holds the copyright to the lyrics, which may be the person or persons who wrote them, or the writer may have transferred those rights to a publisher or record label.

To cover a song, a person does not need to obtain sound recording rights, because, obviously, one is not using anyone's sound recording. It is only necessary to obtain a license from the holder of the musical composition rights. There are two ways to do this. One can pay what's called a "compulsory license." The compulsory license is a royalty rate set forth in the copyright statute. The user would notify the songwriter that they plan to release a cover and then send monthly royalty statements. The law requires the user to pay royalties monthly, and the royalties are set by the copyright statute (called the statutory royalty rate). This option does not require permission of either the songwriter or the artist who originally recorded the song, but this option also does not allow the user to change the words or music in any way. Thus, if the user wants to use a song without paying monthly royalties or if one wants to change a song in some way, then the user should obtain a license directly from the songwriter (or publisher). One would contact the songwriter and negotiate whatever terms of the license one wants. In some cases, it may be possible to cover a song without paying royalties or obtaining a license if the cover is a genuine parody. However, it is not sufficient to simply intend to be humorous. A parody must genuinely qualify as a fair use to be a protected use.

Table 9.1: Required Permissions for the Use of Music.

If you want to:	Then you need:	From the owner of the musical composition	From the owner of the sound recording	From the publisher of the lyrics
Put music in an ad or video or other audio-visual work	A synchronization license	✓	✓	
Make a physical copy of the song	A mechanical license	✓	✓	(you would need permission if you reprinted the lyrics along with the copy)
Broadcast or play the music in a public place	A public performance license	✓ (these licenses are often arranged through a PRO)		
Play the music on the internet or other digital media platform	A digital public performance license	✓ (these licenses are often arranged through a PRO)	✓ (arranged through SoundExchange)	
Cover a song	A compulsory license or other form of permission	✓		
Reprint the lyrics				✓

Fair Use

The copyright statute allows for "fair use," which is the right of a person to use copyrighted material without permission under certain circumstances. (The fair use factors are discussed thoroughly in Chapter 6 on copyright.)

Unfortunately, there is a lot of gray area concerning what is considered fair use. The four-part balancing test does not provide a lot of guidance for specific scenarios. It requires a lot of experience and good judgment to guess in advance when something will be deemed fair use.

Given court decisions, it is clear that it is not fair use to simply download songs for free or swap them on file-sharing sites. In *MGM Studios v. Grokster*, the Supreme Court found that file-sharing sites can be liable for infringement, and Justice Ginsburg noted in her concurring opinion there has been no finding of fair use when such sites are used. It is also not likely to be deemed fair use to use a song on a soundtrack, in a video, or on a website if one is using the whole song for entertainment or commercial purposes and it hasn't been licensed. These are the kinds of uses for which licensing is typically required.

Nevertheless, a search on YouTube will yield thousands of videos where people took a song—the whole thing—and used it in the background for their own montage of video, whether it's a video of funny cats or airplanes or a home video of kids running around the yard. In most of these cases, there is no apparent reason for the use of the song other than the fact that the video creator liked the song. Are these uses fair?

On one hand, there is little, if any, commercial value to the video. But on the other hand, the use is neither educational nor news, nor is there any criticism or commentary. The entire song is often used. It is a use for which royalties are typically expected (synchronization rights), and the use allows people to hear the music without paying for it or without the payment of royalties. Thus, there is a good argument that the use is not fair. And yet, such instances are rampant. Rights holders, relying on the Digital Millennium Copyright Act, often demand that YouTube take down offending videos. However, one case shows that such uses may be fair use under certain circumstances and imposes an obligation on rights holders to take fair use into consideration before sending a takedown notice. In *Lenz v. Universal Music Corp.*, the Ninth Circuit ruled that a 29-second video of young kids dancing to "Let's Go Crazy" by Prince was fair use and should not have been subjected to a takedown notice. Notably, in *Lenz*, the clip of music was short, and it did not substitute for the song as a whole in the marketplace. Moreover, YouTube has offered arrangements to rights holders that allow them to collect a portion of the advertising revenue gained from hits on videos that use their work. YouTube is, in essence, giving a choice between having the infringing content removed or monetizing it. Many rights holders have opted to monetize videos that might be infringing rather than have them removed.

Using music can be fair use when the use is transformative and expressive and uses a small portion of the song. In *Lennon v. Premise Media*, for example, the court held that the use of a 15-second clip of John Lennon's song "Imagine" in the film *Expelled* was a fair use because it was transformative and short. The film used only the portion containing the lyrics "imagine there's no religion" in conjunction with commentary about religion. The court noted that the filmmakers could have licensed the clip, but a license was not required because of the transformative nature of the use, and there would be no long-term harm to the market for licensing the song.

It can also be fair use if the use is for news and the music was captured incidentally. In *Italian Book Corp. v. ABC*, the court found it was fair use to show a news segment about a parade, even though the clip captured music played by a marching band. The point of the story wasn't to feature the music; it was simply an incidental fact that the music could be heard in the parade.

Using a small portion, on its own, however, is not determinative. Sampling, which involves using a small portion of a work, can be infringement. In *Grand Upright Music v. Warner Bros.*, for example, the court found that a short sample in a Biz Markie song was an infringement. That case has been criticized by many commentators who feel that the court failed to do a thorough fair use analysis; however, most experts are concerned that courts would follow that case as precedent, and thus, most people feel that sampling requires permission or the payment of fees, thereby rendering many potential projects impossible because they would be prohibitively expensive.

The use of a whole song doesn't prevent a finding a fair use, as long as the use is genuinely transformative. There has been protection of parodies, for example. In *Campbell v. Acuff Rose Music, Inc.*, the Supreme Court found that 2 Live Crew's parody of "Pretty Woman" could be fair use because it mocked the "white bread" nature of the original, and it did not substitute for the Roy Orbison version of the song in the marketplace. Similarly, in *Brownmark Films, LLC v. Comedy Partners*, the court found that the *South Park* parody of YouTube song "What What (In the Butt)" was a fair use, because the use clearly mocked the song's role in popular culture.

Another troublesome fair use issue is the use of music in political campaigns. There have been several cases in which politicians have been sued for using music without permission. Almost all of them have settled.

One might expect political campaigns to conduct themselves like any other professional communicator. If they wish to play music at a live event, such as a campaign rally, they would simply need to pay one of the performing rights societies (ASCAP, BMI, SESAC, or GMR) for the public performance rights in the musical composition. If they wish to use music in a political advertisement, then they would need to obtain synchronization rights. However, in most of the cases thus far, the campaigns did not bother to obtain a license. They have argued that it is "fair use" to use the songs to illustrate their political points. Since most of the cases have settled, there is little case law on the issue of whether that would be fair use; however, one case that was decided by a court, *Henley v. DeVore*, found that the parody of two Don Henley songs in a political ad were not fair use. The court found that the uses were not transformative because they did not comment on the original work, and any minimal transformativeness was outweighed by the fact that uses adversely affected the market for licensing the work.

The other potential issue in political cases is whether the use improperly uses the name or likeness of the musician or would create the false impression of any endorsement of the politician or a viewpoint expressed by the musician whose work is used. Right of publicity claims require "commercial use." Although advertising is typically considered a commercial use, it is unlikely a court would find political ads to be commercial, and in fact the court in *Henley* noted that other cases have found political ads to be non-commercial, at least for the purposes of intellectual property law. The other option would be to bring a claim under the Lanham Act, but the court addressed that issue in *Henley* as well, and found that the musician could not show false endorsement. However, in that case, the ad used a parody of the original songs rather than Don Henley's original versions. Thus, the court concluded, no one would think Henley actually participated or endorsed the ad. It is possible a court would rule differently if the musician's voice were used.

In sum, fair use determinations are not easy, and music rights holders tend to be very litigious. Record companies have famously sued individuals who download music, and there are numerous lawsuits brought by songwriters who believe their work has been ripped off. If there is any question about what might be fair use, it may be wise to consult an attorney.

Other Provisions Related to the Use of Music Online

The DMCA contains certain provisions about the use of music online. Webcasters cannot publish playlists of upcoming music, and there are limits on the number of songs one can play from a single CD, box set, or artist in a given time frame.

The DMCA also included a provision that required internet radio companies to pay public performance royalties for both the musical composition and the sound recording for each song played. Terrestrial radio companies pay public performance royalties only for the musical composition and not the sound recording. The law adversely affected the internet radio start-ups because they were not generating enough revenue to cover the fees. Several companies went out of business. Those that survived advocated for changes to the royalty requirements, and the rules finally changed. Internet radio companies now have the option pay royalties based on a percentage of revenue rather than a flat per song/ per listener rate. The laws that govern rights will certainly have a determinative effect on whether internet radio and similar businesses survive and how they might provide services in the future.

Practical Options for Using Music

If you work for a big company that has blanket licenses from the PROs and/or SoundExchange to play music as part of a terrestrial broadcast or digital stream, then you won't need to do anything more (other than comply with the terms of those blanket licenses) for those uses. However, most other uses, like making a video or a podcast, will require you to actually obtain a license. What options does a person have?

First, if the use would qualify as fair use, then one wouldn't need to get permission. The challenge with fair use, though, is that it generally only applies to short clips when they are used to illustrate a point or there is direct commentary on them. Fair use wouldn't give you the ability to score a whole video or podcast.

When people need background music for an entire editorial work, the two primary options are either to commission original music or use music from a pre-cleared music library. Hiring a composer to create original music can be a great way to get a unique sound, but it is an expensive and time-consuming process. While it may be worthwhile to hire a composer for discrete projects, like creating a theme song for a show, it can be very expensive to ask someone to score an entire work. Thus, many producers turn to music libraries, which are catalogues of music for which all the rights are cleared in advance, as long as the music is used consistent with the terms of the license agreement. The benefit of such libraries is that it is an easy and relatively inexpensive way to get music. The downside is that the music is somewhat generic; popular songs are not in the catalogues. If one wants to use a specific song, then one must reach out directly to the rights holders to obtain a license. It's important to know that rights holders often restrict the term of the license or the platforms on which the music may be used. And, the more popular the song, the more expensive a license will be. Finally, there is a risk that a rights holder will simply not want to license the music. They have no obligation to let their music be used in a project to which they don't want to be associated, so they can deny any request. Content producers must think carefully about how they want to use music in their projects, plan well in advance, and learn how to navigate the music rights options.

Practical Conclusions

- Whenever you want to use music, you probably need to clear rights. The rights you need depend on what you want to do.

- Music copyrights are complicated because a song will have multiple copyrighted components:
  - The musical composition
  - The sound recording
  - The lyrics

- In most cases, whenever a person wishes to use music, he/she will have to pay a royalty or obtain a license. There are many different kinds of licenses depending on the proposed use, and multiple licenses may be required from multiple parties. Rights needed might include:
  - Synchronization rights to mix the music with visual components
  - Royalties to the musical composition rights holder to perform the work in public or broadcast it.

- Royalties to the musical composition rights holder and the sound recording rights holder to transmit it via digital media, including internet and satellite
- A mechanical license to make any physical copy

- Rights licensing is a complicated system, and there are many different people you may need to contact to obtain the rights you seek.

- It is very difficult to win a fair use case involving music. Courts have ruled that sampling is not fair use and political uses are not fair use. Uses of music are rarely deemed transformative except where there is some direct commentary involving the original work. Courts have found a use to be fair when a very small clip of music is used and the clip illustrates a point the speaker is trying to make. Sharing songs online is not fair use.

- Sites like YouTube are trying to deal with the problem of widespread copyright infringement by giving copyright holders a share of advertising revenue rather than removing the posted video (which the copyright holder could demand under the DMCA). This solution maximizes the amount of content available and also compensates the copyright holder. However, it is up to the copyright holder to decide whether to accept this deal or not. Copyright holders must at least take fair use into account before sending a takedown notification for allegedly infringing material.

- There may be serious consequences for infringement:
  - If a use is not a fair use and was not properly licensed, then the user may be civilly or criminally liable for copyright infringement.
  - The copyright holder can sue the user, who may be required to pay statutory penalties, disgorge profits, or pay for lost profits.
  - Prosecutors generally don't bring criminal charges unless there is widescale piracy. But in such cases, they will prosecute those who make unauthorized copies of movies or songs and sell them.

CHAPTER 10

Negligence Claims Against the Media

Content That May Result in Personal Injury

One serious legal risk that people often overlook is the risk of being sued for negligence if someone is physically harmed as a result of speech. It sounds strange; personal injury cases are most often associated with car accidents, medical malpractice, wrongful death, or other claims that arise from actions, not speech. However, it is possible to be sued for negligence—and in some cases be successfully sued—if speech results in injury to another.

Some of these cases arise from how-to guides or advice. Some arise from encouraging people to do dangerous things. Some arise simply because the information provided turned out to be wrong. Many arise because someone copied a stunt they saw on television, or acted because they were inspired by a song or a movie. These types of claims have had varying degrees of success.

This chapter will discuss the following issues:

1. What is negligence?

2. How does negligence apply to copycats?

3. How does negligence apply to encouragement and advice?

4. How does negligence apply to practical information that is wrong, incomplete, or otherwise harmful?

5. How does negligence apply to other physical harm that happens to be media-related?

What Is Negligence?

"Negligence" is the legal claim that is used in a lawsuit when a person suffers an injury and believes that the injury was caused by another person's failure to exercise "reasonable care." Common examples include car accidents and medical malpractice. For example, if Driver A is injured because Driver B failed to brake at a red light and rear-ended Driver A's car, then Driver A could sue Driver B for negligence. To win a negligence claim, a plaintiff must prove all four of the following elements:

1. The defendant owed a legal duty to the plaintiff to exercise due care. A duty may exist where there is a reasonably foreseeable risk of harm to another. However, there may be no duty if the harm is not reasonably foreseeable.

2. The defendant breached the duty by failing to exercise due care.

3. The defendant's conduct was the cause of the injury. The plaintiff must prove both: "but for" causation (meaning the injury would not have occurred but for the defendant's conduct) and "proximate cause" (meaning that the injury was the natural consequence of the defendant's action, with no interruption or intervening cause that would be the primary cause).

4. The plaintiff suffered a loss. Damages might include medical expenses, "pain and suffering," or other losses.

Considering the example of a car accident, it is easy to see how these elements would be applied:

1. Driver B owes a duty of care to drive carefully, because it is very foreseeable that Driver A will be harmed if Driver B fails to drive carefully.

2. Driver B breached his duty, because he failed to exercise due care and rear-ended Driver A.

3. Driver A's injury would not have occurred but for being rear-ended by Driver B, and the injuries are the natural consequence of Driver B's failure to drive carefully. There was no intervening cause.

4. Driver A suffered medical expenses and other damages as a result.

In media cases, however, there is usually a question as to whether the media company owed a duty to the person who becomes injured, or whether the media's speech was actually the proximate cause of the injury. The chain of events is often not as clear-cut as it might be in a typical car accident case.

Also, when the conduct that allegedly causes harm is speech, there are First Amendment interests at issue; thus, some courts have imposed additional requirements in cases based on speech or expression in order to protect those First Amendment interests.

How Does Negligence Apply to Copycats?

Copycat cases—where a person takes action that copies something he saw on television or acts because he was inspired by a song or movie—are surprisingly common. What is also common is the dismissal of these cases. Sometimes the courts find that there is no duty on the part of the media to foresee a copycat. Sometimes the courts find that the media was not the proximate cause of the action. In either case, courts tend to find that the media should not be liable for copycats, as demonstrated by this sampling of cases:

- *Davidson v. Time Warner*, finding that a record label was not liable when a man shot a police officer after listening to Tupac Shakur's "2Pacalyse Now."

- *Byers v. Edmonson*, finding film makers not liable for a shooting spree allegedly inspired by *Natural Born Killers*.

- *McCollum v. CBS Records*, finding Ozzy Osbourne and his record label not liable for a suicide prompted by a song.

- *DeFillipo v. NBC*, finding no liability on the part of NBC when a teen boy accidentally hung himself after watching a noose stunt on *The Tonight Show*.

- *Sakon v. Pepsi*, finding no liability on an advertiser when a boy broke his neck copying stunts in a Mountain Dew commercial.

- *James v. Meow Media*, finding a video game company not liable when a boy went on a killing spree and blamed it on violent television and video games.

In all of these cases, the courts have found that there is too tenuous a connection between the expression of an idea (whether in a song, on a television show, or otherwise) and the copycat action that followed.

One of the most well-known copycat cases is *Olivia N. v. NBC*, brought by a teen girl who was raped by other girls using a bottle, copycatting a scene from the television movie *Born Innocent*. The court ruled that, in order to recover damages for a copycat action, the plaintiff must not only prove the four elements of negligence, but also prove that the defendant incited the action. Merely depicting an event or idea is not enough to justify liability for negligence. The defendant must have actively encouraged the action in order to be liable. Such a rule was developed to ensure that the speaker's First Amendment interests are protected. Thus, one must consider what constitutes encouragement.

How Does Negligence Apply to Encouragement and Advice?

The classic example of liability based on encouragement is *Weirum v. RKO General, Inc.*, where a radio personality told listeners to rush to a particular location to win a contest. Listeners did, indeed, rush and one of them got into a car accident as a result, causing injury. Clearly, there is more of a link in such a case between the speech and the harm that occurred than there would be in a case where someone saw speeding on television and decided to copycat the speeding on their own.

Encouragement can also be found from how-to guides or advice. For example, the publisher of *The Hitman Manual* was sued when a purported "hitman" bought the book and followed its advice, resulting in the death of a woman and her children. In that case, *Rice v. Paladin Enter. Inc.*, the court refused to conclude that the First Amendment protected the book because it thought the language of the book could be considered encouragement or incitement. The court felt that the book was not an abstract discussion of the issues, which may have been protected, but rather provided actual instructions, bordering on "aiding and abetting" a crime. Thus, the court allowed the case to proceed to trial. Rather than face trial, the publisher settled.

How Does Negligence Apply to Incorrect, Incomplete, or Otherwise Harmful Information?

Aside from encouragement, there have been cases where people have sued because they were injured after relying on books, guides, articles, or advertisements that were incorrect or indirectly caused harm. In almost all of these cases, the courts have said that the publisher/speaker is not liable where they had no reason to know of the error or harm. In some cases, the court has suggested that the reader has a duty to check out the material on his own to ensure the information is true or the product/service discussed is safe.

In *Winter v. GP Putnam's Sons*, the publisher of a mushroom guide was sued. The book purported to tell mushroom fans how to tell the difference between safe and poisonous wild mushrooms. One mushroom was listed as safe, but nearly killed a man who ate it, causing extensive liver damage. The plaintiff sued for negligence, and he also brought claims for products liability, breach of warranty, and misrepresentation. However, he was not successful on any of his claims. With respect to the products liability and warranty claims, the court noted that there was a difference between the book as a product (paper bound together) and the book as a source of information (the content). The product itself—the paper—did not cause the injury and therefore those claims were not appropriate.

With respect to the content, the court found that the publisher was not liable for negligently publishing the content because the publisher had no duty to research the truth of the claims in the book. It was the author, not the publisher, that was the mushroom expert, and thus the author was the person who breached the duty and caused the loss. As a practical matter, the court's decision may have dissuaded others from bringing similar claims. Authors generally do not have "deep-pockets," and plaintiffs' lawyers do not like to sue people who have no money because the chance of actually recovering damages is low. If only the authors of such books can be liable, it might not be worthwhile to file such claims. In any event, the outcome of *Winter* is consistent with other cases involving incorrect information. There have been similar outcomes in cases involving plaintiffs who were injured after relying on travel guides, diet and health books, weather reports, product advertisements, attorney listings, and financial listings. A sampling of cases shows that the courts have consistently ruled that the speakers are not liable:

- *Birmingham v. Fodor's Travel Publications Inc.*, finding that a publisher had no duty to warn that the plaintiff could be injured bodysurfing in Hawaii.

- *Yanase v. Auto Club*, finding that a publisher had no duty to investigate the safety of locations for motels listed in a tour book.

- *Gutter v. Dow Jones, Inc.*, finding a newspaper not liable to a reader who lost money relying on erroneous financial information.

- *Smith v. Linn*, finding no liability in a case where a woman died following a liquid protein diet described in a book.

- *Brandt v. Weather Channel Inc.*, finding the Weather Channel not liable when a man died in a storm after relying on a weather report and no bad weather was predicted.

- *Walters v. Seventeen Magazine*, finding a magazine not liable to a girl who suffered Toxic Shock Syndrome when she purchased tampons advertised in the magazine.

Despite the large number of cases finding the media not liable for harm, it is important to note that a publisher can be liable if there is reason to know that something could cause harm. Two cases involving *Soldier of Fortune* magazine illustrate the difference. In one case, the magazine published a classified ad by someone looking for work. The advertiser turned out to be a hitman, and the family of the person killed sued for negligence. However, in *Eimann v. Soldier of Fortune Magazine*, like in most negligence cases against the media, the court found that the magazine had "no duty to refrain from publishing a facially innocuous classified advertisement." The court ruled that the magazine was not liable because there was nothing about the ad that would have let the magazine know the advertiser was willing to kill someone for money.

But in *Braun v. Soldier of Fortune Magazine*, another case with similar facts, the court ruled that the magazine could be liable, because the ad on its face indicated that there was a potential for harm. It advertised a "gun for hire" who would "consider all jobs." Thus, the court reasoned, the magazine should have known that harm could occur.

There have been a few other cases where publishers have been held liable, but they involve direct instructions for dangerous activities. In *Brocklesby v. U.S.*, errors in a chart describing flight procedures resulted in a plane crash that killed several people. The court concluded that the publisher could be liable, but the decision relied heavily on a substantial body of case law that imposes liability in cases involving obviously dangerous activities. Similarly, in *Carter v. Rand McNally & Co.*, a textbook publisher was found liable for injuries caused by a chemical explosion. The textbook at issue failed to warn of the possibility of a dangerous chemical reaction. But again, the court's reasoning can be distinguished from other cases because chemical experiments are the kind of thing one would expect to be dangerous, as opposed to other kinds of general information.

How Does Negligence Apply to Other Media-Related Harm?

There are some cases that are not based on any content that was disseminated but are nevertheless somehow related to media. For example, in 2006, a teen sued MySpace because a man she met through the site sexually assaulted her. MySpace didn't publish anything that she relied upon, but simply provided the forum through which they met. The case, *Doe v. MySpace*, was dismissed, although not on First Amendment grounds. Instead, the dismissal was based on the immunity for Internet Service Providers, as defined in Section 230 of the Communications Decency Act (which is discussed in more detail in Chapter 20).

In some cases, the injury resulted from conduct that occurred while a program was being recorded. The family of Jennifer Strange, for example, sued radio station KDND because Strange died after participating in the "Hold Your Wee For A Wii" contest. The contest involved drinking a lot of water without going to the bathroom, and she died from water intoxication. Similarly, Megan Hauserman sued Sharon Osbourne over the final episode of the reality television show *Rock of Love Charm School*, where Megan insulted Sharon, and Sharon dumped a drink on Megan. Neither case resulted in a published court opinion, so it is difficult to say with certainty how a court would decide such cases. But it is possible that courts would treat these defendants as they would in any other tort case because it is not their speech that is the basis for liability. The claims are based on their conduct for which any other kind of non-media defendant could potentially be liable.

Along the same lines, there are a few cases where reporters have been sued for negligence as a result of their newsgathering conduct. For example, in *Clift v. Narragansett Television*, a television station was sued for negligence after a suicidal man barricaded inside his home in a standoff with police spoke to a TV reporter and then killed himself after the interview aired. The court refused to dismiss the case, finding that a jury may find the station's behavior negligent.

In sum, if the court finds that the conduct of the media is the direct cause of harm, there will be no special consideration given on First Amendment grounds simply because the media is somehow involved.

Practical Conclusions

- It's possible that content could contain dangerous information or errors that can harm people.

- If you're describing something that's inherently dangerous, like how to fix an airplane, make sure you get all the details right.

- If you encourage someone to do something harmful or dangerous, actually do the harmful thing yourself, or know that there is a likelihood of harm from an advertised service, then you could be found liable for negligence.

- Otherwise, courts typically do not hold media or other speakers liable for injuries that occur that are somehow traceable to their content.

PART III

How Does One Get Information to Publish?

Is There a Right of Access to Information, Places, or Events?

For those who wish to gather information or materials for the purpose of disseminating them— whether as a traditional journalist or otherwise—there are certain legal issues to consider:

1. Do you have a right to access to the information you want?

2. Can you be sued or prosecuted for accessing it?

These questions are related, but do not necessarily overlap. For example, you might not have a right to a particular document, but, on the other hand, it's not necessarily illegal to obtain it, nor can anyone sue you for possessing it. The same may be true for taking photos. Depending on the circumstances, you might not have an affirmative right to take a photo, but on the other hand, there is nothing illegal about taking one. There is a difference between not having an affirmative, enforceable right to something, and it not being illegal or tortious to get it. There is a lot of information that exists in that middle ground.

This chapter will address the first question: when you have a right of access to information or places. The second question of whether you can be sued or prosecuted is addressed in Chapter 12. This chapter will be divided into three sections:

1. General rules with respect to whether you have a right of access to information

2. Specific laws that might affect your ability to access particular types of information

3. Rules that govern whether there is a right of access to places and events

General Rules With Respect to Whether You Have a Right of Access to Information

Different rules have developed over time to cover different kinds of information. Thus, the first step in determining whether you have a right of access to information is to figure out what kind of information it is or where it is located.

For the purposes of determining whether you have a right of access, information can be divided into two categories: private and government. Government information can be further subdivided into three categories, based on the branch of government that holds the information: executive, legislative or judicial. Executive and legislative information can be further split into two categories: federal and state. To determine whether there is a right of access to information, one must know who holds the information sought. The following chart shows how these categories are divided and the generally-applicable rule, and each of these rules will be expanded upon below.

TO DETERMINE IF THERE IS A RIGHT OF ACCESS,
ONE MUST KNOW WHO HOLDS THE INFORMATION SOUGHT

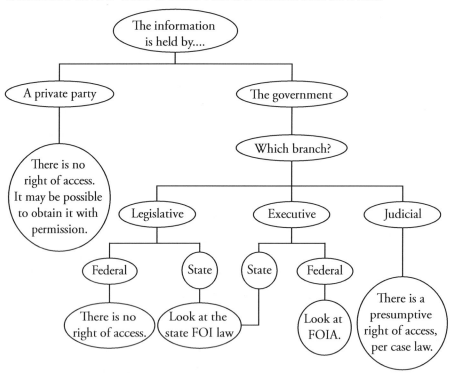

Figure 11.1: Understanding Whether a Right of Access to Information Exists.

Private Materials

The easiest question is whether one has a right of access to private places or documents owned or held by private parties. The answer is usually no. A journalist (or any other person) can certainly request access but has no right to demand it. One needs permission of the owner or host to obtain access.

Private companies that host events are entitled to impose restrictions on press access. Restrictions have become more common to obtain access to sporting events or concerts. There aren't many cases on the subject to help evaluate whether any of the owner's restrictions can be invalidated, so journalists must use their best judgment—and ethics—to determine whether they are willing to conform to an owner's demands.

Ethical considerations are probably more important then legal ones when it comes to evaluating the kinds of restrictions that private owners place on access to events. There have been some high-profile examples where, in order to get press access to a concert or sporting event, the host requires the journalist to let them review the story in advance, or to turn over the copyright in all photos taken. Journalists are supposed to be independent and not cater to those in positions of power, and so a journalist should probably decline such requests, as such actions would be considered unethical. It may mean that the journalist is denied access to the event, but it may be better to report from another angle or not to cover the event at all than to comply with unethical demands.

Even though there is no right of access to materials held by private parties, there may be a right of access to private materials if they come into the possession of the government. For example, if documents are filed with a court as evidence in a lawsuit, there may be a right of access to those documents. Or, a government agency may come into possession of a company's records and, in some cases, those may be accessible through the agency. Access to such materials would be governed by the appropriate rules discussed below.

Federal Agencies

Congress created a statutory right of access to federal executive branch materials by enacting the Freedom of Information Act (FOIA) in 1966. E-FOIA amendments were adopted in 1996 to extend the right to electronic records, and the OPEN Government Act of 2007 amended FOIA to require tracking numbers on FOIA requests (among other things). Congress also created a statutory right of access to federal agency meetings by enacting the Sunshine Act of 1976. Each are explained below.

WHAT DOES FOIA COVER?

FOIA allows any person to request federal agency records for any purpose. "Any person" means any person. The requester need not be a U.S. citizen or a journalist or fulfill any other requirement. The one exception is that the Intelligence Authorization Act of 2003 bars intelligence agencies from disclosing records requested by foreign governments, international governmental organizations, or their representatives; however, foreign governments may request other kinds of records under FOIA.

"Agency" means all executive branch agencies (FCC, FTC, SEC, FBI, IRS, and the entire alphabet soup of federal agencies), the military, presidential commissions, the post office, and other government-controlled entities. However, it does not include the President himself, Congress, states, or any courts. One of the more interesting questions is whether private entities that receive government funds can be subject to FOIA. Receiving government funds, on its own, is not a determinative factor with respect to whether an entity is an "agency" that must comply with FOIA. Amtrak is covered by FOIA, but the Smithsonian is not, nor are public radio and televisions stations. The right of access under FOIA is a statutory creation, and thus Congress has the power to change the scope of FOIA, including or deleting entities subject to coverage. Courts also have the ability to interpret ambiguous provisions of FOIA to determine whether a particular entity should be subject to the law. Thus, any ambiguities must be resolved either through litigation or statutory amendment.

"Records" means any paper or electronic record. It includes paper records, documents, computer files, databases, photographs, videos, audio recordings, and any similar materials. It also includes emails. Government officials are supposed to use their government accounts to conduct official business; however, they sometimes use personal accounts. For the purposes of FOIA, the only relevant question is whether the email concerns official business. For example, in *Competitive Enterprise Inst. v. OSTP*, the Competitive Enterprise Institute (CEI) requested work-related records from the personal email of OSTP's director, triggering a debate as to whether those records were public or private. Ultimately, the court held that, even though the email service was through a private company, the OSTP director used it for a public purpose, and so its contents were still in OSTP's "control" for the purposes of the FOIA. There have been complaints that officials sometimes use text messages on their phones to avoid creating a record that can be requested, but such tactics are unlikely to work, as courts will generally apply a broad definition of record if the subject matter is official government business. Government social media use would probably also be deemed a "record."

The definition of a "record" does not include physical objects in the government's possession. A requester cannot demand to inspect a person's computer, look through a file cabinet, or obtain an object. For example, a transcript of FBI interviews with witnesses about the assassination of President Kennedy would be a "record," but, as the court ruled in *Nichols v. U.S.*, the guns, bullets, and clothing gathered as evidence would not. Also, the Court ruled in *Kissinger v. Reporters Committee for Freedom of the Press* that the government is obligated to provide only those records it actually has in its possession; it is not obligated to obtain materials from third parties or to keep materials forever in the event someone requests them. Nevertheless, the government must provide records over which it has control; thus, the fact that a record is kept or maintained by a government contractor is irrelevant if the agency actually has control over the record. In *Burka v. HHS*, for example, the court found that materials that were created and held by a federal contractor were agency records, because the agency had constructive control over the materials.

"Any purpose" means any purpose. The requester does not have to explain why he wants the records. However, that said, there are certain provisions of the FOIA that may depend on the requester's purpose. For example, the fee waiver provision, explained below, does depend on purpose. Fee waivers are granted only in certain circumstances, and the requester will have to show that his use qualifies for a waiver. But the requester has the option of not declaring his purpose and declining the opportunity for a fee waiver. Also, the requester's purpose may be taken into consideration when there are privacy interests at issue. As noted below, some of the reasons for withholding documents may involve privacy concerns, and the Supreme Court has factored in the potential use of the information as a consideration in such cases. In *NARA v. Favish*, the Court declared that a requester must "establish a sufficient reason for the disclosure" when privacy concerns are being weighed against public interest in the material.

MAKING A FOIA REQUEST

A requester must request the records in writing. Each agency has regulations that define what must be included in the request and how requests are accepted (by mail, email, online submission, or otherwise). Thus, a requester should look at an agency's regulations before making the request. All agencies post their procedures somewhere on their website, and many provide the option of making the request online. As an alternative, the Reporters Committee for Freedom of the Press created an excellent FOIA letter generator and tracking system (available at www.ifoia.org) that allows users to fill out a form that generates a letter that can be automatically emailed to the appropriate agency.

Requests for records must reasonably describe the record sought. As a practical matter, it is important to describe the records sought as specifically and narrowly as possible, because it is much easier—and faster—for the agency to fulfill a request if they can understand exactly which documents would be responsive. Moreover, agencies are not obligated to fulfill requests that are so vague as to essentially amount to a fishing expedition or require the agency to do research on the requester's behalf. For example, in *Lamb v. IRS*, the court stated that requests are improper when they essentially require the agency to act as the requester's researcher and answer questions. Similarly, in *Massachusetts v. HHS*, the court found that a request for all records "relating to" a subject was overbroad and unreasonable; requesters cannot expect to get a response to a sloppy request. In essence, the requester must already have enough information to be able to describe with some specificity what he wants. The fact that a request may involve a large number of documents in response is not determinative; the question is whether the agency can reasonably figure out what those documents are without extensive independent research. Thus, in *Yeager v. DEA*, the court ruled that a request for over a million electronic records was valid because the records were precisely identifiable. In contrast, the court in *Burns v. DOJ*, ruled that asking an agency to listen to several volumes of unindexed audio tapes to find one specific recorded conversation was unreasonable. The record was not sufficiently identifiable.

The statute says that agencies have 20 days to grant or deny the request, although as a practical matter, it may take longer to get the records. A requester may file a lawsuit to seek enforcement of FOIA if the agency unreasonably delays responding to a request. However, the law also acknowledges that there are times when an agency cannot promptly respond because it is flooded with requests and lacks the resources to respond to all the requests in a timely manner. Thus, if the agency is otherwise acting diligently, the courts will not punish them merely for being overwhelmed and understaffed. The requester may simply have to wait his turn, and that may take months or even years.

A requester may also have to pay fees for search and copying costs. It is possible to get a fee waiver if the requester can show that the records sought are of great significance to the public's understanding of the operations or activities of government. The standard is fairly high, and a waiver is not guaranteed. If the fees are not waived, then the requester will be placed in a "fee category." There are three: (1) commercial users, who pay all costs, (2) noncommercial educational, scientific, or journalistic users, who pay nothing for the first 2 hours of research and first 100 pages of copies, but may have to pay fees beyond that, and (3) all others, who pay for search and copy costs, but not for review costs. Journalists should include in their FOIA request both a fee waiver request, showing how they intend to use the information sought to improve the public's understanding of government operations, and a statement that if the waiver is not granted, that they should be in the journalism fee category. If the fees will be over a certain amount (typically around $25, but it varies by agency), the agency will inform the requester so he can decide whether or how to proceed.

WILL THE REQUESTER OBTAIN THE REQUESTED DOCUMENTS?

In theory, the government should provide records responsive to the request unless one of the nine statutory exemptions applies. If an exemption applies, the government may withhold the record.

There is a concept called "discretionary disclosure," which means that an agency may choose to release the record even if it falls within an exemption, but as a practical matter, discretionary disclosure applies only to exemptions 2 (agency rules and practices) and 5 (agency memoranda). The other exemptions reflect laws or legal principles that prevent disclosure and cannot be overcome simply on the basis of discretion. Instead, the question will be whether the exemption truly and properly applies to the record at issue.

The exemptions are:

1. National Security. Congress granted the executive branch the authority to determine which records should be withheld due to national security. The agencies are expected to follow classification procedures, and if a record is properly classified, it may be withheld from disclosure. When the government claims that exemption one applies, the requester may sue on the issue of whether the documents were properly classified.

2. Agency Rules & Practices. Exemption two applies to records "related solely" to internal personnel rules and practices. Over time, courts divided this exemption into two categories, called "high two" and "low two." "Low two" referred to records of "mundane" activities of no interest to the public; courts typically apply this to records concerning the agency's basic functioning, such as where employees park, or what break policies employees have, or the policy on sick leave. "High two" refers to records that are vital to how an agency functions as an enforcer of law and that could be misused by people looking to circumvent the law. An example of what would have been exempt from disclosure under the high two exemption is the Secret Service Manual that explains how agents protect officials. If would-be assassins wanted to circumvent the Secret Service protections, then, in theory, they might request the manual and learn how to do so. However, in *Milner v. Department of Navy*, the Supreme Court rejected the high two concept and narrowed the interpretation of exemption two to cover only personnel records. In *Milner*, the plaintiff sought records pertaining to weapons kept by the government near Puget Sound. The Navy had denied the request, finding that the records were exempt under high two. The Supreme Court, after considering the exemption's legislative history, ruled that exemption two could not be applied because the records were not personnel records. Thus, exemption two is now applied only to those documents previously considered low two, and any documents that fall within high two can be withheld only if it falls under some other exception.

3. Statutory Exemptions. This exemption applies to records that have been declared confidential under other laws. For example, tax returns, patent applications, and census records are subject to limits on access under other laws. In short, FOIA cannot be used to circumvent other confidentiality provisions.

4. Confidential Business Information. If a record would otherwise qualify as a trade secret, then it may be withheld. Businesses are often required to turn over information to federal agencies, such as the SEC, FDA, or others. They do not lose their trade secrets merely because the government is permitted to exercise some oversight of the business. If a FOIA request seeks a record that may include trade secrets, the agency will inform the business and provide them an

opportunity to suggest what should be redacted or withheld. The agency may take the company's suggestion under advisement, but is permitted to make its own final determination as to what should be withheld. Sometimes, this results in what is called a "reverse FOIA," which is when the business sues to stop the agency from releasing information pursuant to a request. In *Chrysler Corp. v. Brown*, the Supreme Court ruled that claims to enjoin disclosure of records may be brought under the Administrative Procedures Act, and thus, companies that wish to prevent the release of records pursuant to a FOIA request can bring these reverse FOIA lawsuits.

5. Agency Memoranda. Exemption five allows agencies to withhold "working documents," which are things like first drafts of documents, internal notes, proposals, and other preliminary materials that agency employees may create or obtain in the course of doing their jobs. The reason for this exemption is to allow employees to propose ideas or have honest discussions of policy without fear that the material will be disclosed and potentially used against them in some way. After all, everyone can make mistakes or propose ideas that need to be refined. This exemption allows for a full and complete internal process so that agencies may do their jobs best. However, as noted above, this exemption is discretionary, so it may be possible to get a first draft or some other preliminary document if the agency decides, in its discretion, to release it.

6. Personnel, Medical and Other Personal Files. Exemption six is often called the "privacy exception," and it potentially applies to any information about a particular individual. The question is whether the disclosure of records "would constitute a clearly unwarranted invasion of personal privacy." Thus, the first question is whether there is information in the records that would raise a privacy issue, no matter how minor. Then, the privacy interest must be weighed against the interest in disclosure. The courts interpret "privacy" broadly, giving generous consideration to people's feelings. In *New York Times Co. v. NASA*, the court denied access to the audio tapes of the Challenger shuttle before it exploded, because the "sound and inflection of the crew's voices during the last seconds of their lives" was personal information. Similarly, in *NARA v. Favish*, the Court concluded that the family's concern with media coverage outweighed the public interest in photos of the death scene of White House counsel Vince Foster. In *Favish*, one argument in favor of disclosure was that that many people suspected that Foster's death was not a suicide, as originally reported, but actually a murder that was made to look like a suicide. The photos were sought by those who wanted to see whether the images provided evidence of murder versus suicide. Nevertheless, the Court gave greater weight to the family's feelings. Interestingly, if the information had somehow been obtained by the press and published, it is unlikely that anyone could have successfully sued under the privacy torts, due to the newsworthiness of the information. Yet such privacy considerations have been considered grounds for not releasing the information in the first place. In *Dept. of Air Force v. Rose*, the Court held that if privacy interests can be adequately satisfied by redacting certain information, then the document should be released with redactions. Such a rule maximizes disclosure while still protecting privacy. This kind of scenario arises most frequently in cases where there is a report that happens to contain names or addresses or other private information that can easily be parsed from the non-private information.

7. Law Enforcement Investigations. The government may withhold records compiled for law enforcement purposes if disclosure would (a) interfere with law enforcement investigations, (b) deprive a defendant of a fair trial, (c) invade personal privacy, (d) disclose the identity of a confidential source, (e) reveal enforcement techniques, or (f) endanger someone's life. As a practical matter, the broad language of exemption seven means that it is very difficult to get law enforcement records, at least until a matter is closed. Even then, portions of the record may be redacted to hide names of sources or witnesses, or to prevent the disclosure of enforcement techniques. Exemption seven contains a privacy provision within it, which is very much like exemption six, and the two privacy provisions are interpreted similarly. In *FCC v. AT&T*, the Supreme Court ruled that corporations do not have privacy interests that can be protected by this provision, but the concept of privacy can be interpreted broadly when it comes to people. One of the most important cases interpreting 7(C) is *U.S. Dept. of Justice v. Reporters Committee for Freedom of the Press*. The Reporters Committee had filed a FOIA request with the Department of Justice (DOJ) for the "rap sheet" of Charles Medico, an alleged mobster. Rap sheets are a compilation of criminal records (such as arrests, charges, and convictions) based on information gathered from local, state, and federal law enforcement agencies. In many cases, information about arrests, charges, and convictions are public records. But the DOJ denied the request based on FOIA exemption 7(C), and the Supreme Court upheld that decision, finding that disclosure would constitute an unwarranted invasion of personal privacy. The Court correctly noted that most of the information in a rap sheet is a matter of public record and could be obtained by searching court records. Yet the Court distinguished between the "scattered disclosure of the bits of information contained in the rap sheet and the revelation of the rap sheet as a whole." The Court reasoned, "[t]he very fact that federal funds have been spent to prepare, index, and maintain these criminal-history files demonstrates that the individual items of information in the summaries would not otherwise be 'freely available' either to the officials who have access to the underlying files or to the general public. Indeed, if the summaries were 'freely available,' there would be no reason to invoke the FOIA to obtain access to the information they contain." The Court therefore noted a "vast difference between the public records that might be found after a diligent search of courthouse files, county archives, and local police stations throughout the country and a computerized summary located in a single clearinghouse of information." The Court concluded that "[t]he privacy interest in a rap sheet is substantial," because "the computer can accumulate and store information that would otherwise have surely been forgotten long before a person attains age 80, when the FBI's rap sheets are discarded." This concept, which has been called "practical obscurity," is an important component of the Court's decision. The Court was concerned with the power of the government to compile vast amounts of information in computer databases, and it did not want such power to be abused. The Court seemed to feel that it would help protect privacy if it were still difficult to compile this kind of data, even if the government were able to do it. With that in mind, the Court considered what would constitute a "warranted" invasion of privacy. Noting that the FOIA was intended to let citizens understand the role and functioning of government, the court concluded that purpose "is not fostered by disclosure of information about private citizens that is accumulated in various governmental

files but that reveals little or nothing about an agency's own conduct." The Court therefore determined that in cases of this sort—where one citizen is seeking information about another citizen and the requester does not intend to discover anything about the agency in possession of the record—the disclosure is unwarranted. The Court admitted that information about Medico was of public interest, but found that such an interest "falls outside the ambit of the public interest that the FOIA was enacted to serve." Again, if the media had found conviction records about Medico at the courthouse and published the information therein, he would have no valid privacy tort claim against the media, as the information would be newsworthy and a matter of public record. The Court merely found that the media cannot use the FOIA to obtain the information. Three courts have also applied Exemption 7(C) to mug shots. The courts have found that privacy interests can, in some circumstances, outweigh the interest in disclosure. In *Detroit Free Press, Inc. v. U.S. Dept. of Justice*, the Sixth Circuit overruled its own prior decision that had found no privacy interest in mug shots. Instead, the court ruled that "[b]ooking photos—snapped 'in the vulnerable and embarrassing moments immediately after [an individual is] accused, taken into custody, and deprived of most liberties'—fit squarely within [the] realm of embarrassing and humiliating information." In the new decision, the court noted that times had changed and that the Exemption 7(C) privacy interest "must be understood … in light of the consequences that would follow" from disclosure. Modern technology heightens the consequences insofar as material is archived online in perpetuity, meaning that a person can never escape the past. The court was also influenced by the fact that there are websites devoted to collecting and displaying mug shots. And, importantly, the court noted that both the Tenth Circuit, in *World Pub. Co. v. U.S. Dept. of Justice*, and the Eleventh Circuit, in *Karantsalis v. U.S. Dept. of Justice*, had determined that Exemption 7(C) should allow agencies to withhold mug shots. Therefore, the Sixth Circuit ruled that requests for such records should be considered on a case-by-case basis, allowing the government to withhold them when they believe privacy interests so require.

8. Banking Reports. This exemption applies to information "contained in or related to examination, operating, or condition reports prepared by, or on behalf of, or for the use of an agency responsible for the regulation or supervision of financial institutions." The legislative history of the exemption suggests that it is designed to promote openness and honesty between bank employees and examiners, and also to protect financial institutions from the release of honest evaluations about their stability. Thus, records that might harm those interests could be withheld under exemption eight.

9. Information about Wells. Probably the least used of the FOIA exemptions, exemption nine covers "geological and geophysical information and data, including maps, concerning wells." The legislative history of this exemption suggests that Congress intended to protect the oil and gas industry from unfair competition, but the exemption has been applied to other kinds of information. In *Starkey v. U.S. Dept. of the Interior*, for example, the exemption was applied to records about water wells. In any event, the exemption exists and may apply where the records sought involve wells and disclosure may cause harm.

WHAT CAN YOU DO IF THE GOVERNMENT IGNORES OR DENIES YOUR REQUEST?

If the agency denies your request, whether in whole or in part, it should tell you why it is denying your request. In most cases, the agency will deny a request because the request is invalid for some reason, such as failing to specify an identifiable record, or because an exemption applies, in which case, the agency should specify which exemption applies. If the requester believes his request was improperly denied, he should appeal to the agency. Each agency has different deadlines for its administrative appeal, so it is important to figure out what the deadline is and comply. A requester must exhaust all administrative remedies before a lawsuit can be filed, so the administrative appeal would be required before filing suit.

The exception to that rule is that if the agency simply ignores your request, a requester may sue claiming "constructive denial," which means that the failure of the agency to respond in any way is the equivalent of a denial and a denied appeal.

Once a suit is filed, the parties will go through the discovery process and litigate the dispute, just like any other case. Then the court will determine whether the agency acted properly or not. If the requester wins the suit, the court can order the government to pay attorney fees and costs. Under the OPEN Government Act of 2007, agencies can be compelled to pay attorneys fees if an agency changes its position and suddenly turns over the requested documents after a lawsuit is filed. The provision is designed to prevent agencies from acting disingenuously.

There are two special kinds of denials that sometimes come up in cases where the documents sought involve national security or some other highly sensitive subject matter. A requester might get what is called a "Glomar response," which is when the government refuses to admit or deny the existence of a record. Also, under certain circumstances, the government can state that "no records responsive to the FOIA request exist." This provision applies to certain law enforcement records if (1) there is a criminal investigation or proceeding and the subject doesn't know it yet; (2) a third party requests records about an unconfirmed informant according to the informant's name/identifier; or (3) a request is made to the FBI for classified information about foreign intelligence, counterintelligence, or international terrorism. These provisions allow the government to avoid disclosing sensitive information without having to directly lie about their existence. In either case, the requester may appeal and sue if he is unhappy with the agency's decision, but because these responses are given in extremely sensitive situations, it is highly unlikely that the requester will prevail.

Another resource for requesters who are unhappy with the responses they've received is the Office of Government Information Services (OGIS). OGIS was established by Congress as part of the OPEN Government Act of 2007 to be the federal FOIA ombudsman. The agency serves as a bridge between FOIA requesters and the agencies, smoothing the communication process by mediating any disputes that arise. They are also authorized to report to Congress on the agencies' FOIA compliance and recommend policy changes. Requesters who would like help can easily request assistance from OGIS through the agency's website, ogis.archives.gov.

SUNSHINE ACT OF 1976

The Sunshine Act provides public access to meetings of agencies that are subject to FOIA. Agencies must place a notice of meetings in the Federal Register at least a week in advance. If the agency plans to close a meeting, it must provide reasons in advance. Meeting should be open unless one of ten exemptions applies. Seven are very similar to FOIA exemptions, and three are unique.

Meetings can be closed if there are discussions about:

1. National security

2. Agency rules

3. Matters exempt from other laws

4. Confidential business information

5. Personal privacy

6. Law enforcement investigations

7. Banking reports

8. Accusations of criminal activity

9. Regulation of financial institutions

10. The issuance of a subpoena or pending lawsuit

In many cases, it is not necessary to close the entire meeting. In *Philadelphia Newspapers, Inc. v. Nuclear Regulatory Comm'n*, the court clarified that a whole meeting may not be closed if only a small portion of the meeting is covered by an exemption. The sensitive discussions can be closed while the remainder of the meeting remains open to the public. If any meetings are closed, the agency must make a transcript of the closed proceedings, and people can sue for disclosure of the transcript if the meeting was improperly closed.

Federal Legislature

Although Congress passed the Freedom of Information Act (FOIA) to provide a right of access to federal agency records and the Sunshine Act to give citizens a right of access to federal agency meetings, it exempted itself from the laws. There is therefore no law or court decision that gives citizens a right of access to Congressional records or meetings.

Nevertheless, members of Congress seem to understand that they are the representatives of the citizens and that access to documents and hearings are important for the purposes of transparency and communicating to their constituency. They are therefore usually pretty good about keeping hearings open to the public or providing documents upon request. However, they are not required to do so. If Congress closes a hearing or refuses to hand out information, there is little recourse except to appeal to their conscience—or to their political opponents, who may be willing to turn over the information if they have it and it is not otherwise illegal to do so.

State Laws

Every state has its own law for open records and open meetings of state agencies. Some states' laws also cover their legislature, but others don't. Some states require written requests, others will let a requester show up at an agency and ask to see records in person. Each state is different, both in terms of the procedures required for and the rules governing disclosure. One must therefore look at the law for the state where one wants to access records. The Reporters Committee for Freedom of the Press provides a state-by-state compilation of laws called the Open Government Guide, which is an excellent reference and readily available on the organization's website (www.rcfp.org).

The kinds of records state agencies would possess include police records, autopsy records, 911 calls, and other records that would be useful for news reporting. While states may generally make these kinds of records available to the public, they have many exemptions that allow agencies to withhold them. In particular, states try to balance the privacy interests of people identified in the records against the public interest in disclosure. Whether one can access 911 calls, for example, perfectly illustrates the intersection of transparency and confidentiality. States have taken different approaches in striking a balance. In Indiana, 911 calls are presumed to be public records. South Dakota requires a finding that "the public interest in disclosure outweighs interest in nondisclosure." Wyoming completely exempts them from disclosure. Thus, the ability to obtain recordings of 911 calls will depend on the law and procedures of the state that holds the records. Moreover, as 911 calls often contain intimate snapshots of harrowing moments, many states provide for the redaction of private information from the recordings before release to the public.

Much like 911 audio recordings, autopsy reports often contain a mixture of important public information and disconcerting private details. Therefore, with a number of exceptions, states avoid making these reports public record, instead adopting their own variations on the disclosure process in order to maintain some level of discretion regarding dissemination of the reports. For example, California applies the exception that the report will not be released if it was compiled for law enforcement purposes, Washington, DC requires that a person possess a "legitimate interest" in order to gain access to the reports, and Washington state declares these records to be confidential. Each state has its own rules governing whether such records can be accessed.

In recent years, one of the most interesting questions has been whether police body camera footage should be available as a public record. In general, body camera footage could be subject to disclosure as they are a part of the official records made by local police departments. However, body camera footage may depict sensitive material that raises privacy concerns for those depicted, which often compels police departments to redact the footage before releasing it. Footage depicting an ongoing investigation may also be restricted, subject to a balancing test between public interest and impairment of the investigation. Again, access to such materials would be governed by the relevant state law, and the states vary. For example, Oklahoma passed a bill that allows for the release of police body camera footage unless the footage depicts death or the infliction of serious bodily harm that was not caused by the law enforcement officer. On the other hand, California considers body camera footage to be "evidence" and therefore exempt under the California Records act. Overall, local regulations regarding the release of body camera footage strive to strike a balance between public interest in transparency and privacy. The Reporters Committee has created a map (available at https://www.rcfp.org/resources/bodycams/) that shows how different states have treated the issue and is an excellent resource for those who are interested in whether such footage can be obtained.

Like the federal government, states contract with private companies to provide services, and courts have not always interpreted the state laws to apply to third parties. For example, in *Oriana House v. Montgomery*, the court ruled that a private correctional facility under contract with the state was not subject to the state public records act.

Interestingly, some state officials have argued that being required to comply with state access laws is an infringement of the official's First Amendment rights because it forces them to disclose information. It is a traditional principle that both banning speech and compelling speech can violate the First Amendment, and thus, they argue that access laws are a form of compelled speech. So far, courts have held that state access laws do not infringe the First Amendment. In *Asgeirsson v. Abbott*, for example, the court upheld provisions of the Texas Open Meetings Law and decided that the law does not violate the officials' First Amendment rights.

Some states limit records requests only to residents of the state. Virginia's Freedom of Information Act, for example, specifies that "public records shall be open to inspection and copying by any citizens of the Commonwealth." Requests are therefore denied when the requestor is out of state. This practice was challenged as unconstitutional, but the U.S. Supreme Court ruled that it is not. In *McBurney v. Young*, the Court ruled that access to public records is not a "fundamental" right that would create a claim under the Privileges and Immunities Clause of the Constitution and therefore affirmed the right of states to limit requests to citizens of the state. There are a handful of states that have such restrictions.

Judicial Branch

Although access to executive branch records is governed by statute, access to the judicial branch is generally governed by case law. Courts have ruled that there is a First Amendment right of access to court proceedings and a common law right of access to court documents. However, the courts will sometimes permit restrictions on access, either by closing courtrooms, sealing documents, placing a gag order on participants, or otherwise restricting access to proceedings. This section will discuss how those principles have been applied to the following issues:

1. Access to criminal proceedings

2. Access to civil proceedings

3. Access to juvenile proceedings

4. Access to military proceedings

5. Access to Alternative Dispute Resolution (ADR)

6. Access to court records and electronic court records

7. Access to discovery documents

8. Pretrial publicity and gag orders

9. Use of cameras and other technology in the courtroom

10. Social media use in the courtroom

11. Access to juror names and identities

12. Access to jurors (prohibitions on juror contact)

13. How the press would challenge a restrictive order.

ACCESS TO CRIMINAL PROCEEDINGS

In *Richmond Newspapers v. Virginia*, the Supreme Court established a First Amendment right of access to criminal proceedings. The Court noted several policy reasons why the public should have access to criminal proceedings; mostly, because it enhances the credibility of the courts. If the public has access to the testimony and evidence presented, it can have faith that the system is not corrupt and that decisions are not being made unfairly. The Court also noted that the press acts as a surrogate for the public who can't get to the trial. Thus, the Court concluded that if a court is going to close a courtroom, it must make findings to explain why closure is necessary, and alternative solutions must be considered first.

Since *Richmond Newspapers*, the Court has ruled in favor of granting access to sensitive testimony, jury selection, and pretrial hearings. In fact, in every case that has come before the Supreme Court on the issue of access to criminal proceedings, the Court ruled in favor of openness:

- In *Globe Newspaper Co. v. Superior Court*, the Court held that a statute mandating closure of courtrooms during minor victims' testimony was unconstitutional.

- In *Press Enterprise Co. v. Superior Court* (*Press Enterprise I*), the Court reversed a California state court's closure of voir dire.

- In *Waller v. Georgia*, the Court held that the closure of a criminal suppression hearing was overbroad and unconstitutional.

- In *Press Enterprise Co. v. Superior Court* (*Press Enterprise II*), the Court held that there was a qualified right of access to pretrial hearings, noting that First Amendment scrutiny must be applied and establishing a test to be used to determine when closure might be proper.

- In *El Vocero de Puerto Rico v. Puerto Rico*, the Court found that closure of a preliminary hearing was unconstitutional.

The right of access should apply regardless of whether the hearing is held in a courtroom or elsewhere. In *Boston Herald v. Superior Court*, the court held that the right of access will apply even when a suspect is arraigned in a hospital room.

Although there is a presumptive right of access to criminal proceedings, a judge may close a courtroom under certain circumstances. The Supreme Court set forth a two-part test for determining when closure might be appropriate in *Press Enterprise II*.

First, the court must determine whether there is a presumptive right of access to the proceedings, taking into consideration both experience and logic. With respect to experience, the question is whether the type of proceeding at issue has historically been open to the public. With respect to logic, the question is whether openness would play a positive role in the functioning of the process. Most proceedings have been historically open, and logic usually suggests that openness helps facilitate smooth proceedings for the reasons set forth in *Richmond Newspapers*. Thus, in most cases, the courts find that there is a presumptive right of access.

Second, if there is a presumptive right of access, the court must determine whether there is an interest would require closure. The Court said, "[p]roceedings cannot be closed unless specific, on the record findings are made demonstrating that 'closure is essential to preserve higher values and is narrowly tailored to serve that interest.'"

An example of a higher value is national security. Sometimes, court proceedings are closed when classified information is used at trial. But, in such cases, the closure should be limited only to the portion in which the sensitive information is discussed; it is usually not necessary to close the entire trial.

After September 11th, 2001, two courts considered the constitutionality of the federal government's blanket closure order on deportation proceedings. The government had detained numerous men whose visas had expired, and argued that national security concerns required secrecy in these proceedings. If terrorists could follow the cases, the government argued, they might gather valuable information about the status of potential operatives; and, since the U.S. did not know who the operatives might be, all proceedings should be closed out of caution.

Both courts applied the *Press Enterprise II* test, but came to different results. In *North Jersey Media Group v. Ashcroft*, the Third Circuit found that the experience and logic test did not require a presumptive right of access to deportation proceedings. Such proceedings were relatively new in the nation's history and lacked the long history of openness that other kinds of proceedings had. Also, logic suggested that there was a potential threat to having such proceedings open if, in fact, there were secret operatives in the United States. But regardless of whether there was a presumptive right, the court found that national security was an interest that required complete closure.

In *Detroit Free Press v. Ashcroft*, the Sixth Circuit came to the opposite conclusion. It found that deportation proceedings were like any other kind of proceeding, and that history and logic indicated that there should be a presumptive right of access. Although national security might be a higher interest that could justify closure, the government failed to meet the burden of showing that total closure of all proceedings was justified. Closure orders must be narrowly tailored, and a blanker order was not in any way "narrowly tailored." The government could seek closure in cases where there was some evidence that national security could be compromised.

The deportation cases illustrate the point that courts can come to different conclusions and that cases can generally be argued on both sides. There are no guarantees that a court will agree with a particular viewpoint, even if it seems like the law should be clear.

Another important interest that can result in closure is the defendant's Sixth Amendment right to a fair trial. If the defendant argues that openness will impair his rights, the court must make specific findings that show a substantial probability of prejudice to a fair trial; that closure would prevent such prejudice; and that reasonable alternatives would be insufficient.

Aside from closure orders, the other exception to the general principle of openness is that grand jury proceedings are secret. Restrictions have been allowed on the disclosure of information obtained during grand jury proceedings; however, witnesses are generally permitted to discuss their own testimony if they wish. In *Butterworth v. Smith*, the Court determined that the government could not show a compelling interest sufficient to justify prohibiting a grand jury witness from disseminating information about his testimony after the grand jury had concluded its investigation. Thus, in the absence of a compelling interest, witnesses may speak at their own discretion.

ACCESS TO CIVIL PROCEEDINGS

The Supreme Court has never addressed the question of whether there is a right of access to civil proceedings, but courts have assumed that the right of access described in *Richmond Newspapers* applies equally to civil proceedings. As the court noted in *Grove Fresh Dist., Inc. v. Everfresh Juice Co.*, courts have extended the right of access to civil proceedings, because "the contribution of publicity" is equally as important in civil cases as it is in criminal cases. The importance of transparency and fairness does not diminish merely because the potential penalty to the defendant is likely to be the payment of money damages rather than jail. Thus, courts apply the test set forth in *Press Enterprise II* in civil cases as well as criminal ones.

ACCESS TO JUVENILE PROCEEDINGS

The Supreme Court has also never ruled on whether there is a right of access to juvenile proceedings. For now, the issue is covered by state statutes or court rules. Some states require open proceedings, some states require closed proceedings, and some states leave each case to the discretion of the judge. Nevertheless, it is generally understood that if the press learns information about a juvenile proceeding, it is free to publish it. In *Oklahoma Pub. Co. v. District Court*, the Supreme Court reversed a prior restraint on the publication of a juvenile murder suspect's name and photo, because the press lawfully obtained the information during court proceedings and because prior restraints are disfavored. The fact that the murder suspect was a minor was, in itself, an insufficient basis for restricting speech. Also, in *Smith v. Daily Mail Pub. Co.*, the Court held that it would be unconstitutional to charge the press with a crime for printing the name of juvenile offender. Again, the fact that a minor is involved, in itself, is an insufficient basis for punishing speech. Thus, a person may or may not have a right of access to juvenile proceedings, depending on state law; but the use of any information lawfully obtained may be protected by the First Amendment.

ACCESS TO MILITARY PROCEEDINGS

The Supreme Court has never directly ruled on whether there is a right of access to military proceedings. However, military courts usually permit access. The Rule for Courts-Martial 806(b) states that military courts are presumptively open to the public; however, they may be closed if classified evidence is used or if there are other security concerns. In *ABC, Inc. v. Powell*, a military court acknowledged that there is a First Amendment right of access to military proceedings, but that right accrues to the "public," and there is no special right of access for the press.

ACCESS TO ALTERNATIVE DISPUTE RESOLUTION (ADR)

The Supreme Court has never ruled on whether there is a presumptive right of access to ADR, which includes settlements, mediation, and arbitration. However, these kinds of proceedings are almost always coordinated by private parties, even if they are required by a court. Thus, there is probably no right of access to such proceedings, because they would be considered private events, not government proceedings.

However, even if the press does not have a right of access to ADR proceedings, it may be able to access documents, such as settlement agreements or arbitration decisions, in some circumstances. The press has the best chance of getting a document if (1) it is filed with a court, because then it becomes a court record, or (2) a party is a state agency and the state open records law allows for access to settlement agreements.

ACCESS TO COURT RECORDS AND ELECTRONIC COURT RECORDS

In *Nixon v. Warner Comm.*, the Supreme Court recognized a right of access to court records, which includes pleadings, motions, evidence, and other documents or materials held by a court. The Court said that the right was based on "common law," meaning that access to court documents has been a traditional aspect of the U.S. court system. Several federal circuit courts have also found a right of access to court records based on the same First Amendment principles that apply to access to proceedings. Regardless of the source of the right, it is pretty clear that court records should be presumptively open to the public. Thus, in most instances, any person should be able to go to a courthouse and request a copy of a record from a court file.

In September of 2001, the federal judiciary permitted electronic access to most civil court records. At the time, they excluded criminal records from electronic access, although some access to such files is now permitted. To get access to federal records electronically, one must use the PACER system, which requires a subscription. State records are sometimes available electronically, depending on state rules, but access varies substantially. Wisconsin, for example, has a very useful website that allows users to search for records, but West Virginia has no electronic access at all.

Although there is a presumptive right of access to court records, a judge may seal certain documents or files, if necessary. Rules of procedure usually permit a party to request a sealing order where there is "good cause." A party will file a motion, and if there are no objections, and if the judge determines there is good cause, the file may be sealed. Parties will often request sealing orders simply because a document contains sensitive or embarrassing information, and judges tend to grant them. However, the press can challenge sealing orders.

Many courts have found that when the press challenges a sealing order, it is proper to use the test set forth in *Press Enterprise II*. Thus, a court will determine whether there is a higher interest to protect and whether the order is narrowly tailored. If the entire document need not be sealed, courts can release a document with redactions of sensitive information.

Although grand jury proceedings are typically secret, it may be possible to request grand jury transcripts, as court records, once the secrecy interest in them has expired. In *Carlson v. U.S.*, the Seventh Circuit considered whether to provide a historian access to grand jury records from the World War II era. The court noted that the grand jury is part of the judicial process, and therefore its "minutes and transcripts" are court records to which the public would have a presumptive right to request access. Rule 6(e) of the Federal Rules of Criminal Procedure gives a trial judge discretion over whether grand jury materials should be disclosed. The Rule identifies particular situations in which the court may disclose records, but the court found that the list was not intended to be exclusive. The court retains the authority to release them when in the interests of justice. In this case, because the secrecy interest in the records had long since passed, the circuit court found that the trial court did have the authority to release the records.

ACCESS TO DISCOVERY DOCUMENTS

Discovery documents are not necessarily court records. They are private documents gathered by the parties to the case. There is therefore no right of access to most discovery documents. However, if a discovery document is filed with the court to be used as evidence, then it becomes a court record and may be accessed unless it is subject to a sealing order.

A party or an attorney may voluntarily give the press a discovery document, but they have no obligation to do so. Sometimes a court will issue a protective order that prohibits parties or attorneys from disseminating material gathered during discovery and subjects them to penalties if they do. The press may challenge the protective order. If the protective order is lifted, then the party or attorney may provide the records, but they are still not required to do so.

Also, if the press is a party to a lawsuit and obtains discovery documents only because of its status as a party to the suit, the court can impose a protective order to prevent publication of the information, just as it could against any other party to a suit. This was the case in *Seattle Times v. Rhinehart*, where the Court ruled that the newspaper could not publish information it had obtained during the course of the lawsuit in which it was involved. This is an exception to the general rule that prior restraints against the press are usually unconstitutional.

PRETRIAL PUBLICITY AND GAG ORDERS

Courts have long had mixed feeling about the press. On one hand, the press is vital to the task of keeping the public informed about matter of public concern, which includes trials and proceedings. On the other hand, there are some cases where media coverage becomes so pervasive that courts fear that they won't be able to properly manage the case.

The classic example of the latter instance is *Sheppard v. Maxwell*. That case involved a high-profile murder, and it is often cited as the inspiration for the television show *The Fugitive*. The coverage of the case was considered a media circus, and the Supreme Court ruled that the pervasive pretrial publicity prevented Dr. Sheppard from getting a fair trial. Although *Sheppard* is often cited as a case concerning media rights, media rights weren't really threatened in any way. It was taken for granted that the media had a right to cover the trial, and the Court never punished the press. The Court's decision affected only the defendant's conviction and discussed strategies courts could use to avoid prejudicial publicity.

Courts are greatly concerned with ensuring that the defendant gets a fair trial. They want to avoid any publicity that might be prejudicial. Pretrial publicity is prejudicial if jurors are so biased that they cannot set aside their preconceived notions and decide a case solely on evidence presented at trial.

However, "unbiased" does not mean "uninformed." Jurors can know about the case, they just can't have made up their minds already. Courts cannot enjoin the press, so they use other means of counteracting any potentially prejudicial pretrial publicity. There are several alternate means of providing an unbiased jury, such as change of venue, voir dire, sequestering the jury, importing a jury, delaying trial, and admonishing jurors—and these efforts are often sufficient to ensure a fair trial. For example, in *Skilling v. U.S.*, the high-profile criminal trial against former Enron executive Jeffrey Skilling, the Court found that the use of voir dire gave sufficient protection to pick an unbiased jury, even though there was widespread pretrial publicity.

One tactic that courts sometimes use is to impose gag orders. Gag orders directly on the press—ordering them not to publish information about a case—are usually struck down as unconstitutional. In *Nebraska Press Assoc. v. Stuart*, the Supreme Court reinforced the idea that prior restraints should not be imposed, finding that a gag order on the press was unconstitutional. An important factor in the case was that there was no solid proof of prejudice to a fair trial. The assertion that media coverage would harm the defendant's rights was merely speculative. The Court also noted that alternatives to a prior restraint should always be considered first. A court can change the venue, engage in voir dire, sequester the jury, import a jury, delay trial, and/or admonish jurors concerning their responsibility to be unbiased. These steps should minimize or eliminate any risk of prejudice to the defendant.

U.S. v. Noriega is a rare case that allowed a prior restraint. The case involved the criminal prosecution of Manuel Noriega, who had been the leader of Panama. He was captured when the United States invaded Panama in 1989 and was tried in the United States on charges related to international drug trafficking. In that case, the court barred the press from broadcasting tapes that had been made of conversations between Manuel Noriega and his attorneys until the court could review the tapes. The court was likely concerned with preserving attorney-client privilege. In essence, the court concluded that the potential harm to Noriega was not merely speculative. The waiver of his rights with respect to confidential communications with his lawyers would cause serious and irreparable harm. It is one of the few cases where a court found that there was a compelling interest to protect, and the ban on publication was the only way to protect the interest.

The more difficult question that arises is whether it is unconstitutional for a court to issue a gag order on trial participants, such as attorneys, parties, witnesses, or others, barring them from speaking with the press. A gag order on the source of information has the same effect as a prior restraint: information does not get to the public.

The Supreme Court has not yet decided a case involving a court's gag order on trial participants. The closest case is *Gentile v. State Bar of Nevada*, which involved the interpretation of a state bar association rule that prohibited lawyers from making statements to the press if the lawyer "knows or reasonably should know" that the statement would have a "substantial likelihood of material prejudice" on a proceeding. Although the Court struck down aspects of the Nevada rule for being vague, the Court found that the "substantial likelihood of material prejudice" standard reflected the appropriate balance between the First Amendment interest of the speaker and the state's interest in protecting the integrity of trials.

Some lower courts have upheld gag orders on trial participants using similar tests. In *U.S. v. Brown*, for example, the court held that a court may impose a gag order on parties and other trial participants if it determines that their speech would present a "substantial likelihood" of prejudicing the court's ability to conduct a fair trial. The court then concluded that there was a substantial likelihood of prejudice because there was widespread media coverage of the trial, and the parties had "demonstrated a desire to manipulate media coverage to gain favorable attention."

Thus, although prior restraints are disfavored and are almost always unconstitutional when applied to the press, there are cases where courts uphold gag orders on trial participants if it seems justified to preserve the court's ability to conduct a fair trial.

USE OF CAMERAS AND OTHER TECHNOLOGY IN COURTROOMS

Cameras, whether for photos or video, have been considered a disruptive element at court proceedings. One of the primary concerns in *Sheppard* was the presence of cameras, including the intimidating effect they may have had on witnesses and the distraction they caused during the trial. Some felt that the presence of cameras, on its own, was enough to prejudice a defendant's right to a fair trial. Courts often banned cameras from the courtroom for fear that they would create a prejudicial distraction.

Then, in the 1980 case *Chandler v. Florida*, the Supreme Court held that camera coverage is not necessarily prejudicial and gave states permission to craft their own rules regarding cameras in the courtroom. Many of the historical concerns about camera coverage had to do with their size and the amount of lighting required; but as cameras have gotten smaller and less obtrusive, those concerns have diminished. Also, courts have noticed that other concerns or fears about camera coverage have turned out to be unfounded. Judges are often concerned that the presence of cameras will cause lawyers to put on a show or cause witnesses to edit themselves too much. While the now-notorious O. J. Simpson trial is Exhibit A for those who express this concern, there is a lot of anecdotal evidence that such behavior is a rarity. Cameras usually have no effect on participants or proceedings, except that they might try to behave better than normal, knowing that they are being recorded.

But the fact that cameras *could* be permitted doesn't mean they *will* be permitted. In state courts, the question is usually left to the discretion of the judge. All states have rules that govern when cameras may be permitted, and judges typically have some discretion and authority to determine when and where they will be permitted.

The federal courts have taken a different approach. The Supreme Court has refused to allow cameras in any of its proceedings. It does, however, make audio recordings of oral arguments and those recordings are publicly available. Federal appellate courts may allow cameras at their own discretion. The Second, the Third, and the Ninth Circuits have adopted rules that allow camera coverage, and audio recordings of arguments are often available in all of the circuits. With respect to federal trial courts, the judiciary created a pilot project, which ran from June 2011 to July 2015. Fourteen trial courts recorded proceedings and made them available online. After studying the results, the federal judiciary affirmed its policy for trial courts, which reads:

> A judge may authorize broadcasting, televising, recording, or taking photographs in the courtroom and in adjacent areas during investitive, naturalization, or other ceremonial proceedings. A judge may autho-rize such activities in the courtroom or adjacent areas during other proceedings, or recesses between such other proceedings, only:
>
> 1) for the presentation of evidence;
>
> 2) for the perpetuation of the record of the proceedings;

3) for security purposes;

4) for other purposes of judicial administration;

5) for the photographing, recording, or broadcasting of appellate arguments; or

6) in accordance with pilot programs approved by the Judicial Conference.

When broadcasting, televising, recording, or photographing in the courtroom or adjacent areas is permitted, a judge should ensure that it is done in a manner that will:

1) be consistent with the rights of the parties,

2) not unduly distract participants in the proceeding, and

3) not otherwise interfere with the administration of justice.

Thus, at this time, there is no affirmative right to use a camera in a courtroom, but cameras may be allowed if permitted by law and allowed by the presiding judge.

SOCIAL MEDIA USE IN THE COURTROOM

A hot topic is whether courts can limit social media use during a proceeding, and the answer so far seems to be yes. The first kind of limit the courts impose is on social media use by jurors. Jurors are given instructions at the beginning of a trial, and such instructions usually require that they avoid news media, lest they see any coverage of the trial that improperly sways their verdict. Courts are beginning to expand their instructions to avoid use of social media, particularly Facebook and Twitter, prohibiting jurors from commenting about the case as it proceeds and from exchanging information with "friends." In particular, courts do not want jurors to "friend" each other during the trial and have conversations outside of the deliberation room. There are also ethical issues raised by the friending of jurors by judges and lawyers. Improper use of social media by a juror can result in a mistrial or an overturned conviction. In *Dimas-Martinez v. State of Arkansas*, for example, a court overturned a conviction because of juror use of social media. The court ruled that social media use constituted "juror misconduct," which impairs the integrity of the proceeding.

Courts have also imposed restrictions on journalists, ordering them not to tweet or post directly from the courtroom. (Some judges do allow tweeting, blogging, or other in-court communication, but other have restricted it.) There are no cases yet interpreting whether such rules violate the First Amendment, but on their face, rules of such nature appear to be classic prior restraints, which should not be permitted absent a compelling government interest and unless the rule is applied in a narrowly tailored fashion, prohibiting only the minimum amount of communication required to serve any valid compelling interest.

ACCESS TO JUROR NAMES AND IDENTITIES

Historically, jurors have not been anonymous. In colonial times, jurors were members of the community, and in many cases they already knew the defendant. In the modern era, jurors must not already know the defendant, they are citizens of the community doing a public service, and their names are read in court. The first instance of an anonymous jury, used in *U.S. v. Barnes*, did not occur until 1977 at the trial of a notorious drug dealer in New York.

Anonymous juries have since been considered a possible remedy in extreme circumstances, usually when the defendant is notoriously violent, has ties to organized crime, or has a history of jury tampering. However, in *Gannett Co. v. Delaware*, the court upheld the use of an anonymous jury merely for the sake of juror privacy. In high-profile cases, jurors are often sought by the media, and many jurors are upset by the intrusion.

Courts are also concerned about the implication of using anonymity in only some cases, because it leaves the impression that the defendant is dangerous, which can prejudice the jurors. In *Massachusetts v. Angiulo*, a court overturned a conviction because the judge failed to ensure that the jury wouldn't be prejudiced by the fact of their anonymity. Some believe the solution is to make all juries anonymous so there is no prejudicial implication, but such a rule would be in violation of the presumptive right of access to juror names.

As a practical matter, what often happens is that a judge will grant anonymity to a jury out of concern for their safety or privacy, and then it is up to the press to challenge it. But despite concerns about juror privacy, many courts acknowledge that transparency in the court system is crucial to the public's trust in the system, and therefore juror names, and even hometowns, can be made public. In *U.S. v. Chin*, the First Circuit reaffirmed the principle that "the identities of the jurors 'must be made public' after a verdict is rendered, unless the Court makes 'particularized findings reasonably justifying nondisclosure.'" In *Chin*, WBUR sought access to the identities of jurors in a criminal trial, but the trial court did not want to release their names and addresses, reasoning that nondisclosure was a "necessary precaution in an age in which traditional boundaries of personal privacy are under assault." The appeals court, however, noted that "[k]nowledge of juror identities allows the public to verify the impartiality of key participants in the administration of justice, and thereby ensures fairness, the appearance of fairness and public confidence in that system." While there are circumstances that would justify nondisclosure, such as a credible threat of jury tampering or a risk of personal harm to individual jurors, there were no particularized findings of such exceptional circumstances in this case. The court noted that the general rule favoring disclosure of juror identities was decided "decades ago and thus well before the first tweet was tweeted." The court also acknowledged, "there is now a greater potential for the public release of a juror's name, and, especially, a juror's address, to be more intrusive and concerning than would have been the case in an era in which social media was unknown." Nevertheless, the court concluded that "these technological changes have by no means diminished the need for accountability and transparency in our system of justice. ..." In the absence of particularized findings justifying nondisclosure, juror identities should be made available to ensure the integrity of the judicial system.

ACCESS TO JURORS (PROHIBITIONS ON JUROR CONTACT)

Even in cases where the identities of the jurors are known, there have been instances where judges have issued orders barring the press from interviewing jurors. The press cannot speak to jurors during the trial—that could be considered jury tampering. But the media traditionally have been allowed to interview jurors when the trial is over.

In a few high profile cases, judges have issued orders barring any juror interviews, ever. In 2001, the Fifth Circuit upheld an order that prevented the press from ever contacting any juror in a wrongful death lawsuit against Firestone Tires. A similar order was issued in the 2002 Texas murder trial of Andrea Yates, a mother who killed her children, and the New Jersey murder trial of Rabbi Neulander, who was accused of hiring a hit man to kill his wife. These kinds of orders are rare and have been issued only in a few high profile cases where the jurors have indicated that they do not want to be contacted.

Jurors have always had the option to simply decline to speak to the press when asked for an interview. There are therefore serious constitutional concerns about a court order that prevents the press from making any contact, but, so far, there have been no clear rulings about the scope of constitutional protection for the press in these kinds of cases. The Supreme Court has never addressed the issue.

HOW DOES THE PRESS CHALLENGE A RESTRICTIVE ORDER?

If the press wishes to challenge an order, whether a closure order, sealing order, gag order, or restriction on juror contact, the press must either intervene or seek a writ of mandamus. Which of the two procedures should be used depends on rules of the jurisdiction where the proceeding takes place.

Intervention is when the press asks the trial court for permission to become a party to the lawsuit for the limited purpose of challenging the order. The press may file briefs and appeal, just like any other party.

A writ of mandamus is, essentially, a request to an appellate court to issue an order telling the trial court to reverse its order.

If a restrictive order is issued, it is imperative to challenge the order in court rather than simply violate the order and hope it is later overturned. Judges have "contempt power" to punish people who violate court orders, including journalists. A journalist who violates an order can be held in contempt, resulting in jail time or fines, even if the original order is struck down as unconstitutional. Thus, it is important to challenge the order and not simply ignore it.

Specific Laws That Might Affect Your Ability to Access Particular Types of Information

There are several federal laws that specifically limit the ability of an entity to release certain kinds of information, all of which involve some notion of privacy. As a practical matter, these laws can affect the press' ability to gather information, although if the information is somehow obtained, they do not impose any limits on publication.

The Privacy Act of 1974

The Privacy Act of 1974 is a law that has two purposes. First, it gives people the right to obtain and amend government files containing personal information about themselves. Congress granted this right in response to concerns that federal agencies were compiling dossiers on dissidents. The law ensures both that such records will not be kept in secret and that there is an opportunity to correct any errors. Second, the law prohibits the government from using in an abusive way any information it has obtained. The government is supposed to use information only for specific, legitimate reasons, and it should otherwise limit the disclosure or use of personal information. If the government discloses information about a person improperly, the person may sue the government for damages.

The Family Educational Rights and Privacy Act

The Family Educational Rights and Privacy Act ("FERPA," a.k.a. the Buckley Amendment) prohibits federally funded educational institutions from releasing educational records without consent. First, it is important to note that, for the purposes of this law, "federally funded" means that the institution receives any federal funds at all, whether directly or indirectly. Colleges that allow students with federally supported student loans, for example, are considered federally funded for the purpose of FERPA. Thus, almost all schools in the United States are subject to the law. Second, it is important to note that the U.S. Supreme Court held in *Gonzaga Univ. v. Doe* that FERPA does not provide a private right of action. If a student's information is released without consent, he cannot sue the school. The only remedy is that the government has the option of withdrawing federal funds. Third, there is an issue of what constitutes educational records. Grades or assignments may certainly not be released without consent, but directory information may be released. Things like disciplinary records might be protected, depending on where and how they are kept. Finally, there is the question of whose consent must be obtained to release the records. Until the student is 18, the parent must consent. However, after that, only the individual student can consent; parents can no longer obtain their child's records. There has been a lot of controversy over whether schools use FERPA as an excuse not to disclose information that could be embarrassing to the school. Courts, however, have rejected schools' claims when they are challenged. In *DTH Media Corp. v. Folt*, a court found that the University of North Carolina could not use FERPA as an excuse to withhold sexual assault-related disciplinary records. Similarly, in a 2018 opinion, the Kentucky Attorney General determined that Kentucky State University was required to disclose disciplinary reports about a professor's alleged misconduct and could not use FERPA as an excuse to keep the records secret. Nevertheless, journalists often have to sue to disgorge such records, as schools often do not voluntarily release them.

The Driver's Privacy Protection Act

The Driver's Privacy Protection Act (DPPA) is a federal law that was passed after high-profile incident where an actress was murdered by a stalker who got her address from the DMV. Prior to the DPPA, it was possible to obtain a driver's address from the DMV. The law now prohibits states from releasing personal information in DMV records without consent. It does not restrict disclosure of information about accidents, driving violations, suspended licenses, or similar matter; it only restricts personal information such as name, address, social security number, height, and weight. It should be noted, however, that the media may be civilly liable if it somehow does obtain such information. In *Dahlstrom v. Sun Times Media, LLC*, a newspaper obtained the birthdate, height, weight, hair color, and eye color of several police officers from the Illinois motor vehicle records, and they used that information in a story that criticized a homicide investigation lineup in which the officers participated. The officers sued the paper, because the DPPA provides a private right of action to anyone whose personal information is obtained. The court noted that the law makes it unlawful for "any person knowingly to obtain or disclose personal information" from a motor vehicle record and found that there is no exception for journalists under the First Amendment. Citing the Privacy Act and cases that restrict access to prisons, the court concluded that the First Amendment does not require access to particular information held by the government and that the safety rationale behind the law was sufficient to justify the restrictions on obtaining or disclosing personal information.

The Health Insurance Portability and Accountability Act

The Health Insurance Portability and Accountability Act (HIPAA) prohibits health care providers from releasing protected information such as medical records without the consent of the patient. The law applies to health care providers and their business associates only. It does not apply to law enforcement or other entities. For example, in *Abbott v. Texas Department of Mental Health and Mental Retardation*, the court found that HIPPA does not bar the state from releasing statistical information concerning abuse allegations at state facilities. Also, the law does not apply to journalists. HIPAA affects journalists in the sense that it can create barriers to obtaining medical information from health care providers, but it imposes no restrictions on journalists if they obtain the information. However, journalists should be aware that the publication of medical information can give rise to a privacy lawsuit as a matter of tort law, and should therefore think carefully about whether publication of the information would give rise to a claim.

Rules That Govern Access to Places and Events

Is There a Right of Access to News Scenes?

The press does not have a special right of access to news scenes. If there is a fire, crime scene, accident, or other newsworthy event, reporters and photographers can try to obtain access to the scene, but they are subject to the same rules as any other member of the public, and they must obey whatever safety rules are established by officials.

If a reporter or photographer disobeys an order to move, he can be arrested. The charges usually consist of trespass, obstruction of justice, disorderly conduct, or similar crimes. Courts have generally upheld these charges in cases such as *Durruthy v. Pastor*, finding that the press does not have special rights of access. However, *Connell v. Hudson*, the court ruled that it violates a photographer's First Amendment rights to restrict access to an accident scene any more than necessary to preserve order. Nevertheless, officials are usually granted wide latitude in determining what is necessary to preserve order.

As a practical matter, it is helpful to maintain good relationships with emergency personnel. Although they are not required to give the press special access to a news scene, they may. Reporters who have a reputation for professionalism and cooperation with emergency responders are often granted access as a courtesy. It is, however, not an enforceable right.

One case suggests that courts may be willing to grant greater First Amendment protection to newsworthy events that are controlled by government agencies. In *Leigh v. Salazar*, a photojournalist claimed that the Bureau of Land Management (BLM) violated her First Amendment rights by imposing restrictions on newsgathering during a wild horse roundup. The Ninth Circuit ruled that the *Press Enterprise II* test, originally applied to evaluate the closure of criminal court proceedings, has been used in a variety of contexts and should be applied to evaluate the propriety of the restrictions imposed by

BLM. If such reasoning is adopted more widely by the courts, it would give great protection to journalists in covering newsworthy events.

Is There a Right of Access to Press Conferences?

There are two issues with access to press conferences: (1) what is required to get a press pass or credential in the first place, and (2) can a politician deny access to a reporter because of his coverage?

Government entities are not required to give a press credential to anyone who asks. In *Los Angeles Free Press v. City of Los Angeles*, the court found that there is no affirmative right to a press credential. Government entities are permitted to restrict access to press conferences to ensure that the room is not overcrowded and to otherwise protect the safety of participants. However, there should be some policy that sets out procedures for granting and denying credentials to ensure that the government is acting fairly and not discriminating on the basis of viewpoint. In *Sherrill v. Knight*, the court ruled that a reporter can be denied White House press pass as long as there is a procedure followed for granting and denying passes.

The trickier question is whether a credentialed member of the press can be denied access because a politician is unhappy with the reporter's coverage. In *Borreca v. Fasi*, a reporter sued the mayor of Honolulu for denying him access to news conferences. The major felt that Borreca was "irresponsible, inaccurate, biased and malicious" in his reporting on the mayor. The mayor told the newspaper that any reporter other than Borreca would be welcome to attend.

The court found that "[r]equiring a newspaper's reporter to pass a subjective compatibility-accuracy test as a condition precedent to the right of that reporter to gather the news is no different in kind from requiring a newspaper to submit its proposed news stories for editing as a condition precedent to the right of that newspaper to have a reporter cover the news. Each is a form of censorship."

The court noted that the mayor need not hold any press conferences, nor was he required to answer any questions from Borreca. The mayor was also free to criticize Borreca's coverage. However, the reporter could not be barred from the conference absent a showing of a compelling interest, and the court ruled that the mayor had failed to show one.

Similarly, in *Westinghouse Broadcasting Co. v. Dukakis*, the court ruled that a politician could not deny a nonunion cameraman access to press conferences merely because the politician felt sympathy for the union in the midst of a labor dispute; such sympathy was not the kind of compelling interest to justify a denial of access.

However, in *Snyder v. Ringgold*, the court found that it was acceptable for a police department official to refuse to talk to a particular reporter. The court distinguished *Borreca*, because the facts of *Snyder* did not involve a press conference that was otherwise open to all members of the press. The case involved a particular reporter who attempted to make particular contacts within the police department and wanted what were essentially exclusive interviews rather than generally accessible information. Under such circumstances, the police had no obligation to accommodate the particular reporter.

Similarly, in *Youngstown Publishing Co. v. McKelvey*, the court found that the mayor's "no comment" policy was not a violation of the newspaper's rights. The mayor had no obligation to comment on stories or to provide information that was not generally available to the public. This principle was also applied in *The Baltimore Sun Co. v. Ehrlich*, a case where the politician was willing to speak to other reporters and simply blacklisted a particular reporter from comment.

The most recent case on the topic arose when the White House revoked the "hard pass" credential of CNN reporter Jim Acosta, because they thought he was "rude," "disrespectful," and asked too many questions, refusing to turn over the microphone when asked. CNN and Acosta sought an injunction to get Acosta's credential restored. The judge did not rule on First Amendment grounds, but correctly noted that the due process requirements of the Fifth Amendment required notice and an opportunity to be heard—neither of which occurred before the pass was revoked. Relying on *Sherrill v. Knight*, the court noted that the White House needed appropriate procedures in place before revoking credentials.

Thus, the courts seem to be inclined to allow politicians leeway in deciding to whom they will give comment, but access to otherwise public events cannot be denied absent a compelling interest, and government entities are required to follow basic due process procedures.

Is There a Right of Access to Government Social Media Accounts?

If government officials use social media accounts, may they block particular users? So far, the answer has been "no." The first case to address this issue was *Knight First Amendment Inst. at Columbia Univ. v. Trump*. President Trump blocked several users from his Twitter account because they used their accounts to criticize him. The users claimed that Trump had violated their First Amendment right to freedom of speech, because he had prevented them from viewing and responding to his tweets. The court agreed with the critics. A key factor was that the President blocked the users in response to the political views they expressed, which constituted "viewpoint discrimination." In addition, the court determined that this Twitter account was a public platform because President Trump, and not Twitter, maintained control over the content of the account. Trump argued that this was a private account, because he had created it in 2009, well before he became President. However, the court held that the present nature of the account is most dispositive, reasoning that, much like how a former military base that has been decommissioned and repurposed into a public park is intended for public use, this account is presently being used for a public, and not private, purpose. Finally, the court found that the content of the speech on this twitter account was related to public government affairs, indicating that government officials did not have the right to deny members of the public access to it.

Then, in *One Wisconsin Now v. Kremer*, a judge ruled that three government officials acted unconstitutionally by blocking One Wisconsin Now ("OWN"), a liberal advocacy group, on Twitter "because of its prior speech or identity." With its account blocked, OWN was unable to view the politicians' tweets or respond directly to the tweets with their opinions. The judge determined that, "by operating those accounts, (the politicians) chose to participate in an interactive forum open to the general public," meaning that the public had a First Amendment right to this information. The judge also elaborated that, "having opted to create a Twitter account … and benefit from its broad, public reach, defendants cannot now divorce themselves from its First Amendment implications and responsibilities as state actors." The politicians argued that Twitter was a private platform and that using Twitter was not an official part of their job, but the court rejected these arguments and held that their Twitter accounts were too heavily intertwined with their public capacity, noting that the accounts were "heavily swathed in the trappings of the office" and were used for official duties such as spreading information about legislation. The court also found that the public comment section of Twitter was a public forum because the politicians intentionally created their accounts as a way to interact with the public. Therefore, even though Twitter is a private entity, the government officials were still acting in an official capacity when they posted information on the platform, and therefore the use of the account was subject to First Amendment principles.

Is There a Right of Access to Prisons?

The Supreme Court has ruled that there is no right of access to prisons. In fact, they've ruled it three times. In *Pell v. Procunier*, the Court held there is no First Amendment right to interview prisoners in state prison, because journalists have no right of access beyond the rights of the average citizen. In *Saxbe v. Washington Post*, the Court held there is no First Amendment right to interview prisoners in federal prison. And in *Houchins v. KQED*, the Court held there is no special right of the press to investigate prisons. However, even if there is no constitutional right of access to prisons, one may still obtain access. The federal Bureau of Prisons may permit a reporter access if it so chooses. Requests can be made with the Bureau, and access is sometimes granted. Similarly, the equivalent state agencies may grant reporters access to prisons. In some states, there may be a statutory right of access. For example, some state laws grant prisoners the right to allow visitors, including journalists, so it may be possible for a reporter to write to a prisoner and have him include the reporter as a guest.

Is There an Enforceable Right to Take Photographs or Use Video Cameras in Public Places or at Public Meetings or Events?

With respect to public meetings, many states expressly allow recording equipment, either by statute or case law. However, the particular rules vary substantially by state. Alabama, for example, allows meetings to be recorded by any means as long as it is not disruptive. Minnesota law allows each individual government body to decide whether to allow recording or not. Oregon law does not address the issue at all. Thus, if a particular state has a clear law on the subject, there may be an enforceable right by statute. If there is no such rule, then the law remains ambiguous. With respect to court rulings, courts have differed on whether there is a constitutional right to record meetings. For example, in *Iacobucci v. Boulter*, the court found that there was a constitutional right to record public meetings but in *Whiteland Woods, LLP v. Township of West Whiteland*, the court found no constitutional right to record public meetings. The Supreme Court has not addressed the issue to resolve it.

In general, with the exception of nuclear facilities and military installations, there is no law against taking photographs in public places. However, the fact that it is not illegal does not mean that there is an enforceable right. Police may instruct photographers to stop taking pictures at crime scenes or protests, and in many cases, such as *Durruthy v. Pastor*, courts have upheld charges against photographers that refuse to comply with police orders.

There is, however, a growing body of case law stating that there is a First Amendment right to use cameras and other recording equipment. In *Gilles v. Davis*, the court noted that photography enjoys some First Amendment protection; in *Smith v. Cumming*, the court acknowledged a right to record police, but subject to restrictions; in *Fordyce v. City of Seattle*, the court recognized some First Amendment interest in filming events; and in *Pomykacz v. Borough of West Wildwood*, the court found a First Amendment right to photograph police. The issue becomes somewhat more complicated when there is an audio element to the recording, such as with microphones or video cameras, because there are usually state laws that govern when consent is required to capture audio recordings of other people. Yet, even in such cases, courts have found a First Amendment right to record police officers performing their jobs. In *Glik v. Cunniffe*, the First Circuit ruled that there was a "clearly established" First Amendment right to record police performing their duties in Boston Common, a traditionally public place. Similarly, in *ACLU v. Alvarez*, the ACLU challenged the constitutionality of the Illinois eavesdropping statute as applied to individuals who record police officers performing their duties. Illinois had long a reputation for having the most restrictive law that made it a crime to make any audio recordings without consent, which included making video (with an audio component) of police officers acting in public places. The suit was filed in contemplation of the G-8 summit, which was to be held in Chicago, in May of 2012. The ACLU anticipated that there would be many protests and other events where police officers would be present, that may citizens and journalists would attempt to record such events, and that there may be many arrests as a result. The Seventh Circuit ruled, in a very short opinion, that the law raised serious First Amendment issues and was more restrictive than necessary to protect any legitimate interests that might exist. In 2017, two more federal circuits decided similar cases. The Third Circuit ruled in *Fields v. City of Philadelphia* that there is a First Amendment right to record police officers in the field, and the Fifth Circuit ruled similarly in *Turner v. Driver*. Thus, the courts are acknowledging a right to record police officers in the course of duty.

Practical Conclusions

- In order to figure out whether you have an affirmative right of access to documents or places, you need to know who owns or controls them.
  - There is no right of access to privately owned documents or places.
  - There is no right of access to Congressional records.
  - There is a right of access to federal agency records and meetings to the extent allowed by the FOIA and the Sunshine Act.
  - There may be a right of access to state agency or legislative records and meetings to the extent allowed by each state's open records or open meetings laws.
  - There is a presumptive right of access to all federal and state judicial proceedings and records, although access may be restricted if there is a compelling interest and the restriction is narrowly tailored.

- You are almost certainly not getting any documents requested under FOIA within the statutory 20-day time frame. Plan ahead. It may take up to a year or more to get them. You may need to sue the government to get the records, but if you win, you may be able to recoup your attorney's fees.

- You are not going to get any documents that relate to national security, involve law enforcement proceedings (unless they are long over and there are no confidential sources to protect), or would intrude on privacy, which the government and courts interpret broadly.

- State access laws vary substantially. It's really important to look at the law of the state to see what your rights and obligations are.

- Although some federal laws may restrict schools, medical providers, and other entities from providing information without consent, those laws do not restrict others from using or publishing whatever information they are able to obtain.

- With respect to news scenes, press conferences and other government places:
  - The press has the same rights as any other member of the public when it comes to accidents and other news scenes. Law enforcement and safety officials can set up barriers, and the press has no right of access beyond what any other person has.
  - Politicians are not required to speak to any journalist and may chose to speak to some and not others. However, if events are open to the public or press conferences are held, they cannot discriminate against a particular person. Credentials must be distributed according to a fair process.
  - There is no constitutional right of access to prisons. The Court has been pretty clear about that. But one might obtain access to a prison if a request is made with the appropriate (federal or state) Bureau of Prisons, or there might be a right of access pursuant to a state statute.
  - Some courts have held that there is an affirmative right to take photos or video in public places and to record police. There might be a right to photograph or record public meetings under a state's open meetings law, but one would have to look at the particular state law to see whether it applies to a particular meeting.

CHAPTER 12

Can One Be Sued or Prosecuted for Gathering News?

It is difficult to overestimate the importance of the newsgathering process. A reporter's diligence in gathering information will often be reflected in the quality of the story that is eventually published. A reporter needs access to as much information as possible to ensure a story is complete and fair. However, reporters must comply with generally applicable laws in the course of newsgathering. Courts have not granted the media special rights that allow them to break laws or do things that ordinary citizens cannot do.

As noted in Chapter 11, there are many instances where there is no right of access to places or materials, but it may be permissible to obtain access nevertheless. However, there are also instances when trying to obtain access can result in civil or criminal liability. This chapter will discuss the kinds of things people might do to gather information that could result in civil or criminal liability:

1. Going on property (trespass)

2. Misrepresenting oneself

3. Making audio recordings or eavesdropping

4. Taking photos/video

5. Using hidden cameras or microphones

6. Accessing emails or secure electronic systems; or using passwords, badges, and other security materials

7. Scraping, using bots, or other technology-based newsgathering

8. Looking through or taking someone's belongings

9. Violating ordinary criminal laws

10. Getting access to subjects or sources

11. Making promises of confidentiality

Going on Property (Trespass)

Going onto private property can result in a trespass lawsuit or criminal charges. Trespass means entering onto private property without consent, or refusing to leave once asked. States may have different interpretations of precisely what this means, but trespass is a legal concept for which there are both civil and criminal provisions, so either could be applied.

In most states, it is acceptable to approach a person's home or business for a legitimate purpose, so ringing a doorbell to see whether someone will be interviewed is usually not a problem, unless there is a "No Trespassing" sign in plain sight. However, once the person refuses to speak or asks the reporter to leave, remaining on the property could be considered trespass.

It is necessary to have the consent of a landowner or resident to enter a home. Ordinary people cannot simply walk into a person's home without consent, and that rule applies equally to the media. In *Miller v. NBC*, for example, the plaintiff was permitted to pursue claims against a TV station that entered her home with paramedics. The television crew was filming the paramedics, and the TV station claimed it had the right to follow them into the home. However, the court said that the press did not automatically have a "newsgathering" right to enter a home. In fact, there are several cases involving ride-alongs, and the courts, including the Supreme Court, has made it clear that the press does not have the right to enter onto private property or homes just because they are following police, fire crews, or other emergency personnel. Moreover, in *Wilson v. Layne*, the Supreme Court ruled that it is a violation of a person's Fourth Amendment right against unreasonable searches and seizures for law enforcement to permit the media to enter a home without the consent of the residents. Thus, in *Wilson*, the government was held liable for allowing the press to enter a home, and in *Miller*, the press was sued directly and found liable. The takeaway for both government and media is that either one or both can be liable if the media goes into a home and the residents have not granted permission. The police (or others) do not have the authority to grant permission. Since *Wilson*, law enforcement agencies will often require reporters who go on ride-alongs to sign an agreement that specifies the rights and obligations of the police and the media. Journalists should scrutinize such agreements very carefully to ensure that the terms do not require anything that would be journalistically unethical. The agreements often state that the police cannot grant you permission to be on private property, which is simply a reflection of the law.

One need not own the home to have a claim. In *Mitchell v. Baltimore Sun Co.*, a resident of a nursing home was allowed to sue for trespass when reporters refused to leave the premises. Thus, trespass claims may also be brought by individuals with a right to reside on property, even if they are not the owner.

Misrepresenting Oneself

Failure to properly identify oneself may create liability in certain circumstances. Fraud is defined as knowingly and intentionally making a false statement or omission of material fact (which is something that would be a significant factor in making a decision) to induce action or inaction and causing damages. Under normal circumstances, using a fake name is not enough, on its own, to constitute fraud. But it can rise to the level of fraud if the misrepresentation was for the purpose of inducing some response that caused another person harm.

Fraud claims were alleged against investigative journalists in *Food Lion, Inc. v. Capital Cities/ABC, Inc.* Two television reporters used false resumes to get jobs at Food Lion supermarket. They secretly videotaped what appeared to be the sale or reuse of meat that was past its expiration date and used the footage in a *PrimeTime Live* broadcast. Rather than suing for libel, Food Lion focused on how ABC gathered its information. It brought claims for fraud, breach of duty of loyalty, trespass, and unfair trade practices. Food Lion won compensatory damages of $1,402 plus punitive damages. The Fourth Circuit reversed the judgment for fraud and unfair trade practices, but affirmed the judgment for breach of duty of loyalty and trespass. In its decision, the court noted that a fraud claim would have been viable except for a technicality—Food Lion did not actually suffer damages because of the fraud. The court found that the reporters did what they were supposed to do, which is work at the store, and any damage that Food Lion suffered was due to the broadcast, not to their work as employees. If the reporters had quit their jobs in a short time, however, it is possible that the court might have been more sympathetic to the fraud claim. The misrepresentations, though, are part of what allowed the court to uphold the trespass claim. Because the reporters had misrepresented themselves, the "consent" they had to be in non-public areas of the store was vitiated, or invalidated, and thus, the damages for trespass were upheld.

Aside from the legal issues, misrepresentations raise ethical issues for reporters. Most respectable news organizations typically require reporters to identify themselves as a reporter and for whom. In some cases, journalists may go undercover, but such efforts should not be undertaken lightly, as the decision will be subjected to ethical scrutiny.

Audio Recordings and Eavesdropping

There are federal and state laws that govern audio recordings. Sometimes they are called "wiretap" or "eavesdropping" laws, but regardless of the name assigned, the idea is that there are circumstances under which it is illegal to record or listen into a conversation. The laws may apply not only to the surreptitious capture of phone conversations, but also to live, in-person communications and other electronic communications. Also, there may be liability when audio is captured in video, because video has audio components as well as visual ones. Thus, these laws must be considered whenever audio is captured in any circumstance.

The one rule that is very clear and consistent is that it is always illegal to intercept or record a phone conversation between other people. (Unless, of course, you happen to be a law enforcement official and have a proper warrant.) When most people think of wiretap laws, this is what they think of—and it is the most basic rule. A person may not intercept a call between other people. This rule is quite strict, and as strange as it may seem, the rule has been applied even in cases where parents listen in on their children's phone conversations. In *State v. Christensen*, for example, a court reversed a robbery conviction because the evidence was based on an illegally obtained phone conversation where a mother listened in on her daughter's phone calls with her boyfriend.

The eavesdropping rule may also apply to in-person communications, but only where there is a reasonable expectation of privacy. There should be no need to worry about liability for overhearing a conversation between two very loud people at your neighborhood restaurant. But surreptitiously recording a conversation between two very quiet people whispering in the corner might be more likely to give rise to liability.

When someone is actually a party to a conversation, whether in person or on the phone, it may be permissible to record the conversation. The federal recording law is called a "one-party consent" law. Any one party to the conversation can consent to recording. The person recording can be the same person consenting, and no notice is required to the other parties.

In addition to the federal law, every state has a recording law. Some states have one-party consent laws, and thus a recording may be made by one party to the conversation. However, some states have "all-party consent" laws, which means that you must obtain the consent of all parties to the conversation in order to record it. California, Connecticut, Florida, Illinois, Maryland, Massachusetts, Michigan, Montana, Nevada, New Hampshire, Pennsylvania, and Washington have all-party consent laws, and the scope of these laws has led to some interesting cases.

In Maryland, for example, a man on a motorcycle, Anthony Graber, was pulled over by a police officer. Graber had a helmet-mounted camera and recorded the traffic stop. He later posted the video of the traffic stop on YouTube. Graber was then indicted by a grand jury for violating Maryland's recording law, which is "all-party consent," because the officer did not consent to the recording. A judge, however, dismissed the wiretap charges, finding that the officer had no reasonable expectation of privacy in the performance of his duties at a traffic stop. This ruling is consistent with cases from other jurisdictions, which often find that recording laws apply only where there is otherwise a reasonable expectation of privacy.

Illinois was notorious for having the most restrictive recording law in the country, one that specifically barred recording police officers. One of the most controversial cases, involved charges against Tiawanda Moore. In that case, a police officer responded to a domestic disturbance call at Moore's home. The officer then allegedly fondled and harassed Moore. She complained and two other officers attempted to intimidate her into dropping her complaint. Moore secretly recorded the officers, as she felt that they were acting improperly. When she went to the police with evidence of the harassment, they arrested her on charges of making an illegal recording. She was tried, and the jury, applying common sense if not the law, acquitted her. A few months later, the Seventh Circuit ruled in *ACLU v. Alvarez* that the law raised serious First Amendment issues and was more restrictive than necessary to protect any legitimate interests that might exist. On remand, the trial judge found that the law was unconstitutionally overbroad and issued a permanent injunction against enforcement of the blanket ban on recording police.

Even if the courts are willing to limit the scope of these laws to allow some recording, particularly of police officers or in public places, one must be careful to consider whether consent might be required under a particular state's law.

To make matters more complicated, it is not always clear which state's law applies. If a person lives in Virginia, but has a D.C. cell phone number, is on vacation in California and receives a call from a friend in Massachusetts, which state's law governs? Good question. In *Kearney v. Salomon Smith Barney, Inc.*, brokers in Georgia, a one-party consent state, recorded calls with clients in California, which requires the consent of all parties. The court held that California law protects California residents regardless of where the call originated, and thus callers from other states are expected to comply with California law when calling California residents. Thus, in cases where multiple state laws may apply, it might be prudent to comply with the most restrictive rule.

Even if it is illegal to record a conversation, it is not necessarily illegal to publish the conversation, as long as the person publishing played no role in the recording. In *Bartnicki v. Vopper*, the Supreme Court ruled that the First Amendment protected a radio station from liability for publishing the contents of an illegal intercepted phone call, as long as the station hadn't participated in or encouraged the illegal taping. In *Bartnicki*, someone else had illegally recorded a call between two local leaders who referred to "blowing up" people's porches. The station merely received the mysterious tape in the mail. A reporter or news outlet may be liable, though, if they encourage or participate in the recording. In *Peavy v. WFAA-TV*, for example, a reporter encouraged and helped a family to monitor and tape a neighbor's cordless phone conversations. Thus, the court found that the reporter could be sued even though the tapes were not broadcast and the material was highly newsworthy, because he had participated in the illegal activity.

Taking Photos/Video

As noted in Chapter 11, courts have recognized an affirmative right to take photos or video in public places and of police officers acting in the course of duty. Generally, when there is no reasonable expectation of privacy, it is fine to take pictures or record video. People take photos of buildings, events and other people all the time, and there are no penalties in most cases.

That said, there may be circumstances that can result in civil or criminal liability for taking photos or video. A photographer or videographer may be liable for trespass if he/she is on private property without permission, as discussed above. Or, a video may also capture audio components that may violate a state's wiretapping law, as discussed above. But in addition to those issues, there are three other scenarios that could create liability:

- Intrusion into seclusion (taking photos or video where a person has a reasonable expectation of privacy),

- Failure to obey reasonable orders by police and security, and

- Violation of criminal prohibitions on taking photos and video of certain federal facilities relating to national security.

Intrusion Into Seclusion

Intrusion into seclusion is a tort that allows a person to recover damages for "an offensive or intrusive physical, electronic, or mechanical invasion of solitude or seclusion." This tort covers a wide range of activities that might invade someone's privacy. The main question is whether the person has a "reasonable expectation of privacy" in where they are or what they are doing.

Some states recognize this tort as a matter of common law and others have a statute. Some states may have additional laws that cover similar conduct. For example, California has passed an anti-paparazzi law, which punishes conduct similar to intrusion. Under this law, it is an invasion of privacy to attempt to capture images or sounds of "personal or familial activities" on private property where there is a reasonable expectation of privacy, if the journalist uses "enhancing devices" or trespasses.

Under U.S. law, there is no reasonable expectation of privacy in public spaces, such as streets, parks, and large public gatherings. (This is not necessarily true in other countries. See Chapter 20 for more information about differences in international law.) Thus, it is generally acceptable to take photos in public places. The issue becomes trickier when people are in quasi-public places, such as hotels, restaurants, shops, offices, or other places where there might be some expectation of privacy. The issue of whether there is a reasonable expectation of privacy will depend on several factors, including the degree of control the person has over the space, whether other people can freely or easily obtain access to it, and whether anyone has indicated that they expect privacy. Thus, for example, a person probably has a reasonable expectation of privacy in his hotel room for which he has paid and to which he has exclusive access, but he would not have an expectation of privacy in the hotel lobby, where people may freely come and go. Similarly, a person may have an expectation of privacy in a clothing shop's dressing room, but not on the floor when browsing for items.

The principles are well illustrated by *Shulman v. Group W. Productions*, where a woman injured in car accident sued for intrusion into seclusion. The press had recorded her rescue from the accident scene, but the court found she had no reasonable expectation of privacy with respect to that incident, because the accident was on a public roadway and anyone passing by could see the rescue. However, the court did allow her to go forward with a claim based on the recording of her conversations with a nurse at the accident scene. The court found that she may have had a reasonable expectation of privacy in those conversations, because she didn't know the conversation was being taped and it is not the kind of thing that would be generally accessible to the public.

Similarly, in *Vera v. O'Keefe*, James O'Keefe, an openly partisan conservative activist/journalist was sued for secretly recording conversations with an employee of a liberal activist group called ACORN. O'Keefe met with the employee in a private conference room and asked the employee to assure him that the conversation was confidential. The recordings were then edited and posted online. Because of the private location and the request for confidentiality, the court found that the employee had a reasonable expectation of privacy, and allowed the claim against O'Keefe to go forward.

Photographers and videographers must therefore be sensitive to their location and to the notion of whether their conduct intrudes on anyone's reasonable expectations of privacy. The fact that one works for the media may not provide special rights to make recordings that invade privacy.

Failure to Obey Reasonable Orders by Police and Security

In general, a person may be in public and take photos. However, if the police (or other law enforcement entity) ask someone to stop, tricky legal issues are raised.

In general, police have the authority to keep order and enforce laws, which can include asking photographers to move or stop taking photos, particularly if they believe the photographer is in the way of traffic or emergency vehicles or is otherwise interfering with their ability to investigate a crime scene or do their jobs effectively. Photographers are usually expected to comply with police requests, and they can be arrested and charged with petty crimes for failure to comply. In *Durruthy v. Pastor*, for example, a court upheld charges against a photographer for failing to obey police orders. That said, there may be some limits on police power. Police should not make unreasonable demands, nor should they impose restrictions beyond that which is truly necessary for safety and security. In *Connell v. Hudson*, for example, the court found that those who gather news have a right not to be interfered with by the police so long as they do not unreasonably obstruct or interfere with police investigations of physical evidence or gain access to any place from which the general public is prohibited for safety purposes. In that case, the court found that the police had imposed unreasonable and excessive demands on a freelance photographer who was shooting photos of an accident scene. The photographer had complied with all safety requests, and the police had exceeded their authority by attempting to stop him from taking pictures. Even though they were motivated by a desire to preserve the privacy of the person killed in the accident, the court found that trying to exert control over those privacy interests was not part of the officers' jobs.

Despite these principles, difficult situations arise. Photographers and videographers must obey police orders and expect to be treated as any other member of the public would be. One does not have special rights to film or photograph, even if one is a member of the press. However, when the police overstep their bounds, it can be excruciatingly difficult to figure out how to respond to such situations in the heat of the moment, so it is wise for photographers to think about such situations before they arise. Remaining calm is important because, even if the officer behaves badly, the photographer can be arrested and charged with crimes like obstruction of justice or interfering with police activity if the photographer behaves badly too.

In many cases, the remedy must occur after the fact. In the best-case scenario, a photographer will be able to call their editor or attorney for assistance. Freelance photojournalists might call the Reporters Committee for Freedom of the Press, a nonprofit that provides free legal information to journalists and will help find attorneys to assist those without one. Their hotline number is (800) 336–4243. But if there is no opportunity to call for help, the photographer may lose the chance to get a photo or risk being arrested. In the worst scenarios, when an officer has clearly violated the law, a photographer can file a "Section 1983" lawsuit for violating his rights. Section 1983 is a portion of a federal law that allows people to sue a government official if that official has violated a "clearly established right." The practical problem with those cases is that they are expensive and time-consuming, and in many cases the courts refuse to grant relief, finding that the officers did not violate a clearly established right. It is only when the police are clearly acting outside the scope of a recognized right that such actions are fruitful. For example, in *Glik v. Cunniff*, the court ruled that officers violated clearly established rights in arresting a man for recording the police.

In theory, police do not have authority to seize a person's camera, film, or memory card unless the person is under arrest; and even then, they may not delete photos or force the photographer to delete photos. Nevertheless, such situations have arisen. Those who use digital cameras will often use software or apps that automatically upload photos or video so a copy is preserved somewhere even if the camera is taken or destroyed. There may be other technological means of preserving images in the event a camera is seized or destroyed. It may be wise to consider using such technology. Even if one can sue the police after the fact and prevail, one suspects a photographer would rather have had the picture.

It is also worth noting that some states grant private security officers powers similar to those of police officers, while other states limit their authority. The authority of security officers is outside the scope of this book, but it should be noted that reporters should become familiar with the rules applicable to the jurisdiction in which they are located in the event they are faced with demands by private security officers. However, even in states where security officers lack official power, they can nevertheless call police to the scene.

Violation of Criminal Prohibitions on Taking Photos and Video of Certain Federal Facilities Relating to National Security

There is a federal law, 18 U.S.C. sec. 795, that prohibits taking photos of (or drawing or representing) certain military facilities without consent. Another law, 42 U.S.C. sec. 2278b, makes it a crime to photograph (or draw or otherwise represent) certain defense installations and equipment, such as nuclear facilities, without consent. Thus, photographers who need images of defense installations may have to obtain consent from the officer in charge of the facility.

Using Hidden Cameras or Microphones

As if the issues surrounding photography and audio recording weren't tricky enough, the use of hidden cameras or microphones adds another layer of complexity. Several states have laws that prohibit the use of hidden cameras in certain circumstances. In many states, it is a crime. In Maine, it is a felony. And, to the extent a camera captures audio, there may also be liability for violating a state's wiretapping law, as discussed in the section above on audio recordings.

The use of a hidden camera might also create civil liability, as it might constitute an intrusion into seclusion, if the person would have a reasonable expectation of privacy. Several cases have permitted intrusion claims when hidden cameras were used. In *Lieberman v. KCOP*, for example, a court allowed a doctor to sue for intrusion when undercover reporters used a hidden camera to reveal that the doctor was improperly prescribing Vicoden to patients. In *Sanders v. ABC*, a court allowed a claim to go forward against *Prime Time Live* for having a reporter pose as a psychic and use a hidden camera to videotape conversations among the psychics who worked for phone service. And, in *Alpha Therapeutic Corp. v. Nippon Hoso Kyokai (NHK)*, a court permitted a company to sue a Japanese TV station because they secretly taped and filmed an interview with company employee at his front door. The court said there could be a "reasonable expectation of privacy" under state law.

However, the use of a hidden camera may be protected in some cases. In *Desnick v. ABC*, the Seventh Circuit ruled that there was no privacy claim when seven reporters with hidden cameras posed as patients at eye clinics as part of an investigative report about whether clinics were recommending unnecessary surgeries for Medicare patients. Whether a court will protect the media or not will depend on several factors, including the law of the state where the claim is brought, the newsworthiness of the material, and the reasonable expectation of privacy or confidentiality of the persons filmed.

Thus, there are always legal issues that must be evaluated before a hidden camera is used. In addition to the legal issues, there are ethical issues to consider. Journalists are generally expected to be truthful in the news gathering process, and the indiscriminate use of hidden cameras raises issues with respect to whether the journalist is acting appropriately. The use of a hidden camera without adequate justification would erode the trust and credibility that, one hopes, a news organization would have. However, the use of hidden cameras is not always inappropriate. There would have to be a careful analysis of the facts of a particular case to determine whether the use would be ethical. A non-exclusive list of factors one might consider includes:

1. Whether the camera will be used in a public, publicly accessible, or private place

2. The newsworthiness of the subject matter

3. The newsworthiness of the individuals filmed

4. Whether the information can be obtained by other means

5. How much information has already been gathered on the topic

6. How much video footage will contribute to the story overall

7. Whether there are any other relevant factors known that would affect the decision

In sum, the decision to use a hidden camera should not be undertaken lightly. Several legal and ethical issues must be considered.

Ag-Gag Laws: Does the First Amendment Protect Clandestine Investigations of the Agricultural Industry?

Courts have recently confronted the issue of how much protection to afford those who aim to expose alleged wrongdoing the agricultural industry via undercover investigations. Several states have passed what are known as "ag-gag" laws, or agriculture protection laws, which aim to criminalize undercover surveillance at farm sites. Supporters of the legislation argue that it is important to grant autonomy to the agriculture industry and allow them to operate without interference, but opponents of the legislation counter that it important to expose unsavory practices. Many states have considered or passed ag-gag laws, but the three courts that have addressed challenges to them have so far have held that the laws are unconstitutional.

In 2012, after an undercover investigator filmed dairy workers mistreating cows, the Idaho legislature passed a statute that criminalized the use of hidden camera audio and video recordings of farm operations or misrepresenting oneself to gain access to such a facility. In 2018, the Ninth Circuit ruled in *Animal Legal Defense Fund v. Wasden* that the statute violated the First Amendment. The court acknowledged that there can be valid criminal penalties for misrepresentations that rise to the level of fraud, but false statements or omissions that do not cause material harm can be protected speech. The court held that the kinds of misrepresentations criminalized by the law, such as omitting journalistic affiliations, would not cause adequate material harm to the agricultural industry and also are not "made to effect a fraud or secure moneys or other valuable considerations." Therefore, the court held that the First Amendment does indeed protect the "misrepresentation" proscribed by the statute and declared the statute unconstitutional.

Similarly, in *Animal Legal Defense Fund v. Reynolds*, the court struck down Iowa's ag-gag law as unconstitutional. Iowa's law criminalized obtaining "access to an agricultural production facility by false pretenses." The court noted that content-based regulations "target speech based on its communicative content" and are valid only in certain instances, such as when words are likely to incite imminent violent action. The court further found that the statute regulated content-based speech, because one must evaluate what the person said in order to determine if it violates the statute. The court held that although lying may not seem worthy of protection, the law was nevertheless unconstitutional because the justification for the law was not adequately compelling to justify a content-based restriction on speech. And in *Animal Legal Defense Fund v. Herbert*, the court struck down Utah's ag-gag law, which criminalized undercover investigations at agricultural sites, including lying to gain access and filming once inside. The court reasoned that, although the First Amendment does not protect false statements that lead to a "legally cognizable harm," the misrepresentations in this case led to no such harm. The court also found no evidence to support the State's claim that the law was meant to protect the animals because even though a lie about one's qualifications for the job could potentially be detrimental to the employee's ability to care for the animals, the law criminalizes *all* statements used to gain access to the facility, regardless of their relation to animal welfare. The court also held that lying to gain access to a facility does not necessarily cause trespass-related harm, because the mere knowledge that an uninvited guest entered the premises does not cause enough harm to be legally cognizable. The court held that the statute was overbroad, criminalizing trivial lies that result in no harm at all, and therefore, the statute violated the First Amendment.

Accessing Emails, Voicemails, or Secure Electronic Systems; Or Using Passwords, Badges, or Other Security Materials

Accessing emails, voicemails, or other electronic systems without consent can result in numerous legal issues. Such conduct could result in a civil lawsuit for intrusion, because in many instances one would be accessing material in which a person has a reasonable expectation of privacy. There may also be criminal charges under federal or state laws. The Computer Fraud and Abuse Act, for example, is a federal antihacking law, codified at 18 U.S.C. 1030, that might apply if the user has hacked into a government computer or has otherwise engaged in some form of fraud or unauthorized access to an electronic system. Other laws that might apply to such situations could be the Stored Communications Act (which prohibits accessing undelivered email), the federal Wire Fraud statute at 18 U.S.C. 1343 (which prohibits a scheme to defraud using interstate communication), an Identity Theft provision at 18 U.S.C. 1028 (which prohibits the use of the identification, including passwords, of others with intent to violate a law), or Access Device Fraud at 18 U.S.C. 1029 (which prohibits fraudulent access to any account or password). States also have laws that limit access to computer systems and email.

Sometimes, a source will give a reporter a password or code to access computer systems or voicemail. Such access is not necessarily legal. One high-profile example illustrates how such conduct can result in both civil and criminal liability. Investigative reporter Michael Gallagher, who was with the Cincinnati Enquirer, did an investigative report on Chiquita International. In the course of his investigation, he was given the access code to Chiquita's voice mail system. He used the code to access voice messages and wrote stories based on what he learned. When this was discovered, the paper was sued for intrusion and the reporter was criminally charged. The lawsuit was eventually settled and the reporter pleaded guilty. If Gallagher's source had simply told him what was in the voicemails, Gallagher probably would not have been liable. But accessing the system to which he was not officially authorized resulted in liability.

Similarly, using passwords provided by a source does not necessarily protect a user from liability. The same is true for "borrowing" badges or other security materials. The unauthorized use of such materials might create liability for fraud, trespass, intrusion into seclusion, any applicable wiretapping or hacking laws, or any other applicable criminal laws (such as a law prohibiting access to secured federal buildings). Obviously, the potential for liability will depend on the specific facts of a particular case, but a reporter should carefully consider whether any planned course of action would meet the elements of a potentially applicable crime or tort.

Again, reporters are subject to generally applicable laws, including laws that protect electronic systems. Some of those laws might be challenged on the grounds that they are overbroad or unconstitutional as applied, but reporters should not simply ignore the potential that these laws might apply to newsgathering behavior.

Scraping, Bots, and Other Technology-based Newsgathering

Some have argued that the Computer Fraud and Abuse Act could apply to technology-based newsgathering techniques like scraping, creating bots, or creating sock puppets. These techniques often violate the Terms of Service of websites, but the question is whether that should result in criminal liability. In one high-profile case, an internet activist named Aaron Swartz was charged with violating the CFAA because he programmed a system to download articles from JSTOR. His case never went to trial, because he committed suicide, but his case was widely disparaged as an instance of prosecutorial overreach. Nevertheless, some courts have found that violating the Terms of Service of a website can result in CFAA liability. Other courts, however, have found that accessing information that is otherwise publicly available on a website is not a CFAA violation, even if the method used to collect or gather the information violates the Terms of Service. For example, in *Sandvig v. Sessions*, the court found that there was a valid "as-applied" First Amendment interest for researchers who were using bots to test a website. The federal circuits are currently split on this issue, so it may be necessary for the U.S. Supreme Court to take a case to resolve the constitutional issues.

Looking Through or Taking Someone's Belongings

"Trespass to chattels" is a tort that applies when a person interferes with another person's possessions in such a way as to deprive them of the item, even temporarily, or to cause harm. Taking an item, whether permanently or for a short time, would qualify. Taking an item may also result in theft charges.

In 2010, the blog Gizmodo published a story about the new Apple iPhone before it was officially released. Someone had left a prototype phone at a bar, another person found it, and Gizmodo bought it, took it apart, analyzed it, and published its article. It turned out to be a genuine prototype, and Apple was angry. Several commentators noted that Gizmodo might be criminally liable for theft or receipt of stolen goods, and also civilly liable for trespass to chattels or disclosure of trade secrets. Apple never sued and criminal charges were never filed, but there is an open question as to whether Gizmodo would have been liable. Courts typically do not grant journalists exemptions from generally applicable laws, and have held journalists civilly and criminally liable, even for journalistic activities.

Violating Ordinary Criminal Laws

Reporters do not necessarily get a special exemption from criminal laws, not even for the purpose of newsgathering. In 2003, ABC news producers arranged to have a container of depleted uranium shipped from Jakarta, Indonesia to the United States to test whether U.S. officials would find it. In doing so, they violated a federal law against making a false customs declaration, because they didn't truthfully list the contents of the container. Officials considered filing charges, but decided not to do so. In other cases, though, reporters have not been so lucky. In *U.S. v. Matthews*, a reporter who was investigating online child pornography rings was charged with possession of child pornography because he obtained some in the course of his reporting. The Fourth Circuit ruled that he could not raise the First Amendment as a defense at trial. Even if he were legitimately reporting on a newsworthy matter, journalists may not break the law to get a story.

Journalists who buy or sell drugs, steal cars or otherwise commit crimes of any nature in the course of reporting could be prosecuted. There are good arguments discussed throughout this book that the First Amendment may provide protection from some prosecutions, particularly when the alleged crime is the dissemination of information or genuinely expressive activity where there is no compelling government interest in punishing the speech. But courts have demonstrated a reluctance to grant journalists a wholesale exemption from generally applicable laws, and thus reporters must think about when their conduct may constitute an ordinary crime.

Getting Access to Subjects or Sources

In general, reporters are free to approach sources or potential sources to ask questions or try to obtain information. The one exception would be that reporters should not contact jurors during a trial, as that may be viewed as jury tampering, or during any subsequent time period as ordered by a judge. For example, in the Casey Anthony murder trial, the judge barred reporters from contacting jurors for three months for a "cooling off" period because of the intense public interest in and anger about the verdict in that case. (See Chapter 11 for more information about the validity of juror contact orders.)

Even though reporters are free to ask questions, the sources have no obligation to respond. When sources fail to respond, reporters may be persistent. Persistence is fine. At some point, though, one must be wary of crossing the line into stalking or harassment or of engaging in activities that may constitute intrusion into seclusion. Courts may impose restraining orders on overzealous media. In *Galella v. Onassis*, for example, the court ordered a photographer to stay at least 25 feet away from Jackie Onassis and her children after many instances of harassment.

Obnoxious techniques to get to sources or gather news have also resulted in lawsuits for Intentional Infliction of Emotional Distress (IIED). In IIED cases, a plaintiff must prove that the defendant engaged in extreme and outrageous conduct that caused severe emotional distress. In *Baugh v. CBS*, the court allowed an IIED claim to go forward against a TV show when the camera crew allegedly misrepresented themselves to a sexual assault victim as being from D.A.'s office. An IIED claim was also permitted in *KOVR-TV, Inc. v. Superior Court of Sacramento County*, when a journalist approached young children, knowing that their parents were not home, to ask for comment about a neighbor that had killed herself and her children. The courts have not been inclined to extend any kind of special protection to journalists who behave in ways that seem outside the scope of responsible, professional journalism. Being respectful toward sources and victims can go a long way toward minimizing the potential for these kinds of claims.

Making Promises of Confidentiality

Reporters will sometimes promise confidentiality to a source in order to obtain information. The problem with such promises is that reporters cannot always keep them. Sometimes reporters are subpoenaed to testify and the law does not always provide protection to journalists to keep sources secret. Sometimes reporters accidentally or unintentionally reveal a source. Sometimes reporters choose to disclose sources unethically.

From a legal standpoint, the failure to keep a promise may result in liability for breach of contract. The Supreme Court ruled in *Cohen v. Cowles Media Co.* that the First Amendment does not exempt reporters from breach of contract claims if they break a promise of confidentiality.

While many like to theorize that the First Amendment's clause ensuring freedom of the press means that there is some protection for newsgathering, and while the Supreme Court has, from time to time, made statements acknowledging that there must be some protection for newsgathering, *Cohen* is but one of many cases in which courts have been reluctant to provide reporters a special exemption from generally applicable laws. Unwarranted intrusions into the newsgathering process may very well be unconstitutional, but reporters must also be conscientious of the potential for liability in the newsgathering process.

For that reason, it is important for reporters to be very clear with sources about exactly what promises they are making. Reporters sometimes use terms like "on background," "off the record," or "not for attribution." These phrases have no specific legal meaning, and people may interpret their meaning differently. Journalists therefore should strive to be very explicit about their intentions and ask the source what their expectations are, so that the "promise" made is understood clearly by both the reporter and source.

Practical Conclusions

- The fact that someone is a journalist does not give one the right to break laws in the newsgathering process. A journalist that steals an item, even for a good journalistic cause, can be charged with theft. It is therefore important to be wary of trespass, fraud, breach of contract, or any other violation of any other existing law in the course of newsgathering.

- Hacking into email, using passwords, codes, or badges, and "borrowing" equipment can all potentially lead to liability. However, if a source printed the emails and gave them to a journalist, took pictures, or otherwise copied or provided the thing at issue, then the journalist will probably not be liable, as long as the journalist in no way participated in or encouraged any illegal activity.

- Every state has an audio recording law that applies to video that captures audio, as well as phone calls, in-person recordings and other forms of communication.
  - There is usually no liability if the recording is made in a place where there is no expectation of privacy, such as taking a video on a public street.
  - With respect to phone calls, you need to know whether the states where each party is located require the consent of one party or the consent of all parties.
  - If you are a broadcaster, FCC regulations will require you to get consent before recording any phone call intended for broadcast.
  - The law on in-person recordings will vary by state, so check state law.

- The use of hidden cameras is fraught with legal and ethical dilemmas, and any such use must be carefully considered because it may result in criminal or civil liability.

- Police and other law enforcement officials have broad discretion to control crowds to protect safety. Journalists do not have a recognized right to cross barriers set up at news scenes, and they can be arrested for failure to follow police orders.

PART IV

How Does the Government Regulate or Interfere With Speech?

CHAPTER 13

Efforts to Subpoena or Search Journalists

There are times when a reporter is subpoenaed to testify at some sort of proceeding, whether before a grand jury, at a deposition, or in a trial. Other times, a subpoena seeks documents or materials, such as a reporter's outtakes, notes, or other materials relevant to newsgathering or reporting. And there have been some instances of government officials attempting to search a newsroom to obtain such materials. This chapter addresses the issues that may arise in such circumstances. It will cover:

1. Whether there is a privilege from testifying or turning over documents if subpoenaed
   a. Is there an applicable state shield law?
   b. Is there common law protection in the absence of a shield law?
   c. Are there procedural rules that might apply?

2. What happens if there is no applicable privilege and a reporter is forced to testify?

3. Whether search warrants can be executed against a journalist

Is There a "Reporters Privilege"?

In general, a person who is subpoenaed to testify or produce documents in a civil or criminal case is required to comply or be subject to contempt proceedings. However, there are some exceptions, known as "privileges." The most famous privilege is probably attorney-client privilege, which exempts an attorney from testifying against a client in most circumstances. Many, if not all, states also recognize a privilege for doctors, therapists, and religious advisors. In some cases, there is even a privilege not to testify against one's spouse. All of these privileges are based on the conclusion that there is a public policy interest that justifies the exclusion of testimony from certain types of witnesses. For example, the attorney-client privilege stems from a recognition that clients need honest, thorough advice, and they can obtain such advice only if the client is open and honest with the lawyer. Clients won't be honest if they are afraid that their lawyer can later be called to testify against them. There are almost always other witnesses who can testify, and the testimony of a lawyer is not necessary. Thus, over time, rules developed that exempt lawyers from testifying if they are subpoenaed. The same basic considerations are true for doctors, therapists, religious advisors and spouses: we want people to be honest in those relationships and not fear forced disclosure of information, for good reasons (appropriate medical care, assistance with psychological issues, religious forgiveness, and strong marriages, respectively), so the law provides exemptions from testifying.

Reporters have argued that they should also have a privilege for similar reasons. Reporters disseminate newsworthy information to the public, and they rely on sources to provide that information. In many cases, sources will not be honest or disclose crucial information if they fear being punished if their identity is disclosed. As a matter of public policy, we should want to encourage disclosure of wrongdoing or other newsworthy information. There are other arguments in favor of a privilege for reporters, as well. It is the independence of the news media that gives it credibility. If reporters are seen as an investigative arm of the government, then people will lack faith both in their reporting and in trusting them with information. The government should do its own investigative work without co-opting the work of journalists.

The policies underlying a privilege are well stated in *Hutira v. Islamic Republic of Iran*. In *Hutira*, the plaintiff sued defendants for allegedly assassinating her father, an Iranian dissident living in the United States. A journalist for the *Washington Post*, David Ottoway, had written an article detailing the assassination, including information about the assassin's ties to the Iranian government. The plaintiff subpoenaed the article itself and sought the testimony of Ottoway to confirm the accuracy of statements in the article. The court quashed the subpoena and discussed the importance of providing a privilege:

> If the parties to any lawsuit were free to subpoena the press at will, it would likely become standard operating procedure for those litigating against an entity that had been the subject of press attention to sift through press files in search of information supporting their claims. The resulting wholesale exposure of press files to litigant scrutiny would burden the press with heavy costs of subpoena compliance, and could otherwise impair its ability to perform its duties—particularly if potential sources were deterred from speaking to the press, or insisted on remaining anonymous, because of the likelihood that they would be sucked into litigation. Incentives would also arise for press entities to clean out files containing potentially valuable information lest they incur substantial costs in the event of future subpoenas. And permitting litigants unrestricted, court-enforced access to journalistic resources would risk the symbolic harm of making journalists appear to be an investigative arm of the judicial system, the government, or private parties.

Similarly, in *U.S. v. LaRouche Campaign*, the court noted a "lurking and subtle threat to journalists and their employers if disclosure of outtakes, notes, and other unused information, even if nonconfidential, becomes routine and casually, if not cavalierly, compelled." Thus, in an effort to promote the flow of information to journalists and protect them from abusive government action, many states have passed laws, known as "shield laws," that specifically provide a privilege for the news media under certain circumstances. Even in the absence of a shield law, there may nevertheless be some protection because of case law or procedural rules.

Is There an Applicable Shield Law?

A "shield law" is a statute that gives a privilege to journalists so that they do not have to testify or respond to subpoenas in certain circumstances. At this time, 40 states plus D.C. have shield laws. Because the shield laws are state laws, they apply only to proceedings in state courts. There is currently no federal shield law. The 10 states without a shield law are Idaho, Iowa, Massachusetts, Mississippi, Missouri, New Hampshire, South Dakota, Vermont, Virginia, and Wyoming.

Each state shield law is different, so there are certain questions one must ask to determine whether a shield law provides protection in a particular case.

First, who is covered by the shield law? Some laws narrowly define who is considered a "journalist" or member of the "media," limiting coverage to full-time employees of professional news organizations. Other laws might be broader in scope, covering freelancers, book authors, bloggers, student journalists, documentary film makers, or others who gather information for publication. In short, laws tend to define a journalist either by status (working for a news organization) or function (disseminating information for public benefit). The laws that define by function tend to cover more categories of people as journalists.

The second question is what kind of information might be protected by the shield law? Some laws might protect only the identity of a source. Others might protect a reporter's notes or materials they have obtained. Some will protect any information obtained in any way. Some laws require a promise of confidentiality for the protection to apply; others do not. The range of material protected can vary substantially.

Finally, how will the law be applied to the particular facts of the case? Each shield law will set forth certain criteria that must be considered, but there are certain considerations that tend to be consistent across states. Factors that the courts tend to consider are the relevance and importance of the reporter's testimony, whether the information is available from other sources, and what kind of proceeding it is. Courts are far more likely to apply a shield law in civil cases where the reporter is called as a third-party witness only because he interviewed someone involved in the case or researched similar situations. Courts tend to find that the reporter's testimony is not very important in those scenarios. However, in criminal cases where a reporter is an eyewitness to a crime, courts might be more likely to require the reporter to testify, particularly if he is the only witness.

Thus, while shield laws can sometimes provide excellent protection to a reporter, they do not provide absolute protection in all circumstances, and thus, it is not always possible to rely upon them.

Moreover, the absence of a federal shield law creates serious problems for journalists that are subpoenaed in connection with a federal case. Most of the time, when journalists are subpoenaed in federal cases, it is to obtain the identity of someone who leaked classified information. However, there are other occasions when journalists are sought to testify as an ordinary witness in civil or criminal proceedings. Because there is no statute defining a privilege, journalists are left to argue that they deserve protection under the common law or procedural rules (each is discussed below), but those arguments are not always well-received and journalists are often left with no protection.

A federal shield law had been proposed several times but none had advanced very far in Congress until 2009. Senator Chuck Schumer proposed the Free Flow of Information Act, which would have provided a privilege to journalists if the benefit to the public from the release of information outweighs the government's interest in obtaining the information sought. The bill had significant support until 2010, when the Wikileaks website published classified documents related the war in Afghanistan. Several Senators then questioned the wisdom of granting any protection that might hinder the identification or prosecution of leakers, and the bill stalled. Proponents of the bill are still trying to generate sufficient interest to pass a federal shield law, but until it passes, journalists cannot depend upon any statutory protection in federal court proceedings.

Is There Protection Based on Common Law?

If there is no applicable shield law, a journalist must rely on an argument that there should be some common law protection under the First Amendment. This argument was first raised in *Branzburg v. Hayes*.

Branzburg involved reporters who were subpoenaed to testify about information they gathered while investigating drug manufacturing or Black Panther activities. The U.S. Supreme Court issued a plurality decision, which means that a majority of justices agreed on the outcome, but they did not agree on the reasons for that outcome. Five justices ruled against the journalists in that case, deciding that they were required to testify. However, one of the justices who ruled against the journalists suggested that the decision was limited to the facts of the case, and there might be circumstances when the reporter should be protected. After that case was decided, some courts adopted tests to determine when First Amendment considerations should override a subpoena. For example, in *Zerilli v. Smith*, the D.C. Circuit denied a motion to compel discovery from a reporter in a Privacy Act lawsuit, finding that the reporter should not have to testify unless the information cannot be obtained by alternate means and the information is crucial to the case. Similarly, in *Silkwood v. Kerr-McGee*, the Tenth Circuit found that a qualified privilege may exist, and the party seeking materials from a documentary film maker must first seek information from other sources. The Ninth Circuit applied the privilege to a civil lawsuit in *Shoen v. Shoen*, and the Third Circuit applied a qualified privilege not to disclose confidential sources in a criminal case in *U.S. v. Cuthbertson*. Thus, it is clear that some courts feel that some form of privilege should be applied, at least in some cases.

There are three criteria the courts usually consider in evaluating whether there should be a privilege. First, the person seeking to subpoena the reporter must show that they have exhausted all other reasonable alternatives to obtain the information. Courts are aware that forcing a reporter to testify can create problems, and so they prefer not to impose such a burden unless it is truly necessary. If the litigant can obtain the information from other sources, then there is no need to burden the journalist.

Second, the courts usually consider whether the reporter has information that is relevant to the case, and if so, whether it is crucial to proving a claim or defense. Sometimes, a party will subpoena a reporter as part of a "fishing expedition," just to see whether the journalist happens to have some useful information. Courts frown upon this—there should be some evidence that the reporter has relevant information. Moreover, it should be crucial to the party's case. Again, the courts know that it is burdensome to subpoena a journalist, so the information must be very important to overcome the negative aspects of the subpoena.

Finally, the courts will consider what kind of case it is and whether there is an overriding interest in the information. Courts are more likely to grant a privilege in civil cases rather than criminal cases, with the exception of Privacy Act lawsuits.

Privacy Act lawsuits arise when a government employee leaks information about a citizen. A common scenario is when an official leaks the name of a suspect. These cases create unique problems for two reasons: first, they are almost always filed in federal court where there is no shield law, and second, the reporter is often the only source of information—thus, the subpoenaing party can usually show that he exhausted all other alternatives and that the information is crucial to the case.

Two cases illustrate the danger of being drawn into a Privacy Act lawsuit. The first, *Lee v. DOJ*, involved Dr. Wen Ho Lee, a scientist at Los Alamos National Labs in Santa Fe, New Mexico. He was investigated for spying for China, but was indicted only for mishandling files, and his case was settled by a plea agreement. He then sued the government for improperly leaking information about the investigation. Several reporters were asked to testify about their sources, they all refused to disclose their sources, and they were all held in contempt. They were fined $500 per day for each day they refused to testify. On appeal, the court affirmed the contempt ruling for all but one of the journalists (one being excluded because of lack of evidence that he knew who the sources were). The journalists were therefore subject to the fines and to potential additional sanctions, including jail time. The government eventually settled the case with Lee, and in an unprecedented move, the news organizations contributed $750,000 to the settlement in an effort to avoid any sanctions.

The second case involved Steven Hatfill, who was cited as a "person of interest" after the Anthrax attacks in 2001. Information about him was leaked to reporters, and Hatfill sued the government for violating the Privacy Act. Toni Locy, who had been a reporter for USA Today, was subpoenaed to testify about who her sources were. She refused to testify and was held in contempt. The judge ordered her to pay fines for failing to cooperate: $500 per day for the first seven days, $1000 per day for the next seven days, and $5000 per day for the next seven days. The court also ruled that no one could reimburse her. Locy appealed the ruling. Hatfill settled his case with the government a few months later. Thus, the appellate court dismissed the appeal and vacated the contempt order because there was no longer a case pending.

If not for the settlements in each case, there could have been disastrous consequences for the reporters.

In recent years, courts have been more hostile to arguments that there should be a common law privilege for journalists. Some courts are rejecting outright the notion that *Branzburg* allows for a privilege in criminal cases or grand jury investigations. For example, some reporters were subpoenaed to testify before a grand jury to reveal who leaked transcripts of the investigation into Barry Bonds' alleged steroid use. The court, in *In re Grand Jury Subpoenas*, ruled that the reporters must testify because *Branzburg* had rejected a privilege. Similarly, in *In re Miller*, the court ordered reporters to testify as to whether government officials leaked CIA agent Valerie Plame's name to media. Most recently, in *U.S. v. Sterling*, the Fourth Circuit completely rejected the notion that *Branzburg* allowed for any privilege in criminal cases, finding that journalists should be treated no differently than any other citizen, unless it appears that the subpoena is served solely to harass the press. And, in a civil case, *McKevitt v. Pallasch*, a court declined to find a privilege where the source had not demanded confidentiality; the court's opinion was dismissive of arguments that *Branzburg* required protection. Thus, the common law argument is also not always going to protect someone from having to testify. If the trend continues and courts decide that there is no common law privilege, then shield laws will be the only recourse for protecting journalists from subpoenas.

Are There Procedural Rules That Might Apply?

Regardless of whether a privilege exists, sometimes it is possible to quash a subpoena or otherwise avoid complying with a subpoena because of procedural rules.

If a person is subpoenaed under state law, there might be limitations that prohibit certain subpoenas. For example, the Texas rules of civil procedure impose restrictions on subpoenaing a witness who resides more than 150 miles from the county in which the lawsuit is pending. A news organization in D.C. or New York would be out of range to be subpoenaed under the rule.

The Federal Rules of Evidence or their state counterparts might also provide some protection. Evidence rules typically prohibit duplicative testimony. Thus, if other witnesses can testify to the same facts, then an attorney could argue that the reporter's testimony is duplicative.

Finally, if one is subpoenaed by the Department of Justice (DOJ), the DOJ is supposed to follow internal guidelines, codified at 28 C.F.R. sec. 50.10. The guidelines require the DOJ to attempt to obtain information from alternate sources and to obtain express approval from the Attorney General before issuing a subpoena to a member of the news media. In 2013, the DOJ guidelines were strengthened after the department subpoenaed the phone records of AP reporters. The public outcry in response to the subpoenas was strong enough to prompt President Obama to tell Attorney General Holder to propose revisions to the guidelines. On July 12, 2013, Attorney General Holder submitted revisions. Under the old rules, the DOJ would notify news organizations of a subpoena only if the prosecutor decided it would not harm the investigation. Under the new rules, the DOJ must give advance notice of a subpoena unless the Attorney General determines that notification would pose a "clear and substantial" threat to the integrity of the investigation, a grave risk to national security, or the risk of death or serious bodily harm. Such notice gives news organizations the opportunity to challenge the subpoena.

Subpoenas should be issued only in extraordinary circumstances in recognition of the importance of press freedom. However, at least one court, in *In re Miller*, has ruled that the guidelines do not create an enforceable right, and reporters cannot use the DOJ's failure to follow them as a defense. Thus, again, a shield law with defined statutory privileges provides the best opportunity for protection from unwarranted subpoenas.

What Happens If There Is No Applicable Privilege?

If there is no privilege, then the person subpoenaed will be expected to comply. Failure to do so will result in contempt proceedings, which typically means that the person will be found in contempt and either fined or jailed. Several reporters, including Judith Miller, Vanessa Leggett, and Josh Wolf, have gone to jail, and others have subject to burdensome fines. *Time* reporter Matthew Cooper was famously fined $1000 a day until he complied with the judge's order to testify in the investigation of the Plame leak. Jim Taricani of Providence, R.I., was also fined $1000 a day for refusing to disclose the identity of a source.

To make matters worse, if the journalist promised confidentiality to a source but then discloses the source's identity without consent, he could be liable for breach of contract. Contracts do not have to be in writing, so a verbal promise can count as a promise. The Supreme Court specifically addressed the issue of confidentiality promises in *Cohen v. Cowles Media* and held that the First Amendment does not protect the press from breach of contract lawsuits when a reporter breaches a promise of confidentiality. There has not yet been a case where a reporter has been sued for breach of contract after being compelled to testify pursuant to a subpoena, so it is not clear whether such compulsion would create a defense for the journalist.

In sum, here is the problem with making promises of confidentiality to sources: a reporter may end up either going to jail or paying money damages. Neither is a good situation. If the journalist keeps his promise and refuses to testify under subpoena, he can be held in contempt and go to jail. If he breaks the promise and testifies, he can be sued for breach of contract, and it is not clear whether a court would exempt a reporter from liability because of the force of the subpoena. It is therefore wise to consider these consequences before making any promise of confidentiality. Even in situations where no promises are made, journalists cannot rely on the applicability of a privilege in all cases, and thus, it is always possible that they will be forced to turn over materials or testify—or face contempt charges.

Practical Ways to Protect Sources

Modern technology has made it very easy to communicate with others. However, modern technology is also quite dangerous when it comes to protecting sources. Any digital or electronic communication, such as email, texts, shared drives, cloud storage, or other systems, is susceptible to hacking. Any electronic communication is probably stored somewhere, whether on your computer's server or the server of the company that provides the service (like Google or Yahoo). Mobile phones can be traced and smartphones are notoriously easy to hack. Location data is saved and often accessible. These practical matters create some concerns when it comes to protecting sources.

It is important to recognize that if you use these kinds of technologies, you are no longer in control of your information if the information is subpoenaed. Reporters used to be able to keep secrets as long as they could keep their own mouths shut. But now, government officials don't need to subpoena the reporter, because they can subpoena the employer, or the service provider, or the internet hosting company, or any other entity that might have the records of the reporter's communications. Sources can be identified if third parties over whom you have no control disclose communication records.

There are tools reporters and sources use in an effort to maintain confidentiality, such as the use of anonymizing services like Tor, the SecureDrop system, the Signal app, or disposable mobile phones. These tools provide significant protection in different ways. Reporters and sources need to engage in "threat-modeling" to figure out what threats to confidentiality they face and therefore which tools are most likely to help. Trying to protect a source from being discovered by a government agency may require a different strategy than trying to protect an employee from being discovered by a private employer.

Some of the best methods of communication are the most old-fashioned. Receiving documents in an unmarked envelope via U.S. Mail is great, but only if the reporter already knows who sent them; it can otherwise be difficult to verify the authenticity of the documents sent. Finding a drop-off location or meeting area that is not under camera surveillance is wonderful, but the parties must leave their smartphones at home so their location is not traced. The pervasiveness of technology requires reporters to think ahead in order to protect sources in cases where confidentiality and security matter.

A reporter might not be legally liable if a source is outed because the information was obtained from a third party. But ethically, a reporter should try to be aware of the risks posed by technology and take steps to protect confidential sources in cases where it is necessary.

Search Warrants Against Journalists

In addition to the issue of whether reporters should be subpoenaed, there is an issue as to whether they should be subject to search warrants issued in the course of a criminal investigation. In *Zurcher v. Stanford Daily*, the Supreme Court ruled that journalists are subject to search warrants, just like any other citizen, and there is no special protection granted by the First Amendment. However, Congress felt that such a rule would harm the free press, so it passed the Privacy Protection Act, codified at 42 U.S.C. sec 2000aa, a federal law that limits the authority of either federal or state law enforcement officials to search for or seize a journalist's materials. The government is supposed to attempt to subpoena the information rather than execute a search warrant, giving the journalist an opportunity to object. However, there are some exceptions. A search warrant may be issued in these limited circumstances:

1. If there is probable cause to believe that the reporter committed a crime. The law makes clear that "crime" refers to ordinary crimes, not something that involves the possession of materials for journalistic purposes. So, for example, if a reporter kills his wife and hides the murder weapon in his desk drawer, the police can execute a search warrant to look for it. The fact that he is a journalist is irrelevant. However, the police should not get a search warrant to see whether the journalist has a copy of a confidential business document provided by a source simply by declaring it a crime to possess a stolen document.

2. If the journalist is in possession of certain national security or classified information, or child pornography. This provision is essentially an exception to the first exception. Although the possession of documents or materials for journalistic purposes would not otherwise justify a search warrant, Congress made an exception for these two kinds of materials. The law does not permit the possession of child pornography for any reason, not even for journalistic purposes, and thus there is no reason why a search warrant could not be issued for those materials. It is far more likely, however, that a journalist could be in possession of classified or national security information, and there is some ambiguity as to whether the First Amendment would provide some protection against criminal prosecution for any potential criminal charges; nevertheless, the Privacy Protection Act does not prohibit search warrants intended to search for or seize such information. (Whether the First Amendment would protect against criminal charges for possession of classified or national security information is discussed more fully in Chapter 15.)

3. If the seizure of materials is necessary to prevent injury or death. It is unlikely that there would be a need for this exception, but it is there in case it is needed.

4. If the warrant is for "documentary materials" (something other than the reporter's own notes or other work product), then a warrant may be issued if the journalist has already ignored a valid subpoena for the materials or is likely to destroy the materials if they were subpoenaed.

There are two notable points about the language of the Act. First, the law provides protection to any person whose purpose is to disseminate information via some form of public communication. Thus, it applies to traditional news journalists, but also to student journalists, book authors, film makers, and arguably to bloggers and others who speak in public forums.

Second, the protection attaches to the person, not the place. Thus, it should not matter whether the journalist keeps the sought-after materials in a traditional newsroom or at home, in a car, or some other place. Although there is no case on this topic, some lawyers believe that the protection should apply even to searches that take place in public places, such as efforts by police officers to obtain cameras or memory cards from journalists covering live news events.

There are very few cases interpreting the Privacy Protection Act, but it is worth noting that government officials can be sued if they violate it. A journalist might not be able to stop a warrant from being executed improperly, but at least there would be a remedy after the fact.

Practical Conclusions

*   Journalists typically want to protect their sources and materials.

*   If a journalist is subpoenaed by a state court, one should look to the state shield law to see whether there is protection from having to disclose the identity of a source or any material gathered.

*   There is not yet a federal shield law; thus, if a journalist is subpoenaed by a federal court or by a state that has no shield law, one may argue that there is some First Amendment protection from having to testify, although protection is not guaranteed.

*   Because protection is not absolute, a promise of confidentiality may result in a reporter either going to jail or paying money damages. If the journalist keeps his promise and refuses to testify under subpoena, he can be held in contempt and go to jail. If he breaks the promise and testifies, he can be sued for breach of contract, and it is not clear whether a court would exempt a reporter from liability because of the force of the subpoena.

*   Technology has made it harder to keep the identity of a source secret, so journalists should be smart about using anonymizers and other tools so that sources are not outed accidentally.

*   The protection for journalists to be free from searches is clearer. The Privacy Protection Act prohibits law enforcement officials at any level of government from executing searches on journalists, except in narrow circumstances:
    *   You can be subject to search if there is probable cause to believe you committed a crime.
    *   Officials can search for national security information and child pornography.
    *   You can be subject to search if you've ignored a subpoena for documentary materials.

CHAPTER 14

Punishing or Restricting Protests and Other Public Speech

People often think of leafletting or protesting as the most quintessential forms of public speech that should be protected by the First Amendment. The guy standing on his soapbox on a street corner or a march across a city typically are protected in some form, but the Supreme Court has established rules that outline how far speakers can go before they are subject to punishment. This chapter will discuss the rules that govern public speech and protests. The main questions are:

1. Will the First Amendment protect the dissemination of "dangerous" ideas or beliefs?

2. Where or how can ideas be disseminated?

3. Can particular methods of expression be prohibited?

Will the First Amendment Protect Dissemination of "Dangerous" Ideas or Beliefs?

Considering the amount of time the Founding Fathers spent discussing the importance of freedom of speech and press, it might be surprising to know that a lot of political speech, usually involving Communism or anti-war sentiment, was punished until fairly recently in America's history. The courts struggled with how to prevent "dangerous speech" while still acknowledging the importance of freedom and preventing abusive government power. The Supreme Court addressed the issue several times in the early to mid-1900s, and the cases illustrate the difficulty the Court has had balancing the competing interests. Some of the opinions also contained nuggets of wisdom, describing the policies in favor of free speech that are still cited today. The following table shows how the Court's thinking developed across time.

Table 14.1: Development of U.S. Supreme Court Opinions on "Dangerous" Speech.

The Case	What Happened	Notable Points
Schenck v. U.S.	A Socialist was convicted under the Espionage Act for distributing flyers that opposed the draft and encouraged others to resist. The Court upheld the conviction, finding that speech may be punished where there is a "clear and present danger" that speech will "bring about the substantive evils that Congress has a right to prevent."	The Court said that freedom of speech "would not protect a man in falsely shouting fire in a theatre and causing a panic."
Abrams v. U.S.	Men were convicted under the Sedition Act for distributing anti-war leaflets. The Court upheld the conviction, finding that the speech had a "bad tendency" to cause harm, specifically to encourage resistance to the war.	Justice Holmes (who had, ironically, written the opinion in *Schenck*) wrote a dissent including the now-famous "marketplace of ideas" theory: "the best test of truth is the power of thought to get itself accepted in the competition of the market." He felt there was a difference between advocating abstract ideas and advocating action.
Gitlow v. New York	A socialist was convicted under state law for publishing a manifesto urging the overthrow of the government. The Court referred both to the "bad tendency" test and the "clear and present danger" test to uphold the conviction, finding the speech presented a "sufficient danger" to peace and security.	Despite the outcome, this case is notable for acknowledging that the First Amendment applies to the states as well as to the federal government via the 14th Amendment.
Whitney v. California	The Court upheld the conviction of a woman for her involvement with the Communist Labor Party, which the state said was a dangerous group. The court again relied on the "clear and present danger" and "bad tendency" tests.	This case is notable for Justice Brandeis's concurring opinion where he agreed with the outcome for procedural reasons, but noted that free speech was important to democracy, and said that speech should not be punished if there is an opportunity to discuss the merits of the ideas presented. He proposed the idea that "more speech" is a better remedy for defeating falsehood than punishing it.
Dennis v. U.S.	The Court upheld the convictions of communists for violating the Smith Act, which criminalized advocating the overthrow of the government. The Court adopted a test that courts must determine whether "the gravity of the 'evil,' "discounted by its improbability, justifies such invasion of free speech as is necessary to avoid the danger."	The dissent noted that the defendants didn't actually do anything. They merely assembled with the intent of speaking out against the government at some later date. This distinction foreshadowed the decision in *Yates*.

(*Continued*)

Table 14.1: (Continued)

Yates v. U.S.	The Court continued to use the "clear and present danger" test, but it overturned the Smith Act convictions of communists, because their statements were merely a discussion of abstract doctrine rather than advocacy of action.	This is the first case where the Court overturned a conviction founded on a person's ideas, regardless of how pernicious the ideas might be, recognizing that abstract doctrine should be protected by the First Amendment.
Brandenburg v. Ohio	The Court overturned the conviction of a KKK member who advocated violence, finding that advocacy may be punished only if it is likely to incite imminent lawless action.	*Brandenburg* directly overruled *Whitney v. California* and established the test that is still used today when evaluating advocacy of ideas or the potential for incitements to violence.

Since *Brandenburg* was decided, the government has, for the most part, accepted that even the most horrible and pernicious ideas can be presented in public, whether via leafleting, protests, speeches, marches or otherwise, as long as they do not incite violence. The focus has shifted to balancing freedom of speech with the inconvenience, noise, and interruption caused by some speakers. The courts have found that some restrictions on where or how a speaker attempts to speak are valid and others are not.

Our constitutional commitment to free speech is now being tested by cases raising terrorism concerns. For example, Tarek Mehanna is a U.S. citizen who has been convicted of providing "material support" to Al Qaeda, a terrorist group. Mehanna had translated some Al Qaeda documents into English and said that he supported the right of Muslims to defend themselves in their own lands, although he has also said that he does not support the tactic of attacking U.S. citizens in the United States. His conviction was denounced by the American Civil Liberties Union, saying that it "undermined free speech." Others have pointed out that media outlets have published Al Qaeda statements in order to inform the public, and it is difficult to distinguish between translations that are provided simply to inform the public and those that are provided to "incite action." There was no evidence that Mehanna had ever been involved in any plot to harm anyone. Nevertheless, Mehanna was convicted, in part because the *Brandenburg* standard of proving that the speech was designed to incite lawless action was not applied. It seems that courts are willing to allow prosecutions of speech if the speech falls within the scope of the laws that ban providing material support to terrorist groups. The U.S. Supreme Court upheld the constitutionality of such bans in *Holder v. Humanitarian Law Project* (which is discussed more fully in Chapter 15). The question, then, is whether speech about terrorism is now subject to a different test than one would ordinarily apply to disfavored or unpopular political speech—and the answer will be resolved over time.

Where or How Can Ideas Be Disseminated?

The courts have established two related concepts for determining whether the government can impose restrictions on where or how a person speaks in public: the concept of a public forum and the concept of time/place/manner restrictions.

Public Forums

In *Perry Educ. Assoc. v. Perry Local Educators' Assoc.*, the Court distinguished three categories of public property: public forums, limited public forums, and nonpublic forums. There is also private property, of course, but people have no First Amendment right to speak, protest or otherwise disseminate their views on private property. That principle was affirmed in *Hudgens v. NLRB*, where the Court ruled that the First Amendment does not require the owner of private property to permit speakers or protesters on his property. However, state constitutions may provide expanded rights beyond what the First Amendment provides and may permit speech or protests in privately-owned places such as shopping malls. For example, in *Pruneyard Shopping Center v. Robins*, the Court held that the California constitution may protect a citizens' right to speak in a privately-owned mall that otherwise resembles a traditional public forum. But such a rule derives from the state constitution, not the federal Constitution.

When dealing with publicly-owned property, the right to speak will be contingent upon the rules that apply to a particular kind of forum. The rules for restricting speech in each kind of government forum varies, as shown in this chart:

Table 14.2: Types of Public Forums.

Type of Forum	What It Is	What Restrictions Are Allowed
Public Forum	These are places that, traditionally, have been open for citizens to speak freely. They typically include streets, parks, and sidewalks.	A valid time, place, or manner restriction can be imposed. Otherwise, any content-based restriction is subject to strict scrutiny. The *Brandenburg* test may be applied if incitement is at issue. All regulations must be viewpoint neutral.
Limited Public Forum	These are places that are designated for certain types of speech, but are not generally open to the public. A public university's lecture hall or a meeting room are some examples. The side of a city-owned bus open to advertisements is another.	To the extent a forum is opened for use, it is subject to the same rules as a traditional public forum. Government cannot discriminate based on viewpoint. But allowing some use of a forum, does not mean it is open for all purposes. In *Embry v. Lewis*, for example, a court ruled that the fact that a school is open for use as a polling place does not necessarily mean it must be open for collecting petition signatures.
Non-Public Forum	These are government-owned facilities that are traditionally not open to speech. Office buildings, jails, military bases, and airports are examples.	Speech does not have to be permitted and the government is free to impose content-based restrictions. If speech is permitted, then any regulations should be viewpoint neutral.

As the rules make clear, forums that have been opened to speech can impose very few restrictions with the exception of Time/Place/Manner restrictions.

Time/Place/Manner (TPM) Restrictions

These restrictions do exactly what they sound like: they impose some restriction on the time, place, or manner of speech. To be valid, they must apply regardless of the content of the speech. Common TPM restrictions are limiting hours for protests in public, banning the use of amplifiers or bullhorns, requiring permits for protest or marches, establishing protest zones, or setting a distance between protesters and buildings or events. There have been media-specific restrictions, too, such as requiring newspapers or other printed media to be distributed in racks or boxes rather than left on the street.

The Supreme Court has said that TPM restrictions can be valid, as long as they meet certain requirements. In *Heffron v. Int'l Soc. Of Krishna Consciousness*, the Supreme Court set out five factors for evaluating whether a restriction would be a valid TPM regulation: (1) the regulation must be content-neutral; (2) the government must have a valid interest; (3) the regulation must be narrowly tailored; (4) there must be alternate forums for the speaker's speech; and (5) the rule must not be applied arbitrarily.

Heffron involved a request from a religious group to attend the Minnesota state fair. The group was permitted, as other groups were, but the fair required that groups stay in a designated section to talk to fair attendees and distribute literature. The group wanted to wander freely throughout the fair and argued that the restriction violated their First Amendment rights. The Supreme Court concluded that the regulation was a valid TPM regulation because the five criteria were met:

1. The regulation was content-neutral. The government did not care what their message was; all those who sought to disseminate materials were required to be in a particular section of the fair, regardless of the content of the message.

2. The government had a valid interest in ensuring safety and orderliness at the fair.

3. The regulation was narrowly tailored, because it did not prevent the dissemination of any message and did not impose any restrictions beyond the regulation of place, which was directly in furtherance of the interest in safety and orderliness.

4. There were alternate forums for the speaker's speech. The group could disseminate its materials in the designated area or outside of the fair. It was prohibited only from wandering around, interrupting people, inside the fairgrounds.

5. The rule was not applied arbitrarily, as all groups who wanted to distribute materials were subject to the same rules.

Protests are often subject to TPM regulations. For example, in *Clark v. CCNV*, the Supreme Court upheld the National Park Service's regulation against camping in Lafayette Park and the National Mall in Washington, D.C. The protesters had obtained a permit to set up tents and signs to raise awareness for the plight of the homeless. They also wanted to sleep in the parks, and argued that sleeping there was an integral expressive part of their effort. However, the Court found that the regulation was valid and could be applied to prevent sleeping in the tents, because it applied to everyone regardless of message, it furthered a legitimate interest in maintaining the condition of the parks, and it left alternate forums for speech, either by allowing the tents and signs and daytime protests at the National Parks, or by allowing camping at other sites designated for camping. Similarly, in *Mahoney v. Doe*, protesters were convicted of defacing public property after they wrote in chalk on the sidewalk. The court found that the deface-ment law was constitutional when applied in that case because it is a valid, content- neutral regulation that has nothing to do with the message of the protesters.

There have been numerous complaints over the last decade or so that governments are impos-ing unreasonable protest zones, keeping protesters away from the people or events they seek to reach with their message. During both the Republican and Democratic conventions leading up to the 2004 presidential election, protesters complained that the host cities created protest zones that were either absurdly small and incapable of holding the number of protesters who arrived (thereby leading to arrests of protesters outside the zone) or absurdly far away from the venue so that no one was seen or heard. In the more recent Occupy protests, cities have arrested or moved protesters with varying degrees of success. Although several commentators have argued that many of these efforts to restrict protesters are unconstitutional, there is no way to enforce First Amendment rights without incurring the time and expense of filing a lawsuit. The First Amendment is not self-executing, and thus efforts to silence pro-testers will be successful unless someone is willing to bring a claim—and, of course, if a court is willing to find that the government's efforts have exceeded the bounds of a valid TPM regulation.

Not all TPM regulations have been upheld by courts. In *Saieg v. City of Dearborn*, for example, a court found a leafleting law to be unconstitutional because there was no substantial government interest to be served.

Some of the funeral picketing laws have been struck down as well, although in some cases only because the law was poorly written. A buffer zone around a funeral can certainly be upheld as a legiti-mate TPM regulation if it is not vaguely written and not too broad in space or time restrictions. In all funeral protest cases, the courts have found that the laws are content-neutral, as they apply to any speech within the buffer zone. Also, the courts have found in all cases that there is a valid government interest, noting the interest in preserving the peace and sanctity of funerals, preventing unwanted speech imposed on a captive audience, or in protecting the family's exercise of religion at the burial. However, courts have struck down such laws for being vague, failing to specify the prohibited distance or times of protest, or for failing to be narrowly tailored, placing burden on more speech than is neces-sary to fulfill the interest. For example, in *Phelps-Roper v. Nixon*, the court suggested that a law that prohibited picketing "in front of or about any location at which a funeral is held" was too vague. But in *Phelps-Roper v. Strickland*, the court found that Ohio's fixed 300-foot buffer zone from an hour before to an hour after a funeral was a valid TPM regulation because the law was adequately specific about the time and place where picketing was prohibited.

Similarly, rack restrictions for print media could, in theory, be a legitimate TPM regulation, as a city has a legitimate interest in safety and aesthetics, but they fail if they are not narrowly tailored or discriminate based on content. For example, in *Cincinnati. v. Discovery Network, Inc.*, the Court found that a rack law wasn't a fair TPM regulation because it was content-based, discriminating between com-mercial publications and traditional news.

Some of the most difficult cases involve parsing whether a regulation is genuinely content-neutral or whether it is a content-based regulation in disguise. This issue was raised in *Madsen v. Women's Health Center*, where a court had issued an injunction against abortion protesters, imposing a 36-foot buffer zone around a healthcare facility. The Court considered whether the injunction was content-neutral and found that it was. The protesters argued that the buffer zone was really content-based because it was targeted toward them, and they had a particular message, namely, opposing abortion. However, the Court concluded that, although the buffer zone was being applied toward them, the reason for it had nothing to do with the message and only with behavior, such as blocking entrances and creating excessive noise.

It should be noted that, even though the injunction was content-neutral, the Court did not apply the typical TPM analysis because the regulation was derived from a court order, not a generally applicable law. The Court held the injunction to a somewhat higher level of scrutiny. Nevertheless, it affirmed the buffer zone and noise regulations, but struck down some of the other portions of the injunction. The Court later upheld a floating buffer zone—limiting conduct within 8 feet of a person entering a health-care facility—as a valid regulation in *Hill v. Colorado*. Most recently, in *McCullen v. Coakley*, the Supreme Court struck down a Massachusetts law that imposed a 35-foot buffer zone around abortion facilities. The buffer zone included public sidewalks. The Court ruled that the buffer zone was simply too broad, and that less restrictive alternatives should be tried first before blocking off traditional public forums, such as sidewalks.

In sum, determining whether speech can be restricted under a TPM regulation is a fact-specific determination that depends on the exact language of the regulation as well as its relationship to the government interest to be served.

The Internet as a Public Forum

If you've ever used the internet, you know that people use it to express their views on just about everything. However, most of the internet is run by private companies: Google, Facebook/Instagram, Microsoft, etc. Nevertheless, the Supreme Court has noted that some First Amendment principles apply when the government is attempting to regulate the use of the internet, as the internet is the modern version of a "public forum." In *Packingham v. North Carolina*, the Court considered a challenge to a North Carolina law that prohibited registered sex offenders from using social media platforms if the offender knows that the site permits minors to use the site. Packingham was a registered sex offender who posted on Facebook about his experience in traffic court and was subsequently sentenced to prison for violating the law. The Court struck down the law because, even if it were considered content-neutral, it was not narrowly tailored to serve a significant governmental interest. The government had the burden of proving that the law is necessary to protect vulnerable victims, but the government could not show that one must be restricted from *all* social media in order to protect potential victims. The Court noted:

> Even with these assumptions about the scope of the law and the State's interest, the statute here enacts a prohibition unprecedented in the scope of First Amendment speech it burdens. Social media allows users to gain access to information and communicate with one another about it on any subject that might come to mind. … By prohibiting sex offenders from using those websites, North Carolina with one broad stroke bars access to what for many are the principal sources for knowing current events, checking ads for employment, speaking and listening in the modern public square, and otherwise exploring the vast realms of human thought and knowledge. These websites can provide perhaps the most powerful mechanisms available to a private citizen to make his or her voice heard. They allow a person with an Internet connection to "become a town crier with a voice that resonates farther than it could from any soapbox." … In sum, to foreclose access to social media altogether is to prevent the user from engaging in the legitimate exercise of First Amendment rights. It is unsettling to suggest that

only a limited set of websites can be used even by persons who have completed their sentences. Even convicted criminals—and in some instances especially convicted criminals—might receive legitimate benefits from these means for access to the world of ideas, in particular if they seek to reform and to pursue lawful and rewarding lives.

Thus, the Court concluded, the law was not properly tailored to the harm to be prevented, and the First Amendment was violated.

There may therefore be some First Amendment protection to the extent the government seeks to regulate "protests" online. One issue that is not yet resolved in how courts will address "hacktivism." "Hacktivism" is the term applied to digital protests. They can take several forms, including hacking a site, taking over the site's operation, denial of service attacks, or other methods of interfering with the normal operation of a website. In some circumstances, people characterize these activities as a form of terrorism, but in other instances, some people argue that the actions are simply another method of enacting social change, effectively the same as a protest or sit-in in the bricks-and-mortar world. The degree to which hacktivists get sympathy often depends on the degree to which their actions are destructive.

There is little case law on this subject, but one factor to consider might be whether the site is a government website or for a private institution. Another factor might be whether any crimes were committed by the hacktivists. Currently, federal laws like the Computer Fraud and Abuse Act are written broadly, so most hacktivism might be deemed a crime, but individuals might challenge the laws "as applied." Another factor is whether any limits on hacktivism are legitimate time, place, manner regulations or whether they are overbroad. We have not yet figured out, culturally or legally, how groups might protest in the digital space.

Can Particular Methods of Expression Be Prohibited?

If a speaker is using a proper forum and complies with applicable TPM restrictions, then speech should not be punished or restricted, unless it is likely to incite violence or there is some compelling interest and the government can meet the strict scrutiny test. Yet the government will sometimes target certain methods of expression. In these cases, the efforts to suppress speech are not content-based in the sense that the government does not necessarily oppose the point of the speaker's message, but it is also not content-neutral in the sense that there is something about the expression itself that offends the government. It is the particular way in which the message is expressed that causes a problem. Two common areas of concern are profanity (or other offensive language) and symbolic speech.

Profanity, Fighting Words, and Other Offensive Speech

Given the ubiquity of profanity and offensive speech in modern culture, it may be a surprise to learn that profanity in public places was, at one time, considered punishable by law. Most states had profanity laws or other statutes that made offensive language a crime.

The concept of punishing such "offensive" language was upheld in *Chaplinsky v. New Hampshire*. *Chaplinsky* involved a Jehovah's Witness who was standing on a public street, denouncing other religions. In the course of a dispute with another man, Chaplinsky allegedly called him a "God damned racketeer" and a "damned fascist." He was prosecuted under a law that prohibited calling someone by an "offensive or derisive name." Chaplinsky argued that law was vague and violated the First Amendment, but the Court found that certain classes of speech can be punished without Constitutional problems, including "the lewd and obscene, the profane, the libelous, and the insulting or 'fighting' words—those which by their very utterance inflict injury or tend to incite an immediate breach of the peace." According to the Court, fighting words serve no purpose in articulating ideas and are of little social value. They are "not in any proper sense communication of information or opinion safeguarded by the Constitution." The Court found that the law was not vague, concluding that "offensive" words referred to "fighting words." The Court also found the words used to be "fighting words" and thus not protected by the First Amendment.

In *Cohen v. California*, however, the Court overturned the conviction of a young man who wore a jacket saying "Fuck the Draft" inside a county courthouse. He was arrested for disturbing the peace by "offensive conduct." The California appellate court found that "offensive conduct" meant acts that would provoke others to violence, and it was foreseeable that wearing this jacket would cause others to commit a violent act or "attempt to forcibly remove his jacket." But the Court disagreed, noting that content-based punishments are presumptively unconstitutional. The Court first determined that the phrase did not constitute "fighting words" because no reasonable person would have taken it as a personal insult. The Court also stated that "the State has no right to cleanse public debate to the point where it is grammatically palatable to the most squeamish among us. … One man's vulgarity is another's lyric." With that, the Court made clear that the use of profanity, in itself, was insufficient to be a crime.

In *Lewis v. City of New Orleans*, the Court struck down a law that made it a breach of peace "to curse or revile or to use obscene or opprobrious language towards or with reference to any member of the city police while in the actual performance of his duty." The Court found the statute to be unconstitutional as overbroad because "opprobrious" language would encompass more than only those words that qualify as fighting words.

Chaplinsky has never been overtly overruled, but since *Cohen* and *Lewis*, many courts have ruled that state or local profanity laws are unconstitutional. However, courts may uphold convictions based on the "fighting words" doctrine in *Chaplinsky*. If the language used is likely to incite an imminent breach of the peace (*e.g.*, cause a fight to break out), the speech may not be protected by the First Amendment. Even under *Brandenburg*, speech can be punished if it is likely to incite imminent lawless action, so it may be that it's not the words used that matter as much as the context involved in determining whether profanity can be the basis for prosecution.

Symbolic Speech

There are times when protesters wish to convey their message by acting in a way that makes a point symbolically. This is often called "symbolic speech," and includes things like wearing armbands to protest a war, burning a flag, lying on a sidewalk imitating victims, or other actions that convey a message. The fact that the speech is conveyed through conduct does not mean there is no First Amendment protection. The Court said in *Spence v. Washington* that First Amendment scrutiny should be applied when "an intent to convey a particularized message was present, and in the surrounding circumstances the likelihood was great that the message would be understood by those who viewed it."

The Supreme Court addressed the issue of symbolic speech in *U.S. v. O'Brien*. A federal law prohibited knowingly destroying or mutilating a draft card, but burning a draft card became a popular was to express opposition to the Vietnam War. O'Brien burned his draft card at a protest, was promptly arrested and then convicted. The Supreme Court noted that the law did not prohibit any kind of speech, only conduct. However, the Court also noted that there was an expressive element to the action (namely, showing opposition to the war), and queried whether that expressive element would justify First Amendment protection. The Court established a test for symbolic speech: a law will be valid if there is a substantial government interest that is unrelated to the suppression of speech and prohibits no more speech than necessary to further that interest. The Court determined that the draft card law was valid because the cards were an important tool in the draft system, the prohibition on their destruction was not motivated by a desire to suppress speech, and there was no other way to ensure the integrity of the cards except to ban their intentional destruction. Thus, O'Brien's conviction was upheld.

However, in *Texas v. Johnson*, the Court found that flag burning was protected by the First Amendment. Johnson was protesting at the Republican National Convention and burned a flag while protesters chanted, "America, the red, white and blue, we spit on you." The Court reiterated that conduct can have expressive elements, thereby invoking First Amendment scrutiny. Using the test from *O'Brien*, the Court found that the state simply lacked an interest that justified the imposition on speech. The Court found that there were no fighting words, no breach of the peace, and no incitements to violence that would justify a restriction on speech. Wanting to preserve the flag as a symbol of unity for the nation was an insufficient interest. Congress subsequently passed the 1989 Flag Protection Act, but that was similarly struck down as unconstitutional in *U.S. v. Eichman*. The Court reasoned that the law was intended to suppress a particular form of speech, and there was no other valid government interest.

Thus, symbolic speech can be protected if it does not qualify as a breach of peace or incitement to violence, unless there is some generally applicable law that would be a valid, content-neutral regulation.

Practical Conclusions

- The First Amendment usually protects the speech of those protesting or speaking in public, as long as the speaker is not inciting violence. However, the fact that the content of their speech is protected doesn't mean that the manner of expression is protected.

- Governments can impose reasonable restrictions on the time, place, or manner of speech so that citizens aren't awakened by protesters using bullhorns at 3 a.m., for example. Blocking traffic, spray painting buildings, and other disruptive or otherwise illegal forms of communication aren't likely to be protected.

- Traditional public forums, like sidewalks and parks, are typically available venues for speech. However, people do not have a right to use any government-owned property. State universities, for example, are not required to let anyone use their auditoriums. However, when such venues are opened for use, government are not supposed to discriminate based on viewpoint.

- Profanity is usually protected by the First Amendment unless it rises to the level of being likely to incite violence.

- Symbolic speech (like burning things) gets some level of protection, although it's possible to be successfully prosecuted if the government has a tangible interest in preventing the destruction of something (like, say, burning down a building, or a draft card, or something along those lines).

CHAPTER 15

Punishing or Restricting Sensitive or Offensive Topics

T he government will inevitably find topics it deems unacceptable. However, the law is very clear that First Amendment principles generally prohibit the government from banning or punishing speech unless some very high burdens are overcome.

Laws that target a particular kind of speech based on its content are called "content-based" laws. When a law is content-based, the courts examine it more carefully than if the law were content-neutral, or focused on some aspect other than its content, such as the time, place, or manner of speech. When laws are content-based, the courts typically apply "strict scrutiny," meaning that the government will have the burden of proving that there is a compelling interest that must be protected and that the law or regulation is narrowly tailored to serve that interest. Courts may also strike down laws that are vague, overbroad, or give too much discretion to government officials. And there are other legal principles or tests that the courts have applied with respect to particular types of speech. This chapter discusses six subject areas that are popular targets of government regulation:

1. National security and classified information

2. Hate speech

3. Sexual content

4. Violent content

5. Threats

6. Lies

Publication or Possession of Classified Information or Matters That Affect National Security

The publication or possession of classified information or material that may have national security implications creates three potential issues:

1. The government may try to stop publication, either through persuasion (as when the government reportedly asked the *New York Times* not to publish a story about intercepting phone calls with suspected terrorists) or via court order.

2. The government may seek a criminal prosecution under the Espionage Act or other federal law.

3. The government might spy upon or attempt to search the home or office of the person(s) believed to have possession of the materials.

Attempts to Stop Publication

If the government discovers that a news organization plans to publish a story with national security implications, it might attempt to stop publication. A government official may call an executive or high-ranking editor and request that the story not be published. This happens occasionally and it's up to the news organization to weigh the legal risks (mostly the risk of being prosecuted) and the ethical implications (of whatever the practical consequences would be) of publication versus withholding the story. One of the most famous examples is when the government asked the *New York Times* not to publish its story about the NSA's post-9/11 program to eavesdrop on communications without a warrant. The paper withheld the story for a while but eventually published it, creating a storm of controversy.

The government might seek a prior restraint, which is a court order mandating that the story not be published. The strict scrutiny test is used by the courts in these types of cases, meaning that to obtain a prior restraint, the government would have the burden of proof to show that there is a compelling government interest in keeping the information unpublished and that the restraint is narrowly tailored to keep secret only the material absolutely necessary to protect the government's interest. If the material is genuinely a matter of national security, then the court will most likely rule that there is a compelling interest in keeping it secret. The question, then, is usually whether the restraint is narrowly tailored or whether the government has met its burden of proof.

In *Near v. Minnesota*, the Supreme Court stated that prior restraints are disfavored and should not be issued absent exceptional circumstances. Prosecutors attempted to enjoin publication of *The Saturday Press* as a nuisance because of its anti-Semitic content, but the Court ruled that the government could not justify such a broad prior restraint on publication. However, the Court also stated that prior restraints may be acceptable in certain circumstances: if the publication concerns the location of troops during wartime, obscene matter, or incitement to violence. The reference to troops is largely considered to be a justification for prior restraints in cases involving national security matters, or, at least, for the notion that there is a compelling interest in keeping that kind of information secret.

This question was addressed but not completely resolved in *New York Times Co. v. U.S.* The government sought an order barring the *New York Times* and the *Washington Post* from publishing the "Pentagon Papers," documents that discussed events that had occurred during the Vietnam War. The Court issued a short opinion upholding the lower courts' refusals to issue an injunction (in other words, it allowed the papers to publish the material), and then all nine Justices issued separate concurring or dissenting opinions. There was no consensus on the reasons why the newspapers should be allowed to publish the material. The most important factor, it seems, was that the government simply couldn't meet its burden of proving that there would be any serious harm if the information were published. Another factor was that the information covered events that had already occurred. It's possible that there would have been a different result if the material to be published could have affected the future. In such a case, it is more likely that the government could show that there would be serious harm.

Consider for example, the facts of *U.S. v. The Progressive*. In that case, the government attempted to enjoin a magazine from publishing information about how to make a nuclear bomb. The trial court issued an injunction, relying on *Near's* troop movements dicta and finding a more immediate potential for harm. The court expressed concern that publication of the information would lead to nuclear proliferation. The magazine appealed and the government stopped fighting the case during the appeals process. The article was eventually published. Nevertheless, the trial court's opinion shows that courts may consider factors such as whether the information could affect the future and the degree of seriousness of the potential harm.

If a court does issue an injunction and a person publishes the material in violation of that order, the person can be held in contempt, even if the order is later overturned. Being held in contempt often means that the person who violated the order will go to jail.

Criminal Prosecution

Although speech is rarely restrained, there is a question as to whether the media could, or should, be punished after publication for disseminating classified information, or even for possessing it. Some of the justices explicitly stated in their opinions in *New York Times Co. v. U.S.* that such a prosecution was a possibility, even if they did not enjoin publication of the Pentagon Papers. The Espionage Act prohibits the unauthorized possession and dissemination of certain classified information, and the law specifically states that it applies to anyone. The Supreme Court has not interpreted how that law should be applied to the press or whether the First Amendment would provide any protection from prosecution; thus, one must at least consider the possibility that a conviction would be upheld if a journalist (or any other media participant) published the information. After all, strict scrutiny does not mean that the government always loses—only that it has a high burden to overcome to win. For example, in *Holder v. Humanitarian Law Project*, the Supreme Court applied the strict scrutiny test and upheld a law that prohibits providing material support or resources to certain designated foreign terrorist organizations. The Court found that there was no First Amendment right to provide training to such groups because the government interest in protecting national security is of the highest order; moreover, the law did not prevent independent advocacy on behalf of the groups. Although the holding of *Holder* is not necessarily directly applicable to cases involving the use of classified information in news reports, the case illustrates the principle that national security interests are the kind of interests that the Court may find compelling, and that some restrictions on speech will be tolerated to protect those interests.

There has never been an Espionage Act prosecution of a professional journalist, and the case law related to this topic is sparse. In 2006, a grand jury was convened to determine whether anyone from the *Washington Post* or the *New York Times* should be charged under the Espionage Act. The *Washington*

Post had revealed that the CIA had secret prisons around the world, and the *New York Times* reported that the NSA eavesdropped on phone calls without warrants. Although no charges were filed, arguments were made on both sides as to whether the media could, or should, be charged with espionage violations.

In 1942, prosecutors considered Espionage Act charges, prompted by a *Chicago Tribune* article entitled "Navy Had Word of Jap Plan to Strike at Sea." Again, a grand jury was convened but charges were never brought.

Professional media organizations have argued that they should not be prosecuted because they exercise good ethical judgment, refraining from publishing truly sensitive material. And many experts believe that a court would find at least some First Amendment protection for news organizations that publish classified information; but the First Amendment is not absolute, and there is certainly some ambiguity about what would be protected. Commentators have speculated that the news media has been protected from charges for various practical reasons—because of political concerns, or because of the difficulty in general of obtaining criminal convictions, or out of concern that a court might rule that the Espionage Act is unconstitutional as written.

One high profile case illustrates the problems in trying to obtain a conviction. Steven Rosen and Keith Weissman were lobbyists for the American Israel Public Affairs Committee (AIPAC), a pro-Israel lobbying group. They were indicted because they had allegedly obtained and disclosed to journalists, as well as the Israeli government, certain classified information about mid-east policy. The Defense Department employee who gave them the information pleaded guilty to charges, but prosecutors eventually dismissed the charges against the lobbyists. One concern was that classified information might have had to be used at trial. But also, it may have been too difficult to obtain a conviction, because the judge had ruled that, to protect First Amendment considerations, prosecutors would have to prove that the lobbyists knew they would harm the U.S. by releasing the information. Media organizations had been concerned that if Rosen and Weissman were convicted, the precedent would be used to go after journalists. The absence of a conviction shows how difficult it can be to apply the Espionage Act to cases where there are First Amendment interests at stake, as opposed to situations where there is clearly an intent to cause harm to the U.S.

As a cautionary tale, though, there is at one case where an Espionage Act conviction was upheld in a publishing context. In *U.S. v. Morison*, a former government employee left his job to work for a publishing company. He took copies of classified photos from the government and gave them to the publisher. He was convicted of violating the Espionage Act, and his conviction was upheld on appeal. Scholars argue, however, that government employees who leak information may be held to a different standard than journalists because they have different obligations vis-à-vis the government. It's possible that a journalist who was simply given classified photos could be treated differently than the government employee who conveyed them.

The great debate is whether the First Amendment would—or should—protect leaks, at least in some circumstances. Although it is widely accepted that national security is the kind of thing that could be a compelling interest that might outweigh First Amendment rights, there are serious concerns with giving the government broad power to prosecute anyone for publishing anything that might fall within the scope of "national security." Also, there is an obvious danger to journalists if the Espionage Act can be applied to news reporting, which has sometimes involved the disclosure of classified information.

Several scholars have argued that the Espionage Act is inherently flawed. Some have argued that the law is unconstitutional on its face because the language is too vague or overbroad. Others have taken the position that the law must be interpreted narrowly. Geoffrey Stone, a law professor at the University of Chicago, testified before Congress that the First Amendment should protect the disclosure of information that has significant value to the public. Mary-Rose Papandrea, a law professor at the University of North Carolina, has argued that journalists should be protected by the First Amendment unless they had an intent to harm national security. The question is whether a court would adopt any of these considerations if a journalist were charged under the Espionage Act. If, for example, a court were to determine that the Espionage Act requires proof of intent to harm the United States, it may be the case that the government could prove such intent with respect to some websites that post leaked material, but not with respect to a news organization. Those who act in furtherance of journalism may have a different intent than those who seek to interfere with the U.S. government.

Also, journalists traditionally adhere to principles of journalism ethics. When it comes to leaks, journalists are supposed to try to verify the information or authenticate the documents that are leaked, try to identify the source to the leak if they are anonymous, try to determine what motives the leaker may have had, and evaluate whether such motives should be furthered by the publication of the leaked information. Journalists will typically consider whether anyone is likely to be harmed by the disclosure of information, and often, the news organization will call the relevant government agency for comment and consider the government's arguments about why the information should not be published. Sites that allow for massive dumps of hacked data make no such ethical assessments.

The government often distinguishes "leakers" from "whistleblowers." According to the government, whistleblowers follow internal protocols for revealing wrongdoing, corruption, or other problematic behaviors. They are supposed to provide information to superiors within the government and are given protection from retaliation if they follow the proper procedures. Leakers, on the other hand, do not follow internal procedures and reveal information to outsiders, such as journalists, or directly reveal the information to the public. The Obama Administration believed that leakers should be prosecuted as spies, regardless of whether their intent was to harm the United States or simply to remedy corruption or abuse, and that administration prosecuted more leakers than all previous Presidential administrations combined.

The problem with the distinction is that it fails to provide a remedy in situations where "superiors" do not take any remedial action, or when it is the superiors themselves that are corrupt or abusing power. Thomas Drake, for example, was one of the leakers prosecuted by the Obama Administration, and he had leaked information about corruption and waste of taxpayer dollars within the NSA only after attempting to go through the internal protocols for whistleblowers. But no one responded to his concerns. He then leaked to the press. The government prosecuted him under the Espionage Act, although it eventually dropped the prosecution.

The press is supposed to act as a check on governmental power by keeping the public informed and reveal information of relevance to self-government. It would make sense, then, to provide First Amendment protection for publishing leaks when the leaks contribute to the public understanding of government actions. It may also logically require providing First Amendment protection for the leakers themselves, in some circumstances, as long as the revelation of information is for the purpose of keeping the government accountable, as opposed to trying to secretly help foreign powers or harm the United

States. Otherwise, we would give the government the power to silence and punish dissent. Leaking can be a particular form of dissent. On the other hand, one wouldn't want to give free reign to any leaker to reveal information that is legitimately harmful to government interests and within the bounds of the proper role of government. The classic example is the location of troops during wartime. Although one might oppose a war, having troops act during war is typically a recognized function of government, and revealing their location would be legitimately harmful. Thus, a court would need to develop a test that accounts for the various interests at issue. One might argue, for example, that a leak should be protected if it involves (1) access to information that the general public has been denied, (2) a recognition that the information is relevant to the public's understanding of what the government is doing, (3) an understanding that the government action is either illegal, corrupt, wasteful, or otherwise would be the kind of activity that should be subjected to legal or constitutional scrutiny, and (4) there is no reasonable internal avenue to remedy the abuse. This standard might protect some leaks but not others.

In sum, there is still a lot of ambiguity with respect to how First Amendment principles would apply to prosecutions under the Espionage Act and whether or under what circumstances a journalist might be criminally liable for the dissemination of classified information.

Spying on the Media

Wikileaks has long complained that the U.S. government is spying on them. Whether that is true or not, it is certainly true that the government has numerous surveillance techniques at their disposal. Agencies monitor phone calls and emails, customs officials are authorized to search computers and other electronics at borders, and law enforcement officials have broad powers under the PATRIOT Act. At this time, there is no case law declaring that the First Amendment protects journalist from being subject to this kind of surveillance.

As discussed in Chapter 13, the Privacy Protection Act provides some extra protection to journalists when it comes to searches. Government officials cannot get a warrant to search for journalistic materials, except in very limited circumstances. One of these circumstances is when the government has probable cause to believe that the journalist is in possession of classified or national security materials. Therefore, in such a context, the protection of the Act is of little use. The Department of Justice also has internal guidelines concerning the subpoena of journalists' records from third parties such as telephone service providers. However, these guidelines do not have the force of law and may not provide complete protection.

The extent to which journalists are shielded from surveillance probably stems more from political sensitivities than from any clear legal protection, although news organizations would always argue that the First Amendment should extend a certain degree of protection from government abuse, even in cases where classified information is involved, as long as the media is acting responsibly and not with intent to harm the U.S. Whether a court would adopt such a rule has yet to be tested.

Hate Speech

"Hate speech" is a term that people use to refer to statements or symbolic speech acts that are potentially insulting or offensive to another because the speech suggests something negative about the other person's race, ethnicity, gender, religion, sexual orientation, or some other categorization. This includes statements that are overtly hostile, such as the use of racial slurs, but also includes statements that are not intended to be hateful but are nevertheless found to be offensive by the audience.

Because hate speech is considered so offensive in civilized society, there are often efforts to restrict it. Sometimes the government will try to pass laws that ban hate speech; sometimes the government will attempt to punish it via criminal prosecution or other penalties. Private parties also attempt to restrict hate speech, either through organizational disciplinary measures or through civil lawsuits. Given the broad range of approaches people take to punish hate speech, this section will address the following issues:

1. Can the government punish hate speech?

2. Can private entities punish someone for hate speech?

3. Can a speaker be civilly liable in a lawsuit based on hate speech?

Can the Government Punish Hate Speech?

For a while, it was fashionable for colleges to enact "speech codes" that regulated how students should express themselves in an effort to curb or eliminate hate speech. But state colleges and universities are government entities, so to the extent a state school attempted to enforce a speech code, it was acting as a government entity and First Amendment rights were at issue.

The courts have found that laws or codes (such as speech codes on college campuses) are unconstitutional if they are vague or overbroad. Attempts to regulate "offensive" speech, for example, would almost certainly be deemed too vague because a reasonable person cannot always guess in advance what another might find offensive. Regulations are overbroad if they ban too wide a range of statements, so that statements that should be protected are excluded along with those that may be genuinely problematic.

Courts have consistently ruled that speech codes are unconstitutional when they are vague or overbroad or both. For example, in *Doe v. University of Michigan*, the court considered the constitutionality of a University of Michigan code that prohibited any expression that "stigmatizes or victimizes an individual" based on race, religion, gender, or other protected categories. The school's brochure contained numerous examples of behavior that would be considered harassment, including: "You tell jokes about gay men and lesbians," and "You comment in a derogatory way about a particular person or group's physical appearance or sexual orientation, or their cultural origins or religious beliefs." While the statute was probably designed with genuinely cruel conduct in mind, the wording itself raises questions about applicability. Can gay men or lesbians joke about themselves? Would telling someone that they really need a haircut constitute a derogatory comment about physical appearance?

The student who challenged the code was a graduate student in biopsychology, a field that studies the biological basis for differences in personality traits and mental abilities. Some of the theories used in that field might be perceived as sexist or racist, and the student was concerned that any discussion of those theories—which were necessary to his studies, regardless of whether he agreed with them—would be a violation of the policy.

The court noted that there was substantial precedent supporting two points: first, that the government should not establish "orthodox" views and prohibit speech with which it disagrees; and second, that the government may not prohibit speech simply because many people find it to be offensive. Those principles indicated that the code was probably invalid.

The court concluded that the code was unconstitutional because it was both vague and overbroad. It was overbroad because it punished speech that should be constitutionally protected, such as statements made in a class as to whether there was any evidence that being gay was a condition that could be changed through counseling. Under normal circumstances, such speech is constitutionally protected—the government cannot prohibit it merely because it may be offensive. The code was also vague because its language was so broad and poorly defined that it was unclear what would be prohibited or permitted. The court focused in particular on the phrase "stigmatize or victimize," which the court felt was too poorly defined to provide meaningful guidance.

Similar results were obtained in *DeJohn v. Temple University*, where the court found a sexual harassment policy to be overbroad, and *UWM Post v. Board of Regents of the University of Wisconsin*, where the court found a regulation concerning discriminatory and hostile speech to be overbroad. In both cases, the language of the policies was so expansive as to cover speech that should be permitted in an academic environment.

While many schools have tried, no school has yet come up with a policy that has been upheld as constitutional, in large part because of the problem of adequately articulating what would be prohibited without being either vague or overbroad. In short, the government cannot prohibit speech merely because it offends. There has to be something more. (Private universities, which are not governmental entities and therefore not subject to the First Amendment, may have speech codes that they enforce.)

Even in the absence of a speech code, local governments will sometimes attempt to regulate speech by punishing it as a crime. Many of the famous cases involving racist or hateful speech involve public rallies (marches, parades, and other gatherings where views are expressed) or actions (such as burning a cross or beating a victim).

The question in these types of cases is where to draw the line between protected speech and punishable crimes. The Supreme Court has generally ruled that offensive speech cannot be outlawed; however, actions based on offensive motives may be prosecuted if the actions qualify as a crime independently of the underlying offensive belief. Thus, the Supreme Court has generally protected events such as marches or gatherings, as long as the participants are simply expressing their viewpoint and not inciting violence or otherwise committing any crimes.

Probably the most important case on this topic is *Brandenburg v. Ohio*. In that case, the leader of the Ku Klux Klan was convicted under an Ohio law that prohibited the advocacy of using crime, violence or terrorism for political purposes. His conviction was based on a statement he made at a rally: "We're not a revengent organization, but if our President, our Congress, our Supreme Court, continues to suppress the white, Caucasian race, it's possible that there might have to be some revengance taken."

The Court noted that a similar law had previously been upheld as constitutional in *Whitney v. California*, where the Court determined that advocating violence as a means to effecting political change was a threat to security and could be outlawed. But the Court also noted that later cases reconsidered the constitutionality of mere advocacy: "These later decisions have fashioned the principle that the constitutional guarantees of free speech and free press do not permit a State to forbid or proscribe advocacy of the use of force or of law violation except where such advocacy is directed to inciting or producing imminent lawless action and is likely to incite or produce such action." Thus, the Court reversed the conviction because the speech was merely hypothesizing the appropriateness of "revengance," rather than seeking immediate action.

The line between mere advocacy of an idea and actual crime can be difficult to draw, but the two Supreme Court cases involving cross burning illustrate the difference.

First, to understand these cases, it is important to understand a basic principle of criminal law, which is that all crimes must have two components: *mens rea*, which refers to a mental state or intent, and *actus reus*, which refers to a concrete action that is taken. A criminal statute will define what actions and mental states are required for a crime to have been committed, but a court may find a law to be unconstitutional if one or both of those components violate constitutional principles.

In *R.A.V. v. City of St. Paul*, the Court considered the constitutionality of an ordinance that banned placing on public or private property "a symbol, object, appellation, characterization or graffiti, including, but not limited to, a burning cross or Nazi swastika, which one knows or has reasonable grounds to know arouses anger, alarm, or resentment in others on the basis of race, color, creed, religion, or gender." In short, the law prohibited speech or actions deemed offensive based on certain protected categories. The Court ruled the law was unconstitutional because it was specifically designed to prohibit certain speech based upon the fact that the particular content was socially disfavored. Given the precedent that government is not supposed to establish an orthodoxy, and given the other legitimate ways speech can be punished (if it constituted a true threat, for example), the law served no purpose but to punish disfavored speech and was therefore unconstitutional.

In *Virginia v. Black*, however, the Court ruled that cross-burning can constitute a crime if intent to intimidate is proven. As noted in *R.A.V.*, burning a cross could be punished as a crime under already existing laws if the elements of the crime could be proven. For example, it might constitute a trespass or a threat, but a prosecutor would have to prove both the action and the requisite intent for the crime. A law that prohibits burning a cross with the intent to intimidate the victim can be a legitimate crime because it contains both *actus reus* (the act of burning a cross) and *mens rea* (the intent to intimidate), and it serves a legitimate purpose other than proscribing a particular expression or belief merely because the viewpoint is disfavored (namely, the legitimate interest in prohibiting intimidation by other citizens).

Comparing the two cases illustrates the difference between speech that is protected by the First Amendment and speech that is not. Efforts to punish a speaker because of the content of his speech—and only because the content of the speech is disfavored—will most likely be deemed unconstitutional. But the government may nevertheless punish something that otherwise constitutes a genuine crime, consisting of act and a requisite intent, and it serves some purpose other than targeting the content of speech.

The nexus between conduct and thought was also addressed in *Wisconsin v. Mitchell*, a case involving black youths who were convicted of beating a white youth because they were upset by portrayals of racism in the film *Mississippi Burning*. The penalties were enhanced because of a bias motive law that permitted greater penalties for crimes based on racial motivation. The Wisconsin Supreme Court overturned the conviction of one of the people involved because the penalty was based on "offensive thought" and, per *R.A.V.*, should be protected by the First Amendment. The U.S. Supreme Court reversed and upheld the conviction. The Court noted that the law was primarily aimed at conduct, not speech. Although the law did punish a person more severely based on a particular motive, the Court noted that motive has always played a role in the sentencing process, and the question is only whether the motive is relevant to the crime. It would be unconstitutional to punish someone more severely for a traffic ticket merely because they are racist, for example. Yet it would be appropriate to impose a harsher sentence if the racist selected a murder victim to kill because of race.

In sum, a person can be convicted of a crime if the conduct at issue is a crime aside from any viewpoint or belief that happens to be related to it. But the government may not make it a crime only to have a disfavored viewpoint.

Given the foregoing discussion concerning the requirement that a valid crime be demonstrated to impose liability, one might think that a person cannot be punished merely because an official is offended by speech. In most cases, the answer is no; but sometimes, certain punishments are permitted.

A typical example of protected speech is *Iota XI Chapter of Sigma Chi Fraternity v. George Mason University*. A fraternity held an "ugly woman" contest in which a male fraternity member dressed up as a woman, invoking stereotypes deemed sexist and racist. The University punished the students involved, but the court ruled that the University's actions were unconstitutional because it was punishing students solely because it did not like the content of their speech.

However, in *Dambrot v. Central Michigan University*, the court considered whether it would be unconstitutional to fire a basketball coach for referring to his players as "niggers." He told them that he wanted them to "play like niggers on the court," but not "act like niggers in the classroom." He claims to have used the term in a positive sense, meaning someone who is "fearless, mentally strong, and tough." The coach was first punished under the school's anti-harassment policy, and then later fired. Although the court ruled that the university's speech code prohibiting such terms was unconstitutional, it nevertheless concluded that the firing of the coach was not a violation of his First Amendment rights. When it comes to government employees, courts have held that their speech is protected only if it addresses a matter of public concern or deals in the realm of academic freedom. In this case, though, the court determined that the speech did not address a matter of public concern, nor did it advance a message, and the University was within its rights to fire him. The court said:

> The First Amendment protects the right of any person to espouse the view that a "nigger" is someone who is aggressive in nature, tough, loud, abrasive, hard-nosed, and intimidating; someone at home on the court but out of place in a classroom setting where discipline, focus, intelligence, and interest are required. ... What the First Amendment does not do, however, is require the government as employer or the university as educator to accept this view as a valid means of motivating players. An instructor's choice of teaching methods does not rise to the level of protected expression.

There are other cases involving government employees who were fired for speech, such as *Martin v. Parrish*, where an employee was fired for the excessive use of profanity. The court found there was no legitimate purpose to the speech—it did not touch upon a matter of public concern—and thus it is possible for a government entity to impose punishment in cases related to speech if the speech falls outside the scope of what the courts have deemed to be protected by the First Amendment. Government employees, however, are subject to different rules (and those rules are discussed more fully in Chapter 19).

Can Private Entities Punish Someone for Hate Speech?

A person who makes racist or sexist statements at work can be disciplined or fired. The exact nature of how a person might be punished may depend on whether the person is in a union or works under a contract, or what company policy is, because there are employment and labor law issues to consider. Nevertheless, there would be no basis for claiming that the speaker has First Amendment rights in such a context. The First Amendment applies only to government action, not private action, so a private employer may punish employees without infringing their rights. In fact, the employer probably must punish a speaker to comply with anti-discrimination laws, and if the speech is viewed as discriminatory, the employer may be in trouble itself if it fails to take action.

The same is true for private schools and other private organizations. Because they are not government entities, a person would have no First Amendment protection, so the organizations may take action to punish hate speech, as long as the punishment complies with all other applicable laws.

Many websites have terms of service that prohibit hateful or offensive comments, and it is common to remove posts that violate those terms. Again, as long as the site is a private entity, they are free to remove offensive posts, and there are no First Amendment implications.

Can a Speaker Be Civilly Liable in a Lawsuit Based on Hate Speech?

There is a risk that a person offended by hate speech might attempt to sue for damages. The two claims that might arise are libel and intentional infliction of emotional distress (IIED).

In most instances, people offended by hate speech will not be successful if they attempt to sue for libel. In the United States, the law typically does not allow claims for "group libel" based on large groups, such as groups based on race, ethnicity, religion, gender, or other classes. Statements that insult large groups would not be actionable because it they fail to identify any specific individual, which is usually a required element of a libel claim in most states. However, there are two things to keep in mind about group libel.

First, hate speech could potentially be libelous if the statement does identify a particular individual rather than a group as a whole. Thus, making a disparaging statement about women in general would not be actionable, but making a defamatory statement about a specific woman could be.

Second, the notion of group libel is recognized in other countries. If hate speech is published online, it will be accessible in Europe and other nations that do punish group libel, and there is, at least in theory, a risk that the speaker could be punished there. One high profile example in 2008 involved actress Brigitte Bardot, who was convicted in France of "inciting racial hatred" because she published a book in which she called Muslims "barbaric" and generally complained that Muslims were ruining the country. Thus, there is the potential for liability in other countries for making statements that defame a group on the basis of race, religion, sexual orientation or other category. The question in most cases will be whether the speaker could be subject to jurisdiction in the foreign court and whether the foreign court would consider it worthwhile to pursue a claim, a determination that would have to be made on a case-by-case basis. (The topic of international jurisdiction is discussed more fully in Chapter 20.)

Plaintiffs have also argued that hate speech should be covered by the IIED tort. However, most cases have been unsuccessful.

In *Citizen Publishing Co. v. Miller*, the court ruled that an offensive letter to the editor could not constitute a claim for IIED because it did not fall under one of the recognized exceptions to the general rule that political speech is entitled to First Amendment protection. The letter in question said: "We can stop the murders of American soldiers in Iraq by those who seek revenge or to regain their power. Whenever there is an assassination or another atrocity, we should proceed to the closest mosque and execute five of the first Muslims we encounter." The plaintiffs argued that this was hate speech and constituted incitement of violence toward Muslims. However, the court ruled that the speech was protected by the First Amendment. There was no incitement because reading about an idea (in this case, the idea of executing Muslims at some point in the future) does not translate into immediate action.

Another case, *Snyder v. Phelps*, involved protesters who protested a marine's funeral with signs that said "God Hates Fags" and otherwise suggested that soldiers were dying in war because God was angry with America's tolerance towards homosexuality. The father of the deceased Marine sued for IIED. The Supreme Court ruled that the protesters' speech was protected by the First Amendment, and the protesters could not be held liable merely because the speech was offensive. Thus, it is difficult to use civil litigation as a remedy for offensive speech.

Sexual Content

Sex is a topic that has traditionally caused a lot of controversy in the United States. State governments (and the federal government, as well) have made the purchase or sale of obscenity a crime, and they have attempted to regulate sexual content by restricting where it can be found or otherwise controlling access to it. The Supreme Court has said on numerous occasions that obscenity is not protected by the First Amendment, yet sexual content is regularly available in mass media. So when and how can sexual content be regulated, banned, punished, or subject to civil liability? This section will discuss:

1. The difference between "obscenity" and "indecency" and when such material may be criminally punished or banned by the government

2. The regulation of "revenge porn"

3. Child pornography as a special category of content that is regulated

4. Whether sexual content can form the basis of a civil lawsuit

Obscenity and Indecency

To understand the law in this area, one must first understand the terms used. Sexual content is divided into two categories: obscenity and indecency.

The question is what falls into each category. The Supreme Court established a test for determining whether sexual content qualifies as obscenity in *Miller v. California*. According to this test, the government has the burden of proving all three of the following elements:

1. Would the average person applying contemporary community standards find that the material appeals to a prurient interest? This means that the jury must find that the material appeals to an

unhealthy or unnatural interest in sex, and in *Mishkin v. New York*, the Court ruled that this element can be met if the material appeals to the prurient interest of a specific fetish-oriented group.

2.   Does the material depict sex in a "patently offensive" manner?

3.   Would a reasonable person find that the work as a whole lacks serious literary, artistic, political, or scientific value? In *Pope v. Illinois*, the Court ruled that a national reasonableness standard, not a community standard, must be used for the third prong of the test.

If the material appeals to a prurient interest, is patently offensive and lacks serious value, then it is obscene, and it receives no First Amendment protection. Obscenity laws are criminal laws that are enforced by the government via prosecutions or regulatory actions. Because there is no First Amendment protection for obscene material, it may be banned or seized and people may be prosecuted for buying or selling it.

If it is not obscene, it may be indecent. Indecent material is entitled to First Amendment protection. In print media, that means that it cannot be banned, punished, or regulated unless the law meets the strict scrutiny test, just like any other content-based regulation. Strict scrutiny requires the government to prove that it has a compelling interest and its regulation is the least restrictive means of serving the interest. So far, the Supreme Court has treated the internet like print media and ruled that indecent material on the internet cannot be banned or regulated unless the regulation meets strict scrutiny. For example, in *Reno v. ACLU*, the Court found that indecency regulations in the Communications Decency Act were unconstitutional because filtering software was a less restrictive means of dealing with the government's interest in protecting children from indecent material. Then, Congress passed the Child Online Protection Act (COPA), which also purported to regulate decency. Again, in *Ashcroft v. ACLU*, the Supreme Court ruled that the law was unconstitutional because filtering would be a less restrictive alternative.

Congress tried to enforce its view of decency online one more time, passing the Children's Internet Protection Act (CIPA), which required libraries that receive federal funds to use filtering software. That law was upheld as constitutional in *U.S. v. American Library Association*. However, the law was upheld not because the government is permitted to regulate decency, but because the law was a form of government funding, which allowed Congress to impose regulations that it would otherwise not be permitted to impose. (See Chapter 19 for more information about government funding as a basis for speech restrictions.)

Indecency in broadcast media, however, may be treated differently. In *FCC v. Pacifica Foundation*, the Supreme Court upheld the FCC's authority to regulate indecency in broadcast media because of the limited spectrum argument: the idea that broadcast spectrum is limited and thus broadcasters have a special responsibility to serve the public interest. The FCC website defines indecency as "language or material that, in context, depicts or describes, in terms patently offensive as measured by contemporary community broadcast standards for the broadcast medium, sexual or excretory organs or activities." Thus, in broadcast media, indecent material can be punished or restricted during hours that children may be in the audience, which is currently defined as 6 a.m. to 10 p.m., pursuant to FCC regulations. (FCC regulation of content is discussed more fully in Chapter 18.)

As a practical matter, what does this mean? Magazines that depict nudity and suggestive poses (*Playboy*, *Penthouse*, *Hustler*, etc.) are not banned if they are not "obscene." In *Jenkins v. Georgia*, the Supreme Court ruled that nudity alone is not sufficient to constitute obscenity, so there must be more than mere nudity. The same holds true for pornography (depictions of sexual activity). If a government wanted to prosecute the buying, selling, or making of pornography, it would have to prove that the material is obscene under the *Miller* test. To determine what constitutes obscenity, courts would look at precedent to see how the *Miller* factors have been applied to fact patterns in the past.

The one exception is that states may ban the sale of indecent material to minors, if the state law meets the standard set forth in *Ginsberg v. New York*. In *Ginsberg*, the Supreme Court ruled that a state law making it unlawful to knowingly sell to a minor images or magazines that depict nudity and are "harmful to minors" was constitutional. The Court noted that the material was not obscene and perfectly legal to sell to adults. However, the Court also noted that the state has an interest in protecting minors and in providing parents with the support of laws that help them raise their children as they wish. Parents may provide their children with such publications if they so choose, but the law supports parents who don't want their children exposed to such material. The Court considered the legislature's reliance on studies asking whether sexual content was harmful to the moral development of minors, noting that a direct causal link has neither been proved nor disproved. The Court stated that legislatures need not have "scientifically certain criteria" and concluded, "we … cannot say that [the law] has no rational relation to the objective of safeguarding … minors from harm." It is worth noting that the Court did not apply strict scrutiny, even though the law was content based. Instead, it applied a rational basis test, which is often used in cases involving economic regulations, asking only whether there is a rational relationship between the government interest and the law.

Aside from the tests used by the courts, it is important to remember that prosecutors have prosecutorial discretion. That means that even though there may be an obscenity law on the books, they might choose to focus their efforts elsewhere, prosecuting murders, drug deals, or other crimes.

Most movies and songs with sexual themes or content are probably protected under the First Amendment because they are either not patently offensive, or they contain serious artistic value. This is why sexual content can be found in books, movies, music, and other forms of mass media. Even when such uses are questionable, prosecutors may not want to spend their time and money prosecuting borderline cases.

Governments have tried to regulate or limit access to sexual content in a variety of ways other than outright bans. Some efforts have succeeded and others have failed. For example, in *City of Renton v. Playtime Theatres*, the Supreme Court held that zoning ordinances applied to adult theatres are generally acceptable as long as the government can show "secondary effects," meaning that the presence of adult theatres causes other problems, like crime. However, creative efforts to limit negative portrayals of women in pornography have not been successful. In *American Booksellers Ass'n Inc. v. Hudnut*, the court considered an Indianapolis city law that prohibited pornography that was discriminatory towards women and depicted them in subordinate situations. The court found the law to be unconstitutional because the government is not permitted to ban content solely because it disfavors the message.

It is worth noting that, in *Stanley v. Georgia*, the Supreme Court ruled that persons may possess obscenity in the privacy of their own home, but that ruling is limited to pornography that features adults.

Child Pornography

The Supreme Court has ruled that child pornography can be banned and citizens can be prosecuted for its sale or possession, and there is no conflict with First Amendment principles even if the content wouldn't have met the *Miller* test for obscenity. In *New York v. Ferber*, the Court ruled that states may regulate the sale of child pornography, and in *Osborne v. Ohio*, the Court ruled that a person may not possess child pornography under any circumstance. The rationale behind these rulings is that children are harmed by the creation of such material and the harm outweighs any interest in expression.

Although states have their own laws that may vary, there is a federal law that criminalizes the possession, distribution, reception, or production of child pornography, defined as the depiction of a person under 18 engaged in sexually explicit conduct. Unlike the law applicable to adults, nudity alone can be a basis for liability if the image is sufficiently suggestive.

The only exception is that the Supreme Court has ruled that "fake" child porn—where no actual children are used, such as cartoons, or images where the person is over 18 but pretending to be younger—is not subject to the same kind of scrutiny as "real" child porn, which involves actual minors. In *Free Speech Coalition v. Ashcroft*, the Court ruled that a statutory ban on fake child pornography was unconstitutional, in large part because the government interest in protecting children was lessened by the fact that no children are actually harmed in fake depictions.

The child pornography law can have some interesting consequences. For example, minors who take and distribute photos of themselves or their significant other may be subject to prosecution. So-called "sexting" cases are on the rise. Many people may feel that teens who are dating and sext each other shouldn't be subject to prosecution, because it unfairly labels them as sex offenders and negatively impacts their entire life for doing something that was not truly within the intent of child porn laws. Thus, some have argued that there should be exceptions if the photos are taken voluntarily and not disseminated to third parties. However, in *A.H. v. State*, the court found that child pornography laws can be used to prosecute teen sexting cases.

The courts have not been friendly to any defenses in child pornography cases, and at least one court has specifically rejected the argument that there are First Amendment rights for journalists when images of child porn are collected in the newsgathering process. In *U.S. v. Matthews*, the court ruled that there was no protection for newsgathering. A journalist can be prosecuted for possession of child pornography, even if it is obtained for legitimate news purposes.

Regulation of "Revenge Porn"

Since the internet and social media has made it easy to harass people with "revenge porn" (also known as non-consensual pornography), 41 states plus D.C. have passed laws to punish the unauthorized posting of sexual images. In *State v. Van Buren*, the Vermont Supreme Court upheld the state law in the face of a First Amendment challenge. The Vermont law criminalizes the knowing disclosure of images depicting an identifiable person who is nude or engaging in sexual conduct, without that person's consent and with the intent to harm, harass, intimidate, threaten, or coerce the person depicted. There are exceptions for images involving voluntary nudity or sexual conduct in public or places where a person has no reasonable expectation of privacy and disclosures made in the public interest or constituting a matter of public concern. The court found that the law was a content-based restriction on speech, and therefore applied strict scrutiny. However, there was a compelling interest in protecting citizens from nonconsensual pornography, and the law is narrowly tailored because it does not implicate matters of public concern. The images at issue in the case were private images that had no impact on any public issue, and the court found no First Amendment interest in their unauthorized disclosure.

However, other revenge porn laws have been deemed unconstitutional. For example, in *Ex Parte Jones*, a Texas court found that the state law could not withstand strict scrutiny because it was not narrowly tailored. The law states:

A person commits an offense if:

(1) without the effective consent of the depicted person, the person intentionally discloses visual material depicting another person with the person's intimate parts exposed or engaged in sexual conduct;

(2) the visual material was obtained by the person or created under circumstances in which the depicted person had a reasonable expectation that the visual material would remain private;

(3) the disclosure of the visual material causes harm to the depicted person; and

(4) the disclosure of the visual material reveals the identity of the depicted person in any manner.

The court found that this law could be applied in circumstances where the person was not aware of the expectations of the person depicted and therefore it was overbroad. It also does not contain an exception for matters in the public interest (although the court did not acknowledge that aspect of the law). In sum, the constitutionality of such laws will likely depend on whether they are drafted narrowly enough to withstand strict scrutiny.

Civil Lawsuits

Technology has made it easier for ordinary citizens to capture and distribute sexual images. Cameras are so small and unobtrusive that pictures can be taken surreptitiously. Images can be emailed, posted, downloaded, and copied in a variety of formats. If images are taken and distributed without the consent of the person depicted, they may have the ability to sue for invasion of privacy, violation of the right of publicity, intentional infliction of emotional distress, or other claims. *Bollea v. Gawker* (discussed more fully in Chapter 4) is an excellent example of where someone won a privacy lawsuit based on the publication of a sex tape. Of course, the issue is always whether the person sued will actually have money to pay any damages awarded. This is why states seek to pass criminal "revenge porn" statutes—as a deterrent to making such online posts when the perpetrator does not fear civil liability.

Violent Content

Depictions of violence are difficult to regulate. Every now and then, a law will try to regulate violent images, but lawmakers have yet to create a law that would withstand constitutional scrutiny. Some have argued that violence should be regulated as a form of obscenity, but such efforts have been unsuccessful.

In other cases, government efforts to regulate violence are stuck down for being too vague or too broad. It has proved difficult to define what exactly is prohibited and what is acceptable.

The leading Supreme Court case on this topic is *U.S. v. Stevens*, in which the Supreme Court struck down a law that criminalized the creation, sale, or possession of depictions of animal cruelty. The problem with the law was that it applied to the portrayal of animal cruelty, not the act itself. Specifically, the law applied to depictions "in which a living animal is intentionally maimed, mutilated, tortured, wounded, or killed," if the act would violate state or federal law in the jurisdiction where the creation, sale, or possession takes place. The law exempted depictions with "serious religious, political, scientific, educational, journalistic, historical, or artistic value."

Although laws that prohibit the cruelty itself may be valid, the Court ruled that the prohibition of depictions was overbroad for two reasons. First, the definition of "cruelty" didn't necessarily require a cruel method of causing harm because it applied to any wounding or killing. Second, the law permitted prosecution even if the activity was legal where it was filmed. Hunting is legal in many states, but is illegal in D.C., for example. Thus, if a person in D.C. possessed a video depicting an animal shot while hunting legally in another state, he may be subject to prosecution under this law.

Several cities and states have attempted to pass laws that criminalize the use by or sale to minors of violent video games, but so far, these laws have been deemed unconstitutional. The Supreme Court struck down such a law in *Brown v. Entertainment Merchants Ass'n*. In *Brown*, the Court found that video games were a form of expression that are presumptively entitled to First Amendment protection, just like movies, books, and other forms of media. The question, then, is whether there was any reason to justify a restriction on such speech. Importantly, the Court rejected the idea that violence is obscene or comparable to sexual content, and therefore it distinguished *Ginsberg v. New York*, which upheld restrictions on the sale of sexual materials to minors. Because the law was a content-based restriction on speech, the Court found that the law would be invalid unless it could meet the strict scrutiny test: there must be a compelling government interest and the law must be narrowly drawn to serve that interest. The Court refused to defer to the California legislature's determination that studies showed a link between violent video games and adverse effects. The Court concluded that there was no proof of adverse effects, and thus it was not clear whether California was actually serving a legitimate interest or simply disfavoring a particular form of speech.

Although violent content may be unregulated, many entertainment industry groups voluntarily rate materials or disclose the nature of any violent material to appease consumers. News organizations will also sometimes warn readers/viewers when violent material will be shown so that those who think the material is offensive or inappropriate can avoid it. This form of self-regulation helps avoid controversy.

Threats

Threats are punishable as crimes. Just because they are speech doesn't mean they are protected. However, statements that might sound like threats if taken literally but which should not be taken seriously because they are political hyperbole or figures of speech are not punishable as crimes. The difficulty is in distinguishing a true threat from expressive speech.

This issue has been addressed in several contexts. One of the first cases on the issue of whether "threats" can be protected by the First Amendment went all the way to the Supreme Court. In *Watts v. United States*, the Court overturned the conviction of a young man who, during the Vietnam War, had attended an antiwar rally on the National Mall in D.C. He referred to the fact that he had just received a draft notice, said that he did not want to go to war, and then said, "If they ever make me carry a rifle, the first man I want to get in my sights is L.B.J.," referring to then-president Lyndon B. Johnson. He was convicted of making a threat against the President, but the Court found that the statement was not a true threat. It was a hyperbolic statement to make a political point and demonstrate opposition to being drafted. As such, it should be protected by the First Amendment.

A threat that appears to be genuine, however, may be punished, regardless of whether it will be carried out. One of the most difficult and controversial cases on this topic is *Planned Parenthood of the Columbia/Willamette Inc. v. American Coalition of Life Activists*. The case involved a website maintained by the American Coalition of Life Activists (ACLA) of "wanted posters" of abortion doctors. It listed their names, addresses, and other information about them and put a red X through their "poster" each time a doctor was killed. Planned Parenthood sued for an injunction against the site, arguing that the site violated the Freedom of Access to Clinic Entrances Act, which provides a right of action against anyone who by "threat of force … intentionally … intimidates … any person because that person is or has been … providing reproductive health services." The ACLA argued that its website was protected by the First Amendment. Although one 9th Circuit panel said that the First Amendment protected the site, another panel on rehearing determined that the site constituted a true threat and was not pro-tected. The courts struggled with whether the site was encouraging murders or whether it was simply making note of the fact that murders occurred. The panel finally determined that a true threat was made because the "wanted poster" design used by the site could reasonably be interpreted as making a threat of death or bodily harm.

Similarly, in *U.S. v. Dinwiddie*, a court found that an abortion protester made true threats to a doctor, because she issued "reminders" about other doctors who were killed, and she had noted her approval of the idea of killing abortion doctors. Thus, even though the expression of ideas or beliefs is normally protected by the First Amendment, a person can be prosecuted when those beliefs are expressed in a way that appears to be a true threat to harm another.

Modern technology, specifically the internet, email, and social media, makes it even more diffi-cult to determine what is a true threat and what is a joke because tone and context are often missing. Email and tweets are notorious for conveying a tone that was not intended by the author, and in some instances, that has raised questions about whether threats are true threats or not. In one instance, a man who opposed health care legislation tweeted that he wanted to kill President Obama. Other Twitter users asked whether he was joking, because it wasn't clear from the context whether he was joking or not. He insisted that he was serious, but other users were still not sure whether he was serious or simply being outrageous. The Secret Service questioned him and he later recanted, saying that he merely spoke out of anger.

The most high profile case on this topic was decided by the Supreme Court in 2015. In *Elonis v. U.S.*, the Court considered whether to uphold the conviction of a man who had allegedly made "threats" on his Facebook page. Anthony Elonis wrote several posts, stating that they were "rap lyrics," and he included disclaimers on his page stating that the lyrics he posted were fictitious. He also referenced exercising his First Amendment rights. However, several people felt threatened by the posts. Among other things, he wrote:

> Did you know that it's illegal for me to say I want to kill my wife?
> It's illegal.
> It's indirect criminal contempt.
> It's one of the only sentences that I'm not allowed to say …
>
> ***
>
> Art is about pushing limits. I'm willing to go to jail for my constitutional rights. Are you?

And:

> Took all the strength I had not to turn the bitch ghost
> Pull my knife, flick my wrist, and slit her throat.

He was fired from his job because his boss interpreted the posts as threats, and the former employer also notified the FBI of his behavior. Elonis was prosecuted for making a threat over interstate lines, pursuant to a federal law, 18 U.S.C. sec. 875(c), which says: "Whoever transmits in interstate or foreign commerce any communication containing any threat … to injure the person of another, shall be fined … or imprisoned not more than five years, or both."

It is well known in criminal law that in order to be guilty of a crime, one must have the intent to commit it. However, what is not always clear is how prosecutors must prove intent. The question in this case was whether they needed to prove that he subjectively intended to harm anyone or whether it was sufficient to show that a "reasonable person" would interpret the statement as a threat. In other words, do you need to prove intent from a subjective or objective point of view?

The Supreme Court ultimately decided that the prosecutor must prove that he had the subjective intent to harm someone. The "reasonable person" standard is a feature of civil liability, and the Court felt that such a standard would be inconsistent with the conventional criminal requirement that a person have "awareness of some wrongdoing" to be convicted.

A threat that appears to be genuine, therefore, may be punished, regardless of whether it will be carried out, if the prosecutor can demonstrate the intent of the defendant to cause harm. Prosecution may be based on a specific statute, such as the Freedom of Access to Clinic Entrances Act or the law against making threats against the President, or the prosecution can be for assault, which is an ordinary crime.

Can Emoji Be a Threat?

Emoji are adorable and fun icons that people can use in text messages or social media to convey thoughts or feelings. They are subject to interpretation, though. They are sometimes meant to be interpreted literally, but are often used in non-literal ways. They may be used earnestly or sarcastically. They are subject to cultural quirks and trends. And some people simply exercise poor judgment in their use of emoji.

There have been several cases involving emoji as "true threats." When people use the gun, knife, or bomb emoji (or all three together), courts have easily found that such images can convey the intent to threaten.

In *In re L.F.*, a student was prosecuted for making threats. She tweeted multiple times about shooting people at her school; however, the tweets also contained nearly 40 emoji, most of which were the so-called "laughing emoji," as well as terms like, "jk" and "lmao." The court found that the statements could reasonably be interpreted as threatening despite the use of the emoji. Although it may have been clear that she was "laughing," it wasn't inherently clear whether that meant she was joking or entertained by the prospect of killing people.

Emoji have been used as evidence in criminal cases as well. In *Kinsey v. State*, a man who was prosecuted for sexual assault argued that his victim had consented—because one text message she sent prior to the incident contained a "winkie face." The judge did not agree that a "winkie face" meant that a person consented to sex, and the man was sentenced to 10 years in prison.

Lies

Lies are morally and ethically problematic. They are nevertheless protected by the First Amendment in many circumstances.

The U.S. Supreme Court addressed the constitutionality of prosecuting lies in *U.S. v. Alvarez*. In that case, Alvarez had lied about being awarded a Congressional Medal of Honor. He was prosecuted under a federal law called the Stolen Valor Act, which made it a crime to falsely claim receipt of military decorations or medals. The Supreme Court noted that there are only a limited number of categories of content-based speech restrictions that have been constitutionally permitted, including libel and fraud. While those categories involve lies, they also involve some additional harm: damage to reputation in the case of libel, or economic loss in the case of fraud. They do not target falsity on its own. In other criminal prosecutions of "falsity," there needs to be an adequate justification to criminalize the speech. In perjury cases, for example, the harm at issue is that perjury substantially undermines the integrity of the judicial system. The Court found that falsity alone is not enough to justify punishment. Any such regulation would be subject to strict scrutiny because it is content-based, and the government had not demonstrated that lies about medals caused an adequate harm to justify the punishment of such speech.

While the Supreme Court opinion was rather dry, Justice Kozinski, who wrote a concurring opinion in favor of Alvarez when the case was at the Ninth Circuit, did a much better job of explaining the practical rationale for why the First Amendment should protect many kinds of lies:

> If false factual statements are unprotected, then the government can prosecute not only the man who tells tall tales of winning the Congressional Medal of Honor, but also the JDater who falsely claims he's Jewish or the dentist who assures you it won't hurt a bit. Phrases such as "I'm working late tonight, hunny," "I got stuck in traffic" and "I didn't inhale" could all be made into crimes. Without the robust protections of the First Amendment, the white lies, exaggerations and deceptions that are an integral part of human intercourse would become targets of censorship. …

***

Saints may always tell the truth, but for mortals living means lying. We lie to protect our privacy ("No, I don't live around here"); to avoid hurt feelings ("Friday is my study night"); to make others feel better

("Gee you've gotten skinny"); to avoid recriminations ("I only lost $10 at poker"); to prevent grief ("The doc says you're getting better"); to maintain domestic tranquility ("She's just a friend"); to avoid social stigma ("I just haven't met the right woman"); for career advancement ("I'm sooo lucky to have a smart boss like you"); to avoid being lonely ("I love opera"); to eliminate a rival ("He has a boyfriend"); to achieve an objective ("But I love you so much"); to defeat an objective ("I'm allergic to latex"); to make an exit ("It's not you, it's me"); to delay the inevitable ("The check is in the mail"); to communicate displeasure ("There's nothing wrong"); to get someone off your back ("I'll call you about lunch"); to escape a nudnik ("My mother's on the other line"); to namedrop ("We go way back"); to set up a surprise party ("I need help moving the piano"); to buy time ("I'm on my way"); to keep up appearances ("We're not talking divorce"); to avoid taking out the trash ("My back hurts"); to duck an obligation ("I've got a headache"); to maintain a public image ("I go to church every Sunday"); to make a point ("Ich bin ein Berliner"); to save face ("I had too much to drink"); to humor ("Correct as usual, King Friday"); to avoid embarrassment ("That wasn't me"); to curry favor ("I've read all your books"); to get a clerkship ("You're the greatest living jurist"); to save a dollar ("I gave at the office"); or to maintain innocence ("There are eight tiny reindeer on the rooftop").

And we don't just talk the talk, we walk the walk, as reflected by the popularity of plastic surgery, elevator shoes, wood veneer paneling, cubic zirconia, toupees, artificial turf and cross-dressing. Last year, Americans spent $40 billion on cosmetics—an industry devoted almost entirely to helping people deceive each other about their appearance. It doesn't matter whether we think that such lies are despicable or cause more harm than good. An important aspect of personal autonomy is the right to shape one's public and private persona by choosing when to tell the truth about oneself, when to conceal and when to deceive. Of course, lies are often disbelieved or discovered, and that too is part of the pull and tug of social intercourse. But it's critical to leave such interactions in private hands, so that we can make choices about who we are. How can you develop a reputation as a straight shooter if lying is not an option?

There is therefore a very high bar that must be met for the government to punish lies. Libel (discussed in Chapter 3), fraud (discussed in Chapter 12), and false or misleading advertisements (discussed in Chapter 17) are examples of false statements that can be punished, at least in some circumstances. But laws targeting general lies and false statements in political campaigns (discussed in Chapter 16) are subject to a high degree of First Amendment scrutiny.

Practical Conclusions

- The government loves to regulate speech.

- The disclosure of classified information is one of the few kinds of information that can be enjoined, but the government must meet the burden of proving that there is a compelling interest and there is no less restrictive alternative than banning publication.

- The Espionage Act provides for prosecution for the disclosure of classified information. Many people think the law is unconstitutional, especially as applied to journalists. However, other people have been prosecuted under the Act, and there is no clear case law granting a First Amendment exception. One must therefore carefully consider what one is doing.

- Hate speech is generally protected by the First Amendment unless it rises to the level of being likely to incite violence or otherwise constitutes a crime (like a true threat).

- Sexual content receives First Amendment protection unless it is deemed obscene under the *Miller* test. If it is merely indecent, then the government cannot ban or prosecute it without meeting the burden of strict scrutiny. However, broadcast media is subject to more rigorous regulation of indecent content by FCC regulations, and the Court has found those to be constitutional, at least during the times that children are likely to be listening.

- Child pornography is never protected.

- Violent content receives First Amendment protection, meaning that the government must meet the burden of strict scrutiny to ban or punish it.

- True threats can be prosecuted as crimes. However, a hyperbolic threat—where the speech is figurative and the speaker doesn't intend to actually harm anyone—should receive First Amendment protection.

- Any other content-based regulation the government can think up is probably going to be subject to the strict scrutiny test.

CHAPTER 16

Regulating Political Speech, Elections, and Campaigns

From a First Amendment perspective, political speech is the most sacred form of speech. It is difficult for the government to restrict political speech, because such regulations are subject to strict scrutiny, the highest form of protection. Nevertheless, the federal and state governments have attempted to regulate political speech in certain forms. This chapter will address those regulations, including:

1. The constitutionality of laws and regulations that directly target election or campaign speech

2. Anonymous political speech

3. "Right of reply" laws, which give individuals the right to reply to criticism

4. False statement laws

The Constitutionality of Campaign Laws

The idea behind campaign speech laws is not to regulate political speech in terms of the exact content, but to regulate how that speech is financed and whether there is any accountability. The concern is that there is so much money invested in advertising and promoting political views or candidates that there is a possibility of corruption or a quid pro quo exchange of money for favors. The question, therefore, is how to properly balance the need to prevent corruption with the right to speak freely about politics. Congress and the state legislatures have periodically established rules to balance those interests, and those laws are inevitably challenged as violations of the First Amendment because they affect one's ability to disseminate a message, whether directly or indirectly. Several cases challenging the constitutionality of federal or state campaign laws have gone to the Supreme Court.

In 2010, the Supreme Court addressed regulations on campaign speech in *Citizens United v. FEC*. However, there is a long and tortured history of campaign finance laws that must be understood in order to understand the significance of *Citizens United*.

Over the years, courts have made distinctions between speech by individuals and speech by entities (such as corporations, labor unions, or nonprofits). They also distinguished between the discussion of political issues in general and the express advocacy for or against a particular candidate. Finally, they made a distinction between expenditures, which take place when a person spends his or her own money to make a statement, and contributions, which take place when the person gives money to a candidate or group, and the recipient is free to spend that money in any way. The following table provides a brief summary of the history of the various laws and cases leading up to *Citizens United*. In all cases, the Court has applied strict scrutiny, because the laws at issue are content-based regulations on political speech.

Table 16.1: Developments in Campaign Finance Regulation.

Federal Election Campaign Act of 1971 ("FECA") is passed.	FECA and corresponding state laws imposed restrictions on "expenditures" and "contributions."
Buckley v. Valeo	The Court found that limits on corporate contributions were constitutional as an effort to prevent corruption, but the limits on expenditures were not. There should be more leeway to spend one's own money on one's own message. The Court also upheld the provision of the law pertaining to the disclosure of donors because it was the "least restrictive means" of curbing corruption.
First National Bank of Boston v. Bellotti	The Court ruled that corporations are free to speak about political issues (as opposed to endorsing candidates). The Bank was allowed to make expenditures to advocate a position with respect to changes in tax laws. There was no compelling interest to justify the infringement on speech.
FEC v. Mass. Citizens for Life	The Court held that restrictions on expenditures were unconstitutional as applied to MCFL. Nonprofits should not be subject to the same restrictions as businesses, because nonprofits are organized specifically for the purpose of promoting causes, as opposed to making money.
Austin v. Michigan Chamber of Commerce	The Court upheld restrictions in a Michigan law that prohibited corporations from using general funds to advocate for or against a candidate. Applying the strict scrutiny test, the Court found that there is a compelling interest in preventing corruption in elections, and the restrictions are narrowly tailored to serve that interest.
Bipartisan Campaign Reform Act of 2002 (BCRA) (a.k.a. McCain-Feingold Act) is passed.	This law amended FECA. It sought to regulate soft money and issue ads. It specifically forbid broadcasters from airing ads from special interest groups within 60 days of an election or 30 days of a primary if the ad mentions the name of a candidate.
FEC v. Beaumont	The Court upheld FECA restrictions on contributions from a nonprofit. Groups can be prohibited from contributing to a particular campaign to prevent corruption.

(Continued)

Table 16.1: (Continued)

McConnell v. FEC	The Court upheld the BCRA as constitutional, generally finding that it serves the compelling interest of preventing corruption.
FEC v. Wisc. Right to Life	The Court held that the BCRA regulations were unconstitutional as applied to WRTL. The government had no compelling interest in regulating their speech, which was an ad asking viewers to contact their Senators to oppose a filibuster of judicial nominees.

In 2010, the Supreme Court decided *Citizens United*, in which it overturned *Austin* and partially overturned *McConnell*. In that case, Citizens United had made a film critical of Hillary Clinton. The film was blocked from being aired within 30 days of the primary, pursuant to section 203 of the BCRA. The Court found that section 203 (as well as 2 U.S.C. sec. 441b, which generally prohibited the use of corporate funds for express advocacy) was unconstitutional and that corporations, unions, and non-profits should be allowed to make expenditures for electioneering communications that specifically name a candidate in the time leading up to an election. The Court did not address the issue of whether corporations can make contributions. The Court also found that disclaimer and disclosure requirements can be constitutional, although they may be challenged as applied.

Campaign speech regulations had always contained what was called the "media exception." News outlets were allowed to publish editorials or endorse candidates or otherwise engage in speech about elections, even though news organizations are typically corporations. *Citizens United* leveled the playing field, so to speak, making all corporations equal with respect to their ability to speak about candidates with their own money. Media companies no longer are the only companies that may make endorsements. The Court also noted that, traditionally, First Amendment principles do not support discriminating against certain speakers. Treating corporations differently in the absence of any evidence of actual corruption was not warranted. Finally, the Court noted that the law was, in effect, a prior restraint on speech and gave the FEC a censorial role over campaign speech. For all these reasons, the Court found the portions of the law to be unconstitutional restraints on speech. The Court made it clear that campaign regulations would be subject to strict scrutiny and that Congress must justify regulations with some evidence of actual harm, not mere speculation that there might be some vague sense of corruption in the political process.

In 2014, the Court went a step further, ruling in *McCutcheon v. FEC*, that regulations imposing limits on the aggregate amount of money a person can donate to campaigns over a two year period do not further the government's interest in preventing *quid pro quo* corruption or the appearance of corruption and therefore violate the First Amendment. The limits initially were established by FECA in 1971 and were upheld in *Buckley v. Valeo*. The limits were then amended by the BCRA. In *McCutcheon*, a majority of justices reasoned that there was no reason to limit the number of candidates to which a person can donate money. (It should be noted that there are still restrictions on how much money an individual can donate to a specific candidate; the aggregate limits meant that a person could only donate to a limited number of people before hitting the aggregate limit.) Again, comparing people to the media, Justice Roberts wrote, "[t]he government may no more restrict how many candidates or causes a donor may support than it may tell a newspaper how many candidates it may endorse."

It should be noted that churches and nonprofits may still be barred from advocating for political candidates, but those restrictions are based on tax laws that give them preferred tax status. They could make expenditures for endorsements like other entities, but they would risk losing their tax status.

Anonymity

Campaign laws have attempted to require disclosure of the identity or sponsor of certain speech, including ads or campaign literature. But there is also some support for anonymous political speech, given the rich history of political protest and the potential for government censorship or retribution. The Supreme Court has, on multiple occasions, struck down laws that require information about a speaker on constitutional grounds.

In *McIntyre v. Ohio Elec. Comm'n*, for example, the Court ruled that Ohio's ban on anonymous campaign literature was unconstitutional because anonymous speech is not inherently harmful, and there was no evidence that the particular material distributed by Mrs. McIntyre was false or misleading. The Court spoke favorably of the need for anonymous speech in some instances, particularly where a viewpoint might be disfavored or subject its author to retribution. It noted that many important books and pamphlets have been distributed anonymously or pseudonymously, including the Federalist Papers. Similarly, in *Buckley v. Am. Constitutional Law Foundation*, the Court struck down as unconstitutional a state law requiring initiative petitioners to wear identification badges, and in *Talley v. California*, the court found a law requiring handbills to identify their sponsor to be unconstitutional.

However, the Court has also recognized that people speaking in political contexts cannot remain anonymous all the time. In *Doe v. Reed*, the Court affirmed that the names of petition signers may be available under open records laws, but allowed the possibility that access can be unconstitutional if the names are being obtained for the purpose of harassment. Also, in *Citizens United*, as noted above, the Court upheld the requirement that certain electioneering communications disclose their source.

Because regulations concerning anonymity are usually content-based rules, the courts will typically apply strict scrutiny, and thus the outcome of any case is likely to depend on whether the government has a compelling interest and whether the regulation is properly tailored to serve that interest. Overbroad laws banning all anonymity are likely to be deemed unconstitutional, but narrow laws, such as the disclaimer requirement on electioneering communications, are more likely to be upheld.

Right of Reply Laws

The concept behind a right of reply is that an individual who is personally attacked in the media during discussions of political or social issues should have the opportunity to respond to the attack. These laws are content-based, insofar as they regulate the particular content of speech, and they are a form of coerced speech, which is as equally disfavored as a prior restraint. The Supreme Court has addressed the issue of right of reply twice, with differing results.

First, in *Red Lion Bct. Co. v. FCC*, the Court ruled that it did not violate the First Amendment for the FCC to require a right of reply in broadcast media. As a federal agency, the FCC makes rules as part of its administrative function. The FCC wanted to ensure that all sides of a discussion on a matter of public interest be given fair coverage, so it enacted various rules in furtherance of that goal. Among those rules was a "right of reply," giving any person who has been personally attacked an opportunity to respond at no charge. A broadcaster challenged the rule as a violation of its First Amendment rights, but the Court upheld the FCC's authority to impose such a rule. The Court noted that the broadcasting spectrum is limited; there are only so many spaces available in any geographic area. Thus, anyone who is fortunate enough to obtain a license to use public airwaves must serve the public interest. The Court found that the FCC, as the agency designated to administer the public airwaves, has the authority to impose rules that serve the public interest. The Court therefore concluded that the First Amendment was not violated.

Then, in *Miami Herald Pub. Co. v. Tornillo*, the Court ruled that it was unconstitutional to require a newspaper to provide a right of reply. A Florida law required newspapers to provide political candidates equal space to respond to criticisms or other attacks on the candidate. Those who opposed the right of reply argued that forcing a paper to publish something is as equally pernicious as preventing a paper from publishing something; in either case, the government is interfering with editorial discretion and violating the paper's freedoms. Those who supported the right of reply argued that the government should ensure that a wide range of views reach the public and that maximizing speech in this way is consistent with the principles of the First Amendment. The Court noted the costs of time, effort, and space that the paper would incur, but ultimately found that the law was unconstitutional precisely because it gave editorial control to the government. The Court did not distinguish *Red Lion*—in fact, the Court didn't even mention the prior case. Instead, it focused on several other prior cases to support the principles that newspapers should be free from editorial control by the government and that speech about politics may be robust, even if sometimes unfair.

The difference between the two cases can be understood simply by acknowledging that the Court has treated broadcast media differently from other media. (The treatment of broadcast media is discussed more fully in Chapter 18.) Since these cases were decided, the FCC has abandoned its right of reply requirements. As a practical matter, there is no longer a right of reply recognized anywhere in the United States. However, since *Red Lion* has not been overturned, it is theoretically possible that the rule could be revived with respect to broadcast media. Furthermore, many other countries recognize a right of reply, so sometimes U.S. media companies receive demands for reply space from foreigners who believe they have been unfairly attacked. Although the rules of other nations are not necessarily binding on U.S. companies, the concept of a right of reply is still relevant to discussions of press freedom.

False Statement Laws[1]

Some states have passed "false statement laws," which purport to regulate false statements made during political campaigns. The underlying goal is superficially admirable: to prohibit candidates for office or their representatives from making false statements that mislead the public. Voters need to be informed so they can make good choices in elections. If they are misled into believing false information, election results may be skewed from what the voters would have otherwise intended.

The problem, of course, is how to craft legislation that promotes such a goal, which clearly impacts speech, without running afoul of the First Amendment. Legislators therefore adopted a constitutional principle from the Supreme Court that they thought would withstand constitutional scrutiny: the laws prohibit making false statements in the course of a political campaign if the speaker has acted with "actual malice," which is knowledge that the statement is false or reckless disregard of the truth.

The appeal of the actual malice standard is obvious. It was first used in *New York Times Co. v. Sullivan*, a libel case brought against the New York Times because the paper ran a political advertisement that reflected poorly on southern officials. The Court noted that false statements are "inevitable in free debate" but that lies made with knowledge of falsity or recklessness disregard of the truth are not entitled to constitutional protection. The actual malice standard is supposed to provide "breathing room" for speech on important issues while also maintaining the ability to seek a remedy in egregious cases.

It is worth noting explicitly that the Court found it necessary to offer constitutional protection to speech in libel lawsuits because libel claims were being used abusively during the civil rights era to silence criticism of government officials. Alas, it seems history repeats itself. Two different courts have found that so-called "false statement" laws were being used abusively to silence criticism of those running for office.

In *281 Care Committee v. Arneson*, the U.S. Court of Appeals for the 8th Circuit considered a Minnesota state law that made it a crime to make a false statement in the course of a political campaign if the person knows the statement is false or communicates it with reckless disregard of whether it is false. The court applied strict scrutiny because the law restricts political speech on its face. The court acknowledged that the interest in preserving fair elections and preventing fraud on the electorate could be a compelling state interest, but decided that it need not determine that question, because the law was not narrowly tailored.

The government argued that the law was narrowly tailored because it required "actual malice." Following the logic of *Sullivan*, the government argued that such a requirement provides the "breathing space" necessary to protect free speech while still allowing punishment for known lies. The government also argued that counterspeech is not as effective in ensuring fair elections and preventing fraud.

The court rejected all of the government's arguments. Most importantly, the court found that this kind of false statement law will "perpetuate the very fraud it is allegedly designed to prohibit." First, the court found that it is "immensely problematic" that any person can lodge a complaint under the law. There is a real risk of abusive complaints being filed by political opponents who simply seek to ensnare candidates in lengthy, expensive, and protracted administrative proceedings that take time and money away from actual campaigning.

The court also noted that much of the speech that is subject to complaints may be protected speech, such as opinion, exaggerations, or conjecture, rather than false factual assertions. Thus, many speakers will be forced to defend themselves without cause, and there is clearly "potential for abuse."

The court also directly disputed the government's position, noting that counterspeech is, indeed, the most effective—and least restrictive—response to any potential false speech and cited to the Supreme Court's assertion to that effect in *Alvarez*: "The remedy for speech that is false is speech that is true."

Most importantly, the court concluded that the actual malice standard does not adequately safeguard speech and is constitutionally inadequate under the circumstances, because there aren't any mechanisms in place to halt abuse of the law.

The U.S. District Court for the Southern District of Ohio issued an opinion in *Susan B. Anthony List v. Ohio Elections Comm'n* that struck down a similar Ohio law and more or less mirrored the reasoning in *281 Care Committee*. The Ohio law made it a misdemeanor to make a false statement about a candidate if the statement is made with actual malice, and if the statement is designed to promote the election, nomination, or defeat of a candidate.

The court noted that "political candidates have exploited the statute to silence opponents by strategically deploying OEC complaints to burden and distract their electoral rivals." There is no system to weed out frivolous complaints, and the accused "is forced to use time and resources responding to the complaint, typically at the exact moment that the campaign is peaking and his time and resources are best used elsewhere." Complaints are often timed so that no judicial review can occur before the election. Complainants routinely move to dismiss the complaints after the election is over, having inflicted the desired damage to opponents.

The court emphasized the Supreme Court's statement in *U.S. v. Alvarez* that "[t]he remedy for speech that is false is speech that is true." The remedy should be more speech, not enforced silence.

The court also endorsed the view that the people, not the government, should decide what is true in matters of political concern. The plaintiffs argued that they are not "arguing for a right to lie," but instead for a "right not to have the truth of our political statements be judged by the Government." The court was persuaded that the distinction was "critical" and "based on the quintessential truth that 'the First Amendment itself reflects a judgment by the American people that the benefits of its restrictions on the Government outweigh the costs.'"

The court, citing *Sullivan*, noted that "false statements are inevitable if there is to be open and vigorous expression of views." However, the court distinguished false *political* speech from cases where there are "important private interests," such as fraud or defamation. The court therefore concluded that it must apply strict scrutiny, because the law is a content-based restriction on speech.

Although the court acknowledged that protecting the integrity of elections would be a compelling interest, the court found that the law did not actually protect that interest and it was not narrowly tailored. Among the court's findings, it stated that the law burdens truthful speakers and liars equally; it puts the government in the paternalistic position of being the arbiter of truth; it chills a substantial amount of truthful or protected speech; and it is subject to abuse.

Again, the court specifically disputed the government's contention that the *mens rea* requirement provides "breathing space" for speech, because even truthful speakers are subject to the burdens of an OEC proceeding, including burdensome discovery into the candidate's communications and strategic discussions. The court concluded:

> We can all agree that lies are bad. The problem is, at least with respect to some political speech, that there is no clear way to determine whether a political statement is the lie or the truth, and we certainly do not want the Government (*i.e.* the OEC) deciding what is political truth anyway, for fear that the Government might persecute those who criticize the Government or its leaders.

Practical Conclusions

- Political speech, especially speech about elections and campaigns, receives the highest degree of protection under the First Amendment, so any regulation on political speech will have to meet strict scrutiny, meaning there is a compelling government interest and the regulation is the least restrictive means of protecting that interest.

- When considering restrictions on campaign speech, the desire to prevent actual corruption is a compelling interest. The question will always be whether the regulation is overbroad or adequately supported by evidence of harm.

- The Court has distinguished between expenditures, where someone is speaking for themselves, and contributions, where someone is giving money to another group or candidate. Expenditures get greater protection under the First Amendment than contributions. Also, discussions of political issues in general get more leeway than specific endorsements of or opposition to a candidate.

- There have been two perpetual problems with respect to campaign speech. First, no matter what rules Congress sets up to avoid corruption or the perception thereof, those who want to donate find ways to make their contributions legally. The rules never completely remove money from the electoral process and thus there is a persistent feeling that there is still a potential for corruption. Second, it has been difficult to justify why media companies were permitted to endorse candidates but other companies were not. *Citizens United* leveled the playing field so that all speakers are treated equally. There will undoubtedly be a new and different set of problems that arise, and one should expect political speech cases to continue to be evaluated by the Court.

- There are both state and federal laws that regulate campaigns, and they change regularly, so it is important to stay abreast of any regulation that might apply to your conduct.

- Right of reply laws have been deemed unconstitutional, although some right of reply might be permissible in broadcast media if the FCC were to enforce such a rule (no such rule currently exists).

- It is unconstitutional to ban anonymous political speech or regulate "falsity" in campaign statements, unless the highest standards of scrutiny can be met.

Note

1. This section is adapted from a previously published article. Ashley Messenger, "False Statements and Actual Malice: Courts Rethink What's Required to Protect Free Speech," *Communications Lawyer* 31, no. 3 (Summer 2015).

CHAPTER 17

Regulating Advertisements/ Promotions/Marketing

S hould advertisements receive First Amendment protection? People often complain about advertisements for many reasons: they encourage consumerism, they might be misleading, or they advertise "bad" products. On the other hand, advertisements help inform consumers about goods and services available in the market, and it is sometimes difficult to distinguish commercial speech from other kinds of protected speech, such as discussions of political or social issues. The Supreme Court has tried to balance these competing concerns in its decisions on what is known as "commercial speech." This chapter will address the legal issues related to advertising, promotions, and marketing:

1. What legal issues should be considered by those advertising goods or services?

2. What legal issues arise for those who accept advertising?

3. What special rules apply when promotions include contests or prizes?

Issues to Consider for Advertising Goods and Services

There are four primary concerns for those who want to advertise products:

1. Considering whether there are any local, state, or federal laws or regulations that regulate the ad or medium

2. Avoiding false or misleading statements

3. Regulation of endorsement and "influencers"

4. Complying with other applicable laws or legal principles concerning content

Government Regulation

Government entities at all levels have an extensive track record of regulating advertising or commercial speech. It is common, for example, to have a city ordinance that regulates business signs or billboards. State laws often prohibit a certain type of advertising; Virginia, for example, has passed laws banning the advertising of prescription drug prices and banning ads for alcohol in college newspapers. The federal government has banned tobacco advertising on television and requires certain disclosures on pharmaceutical ads. The FTC also has the power to enact regulations and punish unfair or deceptive advertising. The question is whether these kinds of laws violate an advertiser's First Amendment rights.

The First Amendment is not self-executing, so if an advertiser feels that a law violates its rights, it will have to affirmatively file a lawsuit challenging the law. In most of the cases discussed in this section, that is precisely what happened: a particular entity felt that its rights were infringed and brought a suit to challenge the law.

The Supreme Court initially did not give any First Amendment protection to commercial speech. In *Valentine v. Chrestensen*, the Court ruled that advertising was not as important as political speech, and thus it was not entitled to First Amendment protection. But over time, the Court began to develop some protection for advertisements. The first case where the Court gave any protection to an advertisement was *New York Times Co. v. Sullivan*, a libel case based on statements in a political advertisement. But the Court provided First Amendment protection because it was political speech, even though it was in a paid-for ad. It was not "commercial" in the sense that the speakers were not seeking a profit. The first case giving protection to true commercial speech was *Virginia Bd. of Pharmacy v. Virginia Citizens Consumer Council*, which found that the state could not prohibit truthful advertising of pharmaceutical prices. The Court noted that advertising serves legitimate social purposes: "So long as we preserve a predominately free enterprise economy, the allocation of our resources ... will be made through numerous private economic decisions. It is a matter of public interest that those decisions ... be intelligent and well-informed." Although commercial speech still does not receive the same level of protection as political speech, the Court has clearly established that there is some protection under the First Amendment.

The first question to sort out is whether the speech at issue is "commercial speech" or "political speech." The difficulty in distinguishing the two is illustrated by *Bolger v. Youngs Drug Products Corp.* In *Bolger*, the Court considered a brochure that provided information about sexually transmitted diseases and family planning but was published by a condom manufacturer and was used to promote its product. The Court concluded that, given the economic motive of the speaker and the fact that the brochure was intended to promote a product, the brochures were commercial speech. The Court said that advertisers cannot immunize their statements from regulation simply by making references to public issues. On the contrary, the ad in *New York Times Co. v. Sullivan* was political speech. Even though it took the form of a paid advertisement, its purpose was to convey a political message, not to obtain any economic benefit.

If the speech at issue is commercial speech, then the Court will evaluate the law's constitutionality using the test established in *Central Hudson Gas & Elec. Corp. v. Public Serv. Comm'n*. In *Central Hudson*, the Court considered a New York law prohibiting electric companies from advertising in a manner that would promote the use of electricity. The purpose of the law was to save energy. The Supreme Court struck down the law as unconstitutional, using a four-part test that is still used today:

1. Is the ad false or misleading, or is it for an illegal product or service? False or fraudulent speech is not protected by the First Amendment. Therefore, a deceptive ad may be banned or regulated. Ads for illegal products may also be regulated in some cases. But if the ad is not false or misleading, a court must look to the other factors.

2. Does the government have a "substantial interest" in regulation? The interest need not be a compelling interest, like in the strict scrutiny test, but there must nevertheless be some important interest in government regulation.

3. Does the regulation directly advance the government interest? This element is open to interpretation; there may be a continuum between the severity of the interest and the specificity of the regulation that determines whether the regulation will be acceptable.

4. Is the regulation sufficiently narrow? Is there a reasonable fit between the law and the interest? Regulations should not be overbroad or encompass legitimate speech.

In *Central Hudson*, the Court agreed that the state had a substantial interest in energy conservation. But it found the law to be unconstitutional because it was more extensive than necessary to promote the state's interest. The law restricted advertising of services that would have no impact on overall energy consumption.

The Court has similarly applied the *Central Hudson* test to a variety of scenarios, but the majority of cases seem to involve "vice advertising": regulations that affect the promotion of alcohol, tobacco, or gambling. For obvious reasons, states feel that they have an interest in curbing the promotion of vices, but efforts to restrict advertising are typically broadly written, and the Court has found that the regulations violate the First Amendment in many cases.

For example, in *44 Liquormart, Inc. v. Rhode Island*, a state law banned the advertising of liquor prices anywhere other than the place of sale. The Court ruled that the law was unconstitutional. The state may have a substantial interest in promoting temperance, but the law did not directly advance this interest. There is no evidence that the law would significantly reduce alcohol consumption. Also, there were alternative forms of regulation that would not affect speech such as imposing higher prices on liquor via increased taxes or rationing alcohol purchases.

Similarly, in *Lorillard Tobacco Co. v. Reilly*, the Court considered Massachusetts regulations on ads for tobacco products. One of the regulations was that outdoor ads could not be within 1000 feet of a school or playground. Also, point-of-sale ads could not be within 5 feet of the ground. The Court found that the regulations were unconstitutional, even though the state had a substantial interest in preventing children from using tobacco products. The regulation of outdoor advertising was not narrowly tailored because the distance cited covered most if not all of the state's metropolitan areas. It also regulated oral statements regarding tobacco products as a form of "outdoor advertising," in addition to signs and billboards. The product is legal for adults, and the regulation would effectively prohibit most advertising to adults. Thus, it was too broad. The Court also found that the five-foot requirement failed both the third and fourth prong of the *Central Hudson* test. The idea behind the regulation was that children are typically under five feet tall and will see ads at that height. But the Court noted that not all children are under five feet tall, and, perhaps more importantly, nothing prevents children from looking up. Thus, there was no evidence that the regulation would directly advance the interest, and it was not narrowly tailored.

The Court's rulings with respect to gambling advertisements has been a bit more mixed, in part because gambling is legal in some states and not others.

In *U.S. v. Edge Broadcasting Co.*, the Court upheld FCC regulations as applied to a North Carolina broadcaster who advertised Virginia's lottery, because the lottery was not authorized in North Carolina. FCC regulations prohibited the North Carolina station from running the ads because it was located in North Carolina (a nonlottery state), even though over 90% of its listeners were in Virginia (a lottery state). The Court found that the regulation limiting ads in nonlottery states was a reasonable, common-sense approach for the government to support the nonlottery states' anti-gambling policy without inter-fering with the lottery states' policies. Even though airwaves extend across borders, it is reasonable to enforce the restriction within the nonlottery state. Otherwise, the lottery state's law would be dictating policy to the nonlottery state. Also, nothing prevented other forms of advertising to those in Virginia.

However, in *Greater New Orleans Bct. Assoc., Inc. v. U.S.*, the Court held that FCC regulations that prohibited broadcasters from carrying ads for privately operated casinos were unconstitutional as applied to broadcasters in states where gambling is legal, such as Louisiana and Mississippi. The Court ruled that "the power to prohibit or regulate particular conduct does not necessarily include the power to prohibit or regulate speech about that conduct." Even though the government may have a substantial interest in regulating gambling, the FCC's regulations were contradictory to that interest, as they per-mitted ads for state-run gambling and tribal casinos. There was, therefore, no clear relationship between the stated interest and the regulations. They were therefore unconstitutional under *Central Hudson*.

In a non-vice case, *Mainstream Marketing Services, Inc. v. FTC*, a federal appellate court found that the Do-Not-Call Registry was a legitimate restriction on commercial speech. Using the *Central Hudson* test, the court noted that telemarketing was generally for legal products and was not false or mislead-ing. However, the government had a substantial interest in preventing telemarketers from bombarding citizens with commercial phone calls; the practice had become commonplace and citizens were com-plaining about the volume and persistence of the calls. The court also found that the law would directly advance the government interest by giving citizens the option to opt-out of calls, and it was narrowly tailored because it restricted only unwanted business solicitation, not political or charitable telemar-keting. Thus, despite the strong preference the courts have shown towards First Amendment interests, *Mainstream Marketing* shows that it is possible to have a constitutional regulation of commercial speech when the government creates a narrowly tailored law that directly advances a substantial interest.

False or Misleading Statements

The one thing that a court will never protect is a false or misleading ad. Fraud is not protected by the First Amendment. A false or misleading statement in an advertisement may result in civil lawsuits by consumers who feel defrauded, or by competitors under certain provisions of the Lanham Act, and may also result in FTC action. For example, in *Rezec v. Sony Pictures*, moviegoers sued for fraud because

Sony's poster for *A Knight's Tale* featured a quote from a nonexistent movie reviewer. The court refused to dismiss the claim before trial, and Sony settled the case. Similarly, in *Tambrands, Inc. v. Warner-Lambert Co.*, a company that makes home pregnancy tests successfully sued a competitor to enjoin a misleading advertisement. And, in *FTC v. Colgate-Palmolive Co.*, the Supreme Court upheld the FTC's authority to impose restrictions on an advertisement that falsely implied how a product had been tested. Thus, there are numerous ways that an advertiser may be subject to liability or penalties for false or misleading commercial speech. The potential for civil lawsuits is worth noting, but the main concern is enforcement action by the government.

The FTC is the federal agency with authority to take action against advertisers for false or misleading ads. The question will be whether an ad is deceptive to a reasonable consumer.

The FTC does not file lawsuits in court like other plaintiffs; it files an administrative complaint, which will be heard by an administrative law judge (ALJ). If the advertiser is unhappy with the ALJ decision, it may appeal to the FTC board, then to a federal appellate court, then (possibly) to the Supreme Court. There is no trial court involvement. If the FTC prevails, it may enjoin an ad, require affirmative disclosures or disclaimers, require corrective ads, or take other actions. All determinations will be very fact-specific, and thus it is difficult to make any sweeping statements about FTC actions, except to say that courts are unwilling to give protection to anything that may be false or misleading.

Regulation of Endorsements and "Influencers"

In October of 2009, the FTC issued new guidelines to update its Guides Concerning the Use of Endorsements and Testimonials in Advertising. These are not binding law, but are administrative interpretations of the law, which means that following the guidelines will help avoid any potential FTC action. The guidelines were intended to target the problem of celebrities, bloggers, or "influencers" who accept money or other benefits to endorse a product without disclosing that they have been paid to make the endorsement. The FTC has said that, in such cases, endorsers as well as advertisers can be liable for fraud. Thus, a celebrity or blogger must disclose any "unexpected payments" that were made to them. Celebrities in particular must explicitly disclose endorsement deals in non-traditional advertising contexts, such as when they promote a product on a talk show. Also, FTC regulations now require companies that use the disclaimer, "results not typical," to clearly disclose typical results rather than rely on that disclaimer alone. And with respect to social media posts, the FTC has several guidelines for making sure that disclosures are effective. First, the disclosure should be unambiguous; including #sp or #thanks is not clear enough, but #ad is sufficiently clear. The disclosure should also be in the first three lines of the post because any additional content requires the viewer to hit the "more" button, which viewers often do not do. Finally, the disclosure should not be in the midst of a long jumble of hashtags where it might be difficult for viewers to notice. Failure to adhere to these rules may result in FTC action.

Other Issues Relating to the Content of the Ad

Advertisements are speech, and they therefore must comply with all the other generally applicable laws concerning content. An ad could serve as the basis for libel or copyright claim, for example, so it is always important to consider general tort or criminal laws when creating an ad. The most likely claim arising from advertising would probably be a violation of publicity rights, which specifically apply to commercial uses. (Publicity rights are discussed fully in Chapter 5.)

Issues for Those Who Accept Advertising

Media outlets that accept advertising are sometimes targeted for either running or refusing a particular ad. This section will briefly discuss the kinds of issues that occasionally arise.

Liability for False or Harmful Advertising

Advertisers who run false or misleading advertising are subject to liability themselves, as discussed above, but what about the media outlet that accepts the ad? Many states have laws that exempt newspapers and other publications or news organizations from liability as long as the media outlet didn't know the ad was false. Also, aside from any applicable law, civil litigants or prosecutors who wish to bring fraud claims must show that the defendant knew the statement was false. Thus, as long as the media outlet does not know the statement is false, it should be immune from civil or criminal liability. The issue becomes much murkier, however, if the outlet knows or has reason to know that an ad may contain false or misleading statements.

For this reason, several publishers have voluntarily refused ads for certain weight loss products. The FTC has found that many weight loss ads often contain false or misleading statements and has expressed a desire to make media companies liable for running such ads. The companies that have rejected the controversial ads have done so either for ethical reasons (not wanting to promote fraudulent or ineffective products) or out of concern for liability. There is little law on this subject, so the degree to which the media may be liable is unclear, and thus many act out of an abundance of caution. In any event, media outlets should avoid accepting any advertisement that contains claims the media knows to be false, for both legal and ethical reasons.

Along the same lines, media organizations are usually not held liable if a person is harmed as a result of some form of advertising. For example, in *Walters v. Seventeen Magazine*, the court found that a magazine was not liable to a young woman who suffered from Toxic Shock Syndrome after she purchased tampons that had been advertised in the magazine. However, it is possible that a court might permit a claim in extreme cases where a media outlet knew or should have known that the ad would result in harm. In *Braun v. Soldier of Fortune Magazine*, the court found that a magazine could be found liable when it accepted an advertisement that clearly contained dangerous language suggesting that the advertiser was a hit man. (This kind of liability is discussed fully in Chapter 10.)

Liability for Discriminatory Housing Ads

The Federal Fair Housing Act, 42 U.S.C. sec. 3601 *et seq.*, prohibits discrimination in housing advertisements, and the media can be liable if they permit discriminatory ads. In *Ragin v. New York Times Co.*, the Second Circuit refused to dismiss a lawsuit alleging that the *New York Times* violated the law because housing ads that appeared in the paper either excluded black models or pictured blacks only as maids or doormen. The Sixth Circuit has taken a slightly different approach. In *Housing Opportunities Made Equal v. Cincinnati Enquirer*, the court ruled that newspapers are not liable merely because advertisers provide ads that might be viewed as discriminatory. In order for a paper to be liable, there must be an extended series of ads from a single advertiser, putting the paper on notice of a discriminatory practice. Several ads from different advertisers are insufficient to create liability on the part of the publisher. In either case, though, the court noted that media may be liable under the law.

Websites have also faced claims under the Fair Housing Act for allegedly discriminatory roommate advertisements, and the question in those cases was whether Section 230 of the Communications Decency Act provides immunity to the websites. In *Chicago Lawyers Committee for Civil Rights, Inc. v. Craigslist, Inc.*, the court concluded that Craigslist was entitled to immunity from claims, because the allegedly discriminatory ads were posted by third-party users, and Section 230 is designed to protect websites from liability for content posted by third parties. However, in *Fair Housing Council of San Fernando Valley v. Roommates.com*, the court came to a different conclusion. Unlike Craigslist, which merely provided a space for free-form advertisements, the site Roommates.com provided a drop-down menu from which users may choose attributes one sought in a roommate, including sex, sexual orientation, and familial status. The court concluded that the website was not entitled to immunity because it provided the pull-down menu, rather than leaving content solely to the discretion of the users. The court then remanded the case to the trial court for a determination of whether the ads on the site actually constituted a violation of the Fair Housing Act. The trial court ruled that the ads violated the Act, but the appellate court reversed, finding that the law applied only to the sale or rental of a dwelling, rather than to a roommate situation. Thus, it seems, websites may be liable if they allow advertisements for homes for rent or sale and they participate in providing the allegedly discriminatory options.

Refusal of Ads

A media outlet is not required to accept advertising. At its own discretion, it may reject an ad in order to avoid offending its audience or otherwise fulfilling its own editorial mission. The Supreme Court affirmed this principle in *CBS v. DNC*. In that case, the Democratic National Committee (DNC) argued that the First Amendment gave it an affirmative right to have its views heard on the air and therefore it should be allowed to buy time to express those views. CBS argued that it had a First Amendment right to exercise its own editorial discretion in deciding how issues should be covered. The Supreme Court agreed with CBS that it would infringe the First Amendment right of news organizations to dictate how they must cover issues of public concern. The fact that broadcasters are subject to FCC regulation and may be required to serve the public interest is insufficient justification for forcing them to accept any advertisement from any speaker who wishes to be heard.

Industries may also choose to self-regulate in an effort to avoid government action or lawsuits. For example, broadcasters have had a voluntary ban on liquor advertising. On rare occasion, a broadcaster will run a liquor ad—and it's not illegal for them to do so. But the practice is frowned upon within the industry, and it is not common.

If the government does impose a ban on advertising of some sort, the media outlet may challenge the law, just as the advertiser may. In the cases challenging FCC regulations on gambling ads, discussed above, the plaintiffs were broadcasters who wanted to run the ads rather than the casinos. The media has standing to challenge government regulations on advertising as part of its freedom of speech.

Ethical Issues With Native Advertising

Native advertising is the term used to describe paid stories that look and feel like objective journalism by a publication, but in fact are essentially advertisements or promotional pieces. They are often written by the subject of the story themselves or their paid agents. Ethically, it is important for news organizations to properly label native advertising as "sponsored" so it is not confused with actual editorial content. But there are other ethical issues that arise as well. In particular, there is a question as to whether a news organization should accept native ads from an entity it covers, or whether it should accept ads that contradict the organization's own reporting. For example, if a news organization reports that a particular company has engaged in illegal child labor, should it later accept native advertising that looks like an objective news report but really is written by the company and contains denials or excuses concerning its labor practices? Legally, as long as the advertisement does not contain libel or is not tantamount to fraud or otherwise does not run afoul of any particular regulation, then there is no legal reason to reject the advertisement. But there are significant ethical issues that must be considered as well, and the organization may nevertheless choose not to accept the advertisement.

Lotteries, Contests, Prizes, and Other Promotional Activities

Contests, prizes, and giveaways are popular ways for organizations to promote themselves. The internet has also brought more opportunities for interactivity between companies and consumers, or any other group and its potential audience, and this interactivity often involves "call-outs," asking for submissions, comments, or ideas, sometimes with the potential for a prize, even if that prize is simply publicity or recognition.

These kinds of promotional efforts can raise legal issues. The main issues to be aware of are:

- All 50 states and the District of Columbia have laws that regulate to some degree lotteries and contests. They are concerned with the potential for misleading or defrauding the public. Thus, there are certain requirements that each state imposes to avoid potential problems.

- To comply with state regulations and to avoid claims of liability, those who run contests or giveaways (sponsors) typically create "official rules." The rules act as a contract, spelling out the rights and responsibilities of the contest sponsor and the entrants.

- There are rights issues to consider whenever a contest or promotional activity requests submissions from the audience. If one requests stories, photos, comments, or other creative works, then there are copyright issues to clear. The use of a person's name or photo may require clearing publicity rights.

The first thing to know is that the law distinguishes different kinds of contests: "lotteries," "sweepstakes," and "games of skill." A "lottery" is a promotion that has three elements:

1. Prize: this means that the entrant can win something of value.

2. Chance: this means that the winner is selected by chance; for example, by random drawing. Games of chance are distinguished from games of skill, where a person wins a prize by, say, running the fastest or figuring out a puzzle first.

3. Consideration: this means that the entrant must give something of value to enter the contest. Buying a ticket is a common example.

These three elements clearly apply to state-run lotteries like Megabucks or Mega Millions. The entrant buys a ticket for a random chance to win a prize. All 50 states strictly control lotteries, and in many states, only the state-run lottery is allowed. Charity raffles often have the same elements as a lottery and can be illegal unless they are authorized by the state.

Sweepstakes are contests that do not require the element of consideration. Often the rules allow someone to enter by sending in a postcard or email, rather than by buying something. A sweepstakes must have the language "NO PURCHASE NECESSARY" prominently placed on the call-out.

A game of skill eliminates the element of chance. But when the "skill" is judged by some subjective criteria (such as a submit the best video or poem contest), the sponsor should attempt to get expert judges who establish some criteria for what constitutes "the best" to avoid any allegation that the game has been rigged or that it is actually a game of chance.

Even though many kinds of contests can be legal, they are still usually regulated by states to avoid fraud or deceptive lures. It's important to know that there are regulations imposed on those who plan to sponsor any activity involving a prize, or chance, or consideration. Each state may have specific laws or requirements, and the rules vary by state. A national contest will have to comply with all such regulations, whereas a contest limited to one state will need to comply only with that state's rules.

Official rules for contests of any kind are typically required. They operate like a contract, and entrants and sponsors alike must abide by the rules set forth. If rules are well-written, they can be helpful to the contest promoter because they help ward off potential liability. In *Sargent v. New York Daily News, L.P.*, for example, the court dismissed a case brought against a newspaper that ran a daily numbers game. The game cards inadvertently contained an error, and thus more people won the game than the paper had prizes to award. However, the rules contained a provision declaring that in the event that an error resulted in more prizes being claimed than were stated to be awarded, the paper would conduct a random drawing to determine the actual winner. The court found the rules to be a binding contract, and by entering, the entrants were agreeing to the rules. Since the rules covered the scenario of an error, and the paper had held the random drawing, the other winners were bound by that outcome and had no right to bring a claim. The tricky part, of course, is thinking up all the possible scenarios that could cause some aspect of the contest to go awry, which is why contest rules often contain broad clauses that disclaim liability in the event of computer viruses, security violations, wars, strikes, lock-outs, acts of God, technical difficulties, printing or typographical errors, hacking, loss of power, lost entries, and other events not within the reasonable control of the sponsor.

Rules typically define who can be an entrant, and the typical requirements are that the person must be over the age of 18 and not an employee of the sponsor. The age requirement is due to the fact that minors cannot legally enter into a contract. Thus, if a contest wishes to attract minors, the rules typically require parental consent. Also, if the contest is run online and the minor is under 13, the provisions of COPPA may apply and more care must be taken. (The provisions of COPPA are discussed in Chapter 20.) The requirement that entrants not be affiliated with the sponsor is to avoid any perception of unfairness or rigging of the contest.

Rules also spell out the method of entry. Sometimes, sponsors want to use sites like Facebook, Twitter, or YouTube, asking entrants to post comments, photos, or videos. Each of those sites have their own policies and rules about running contents via their site, and sponsors should be aware of them. Facebook, for example, has had some very strict rules; they have required that certain approved apps be used, and banned certain kinds of contests that require posting replies or comments. Sponsors should make sure that their planned contest comports with the requirements of any site they may wish to use.

Even when the contest is a very simple promotion with a prize of little value, such as giving away a t-shirt to the person who thinks up the funniest caption for a photo, it is a good idea to have at least some basic rules. If the contest or promotion involves asking people to submit photos, poems, videos, comments, or some other kind of original content, the sponsor must take into consideration the copyright issues that are raised. The sponsor will need the entrant to either waive copyright or grant the sponsor a license to use the material. If the submitted material contains images of people, then the sponsor may need a grant of publicity rights if the material is being used for a commercial purpose. The call-out for a contest or submission request may need certain things:

- In the case of a sweepstakes, say "NO PURCHASE NECESSARY."

- Link to the official rules, in the event of any kind of contest.

- Link to the site's terms of use and privacy policy.

- Include a waiver of copyright rights if requesting submissions of original content.

- Include a waiver of publicity rights if you are asking to use a person's name or image.

- If photos are submitted, the submitter must warrant that they own the rights in the photo (*i.e.*, are the photographer) or have explicit permission from the photographer and that people pictured have granted permission to have their image used as part of the promotion.

In any event, due to the complexities of state regulation, those who wish to engage in promotional activities should be aware that they may need the assistance of a legal expert who can help navigate any applicable regulations.

Practical Conclusions

- So far, the Supreme Court has not been willing to extend the same level of protection to commercial speech as it does to political speech. Thus, advertisements and other kinds of speech that might be deemed "commercial" are subject to a greater degree of regulation.

- Even thought the government has more power to regulate commercial speech, the laws must nevertheless be based in some substantial interest and be narrowly tailored.

- The government has the greatest power to regulate false or misleading speech, and the FTC is the agency that most often takes action when it deems commercial speech to be false or misleading.

- It is possible for media outlets to be liable if the advertisements they carry are false or obviously advertise a dangerous product or service. It is rare for media to be held liable unless they know of the falsity or danger, but media outlets should be wary when advertisements seem potentially problematic. Media outlets are also free to reject advertisements that their audience will find offensive or troublesome.

- Contests and other promotional activities are subject to regulation by both federal and state governments. Sponsors must be careful to set forth terms in official rules and make sure that contest and promotions comply with all legal requirements. Regulations often require disclosures (such as saying "NO PURCHASE NECESSARY" on sweepstakes materials), and having well-written contest rules is important, because rules may operate as a contract.

- Interactive promotional campaigns that solicit materials from the audience should be thoughtful about copyright and publicity rights that might arise, and call-outs should clearly state what kind of rights are being requested in submitted materials.

CHAPTER 18

Television and Radio—FCC Regulation

The Federal Communications Commission (FCC) is the federal government agency tasked with regulating the communications media. Print media and in-person speech are not subject to FCC regulation, but television and radio are. Cable, satellite, and phone companies are subject to some regulation as well. As technology changes, it is important to understand what the FCC can do and why. Public understanding of the FCC's role is becoming more important as the FCC attempts to expand its influence over the internet.

This chapter will discuss:

1. What the FCC is and what it does

2. What kinds of entities are subject to FCC regulation

3. What kinds of regulations the FCC can enforce

4. Issues pertaining to public broadcasting

5. Whether the FCC can regulate the internet

What Is the FCC and What Does It Do?

The FCC was established by the Communications Act of 1934. Congress gave it broad authority to regulate interstate and foreign communication by wire or radio. The agency is divided into seven bureaus to handle a variety of issues:

1. The Media Bureau regulates radio, television, and cable.

2. The Wireless Telecom Bureau oversees wireless transmissions, such as cell phones and related technologies.

3. The Wireline Competition Bureau makes policies covering phone and internet service.

4. The Public Safety Bureau addresses emergency preparedness communications.

5. The International Bureau represents the FCC in international matters.

6. The Consumer & Government Affairs Bureau deals with consumer complaints and disability access issues.

7. The Enforcement Bureau investigates violations of any FCC policy.

The FCC is authorized by Congress to make rules consistent with congressional legislation. When it seeks to make or change a rule, it publishes a "notice of proposed rulemaking" and the public has an opportunity to comment. The notices are posted on the FCC's website at http://www.fcc.gov/Daily_Releases/Daily_Digest. Rules change regularly, so industries that are regulated by the FCC must stay on top of the changes and proposed changes.

What Kinds of Entities Are Subject to FCC Regulation?

The FCC has authority to regulate a wide variety of technologies. In some cases, the regulations among them are similar, but in some cases they are different, as each technology raises different kinds of concerns. One of the main problems facing the FCC is how to promote competition and treat the different technologies fairly. Because cable, satellite, phone, and broadcasters all provide television services, for example, each industry wants FCC policies to either benefit its own industry or at least not harm its industry. If one industry were to be heavily regulated, and another were not, it might give the unregulated industry an unfair advantage in the marketplace. The FCC tries not to interfere unfairly with competition among services.

Sometimes, competition issues give rise to First Amendment issues. The various kinds of communications technologies each want the freedom to provide content as they wish.

Broadcast television and radio are subject to the most regulation of content. When the government granted the authority to regulate the airwaves, it recognized that the airwaves are a public good, and the FCC was tasked with devising a systematic way to apportion the airwaves among competing users. The electromagnetic spectrum over which signals are sent is limited, and there isn't enough room for everyone to have their own signal. This fact is the basis for what is called the "limited spectrum argument," which argues that the FCC needs to regulate use of the airwaves because the spectrum is limited and thus users should be licensed and serve the public interest. Broadcast media is also intrusive in the sense that the content comes freely over the airwaves, and once someone turns on a broadcast station, they will see or hear whatever is broadcast. For these reasons, broadcasters are subject to regulations on profanity and indecency. Regulations also dictate how signals may be transmitted (*e.g.*, the switch from analog to digital television signals was an FCC mandate) and who may own stations.

Although most consumers think of television as a single medium, most people who receive television do so via cable, which does not use public airwaves. Because cable is a subscription service, cable companies are not treated exactly like broadcasters. Indecent content, for example, has received more First Amendment protection when it is delivered via cable as opposed to via broadcast media. In *U.S. v. Playboy Entertainment Group*, the Supreme Court struck down regulations that required "adult" cable companies to scramble indecent material; the Court applied strict scrutiny, which it has not done in the case of broadcast media. However, the Court has been willing to allow some regulation of cable. For example, the FCC has required "must-carry" rules that force cable companies to carry broadcast stations. These rules are designed to preserve on-air broadcasting and prevent cable companies from squeezing out broadcasters. The requirement was upheld by the Supreme Court in *Turner Broadcasting Sys. v. FCC*, where the Court used an intermediate level of scrutiny and ruled that must-carry rules were constitutional because they are content-neutral and advance substantial government interests. The FCC also requires cable companies to comply with its regulations concerning advertising, children's programming, and political affairs. There is a theoretical question as to whether these regulations would be deemed constitutional if challenged. However, the cable companies have never challenged these regulations as violating their First Amendment rights. Remember that the First Amendment is not self-executing. One must challenge a law to have it struck down as unconstitutional. If the companies do not challenge the law, then it may be enforced, regardless of whether it might violate the First Amendment.

Satellite television services are also subject to regulation. Like cable, they must comply with the political content rules and the rules on children's programming. They are also required to "carry one, carry all," meaning that if they carry any one local station, they must carry all local stations.

Telephone companies are regulated by the FCC as "common carriers." Common carriers are required to provide service to all paying customers. They must not regulate the content of their lines, and they generally do not transmit content themselves. Thus, content regulation has not traditionally been a problem on telephone. Most regulations pertain to the rates telephone companies may charge customers.

What Kinds of Regulations Can the FCC Enforce?

FCC rules cover a wide range of matters. They regulate ownership of stations, licensing requirements, technology and distribution requirements, and disability access to media, among other things. This book, however, is targeted towards understanding liability for speech, so this section will focus only on those regulations that affect content, rather than ownership, distribution, or other such issues.

Section 326 of the Communications Act prohibits the FCC from acting as a censor, and, of course, the First Amendment imposes limits on government regulation of speech in general. However, there are some notable areas in which the FCC does engage in content regulation. Almost all of these regulations would most likely be deemed unconstitutional if applied to print media, but the Supreme Court has permitted more expansive regulation of broadcast media because of the limited spectrum argument. As the Court said in *Office of Comm. Of the U.C.C. v. FCC*, a broadcaster receives "the free and exclusive use of a limited and valuable part of the public domain; when he accepts that franchise it is burdened by enforceable public obligations." Although some regulations also have been applied to cable and satellite, they have not yet been challenged, and thus there is no ruling on whether the FCC's expanded regulation of those media are constitutional.

Indecency

As discussed in Chapter 15, indecency is sexual content that does not qualify as "obscene." Indecent content is subject to regulation on broadcast media. In *FCC v. Pacifica Foundation*, the Supreme Court upheld the FCC's authority to regulate indecency in broadcast media because of the limited spectrum argument. Therefore, indecent programming is prohibited during times of the day when there is a reasonable risk that children may be in the audience. Under the current rule, indecent broadcasts aired between 6:00 a.m. and 10:00 p.m. are subject to enforcement action.

The FCC website defines indecency as "language or material that, in context, depicts or describes, in terms patently offensive as measured by contemporary community broadcast standards for the broadcast medium, sexual or excretory organs or activities." That language is quite broad. In *FCC v. Fox Television Stations, Inc.*, the Supreme Court struck down fines against television broadcasters arising from three different shows, ruling that the FCC's indecency policy was vague, because the agency failed to give adequate notice to the broadcasters with respect to how the policy would be enforced. The FCC will be expected to develop rules that are not vague and to give clear guidelines with respect to what is prohibited.

Profanity

The FCC also regulates profanity. The FCC defines profane material as language "so grossly offensive to members of the public who actually hear it as to amount to a nuisance." Profanity is prohibited on broadcast radio and television between 6 a.m. and 10 p.m.

The Fairness Doctrine and Right of Reply

The FCC used to have a rule called the "Fairness Doctrine." The idea was that broadcast media should discuss matters of public concern in ways that were fair and balanced, providing a wide range of views on the topic. Citizens were allowed to complain about unfair coverage and the FCC could require additional coverage in the interest of fairness. Among the particular rules imposed, the FCC required a right of reply, which gave the subject of a personal attack the right to respond to the attack via the same platform. This rule was upheld as constitutional in *Red Lion Broadcasting Co. v. FCC*. The Court reasoned that the FCC should have the authority to impose rules to serve the public interest because there is a limited spectrum and thus those who have the privilege of holding a broadcast license may be subject to more stringent rules than would otherwise be permissible. Thus, the right of reply is not a First Amendment right; it was only an administrative rule, and rules are subject to change. In fact, the rule was repealed in 1987. There is no current "right of reply rule," nor is there any other recognized right to force media to allow people a space to respond to editorial content. The remaining aspects of the Fairness Doctrine, allowing complaints about the fairness or balance of media coverage, have also been repealed. Politicians periodically call for a revival of the Fairness Doctrine, but during the time it existed, it was widely criticized for creating burdensome and time-consuming administrative procedures that were never resolved to anyone's satisfaction; that's why the rule was eventually repealed. There is also an argument that such rules are no longer necessary, because the internet gives everyone a platform to reply to any accusations about them.

Political Elections

The Candidate Access Rule is an administrative rule that requires stations to provide to candidates for federal office "reasonable" access to buy advertising time at the lowest available rate. There is also a rule requiring stations to provide "equal opportunities" for airtime, which includes the opportunity to buy time, but may also include unpaid time, to the extent a station provides access to a competing candidate. These requirements apply once a campaign has begun, although that time may be subject to debate before the FCC.

In *CBS v. FCC*, the Court concluded that the access rule did not violate the First Amendment rights of broadcasters, citing both to the limited spectrum policy argument and also to the fact that the rule was narrowly tailored, limited only to candidates for federal office in the time period before an election. In that case, the Court upheld an FCC determination that the television networks had failed to provide "reasonable time" when the Carter-Mondale campaign requested a 30-minute time segment to show a documentary "outlining the record of [Carter's] administration." The networks objected because of the impact on regular schedules, but the Court affirmed the FCC's broad discretion to impose rules it deems in the public interest. Again, note that the authority to impose this requirement is based solely on the FCC's authority as a rule-making agency and not as a requirement pursuant to the First Amendment. Absent the FCC rule, the candidates would have no right to demand coverage by the networks.

The equal opportunities rule can have some strange effects, as a practical matter. Whenever a legally qualified candidate is permitted to "use" a station, the station must provide "equal opportunities to all other such candidates for that office." However, newscasts, news interviews, on-site news coverage, and other news-related events, such as debates, are exempt from the definition of "use." Thus, media coverage of candidates who appear in the news simply by virtue of their candidacy or their elected position does not invoke the equal time rule. In *Kennedy for President v. FCC*, the court recognized that this policy gives incumbents an advantage because stations are not required to provide equal time to opponents when the incumbent is featured in a genuine news context. The courts will judge the newsworthiness of the appearance as an important factor, and the trend has been to define newsworthiness broadly, so that even interviews on *The Tonight Show* are considered news. However, other appearances can be a "use." Several politicians are former actors, and questions have been raised about whether it would be a use to show movies or television shows in which they appeared during the time that they were campaigning for office. Most recently, when Fred Thompson was campaigning for the Republican presidential nomination, NBC said it would stop airing re-runs of *Law & Order* in which he appeared so that it would not run afoul of the equal time rule. Of course, news coverage is probably more likely to affect voters than old movies, so the practical efficacy of the rule's application may be questionable.

Finally, there is a statutory exemption from liability granted to a broadcaster who provides time to candidates. Once a broadcaster provides time, it cannot censor or edit the candidate. They are given statutory immunity for libel in exchange for not tampering with the politician's speech.

Children's Programming

The Children's Television Act of 1990 contains provisions that affect both requirements for educational programming for children and limits on certain advertising.

With respect to educational programming, the Act requires television licensees seeking renewal to show that they have served the educational and informational needs of children. In 1996, the FCC established a more formal rule requiring broadcasters to include at least three hours of educational programming per week in order to qualify for license renewal. This rule does not apply to cable.

With respect to advertising, FCC rules limit both the amount and content of advertising during children's shows that air on either broadcast television or cable. For children ages 12 and under, ads are supposed to be limited to 10.5 minutes per hour on weekends, 12 minutes per hour on weekdays. Programs based on toys (*e.g.*, GI Joe) cannot show ads for the product within the show, although such ads may follow the show.

Aside from FCC regulation, the advertising industry engages in some self-regulation. The Children's Advertising Review Unit (CARU) sets industry standards for children's advertising, and while it is not a formal government regulation, most advertisers comply with the provisions in an effort to avoid further government scrutiny. The standards are designed to avoid deceptive or misleading ads, inappropriate sales pressure, and the blurring of advertising and editorial content.

Other Advertising Regulations

As noted in the chapter on advertising, most government regulation of advertising comes from other federal or state agencies, such as FTC regulations concerning misleading ads or the FDA's requirement that pharmaceutical ads contain certain disclosures. The FCC also imposes some regulations on advertising in addition to the requirements with respect to children's programming.

The FCC has a rule that requires the source of an ad to be identified in some form. Broadcasters may not run ads that fail to disclose the producer or sponsor of the advertisement.

The FCC also implements a law passed by Congress that regulates the volume of television advertisements. Citizens had complained that ads were much louder than regular programming, and Congress passed the Commercial Advertisement Loudness Mitigation (CALM) Act to address the problem.

Other Content Regulations

The Telecommunications Act of 1996 requires a V-chip in all televisions produced after its effective date. The V-Chip has the capacity to restrict access to programming that contains sex or violence. It relies on a ratings system created by television producers who identify potentially objectionable content so that consumers can block content they find offensive. Studies have consistently shown that consumers love the idea of a V-chip, but they rarely use it.

FCC regulations prohibit hoaxes, which are defined as broadcasting knowingly false information about a crime or catastrophe. If the false information would foreseeably cause substantial public harm and actually does cause such harm, then the station may be fined. If the material is properly labeled as fiction or some other appropriate disclaimer is given, then the FCC presumes it is not a hoax. There is also a rule that prohibits intentional distortion of news. In general, the FCC will not intervene in ordinary news judgments, and the Fairness Doctrine has been revoked. But the FCC maintains a provision that allows action in cases where there is compelling evidence of intentional rigging or slanting of news.

FCC regulations also prohibit fraud, payola, and any rigging of game shows. Payola is a practice that used to be common, where record labels would pay radio stations to play a particular song a particular number of times per week. That practice is now banned. It is also prohibited to give something of value in exchange for a mention of a product or service. For example, if a restaurant gives free food to a station in exchange for station personalities saying on air how much they love the food—*and* they fail to disclose that they received free food—that is a violation of the rule. The idea is that the audience should know when something is sponsored or not. An advertisement must state the sponsor, and promotions should, too. If the DJ discloses that the food was given for free, it is ok. It is also ok if the DJ says he loves the restaurant simply because he is giving his personal opinion and no free food was given in exchange. But it would violate the rule to receive the free food, mention the restaurant on the air, *and* fail to disclose the gift.

FCC rules also require giving notice that a phone call will be recorded if the station intends to broadcast the contents. The notification must be given before the recording begins. The only exception is when it is obvious that the call would be broadcast, such as when a person calls in to a live talk show that airs callers. FCC regulations also regulate when other material may be used on the air. For example, FCC regulations prohibit the rebroadcast of any content that originated with another broadcaster without that original broadcaster's consent.

Finally, each station must periodically make station identification announcements including its call letters and the community in which it broadcasts. Televisions stations are also required to periodically state the location of its public file—the place where citizens can go to see the station's record of programming and compliance with FCC public interest requirements. All licensed stations are required to maintain a public inspection file, which contains certain information about how the station is meeting its public service requirements. Anyone can request to see the file at any time. The file must contain numerous items, including materials related to a complaint or investigation, information about political candidates' request for time, letters and emails from the public, programming reports (including reports about children's programming), and lists of donors (if any). In 2012, the FCC voted to phase in a rule requiring that the political advertising information in the public file be posted online.

Emergency Alert Tones

As part of its public service mission, the FCC regulates emergency alerts. When there is an emergency, broadcasters emit a particular "tone" that signifies to the audience that there is an emergency; that tone is then followed by instructions. Stations must periodically run tests of the emergency alert system. The FCC takes these tests and emergency tones *very* seriously. In fact, FCC regulations prohibit the use of an alert tone in any situation that is not a genuine emergency or authorized test, and the agency will fine any station that improperly airs a tone. For example, Turner Broadcasting System was fined $25,000 for using an emergency alert tone in an ad for Conan O'Brien's talk show. And a trailer for the film *The Olympus Has Fallen* contained an alert tone, and companies that aired the trailer were fined by the FCC. It is therefore very important not to air emergency alerts unless it is a genuine emergency.

Complaints Regarding Broadcast Content

FCC investigations regarding broadcast content are usually prompted by consumer complaints. The FCC will investigate and determine whether a fine is appropriate. The FCC asks complainants to provide the following information: (1) the date and time of the alleged broadcast; (2) the call sign of the station involved; and (3) information regarding the details of what was actually said (or depicted) during the alleged indecent, profane, or obscene broadcast.

The FCC will consider the context of what was said or depicted and determine whether it violated any regulations. FCC makes administrative determinations, and a media company that has been subject to an enforcement action must appeal within the agency's administrative process before appealing to a court. However, if the administrative appeal is unsatisfactory, the company may file an appeal with a federal appellate court.

What Are the Issues Pertaining to Public Broadcasting?

The FCC recognizes a class of licensees that it refers to as "non-commercial educational stations," many of which are public broadcasters. Public television and radio are different from commercial television and radio in two important respects:

1. Public stations are private non-profits or governmental entities, whereas commercial stations are private for-profit entities.

2. Public stations may receive some government funds, whereas commercial stations do not.

Most public broadcasters get their funding from private donors, but they may receive some portion of their finding from the federal or state government. The stations most likely to rely on government funds are small stations in rural areas, because those stations are simply not commercially viable and could not exist otherwise. Advertising as a business model for media works well when there is a large audience to whom many advertisers would like to reach. A small, rural population will not attract many advertisers, and even then, the cost of ad space is typically related to the size of the audience. Stations with a small audience cannot command enough money for ad space to cover the cost of operating a station. Thus, government funds may be available to help maintain these stations, which provide vital information, such as news and emergency information, to the people in the area.

The Corporation for Public Broadcasting (CPB) is an independent entity that disperses federal money for public broadcasting. The CPB is technically not a government agency. It is a private non-profit corporation that was authorized by Congress. It distributes funds according to strict rules, but federal agencies (such as the FCC) cannot interfere with CPB decisions. CPB gives money directly to the stations, and the stations use that money for operations and programming. CPB funds are sometimes used for other purposes, such as to start the production of a show or pay for other special costs.

In public radio, for example, CPB gives money to a station, and the station will probably also get some money from donors or corporate sponsors. The station will then either create its own programming or buy programming from a producer. Public radio producers include NPR, Chicago Public Media, and American Public Media, among others. Listeners are often confused by this system, assuming that if they are listening to an NPR station, then all of the shows they hear are produced by NPR, but that is not necessarily the case. Individual stations may mix and match shows from several producers to create a unique blend of programming that they think best serves their local audience. NPR acts as the trade association for public radio stations, which explains why stations are often referred to as an "NPR station" even though the programming can come from many different sources.

Public television is slightly different. Like radio, local stations are funded by a combination of grants, donations, and sponsorships, and the stations then create their own shows or buy shows from producers. However, there is one central distributor of shows: PBS. Programs are usually produced by individual stations (for example, *Frontline* is produced by WGBH in Boston), and PBS operates as a distributor, licensing the shows to other stations for broadcast.

The FCC has imposed unique regulations on public media, and there are a few issues that have been addressed in court decisions, described below.

Political Opinions

Public broadcasters may not endorse or oppose specific candidates for office. They may provide political commentary on issues. There had been an FCC rule against editorializing, but it was struck down as unconstitutional in *FCC v. League of Women Voters*. It should be noted that even if the FCC did not have the rule concerning candidates, the IRS also prohibits certain non-profits from endorsing political candidates.

Editorial Discretion

Public stations are not open forums. They have complete control over their editorial content. The public has no right to demand time to broadcast particular material or a discussion of an issue. For example, in *Arkansas Educ. Television Comm'n v. Forbes*, the Court ruled that a public station that hosts an election debate can exclude minor party candidates, as long as the exclusion is based on objective criteria, such as requiring a certain level of support from the public.

Sponsorship

Public broadcasters may not sell advertising, but they may make "acknowledgments" of contributions. The underwriting announcements may state the sponsor, a slogan that does not promote the product, value-neutral descriptions of product information, or a location, but they may not include any kind of call to action to buy a product or service, nor may they provide price information, inducements, or comparisons to competitors. Like commercial media, though, public stations may reject sponsors for business reasons, such as a concern about offending the audience. In *Ku Klux Klan v. Curators of Univ. of Missouri*, the court decided that the Ku Klux Klan did not have First Amendment right to sponsor a show on a public radio station. In fact, the station's decision to reject their funds can be a form of protected speech. Thus, stations have discretion to reject potential sponsorships.

Can the FCC Regulate the Internet?

The FCC has expressed an interest in regulating at least some aspects of the internet. There is a dispute about whether the FCC would have authority to do so. On one hand, Congress granted the FCC broadly worded authority to regulate communications. On the other hand, there is an argument that the FCC's authority can be limited on First Amendment grounds, or that the particular regulation at issue must properly be within the scope of the authority granted by Congress.

One of the most hotly contested issues has been whether the FCC can enforce "net neutrality" regulations. These regulations would restrict internet service providers from interfering with the ways customers use broadband service. The FCC's authority to impose such regulations was first tested in *Comcast Corp. v. FCC*. In that case, the federal circuit court in D.C. ruled that the FCC did not have authority to regulate Comcast's internet service. However, the ruling was fairly narrow and was based solely on the issue of whether there was a congressional grant of authority, not on First Amendment grounds. The ruling left open the possibility that regulation could be possible if either Congress were to grant the FCC some additional authority via statute or the FCC enacted a regulation that was already within the scope of its authority.

In 2015, the FCC classified internet service as a public utility, required that broadband be equally accessible to all consumers, and prevented ISPs from charging for faster downloading speeds. In 2016, a federal appellate court upheld the FCC's right to enact these regulations in *U.S. Telecom Ass'n v. FCC*. The classification of services was within the scope of the FCC's authority, and the court found that the agency's decision met the "reasonableness" standard by which such decisions are judged. The regulations did not last long however. In January 2017, Donald Trump appointed Ajit Pai as the new FCC Chairman, and in December 2017, the FCC reversed those rules. The "Restoring Internet Freedom Order" officially took effect June 11, 2018. Since then, a coalition of net neutrality advocates have sued the FCC, arguing that the change in regulations was "arbitrary and capricious." States have also attempted to impose net neutrality by passing their own state regulations; however, the federal government has sued the state of California to stop the state's enforcement of any regulations, arguing that the federal government has exclusive authority to regulate broadband services. That case has been stayed pending the outcome of the lawsuit against the FCC. Thus, it will take some more time for these lawsuits to resolve the issue of whether or how the FCC can regulate net neutrality.

Table 18.1: Arguments For and Against Net Neutrality.

Arguments For Net Neutrality	Arguments Against Net Neutrality
The internet is a Title II Telecommunications Service (which may be subject to more regulation).	The internet is a Title I Information Service (which should be subject to less regulation).
The internet is a basic need.	Promoting competition is good.
ISPs may demand payments from popular services in exchange for not slowing down or blocking that service.	Net neutrality may lead to a lack of investment in the internet.
Without neutrality, some internet users could be denied fast internet service or may even be blocked from some sites.	Existing legal frameworks can prevent harmful internet practices and consumer outrage over discriminatory practices will prevent abuse.
Lack of neutrality puts small companies at a disadvantage if they can't afford to keep up with larger companies that can buy faster delivery speeds, creating a barrier to entry.	Principles of capitalism should prevail.

The FCC has not yet attempted to regulate content on the internet, and the Supreme Court's decisions indicate that it is likely to treat the internet as it treats print media, meaning that any efforts by the FCC to regulate content would be subject to a high degree of scrutiny.

Practical Conclusions

- The FCC serves many functions, and those who work in a regulated industry (broadcast, cable, satellite, telephones) must stay abreast of the ever-evolving regulatory requirements. The burden falls on the media to challenge any regulations that infringe on First Amendment rights.

- The main form of content regulation is the prohibition on indecent and profane material on broadcast media. Such content is prohibited during the hours that children are likely to be in the audience, which is 6 a.m. to 10 p.m. The agency will fine stations that violate this rule.

- Other regulations impose restrictions on children's programs and advertising, hoaxes, and payola. There are also rules that require disclosures of information in a station's public file, consent when recording information for broadcast, and consent for the rebroadcast or retransmission of certain content. During an election season, candidates are entitled to equal opportunities to use broadcast media.

- Enforcement actions are typically prompted by a complaint. The audience may file a complaint with the FCC describing the objectionable material, and the FCC will investigate to determine whether a violation occurred. Stations that violate the rules may be fined, and repeated violations may result in the loss of the station's license.

- Public media operates much like commercial media, except that it is prohibited from accepting advertising. It may receive contributions and acknowledge them on air, but there are strict guidelines concerning what may be in an acknowledgment. There cannot be a call to action in any form. Also, public stations may not endorse or oppose candidates for office, and the public cannot demand time or coverage on a public station.

- The FCC's power to regulate content stems from the so-called "limited spectrum argument," the notion that there is limited spectrum for broadcast media, and thus, anyone who is fortunate enough to obtain a broadcast license must operate in the public interest. As technology changes and it is easier to distribute content in a virtually unlimited digital arena, the courts will have to determine whether the FCC's power to regulate content remains justified.

- The FCC's authority to regulate the internet is still evolving. There are likely to be First Amendment battles in the future if the FCC attempts to regulate content on the internet. Its ability to regulate "net neutrality" is still being litigated.

CHAPTER 19

Special Classes of Speakers

Throughout this book, there are references to the First Amendment applying equally to everyone. The professional journalist does not have a greater constitutional right than the ordinary citizen. The government must treat all speakers equally. These are important and consistent principles in First Amendment jurisprudence.

Alas, there are a few exceptions. The Supreme Court has crafted different rules for a few categories of speakers: students, government employees, and those who are speaking with government funds. This chapter will discuss the rules and circumstances that apply to each of these special classes.

Students

Although the Supreme Court has said that students do not leave their First Amendment rights at the schoolhouse door, the Court has allowed student speech to be punished or censored in many circumstances. Traditionally, the speech that was punished or censored has occurred at school, but in recent years, there have been several cases involving off-campus speech, particularly cases involving internet postings.

This section will discuss the tests and considerations the Supreme Court has used to evaluate the constitutionality of restrictions on student speech and how that has been interpreted or expanded to off-campus speech.

The Court's first decision on student speech was full of promise. In *Tinker v. Des Moines Indp. Community School Dist.*, students wore black armbands to school to protest the Vietnam war and were suspended for violating school policy. The Court ruled in favor of the students, establishing the rule that administrators may restrict speech only if they can meet the burden of proving that the speech materially disrupts classwork, involves substantial disorder, or invades the rights of others. The Court added that school officials must offer compelling evidence of disruption and may not base their punishment on mere speculation about what might occur.

Since that decision, the Court has backtracked on the broad rights that appeared to have been granted to students.

In *Bethel School District v. Fraser*, the Court considered whether a student could be suspended for the speech he gave at a high school assembly to endorse a candidate for student elections. The speech contained numerous sexual innuendoes. The Court upheld the suspension, giving little explanation as to why except that schools are permitted to maintain decorum and suggesting that the sexual innuendos would be disruptive.

In *Hazelwood School Dist. v. Kuhlmeier*, a student newspaper wanted to publish articles about pregnancy and divorce. In both cases, the school was concerned that the article would invade the privacy rights of people referenced in the story. School administrators censored the paper and the Court upheld the censorship. The Court made a distinction between school-sponsored forums and other forms of speech, finding that if a forum is school-sponsored and has not otherwise been declared to be a public forum, a court should uphold censorship when it is reasonably related to legitimate educational concerns. The Court seemed to give the schools fairly broad discretion to determine what was a legitimate concern, noting that school-sponsored speech can be restricted if it is ungrammatical, poorly written, biased, prejudiced, vulgar, profane, or otherwise unsuitable, particularly if the subject matter appears to promote drug use, sexual activity, or other topics that interfere with decency and civility.

The Court has endorsed a school's ability to punish students for their own speech, as well. In *Morse v. Frederick*, the Court upheld the suspension of a student who attended a parade holding a sign that read, "Bong Hits for Jesus." The event was "school supervised," and the Court found that the school had an interest in controlling speech that advocates drug use. Even though the student said that his statement was intended to be nonsensical and not to advocate drug use, the Court apparently decided that the statement was advocacy, regardless of intent.

Thus, aside from *Tinker*, the Court seems to have taken the view that the schools' right to maintain order overrides the students' right to free speech. They seem to give schools wide discretion in cases involving sensitive subject matter, particularly sex and drugs.

One of the most interesting aspects of the *Morse* case is that it involved speech that occurred off campus. The ability of schools to punish speech that occurs off campus has become a hotly contested issue. *Morse* involved a low-tech form of speech: a student held up a sign at a parade. Most off-campus speech cases, however, involve internet postings.

The Supreme Court has not yet decided a case involving student internet postings, and the lower courts have differed on the scope of a school's authority to punish students for such speech. In some cases, the courts have said that students can be punished for off-campus speech if it nevertheless affects the educational process. For example, in *Doninger v. Niehoff*, a student class officer was barred from running for office again because of statements she posted online. The court found that her rights were not violated because the statements caused great disruption in the school. Similarly, in *J. S. v. Bethlehem Area School Dist.*, the court found that it did not infringe a student's rights to punish him for his "Teacher Sux" website, because it was accessed from school, aimed at an audience related to the school, and caused disruption.

In other cases, however, the courts have protected the student's free speech rights. In *Layshock v. Hermitage School Dist.*, the court found that a student's fake MySpace profile of the school principal was protected First Amendment activity because his actions were entirely off-campus and any effect on the school was minimal. Also, in *Emmett v. Kent School Dist.*, the court found that it would be improper for a school to punish a student for his satirical website, because the website was independent of the school and the mock obituaries on the site could not reasonably be construed to constitute a true threat of harm to anyone.

Given the conflicting opinions and the highly fact-specific nature of the courts' reasoning, there is little useful guidance in interpreting how much protection courts will give to student speech online, except to say that if the court believes the school or educational process has been affected in any way, it is likely that the courts will grant schools broad discretion to punish online speech.

Students, therefore, cannot be certain that their speech will be protected. Due to *Hazelwood*, students who work for school-sponsored media may encounter administrative censorship. And they may be punished even if the speech occurs off-campus if the speech is deemed to have caused disruption at school.

One other question is whether and to what degree colleges and universities may censor or punish student speech. The argument for censoring younger students is that they are minors, but college and university students are typically over 18. There is substantially less government interest in "protecting" them. Nevertheless, college students have seen an erosion of their rights over the years.

In *Papish v. Bd. Of Curators of the Univ. of Missouri*, the Supreme Court found that a university had violated the First Amendment rights of a student in expelling him for distributing a privately operated newspaper with indecent and offensive speech. The paper contained an article with the headline, "Motherfucker Acquitted," and the cover featured a cartoon of police officers raping the Statue of Liberty. The Court held that the interests of decency were insufficient to impose punishment for the student's speech. In essence, the Court acknowledged that university students were adult citizens entitled to the standard First Amendment protections.

However, in *Hosty v. Carter*, the Seventh Circuit extended the *Hazelwood* holding to colleges, stating that there was no significant difference between high school and college newspapers and permitting censorship if the paper is school-sponsored. The Supreme Court denied the appeal of the case.

Adverse rulings have not been limited to campus news media. In *Cummins v. Campbell*, the Ohio State University refused to let the Student Union show the film *The Last Temptation of Christ* until it had been approved by university officials. Students argued that the restriction was a prior restraint and therefore unconstitutional. But the court concluded that the Student Union Activities Board was school-sponsored, and therefore the *Hazelwood* rule applied. The restriction was constitutional because it was related to legitimate pedagogical concerns.

Restrictions have also come in the form of funding disputes. In 2009, the Maryland legislature considered a bill that would withhold funding to any university that fails to adopt a policy on "the serious social and health concerns associated with screening pornographic films." The bill, as one might imagine, was in response to a planned screening at the University of Maryland of *Pirates II: Stagnetti's Revenge*, a film that was admittedly pornographic, and yet not deemed obscene. Several universities across the country were hosting screenings in conjunction with discussions about the First Amendment led by professors. The University of Maryland, however, in response to the threat of losing funding, cancelled the on-campus screening, but students and professors simply organized a screening off-campus. The bill eventually failed to pass. There may be no law or precedent set by the incident, but it certainly illustrates the range of threats or difficulties that students may encounter when controversial speech is at issue. Losing funds is as much a threat as outright censorship.

There is a nonprofit organization called the Student Press Law Center (SPLC) that provides legal advice and assistance to student media, and they have had some successes. For example, in 2010, police officers in Harrisonburg, Virginia, executed a search warrant to obtain some photographs in the possession of the James Madison University student newspaper. The Privacy Protection Act prohibits such newsroom searches with few exceptions, but being student media is not one of the exceptions. The SPLC was able to help them obtain an attorney, and the Commonwealth's Attorney who authorized the search eventually apologized and the paper received a $10,000 settlement. Thus, students do not necessarily lose all rights that might otherwise exist, even in light of several unfavorable Court opinions. Another nonprofit organization, the Foundation for Individual Rights in Education (FIRE), provides legal assistance to individual students who are faced with First Amendment issues, and they have been successful, as well.

Government Employees

The government acts as an employer. In that sense, they have some interest in restricting speech to the extent it affects how one does one's job. But the fact that someone is employed by the government doesn't mean that they can't have First Amendment rights in their role as a citizen. The court has developed some rules to balance the rights of government employees to speak in their capacity as citizens while also giving the government employers some rights to punish or restrict speech that harms some government interest.

In *Pickering v. Board of Ed. Of Township High School Dist. 205, Will Cty.*, the Supreme Court considered whether a teacher's letter to a local newspaper should be protected by the First Amendment. The Court noted that the teacher may act as a citizen and comment on matters of public concern. The teacher's interest in doing so must be balanced against the government's interest in promoting the efficiency of the employee's job duties. Thus, the question is whether the school had a greater interest in limiting the teacher's speech than it would in limiting any similar speech by any other member of the public. The Court concluded it did not, and thus the teacher's speech should be protected.

However, in *Garcetti v. Ceballos*, the Court found that speech made in the course of fulfilling one's duties was not protected. Ceballos was a district attorney in California. He criticized a search warrant that had been executed, arguing that the supporting affidavit was inaccurate. There were meetings and arguments within the district attorney's office over the case. Ceballos claimed that, after his criticisms, he was subject to retaliatory actions and denied a promotion. He sued the government, claiming that the retaliation violated his First Amendment rights. Citing *Pickering*, the Court said the question was whether the employee was speaking in his capacity as a citizen on a matter of public concern. If not, then there is no First Amendment claim. If so, then the question is whether the government has justification for treating the employee differently from any other member of the public. The Court concluded that Ceballos was acting in his job capacity and not as a citizen, and thus, he had no First Amendment claim.

The Court's ruling in *Garcetti* raised the question whether there could be any First Amendment protection for whistleblowers if they are merely acting as government employees. The Court's more recent ruling in *Lane v. Franks* addresses some of those concerns. Edward Lane was the director of a state-funded youth training program. He realized that state representative Susan Schmitz—who was later indicted—was being paid as an employee of the program, even though she wasn't showing up for work. Lane fired Schmitz and later testified against her under subpoena. Lane was then fired from his job, purportedly for budget reasons, but he claimed it was retaliation for firing Schmitz. The lower courts ruled that Lane was acting in his capacity as a government employee when he fired Schmitz, and testifying against her was based on his employment role, and therefore, under *Garcetti*, he was not protected by the First Amendment. The Supreme Court, however, overruled those decisions, finding that testifying on a matter of public concern is "a quintessential example of citizen speech." The Court also clarified that the ruling in *Garcetti* is limited to speech as part of one's specific duties, not simply anything related to government employment. It's still not clear exactly when whistleblowing transforms from employee speech to citizen speech; such a determination is likely to be very fact-specific. Nevertheless, there is some indication that some whistleblowing activity by government employees could be deemed "citizen speech."

But the fact that an employee is acting as a citizen and not in the course of his duties doesn't mean that his speech will always be protected. *San Diego v. Roe* is highly illustrative. In that case, a police officer sold items on eBay. Among those items were explicit videos of himself masturbating while wearing a police uniform. The police department was not amused. The officer was eventually terminated, and he sued, claiming that his First Amendment rights were violated. The Supreme Court noted that government employees do not completely relinquish their First Amendment rights merely because they are government employees. Their speech can be protected when they speak as citizens on matters of public concern or when there is no government interest in regulating their speech outside of work. In this case, however, the Court found that the officer's speech was not unrelated to his employment, because he used a police uniform and listed himself as working in the field of law enforcement. Moreover, his speech may have been a "debased parody," but it "brought the mission of the employer and the professionalism of its officers into serious disrepute." The Court found this scenario to be distinct from other cases where government employees spoke out on issues, largely because of the harm to the employer's mission. Thus, government employees must be aware that out-of-office speech may not be protected by the First Amendment when it nevertheless negatively affects the employer.

Speakers Whose Speech Is Government Funded

The Supreme Court has ruled on several occasions that the government may impose requirements on the receipt of government funds, even if those requirements affect the recipient's right of free speech. As a practical matter, this means that persons or entities that accept government funding may have to sacrifice some First Amendment rights.

Rust v. Sullivan, one of the first cases on this topic, involved regulations promulgated by the Department of Health and Human Services (HHS). A federal law prohibited the use of federal funds for programs that use abortion as a method of family planning. HHS regulations prohibited not only the providing of abortions but also any counseling, referring, or advocating concerning abortions as a method of family planning. The regulations were challenged on several grounds, including the First Amendment. The plaintiffs argued that the regulations were viewpoint-discriminatory, but the Court rejected that argument. It ruled that the government was not discriminating based on viewpoint; it was merely funding one activity over another. The government may choose, as a matter of policy, that it wishes to encourage childbirth rather than abortion, and it may further that policy via the use of funds. The Court also noted that the regulations govern only the program that was funded and not the grantee. Entities that received these funds could express views about abortion as long as such expression was done outside the scope of the specific program that was being funded.

In *NEA v. Finley*, artists challenged the constitutionality of a law that required the National Endowment for the Arts (NEA) to consider the decency of any work that received funding. The artists had been recommended for grants, but the recommendations were later revoked, after the law was passed. The Court upheld the decency requirements because the law merely required "considering" decency. It did not ban works that would be indecent, and therefore it did not amount to censorship. The law was also challenged for being vague and viewpoint discriminatory, but the Court found that neither was the case, largely because the NEA must make grants based on "artistic excellence," which is inherently subjective and some leeway must be given to the judges to make determinations of what is appropriate. Such a case is different from one where the government attempted to ban or punish any indecent art; here, they only chose not to sponsor it.

In *U.S. v. American Library Assoc.*, the Court considered the constitutionality of a provision of the Children's Internet Protection Act (CIPA) that requires libraries that receive federal funds to use filtering software to screen out pornography and other inappropriate materials. The Court found that the law was a valid exercise of Congress' spending power. Congress was not banning the material outright, and the refusal to fund an activity is not the same thing as penalizing the activity. Congress spends government funds for specific purposes, and in this case, the purpose is to ensure that federally funded libraries are used for appropriate educational and informational purposes. The Court found that to be sufficient.

Finally, in *Rumsfeld v. FAIR*, the Court upheld a federal requirement that schools that receive federal funds allow military recruiters on campus. Law schools had challenged the law as a violation of their First Amendment rights, because they objected to the military's "don't ask, don't tell" policy, and argued that the law forced them to accommodate a viewpoint it disagreed with. But the Court upheld Congress' authority to impose the recruiting requirement in conjunction with federal funding because there was nothing that prevented the schools from expressing their views in opposition to the military.

Thus, when the government is spending money to promulgate a particular program, it is possible that speech-related restrictions may be imposed on that program. However, the government's ability to impose restrictions is not unlimited.

In *LSC v. Velasquez*, the Court considered a provision of the welfare reform law that prohibited lawyers who receive federal funds from challenging the constitutionality of the welfare law on behalf of their clients. The majority in that case distinguished the other federal funding cases, finding that in those cases, the government was funding its own activity and speaking on its own. In this case, the funding was provided to lawyers to facilitate private speech—namely, the speech of their clients. Moreover, the court noted, the law distorted the way the justice system was supposed to work. Under principles of separation of powers, Congress shouldn't restrict the operation of the judicial system in terms of considering the constitutionality of a law. Thus, the Court concluded that the law truly did infringe on First Amendment rights.

Most recently, in *Agency for Int'l Development v. Alliance for Open Society*, the Supreme Court struck down a requirement that organizations that receive funds to help prevent the spread of AIDS or HIV make an affirmative statement of policy that they oppose prostitution or sex trafficking. Some organizations opposed this requirement because they were concerned that it would inhibit their ability to work with prostitutes to limit the spread of the disease. The Court ruled that the requirement was unconstitutional because it is not acceptable to use funding to leverage restrictions on speech that are outside the scope of the funded program. The Court distinguished *Rust*, finding that in *Rust*, the restriction simply defined the scope of the funded program.

Thus, the government may impose some restrictions on speech as a condition of receiving government funds as long as they are within the scope of the defined program and allow alternate avenues for speech. The government may not use funding as an excuse to leverage restrictions on speech that are outside the scope of the government program. If the grantee does not want to agree to the terms of the defined program, then the remedy is to decline government funding.

Practical Conclusions

- Students, government employees, and those who receive government funds are all subject to having their First Amendment rights restricted, at least in some contexts.

- The government will sometimes condition the receipt of government funding on adherence to restrictions on speech. Those who object can restore their First Amendment rights simply by rejecting the government funds.

- Government employees have First Amendment rights when they are acting in their capacity as citizens. However, as employees, they do not have a First Amendment right to defy their employer's interest merely because their employer is the government.

- Although the Supreme Court once ruled that students have strong First Amendment rights, the courts have slowly eroded that principle, and students are now often subject to the whims of school officials with respect to what they deem educationally appropriate. In recent years, the Supreme Court has given great deference to school officials and has been unwilling to protect speech about sex, drugs, or other controversial issues. But schools are not obligated to restrict student speech, and some schools are quite lenient. Thus, the degree to which students have a right of free speech will depend largely on the temperament of their school officials.

PART V

What Practical Issues Are Related to Media Law?

CHAPTER 20

How the Internet Has Affected Publishing and the Law

The rapid expansion and popularity of the internet, as well as its permanent, searchable, and worldwide nature, have created some interesting questions about how traditional legal principles should be applied to new technologies. In some instances, new laws have been proposed to address particular concerns. Nevertheless, it is important to recognize at the outset that most legal principles and issues have not changed because of the internet. Rules that apply in the bricks-and-mortar world also apply online.

Throughout this book, I have incorporated cases and examples arising out of internet use to illustrate how traditional legal principles are being interpreted with respect to online material. In most cases, the rules applied are the same. For example, with respect to trademark infringement, the courts have used the same test—likelihood of confusion—to evaluate whether a URL infringes a mark as they would have used to evaluate whether any other use is an infringement. The logic and thought-processes used are similar and the outcomes in cases involving the internet are not much different than pre-internet cases.

That said, there are certain areas where the internet has made a noticeable impact and where laws have been introduced to address particular issues. This chapter will discuss some of the issues that are truly novel or unique to internet communication. They include:

1. Terms of Service (or Terms of Use) as a valid contract

2. Privacy policies

3. The General Data Protection Regulation

4.   Laws applicable to gathering information from children under 13

5.   Immunity under CDA section 230 or the DMCA

6.   Online anonymity

7.   International aspects of online publishing, which include foreign censorship (what kinds of things are regulated overseas that are not regulated in the United States), jurisdiction (the question of where you can be sued/prosecuted for your statements), and geo-filtering

8.   Cyberbulling, cyberharassment, and cyberstalking laws

9.   Issues related to social media

Terms of Service

Most websites have Terms of Service, sometimes called "Terms of Use," or "Terms and Conditions," that outline how the site may be used. Most people don't bother to read them, except perhaps on popular social media sites where users may be concerned about copyright or privacy issues, and even then, it is probably a small percentage of users who actually read through all the terms.

Site owners, however, create terms to act as an agreement and set limits on how the site may be used. The question is whether those terms will operate as a binding contract between the site and users.

In one of the first cases to address the subject, *Jessup-Morgan v. AOL*, the court affirmed the principle that terms function as a contract and outline the rights and responsibilities of the parties. In that case, a woman harassed her husband's ex-wife by posting the ex-wife's name and phone number on internet message boards with a request for sex. After several unpleasant phone calls, the ex-wife was able to obtain a subpoena to force AOL to identify the user who posted the messages. The new wife then sued AOL for revealing her identity. The court found that AOL's terms, which permitted them the right to respond to valid subpoenas, were binding and applicable to the situation. Thus, the new wife had no claim against AOL.

But in *Specht v. Netscape Communications Corp.*, the court found that users were not bound to an arbitration clause that was in Netscape's terms because the users hadn't affirmatively agreed to it. The court noted that the terms aren't readily apparent to users. One must typically scroll all the way to the bottom of the page and then click on a link to see the terms, and many people don't do that. Because the terms weren't readily apparent, users weren't bound by them.

Then, in *Ticketmaster Corp. v. Tickets.com, Inc.*, the court found that it might be possible to have a binding contract if there are facts showing that the user knew of the terms and continued to use the site. While the court noted that it would be preferable to have clear consent, there may be facts that indicate assent even in the absence of such clarity. The court noted that other cases have allowed pre-established terms, such as terms on travel tickets or parking garage tickets, to be enforceable.

Thus, whether a particular term or set of terms will be enforceable will typically depend on a few factors, including whether there is clear assent (such as clicking on an "I agree" button) or facts that indicate assent, whether the user had knowledge of the terms, whether the terms were easy to find or readily apparent (as opposed to being hard to find or having to click through several links to see them), and whether the terms seem appropriate and reasonable. Site owners who wish to have terms enforced might consider making the terms readily available and having users click on an "I agree" button. The iTunes website is a good example of a site that incorporates terms and assent into the user experience. Users might want to be aware of what site terms say, particularly with respect to copyright issues, subpoenas, and other issues that may be of concern to them, because the terms could be found to be enforceable, even in the absence of express consent.

Privacy Policies

Data privacy is becoming an extremely important issue. The news media has always had access to valuable data: subscription lists, letters to the editor, information submitted in contests, and other materials. But the explosion of digital media has resulted in vast amounts of information available to media companies or websites. Sites and apps often collect names; IP addresses; email addresses; location data; comments; credit card information; and data about content read or shared, including advertising responses. This information could be used or shared, and the question is whether there should be limits on such use or sharing, and if so, what would the limits be?

In 1999, the FTC issued a report to Congress saying that regulation was not yet required and that industry self-regulation was adequate, but set forth four "Fair Information Principles." The Principles are:

1. Notice: Notify users of what information the site gathers and how it is used.

2. Choice: Give users the opportunity to opt-in or opt-out of the gathering of information.

3. Access: Give users access to the information about themselves and the ability to contest accuracy or delete it.

4. Security: Take reasonable steps to ensure security of the data.

To avoid government regulation, companies have overwhelmingly chosen to adopt some variation of these four principles and develop privacy policies. Most major websites have privacy polices that outline the rights and responsibilities of the site and the user. However, a site that has a privacy policy must adhere to it. The FTC has used its authority to regulate false or deceptive trade practices and will bring enforcement actions against sites that fail to comply with their own policies or otherwise engage in fraudulent behavior. In one high-profile case, the FTC sued Facebook, alleging that it misled consumers because it suggested that user information would be private, but then shared it. Facebook settled the case in 2011. Twitter has also been sued for failing to adequately secure data after hackers obtained non-public information about users. And, aside from government regulation, private parties have filed class action lawsuits for breach of contract, misappropriation, fraud, or other claims as a result of alleged data misuse. Thus, it is important to carefully craft a privacy policy and adhere to it faithfully.

The European Union (EU) has established a rather complex and detailed data privacy regulation that applies to all sites that do business in the EU or have EU users. It has a rather unwieldy name, "EU Regulation on the protection of individuals with regard to the processing of personal data and on the free movement of such data, issued January 25, 2012," and is 118 pages long. It regulates many details about how websites can gather, use, store, and disseminate information about people. One of the most notable features is the so-called "right to be forgotten," which gives individuals the right to demand that websites and other data holders delete information about the individual upon request.

The U.S. federal government has no comparable law, but several states have passed data privacy laws, and the laws apply not only to companies based there, but to those who collect data from any state resident. Thus, most websites will collect data from across the country and will be subject to all these laws. Massachusetts and California are considered the strictest, requiring notification to all consumers if there is a security breach. Massachusetts also requires a written Information Security Program that is supposed to ensure the protection of data. California has enacted a version of a "right to be forgotten" for minors. The law requires websites to provide minors with a procedure for removing things they have posted.

Congress has considered several data privacy bills. In March of 2012, the FTC issued a new report stating that self-regulation was no longer adequate and calls for a federal law, but no law had been adopted yet. One of the most popular proposals is for a "Do Not Track" feature, which would let consumers opt-out of being tracked by advertisers. Another proposal that has some support is the adoption of the EU concept of a "right to be forgotten." The EU rule allows for the deletion of data upon demand by a citizen—and that includes any data, such as photos on Facebook, comments, or any other material that can be linked to an individual. Such a rule would create serious concerns in the United States, as it conflicts with First Amendment right to publish and disseminate information. The EU recognizes that the right to be forgotten must be balanced with the right to free expression, but European laws are far more privacy-friendly than in the United States. There are many instances where governments have forced the deletion of data about criminal convictions and other public records—things that would almost certainly be protected by the First Amendment. How data privacy and free speech will be balanced has yet to be resolved.

The GDPR (General Data Protection Regulation)

Europeans are notoriously protective of their concept of privacy, or what they call "data protection." They view privacy rights far more expansively than American courts do. In response to what it views as abusive and excessive activity by American companies and websites, the European Union adopted data protection regulations, including what is known as the General Data Protection Regulation, or GDPR, in 2016. The regulations went into effect in May of 2018, giving companies about two years to prepare. The EU expects American companies to comply with the GDPR if they have customers or users in the EU; it is therefore important for Americans to be familiar with the requirements and to decide whether to comply or block EU users of a website.

In short, GDPR regulates the collection, use, dissemination, and any other "processing" of "personal data" about people in the European Union. It applies to any person or company that offers goods or services to people in the EU or that monitors the behavior of people in the EU, regardless of whether the person or company is in the EU or not. Thus, American companies have had to either comply with GDPR regulations or stop interacting with them. Many U.S.-based websites, including numerous media companies, have cut off access to EU citizens rather than try to comply with GDPR requirements.

What does GDPR require? In general, companies must protect "personal data," which includes name, address, social security numbers, health information, IP addresses, location data, online identifiers (such as cookie identifiers), information about how users interact with a site, and other information that Europeans view as capable of identifying a person. Certain companies must name a data protection officer who is responsible for overseeing data policies and ensuring that the company is compliant.

A company's first obligation is to have a valid legal basis to collect or process any personal data at all, such as getting consent from a user, relying on a "legitimate interest" that is not outweighed by the fundamental rights and freedoms of the user, or processing as necessary to perform or enter into a contract. To obtain consent under the GDPR, they must explain what data they collect and how they use it for a specific purpose, and the user must affirmatively agree to use it in that way. Websites therefore often have pop-up pages that ask users to agree to the use of cookies for specific purposes when the user first visits them. Companies must get consent again every time they change the purposes for which they collect or use data. And users have a right to withdraw consent at any time, which generally means that the company must delete their data promptly.

As time passes, companies have an ongoing obligation to respect privacy interests. That means they must promptly report any data breaches, and they must respect the EU's "right to be forgotten" policies, which generally require that data be kept only as long as it is needed for a specific purpose. Although the GDPR includes an exception for "processing for journalistic purposes," or news reporting in the public interest, and EU has indicated that such reporting is a legitimate interest, there are serious questions about how the EU will interpret the right of news media to report of sensitive matters and whether there will be a time at which online stories will be forced to be removed.

Gathering Information From Children

The Children's Online Privacy Protection Act of 1999 (COPPA) regulates how companies can collect information from children under 13. Many websites that are not directed at children, such as news sites, prohibit children under 13 from registering in any way, and specify that limitation in its terms of use. However, for sites that do collect information from children under 13, the FTC's website lists these requirements:

1. Post a clear and comprehensive privacy policy on their website describing their information practices for children's personal information;

2. Provide direct notice to parents and obtain verifiable parental consent, with limited exceptions, before collecting personal information from children;

3. Give parents the choice of consenting to the operator's collection and internal use of a child's information, but prohibiting the operator from disclosing that information to third parties;

4. Provide parents access to their child's personal information to review and/or have the information deleted;

5. Give parents the opportunity to prevent further use or online collection of a child's personal information; and

6. Maintain the confidentiality, security, and integrity of information they collect from children.

In addition, federal regulations prohibit websites from conditioning a child's participation in an online activity on the child's providing more information than is reasonably necessary to participate in that activity.

The FTC has sued numerous websites alleging violations of the Act. In most cases, the parties have settled, and thus, there is not a large body of case law interpreting the proper scope of the law.

Immunity From Claims

There are two laws that provide an immunity from liability to "internet service providers" that would not be available to other forms of media.

Section 230 of the Communications Decency Act (CDA) contains a provision that exempts internet service providers from liability for content posted by third parties. The law makes a distinction between "service providers" and "content providers." The content provider is the person who creates the content. This might be the author of an article, or a commenter who posts comments on a website, or a person who tweets, or any other person that creates content online. The content provider is always liable for the content he or she creates.

The "service provider" is the person or entity that allows a website or service to be used. Good examples include Amazon (which provides a way for users to post comments about products they sell), Craigslist (which allows users to post ads or comments on a variety of topics), blog or microblog services like Tumblr, Wordpress, or Twitter (they allow users to write anything they want), social media sites, review sites like Yelp, or news websites that allow users to post comments in response to articles. Under Section 230 of the CDA, service providers are not liable for content generated by the third parties that use their service or site.

The immunity granted to service providers is applicable to a wide range of claims, including libel, privacy torts, negligence, fraud, misprepresentation, unfair competition, breach of contract, IIED, and other civil or criminal laws. For example, in *Doe v. MySpace*, the court deemed MySpace immune from liability for negligence when girl was sexually assaulted by man she met via the website. In *Dart v. Craigslist, Inc.*, a court similarly found Craigslist immune from liability for being a public nuisance even though its "erotic services" section could be used for prostitution. The broad scope of the defense can be illustrated best by surveying the wide range of cases in which immunity has been granted, which includes everything from offensive comments to fraudulent dating profiles to discriminatory housing advertisements:

- *Zeran v. AOL*, finding AOL immune from a libel claim where an anonymous user falsely posted Zeran's name and phone number on internet bulletin board as the seller of offensive T-shirts;

- *Doe v. Oliver*, finding AOL immune from liability for email messages composed by a user;

- *Carafano v. Metrosplash.com, Inc.*, finding a dating service immune where a person falsely listed a woman's information on website;

- *Schneider v. Amazon.com, Inc.*, finding Amazon immune from liability for comments posted on its site by third parties;

- *Chicago Lawyers Committee for Civil Rights v. Craigslist, Inc.*, finding the site not liable for violating fair housing law when it merely provided free-form space for housing ads.

One of the questions is the degree to which one may choose, edit, or moderate content or comments before one becomes the content provider. The law contains a "good Samaritan" provision that gives sites the power to remove offensive content without waiving immunity, and most cases take a broad view of how immunity should be applied. Immunity may be granted, even if the defendant exercised some minor editorial discretion. Again, there are many cases that support this principle:

- *Blumenthal v. Drudge*, finding AOL immune from a libel suit when it licensed content from the Drudge Report;

- *Batzel v. Smith*, finding a network immune from liability for an email, even though it made minor edits to the email;

- *Donato v. Moldow*, finding the owner of a site immune even though he edited, selected, and deleted various comments;

- *Barrett v. Rosenthal*, finding a site immune even though it selected the republished statements;

- *Mayhew v. Dunn*, finding a site immune from liability for allegedly libelous claims posted in comments even though comments are moderated;

- *Global Royalties Ltd. v. Xcentric Ventures, LLC*, finding site immune even though it was notified of an allegedly libelous post and refused to remove it.

Nevertheless, immunity is not unlimited. It is possible that a site could be liable for online postings if it edited comments or third party content in such a way as to change the meaning in a defamatory manner or if the site creates or contributes to the illegal or tortious nature of the material on its own. The website Badbusinessbureau.com, for example, has been denied immunity in two cases, *MCW, Inc. v. badbusinessbureau.com* and *Hy Cite Corp. v. badbusinessbureau.com*, because it provided its own disparaging titles and headlines in addition to the third party content provided by others. In another case, *Woodhull v. Meinel*, a site was denied immunity because the blogger stated her intent to "make fun of" the plaintiff, intentionally contacted people to seek out negative information about her, and then mixed the information she received with her own thoughts and comments.

Also, a site may be liable if it provides the tools or encouragement for users to engage in illegal activity. In *Fair Housing Counsel of San Fernando Valley v. Roommates.com, LLC*, the court ruled that a housing website could be liable for violating the Fair Housing Act because it provided drop-down menus permitting landlords to discriminate on the basis of race, religion, and other protected categories. Craigslist was found immune in a similar case, because Craigslist merely provides space in which people write free-form ads. But Roomates.com was potentially liable because of its own participation in providing the allegedly discriminatory options. (A court later ruled that Roomates.com was not liable because the Fair Housing Act did not apply to roommate ads.) In *FTC v. Accusearch, Inc.*, the court denied immunity to a site because it paid researchers to acquire confidential records that were illegally posted. And, in *NPS, LLC v. StubHub, Inc.*, the court found that a site may be liable if it can be shown that it encouraged illegal ticket scalping.

Even if a site were otherwise eligible for Section 230 immunity, it can nevertheless be sued if it promises to remove the offending material and then fails to do so. In *Barnes v. Yahoo, Inc.*, the court allowed the plaintiff to pursue a promissory estoppel claim (which is similar to breach of contract) when Yahoo representatives promised a woman that they would remove material about her from a site and then failed to do so. Even if Yahoo would have been immune from liability for the content because of Section 230, they found themselves in trouble because of the promise to take action.

However, if the site has not made any promises to remove a post, at least one court has found that it can't be ordered to do so. The California case *Hassell v. Bird* arose after a dispute between attorney Dawn Hassell and former client Ava Bird. Hassell represented Bird in a personal injury claim, but dropped her as a client because Bird did not respond any of the 15 times Hassell tried to communicate with her. Bird then posted negative Yelp reviews of Hassell's firm, claiming that Hassell had failed to reach out to her. Hassell filed a lawsuit claiming that Bird's reviews were defamatory and asking the court to order Yelp to remove the reviews. The lower court ruled in favor of Hassell, finding Bird liable for defamation and ordering Yelp to remove the posts. However, the California Supreme Court reversed the order to Yelp, noting that Section 230(c)(1) says, "no provider or user of an interactive computer service shall be treated as the *publisher or speaker* of any information provided by another information content provider (emphasis added)." Because Yelp is not the "publisher or speaker," it is not the proper party to enjoin. The court therefore concluded that the site has no duty to remove the review. Such a ruling is consistent with the underlying purpose of Section 230, which is to direct all remedies for alleged wrongs to the person who posted the online material rather than the operator of the service where it appears; otherwise, ISPs would have an endless flood of litigation from those who feel aggrieved. The court did affirm the part of the ruling that held Bird responsible and ordered *her* to remove the post.

Section 230 does not cover intellectual property claims. However, there is a provision in the Digital Millennium Copyright Act (DMCA), 17 U.S.C. sec. 512, that provides a "safe harbor" defense to "Internet Service Providers" (ISPs) if they follow certain notice and takedown procedures for alleged copyright infringement by third parties who post on their sites. The person who posted the infringing material may still be liable, but the ISP will not be if the safe harbor provisions are followed.

In short, the law requires ISPs to provide the name and contact information for an agent to whom notice of alleged infringements can be sent. A copyright holder may then send notice that he has a "good faith belief" that the posted material is an infringement. The ISP must remove the material and notify the poster of the removal. The person who posted the material may provide a counter-notice if they believe the material does not infringe someone else's copyrighted material. The copyright holder then has 14 days to file a lawsuit in federal court. Otherwise, the ISP must repost the material.

The DMCA notice and takedown provisions have generated some controversy for several reasons, but the most practical concern is that it creates a game of chicken between a copyright holder and poster in cases where there is genuine dispute. Either party can end up being liable for damages if they are wrong. The ISP, however, will be protected, as long as they follow the procedures set forth in the statute.

Speaking Anonymously

There are times when speakers wish to remain anonymous, and the First Amendment sometimes provides protection from having one's identity disclosed. This section will cover the issue of when one can speak anonymously online and when one's identity must be disclosed. (There are other issues related to anonymity that have been covered in other chapters. The question of whether a source can remain anonymous is covered in Chapter 13. The question of anonymous juries is addressed in Chapter 11. Anonymity in political speech is addressed in Chapter 16.)

Some websites allow commenters to be anonymous, others require a real name or at least require some verified registration. The trend towards using Facebook comments would eliminate the issue of anonymity. However, even sites that permit anonymity don't or can't always preserve it. Whether and under what circumstances they will disclose an identity is usually spelled out in the Terms of Service. Most sites say that they will disclose an identity if required by a court or lawfully subpoenaed. The question, then, is when will the courts order disclosure of a speaker's identity?

Many courts agree that there should be some First Amendment protection of anonymous speech, and they don't want to allow aggressive litigants to use the courts to harass speakers if no claim would truly exist. In *Doe v. 2TheMart.com, Inc.*, the first case to consider the issue of online anonymity, the court acknowledged several important reasons to provide some level of protection, stating that anonymous speech "foster[s] open communication and robust debate," and concluded that "[p]eople who have committed no wrongdoing should be free to participate in online forums without fear that their identity will be exposed. ..." On the other hand, the courts don't want to provide blanket immunity to those who speak anonymously if their speech would be truly tortious or illegal and not otherwise protected by the First Amendment. Thus, most courts have adopted some form of balancing test.

The lowest level of protection given to anonymous speakers was the test used in *In re Subpoena Duces Tecum to AOL, Inc.* In that case, the court ruled it would allow a subpoena to discover a speaker's identity if the claimant has a legitimate, good faith basis to contend that it may be the victim of actionable conduct.

On the other end of the spectrum, some courts have set very high standards for a plaintiff to meet before a subpoena may be issued. In *Independent Newspapers v. Brodie*, for example, the highest court in Maryland adopted a five-part test to determine when a site must disclose the identities of anonymous posters. It instructed trial courts, before requiring disclosure, to: (1) require a plaintiff try to notify the anonymous posters that they are the subject of a subpoena or application for order of disclosure, including posting a notification of the identity discovery request on the message board; (2) withhold action to afford the anonymous posters a reasonable opportunity oppose the application; (3) require a plaintiff to identify the exact statements alleged to constitute actionable speech by the poster; (4) determine whether the complaint has set forth a prima facie defamation action against the anonymous poster; and (5) if all else is satisfied, balance the anonymous poster's First Amendment right of free speech against the strength of the defamation claim and the necessity for disclosure of the poster's identity. The *Brodie* test is very similar to the test adopted by New Jersey in *Dendrite Int'l, Inc. v. Doe No. 3*.

Some courts have adopted a somewhat less stringent test, but one that still provides some protection to anonymous posters. In *Solers, Inc. v. Doe*, the court considered whether the identity of an anonymous tipster who told a trade association that Solers was pirating software could be subpoenaed.

The court evaluated how other jurisdictions handled the issue, and discussed the Virginia and Maryland cases above. The court then decided to use another test. It ruled that trial judges must conduct a five-part analysis before ordering the disclosure of an anonymous speaker's identity: (1) ensure that the plaintiff has adequately pleaded the elements of the defamation claim; (2) require reasonable efforts to notify the anonymous speaker; (3) delay action for a reasonable time to allow the speaker an opportunity to oppose disclosure; (4) require the plaintiff to proffer evidence creating a genuine issue of material fact on each element of the claim that is within its control; and (5) determine that the information sought is important to proceeding with the plaintiff's lawsuit.

Given such tests, the courts are unlikely to issue a subpoena if the statements at issue are unlikely to be actionable. As a practical matter, that means that anonymous speech can be protected if it is clear from the face of the statement that it is opinion subject to protection or if it is not a defamatory statement. In *Highfields Capital Management, L.P. v. Doe*, for example, the court found that the statements at issue were clearly parody and not to be taken seriously, and therefore, they were not actionable. Similarly, in *McMann v. Doe*, the court found that statements criticizing a home builder's business practices were clearly opinion and not actionable. Because courts are willing to extend protection to anonymous speakers when their speech is clearly opinion on its face, it becomes imperative that those who wish to remain anonymous grasp the difference between factual assertions and opinion and to understand how the expression at issue will appear to others. In other cases, where the statements at issue appear to be actionable, courts will order disclosure of the speaker's identity. For example, in *Cohen v. Google, Inc.*, the court did not protect the identity of an online speaker, finding that the statements that plaintiff was a "skank," "ho," and "whoring," in conjunction with sexually suggestive photos were capable of defamatory meaning.

Another issue to consider with respect to posting anonymous statements is who will defend the anonymous speaker's rights and pay for the legal defense. In many cases, the website does not defend the speaker and the anonymous speaker is required to obtain their own counsel to argue against disclosure of their identity. That can be quite costly.

There have been some cases where news organizations have actively tried to defend anonymous commenters, either asserting First Amendment rights on behalf of the speaker or arguing that the state shield law should provide some protection. The shield law cases have had mixed results.

In *Mortgage Specialists v. Implode Explode Heavy Industries*, the New Hampshire Supreme Court determined that a website could assert protection under the state's reporters privilege to protect the identity of online users. The court concluded that websites were no different that more traditional news outlets, and that the information provided by site users fell within the scope of the state statute. Courts in Texas, Montana, Oregon, and Florida have come to similar conclusions. However, it should be noted that the application of the state shield law may be attributable to the broad language of the particular state law. Other states with more narrow language have ruled that shield laws do not apply to commenters.

For example, in *Too Much Media LLC v. Hale*, a judge ruled that the New Jersey shield law did not protect Hale's posts on a porn industry message board. Too Much Media had sued Hale for defamation for various criticisms, including claims that the company had threatened her life. The court ruled that Hale did not qualify as news media under the state shield law. There was no evidence that she had ever published an article in a newspaper or journal, but more importantly, the court felt that comments should not qualify for the same protections as a bone fide news article because there is no fact-checking, no editorial review, and no effort to contact the subject to obtain their side of the story. Courts in Illinois and Kentucky have also ruled that website comments did not fall within the scope of protection given by their state shield laws.

In sum, there may be protection for anonymous speakers in many cases, particularly where the statement at issue does not appear to be truly actionable, but there are practical problems with respect to who will be responsible for defending against disclosure. Unless websites are willing to pay the cost of defense, individual commenters will be left with the expense of defending against subpoenas.

There is an additional practical problem, which is that these First Amendment protections apply only when there is government action or when one is seeking a remedy though the legal system. It provides no protection from being "outed" by someone who discovers your identity through other means. For example, the website Gawker published an article exposing the identity of "Violentacrez," a well-known user on Reddit, a popular and wide-ranging internet forum. Violentacrez started a Reddit forum called "Jailbait," where users could post sexualized photos of underage girls, as well as one called "Creepshots," where users could post upskirt photos and other photos of women they had surreptitiously taken in public places. His other forums were called "chokeabitch," "niggerjailbait," "rapebait," "Hitler," "Jewmerica," "misogyny," and "incest," the titles of which indicate why he was considered to be a horribly offensive internet troll. But Violentacrez didn't merely post online. He attended meetings and interacted with other Reddit users. A small group of people knew his real identity. As he became more powerful and more controversial, the interest in his identity increased, and it's no surprise that, eventually, someone revealed his name to a writer. Adrian Chen, a writer for Gawker, heard a rumor about Violentacrez real name and was able to confirm from publicly available information that he was, in fact, Michael Brutsch, a middle-aged father from Texas. After the article was published, Brutsch was fired from his job as a programmer. The disclosure also prompted several online discussions about free speech, anonymity, and what information should be disclosed or protected. People may debate the ethical aspects of the controversy, but the legal aspects are fairly clear. Under current law, Brutsch doesn't have a legally enforceable right to remain anonymous. In fact, censoring the disclosure of his name would be a prior restraint, which is generally prohibited under First Amendment principles. If he were to sue for publication of private facts, he would have to show that his identity was not already publicly available and that the disclosure was not newsworthy, and those elements may be difficult to prove under the circumstances. As a practical matter, people may discover the identity of an anonymous speaker and disclose it, and, depending on the facts, there might not be a legal remedy available in such situations.

International Aspects of Publishing Online

The internet is great because it provides access to people all over the world. However, that access can cause additional legal headaches because countries vary with respect to laws governing content. Other nations may give more weight to competing interests (such as an individual's interest in his reputation or privacy; or the government's interest in preserving order) and permit civil suits or criminal prosecution of speech that would be protected in the United States. It is therefore imperative that speakers based in the United States understand that there may be consequences to online actions or speech that run afoul of foreign laws.

There are three primary issues that arise:

1. Foreign censorship (topics that are regulated overseas that are not regulated in the United States)

2. Jurisdiction (the question of where you can be sued/prosecuted for your statements)

3. Geo-filtering and other potential remedies

Foreign Censorship

It would take another entire book to list all of the regulations on and prohibitions of speech that exist in other countries. But it is possible to categorize many of these restrictions to provide an overview of the kinds of issues that will give rise to liability in other countries. In sum, they can be divided into four broad categories:

1. Traditional torts and claims

2. Incitement of racial or religious hatred

3. Protection of cultural values

4. Protection of government interests

TRADITIONAL TORTS AND CLAIMS

Other countries impose liability for libel, invasion of privacy, copyright infringement, and other such claims, just as we do in America. The difference is that, in many counties, there are fewer defenses to liability, and it may be more likely to be found liable under the laws of other nations. For example, other nations do not apply fair use as a copyright principle; there is far more protection for creative works. Other nations also have more expansive definitions of "moral rights," giving even greater protection to artistic works. With respect to libel claims, the actual malice test, which is the basis for constitutional protection for free speech in libel cases in the United States, has not been adopted in most other countries. Several countries have adopted some form of a "responsible journalism" defense, allowing the potential for protection if the story is found to constitute responsible journalism, but the balance of interests often favors plaintiffs, as many countries give more weight to protection of reputation or privacy interests than they do freedom of speech.

Some plaintiffs have attempted to file libel lawsuits against U.S. publishers in foreign courts, because they know they cannot win a case under U.S. law, but they can prevail overseas. Some of these cases are discussed below in the section on international jurisdiction. But it has been Google, rather than traditional news organizations, that has suffered the most high-profile consequences of European law. In *Mr. X v. Google, Inc., et al.*, Google was ordered to remove autocomplete results that accompanied a man's name. The case involved a complaint from "Mr. X," a man charged with raping a 17-year-old girl. He was later found guilty on a lesser charge of corrupting a minor. When the man's name was typed into Google's search engine, the Autocomplete feature would suggest terms such as "rapist." The man sued for libel. Google argued that it was not responsible for the terms that were shown in Autocomplete because they are automatically generated using algorithms based on what users have searched for in the past. Yet the court found that the results violated the man's rights under French law (which is very protective of both reputation and privacy), and ordered Google to prevent the result from arising. Similarly, a German federal court ordered Google to remove Autocomplete results that it found to be defamatory in a case involving a German businessman whose name Autocomplete paired with the terms "Scientology" and "fraud."

In the EU, human dignity and freedom of expression are both considered fundamental rights, and when those rights compete, expression does not necessarily prevail. For example, in 2004, Princess Caroline of Monaco won a ruling from the European Court of Human Rights, declaring that her privacy had been invaded by the publishing of photographs showing her engaging in ordinary activities such as playing tennis, shopping, skiing, and the like. However, in 2012, the European Court of Human Rights found that it was not an invasion of privacy to publish a photo of Caroline, Princess of Hanover, skiing in Moritz, because it showed that she was on vacation while her father, Prince Rainier, was terminally ill, and therefore the photo was relevant to commentary on a matter of general public concern. In essence, news organizations must prove that there is a legitimate purpose that justifies the expression; otherwise, privacy interests are likely to prevail.

European countries are also more likely to impose prior restraints on the publication of information that they find to violate human rights, which includes material they deem "private." The U.K. is also known for its practice of issuing "superinjunctions," which are court orders that not only enjoin publication of information, but also include a provision that the existence of the injunction cannot be published. The practice of issuing such prior restraints is generally not permitted in the United States, but it is common in Europe.

The EU's data privacy regulations are much stricter than U.S. rules, and they include the so-called "right to be forgotten," a provision that grants citizens the right to demand that data about them be removed from the internet or archives. It remains to be seen exactly how the right will be enforced, particularly in the United States where such a rule is contrary to First Amendment principles.

In sum, other countries balance privacy and reputation against the right of free speech differently than the United States. Those in America who are accustomed to great freedom of expression must recognize that the laws of other countries may be more restrictive.

INCITEMENT OF RACIAL OR RELIGIOUS HATRED

As noted previously in this book, U.S. law generally does not recognize claims for group libel or hate speech. However, many other nations do. In particular, countries tend to prohibit the incitement of hatred based on race, religion, or other protected categories.

A Russian court, for example, convicted the organizers of an art exhibit for inciting religious hatred because some of the paintings were satirical, including images of Jesus as Mickey Mouse or Lenin. Those who were offended by the paintings argued that works that were "insulting" could not qualify as "art." Similarly, Brigitte Bardot was convicted of inciting racial hatred in France for statements in a book she wrote. She criticized Muslims in Europe for failing to assimilate. Sweden convicted a minister under hate speech laws for calling homosexuality a "deep cancerous tumor" in society, although his conviction was eventually reversed on appeal.

These examples are just a small sample of the kinds of things that subject a speaker to liability in other countries. The constitutional protection given in the U.S. to these kinds of statements, no matter how offensive, is unique, and online speakers should understand that their statements might not be protected in other countries.

PROTECTION OF CULTURAL VALUES

Many nations will ban or punish speech that "harms cultural values." Turkmenistan, for example, has outlawed lip synching. China banned a Nike ad that was "insulting" because it featured cartoon martial arts artists. Cambodia once banned a pop song about a monk who falls in love. The film Monty Python's Life of Brian has been banned in several countries. Many nations criminalize profanity or blasphemy.

In short, it is common for countries to ban materials, especially movies, music, and other expressions of pop culture, that they believe harms their own culture and would have a negative influence. Such rules are quite different from the U.S., which does not consider the protection of "cultural values" to be a compelling interest that justifies restrictions on speech.

PROTECTION OF GOVERNMENT INTERESTS

Many nations will restrict speech to serve government interests. For example, British law bans media from publishing certain information about criminal trials prior to the trial and until it is concluded. The British government once prohibited a newspaper from publishing excerpts of a memo regarding the bombing of Al-Jazeera. And, of course, many countries block internet access and jail dissenters.

The U.S. has taken the opposite approach in the modern era, allowing great latitude in the discussion of court proceedings and political issues, with the exception of national security issues, where the courts have found that there may be a compelling interest that outweighs freedom of speech. Dissenters are rarely jailed for their ideas, although they may be arrested for their particular form of protest (if it involves threats of violence, for example). These protections are rarely available in other countries, which can come as a surprise to Americans overseas.

In one high-profile incident, an American blogger was jailed for "insulting" the king of Thailand. The blogger was a resident of Colorado and an American citizen, but he had been born in Thailand. He had translated a banned biography of the Thai king and posted it online. He visited Thailand in May 2011 and was arrested. In a statement, he said, "[i]n Thailand there are many laws that don't allow you to express opinions but we don't have that in America." He was convicted and sentenced to 2 ½ years in jail. He was eventually pardoned and released from prison after serving about 7 months of his sentence.

Other countries may also punish speech that would be given First Amendment consideration in the United States. For example, a man in Switzerland was fined for causing a public nuisance for using the phrase "Allahu akbar" in a "loud and clear" manner. He had unexpectedly seen a friend at a train station, and used the statement to express pleasant surprise. However, that same phrase has been used by terrorists before carrying out attacks. Therefore, according to police, people nearby may have been afraid. The police emphasized that it was the "shouting" manner in which the words were used that resulted in the fine. The man denied that he had shouted and said, "just because terrorists misuse these two words doesn't mean I have bad intentions when I say them." Nevertheless, such speech was penalized.

Thus, it is important to understand the differences among countries' laws, in case one finds oneself subject to jurisdiction overseas.

Jurisdiction

Jurisdiction is a complicated and tricky legal concept, but there are two basic principles:

1. A court must have subject matter jurisdiction over a case; and

2. A court must have personal jurisdiction over the defendant.

The concept of subject matter jurisdiction refers to whether the case should be in federal or state court and whether there is a legitimate case to be heard. (These are questions of procedure and are outside the scope of this book, except as covered in Chapter 1.) Personal jurisdiction is the concept relevant here, and that is the question of where a person can properly be sued or called into court. Can a person who lives in Virginia be sued in California? Can an American be sued or criminally prosecuted in Thailand? Maybe.

Each country may have different laws concerning jurisdiction. In the United States, a court may have personal jurisdiction over a defendant if he has "sufficient minimum contacts" with that jurisdiction, and in most cases, that means one of the following:

1. The defendant lives or works in the state (or, if it's a corporation, is located or operates there);

2. The incident that forms the basis of the lawsuit occurred there; or

3. There is "purposeful availment," meaning the defendant intentionally made use of the forum in a meaningful way.

A person who lives in Virginia and libels another person in Virginia can definitely be sued for libel in Virginia. The Virginia courts would certainly have personal jurisdiction over the defendant. The question can become more difficult, though, when the parties live in different states.

One of the well-known cases on this topic is *Young v. New Haven Advocate*. In that case, a newspaper in Connecticut posted an article online that allegedly defamed a prison warden in Virginia. The warden filed suit in Virginia, but the court ruled that Virginia did not have jurisdiction over the newspaper. The article was targeted towards the citizens of Connecticut. There were only seven subscribers in Virginia. The court, using the "purposeful availment" test, concluded that the paper had not purposefully directed itself at Virginia and thus it could not reasonably have anticipated being sued there. The ruling is consistent with the analysis courts used before the internet was invented. If a newspaper were sued, the question would be whether it purposely targeted the state, and the court would consider how many newspapers were distributed in that jurisdiction. If there were very few, then the court would likely find that it did not have jurisdiction over the paper.

Some people believe that cases involving internet communications should be treated differently because when a person posts something online, it automatically becomes available to the whole world. In essence, the person posting the material should know that his statements are being disseminated world-wide and therefore knows that he is availing himself of the world, and therefore should be subject to jurisdiction anywhere. This is known as the "effects" test—the idea that a person can be sued in a state when the defendant takes an action "aimed" at a state and the effects of the action will be felt in that state. This was the position taken by the court in *Calder v. Jones*, where the court ruled that California courts had jurisdiction over the National Enquirer, which was based in Florida, because the tabloid's allegedly libelous statements had an effect in California, where the plaintiff worked. Thus, there are cases where courts have concluded that internet postings do subject defendants to jurisdiction in other states because the speaker knew it was likely to cause harm in the plaintiff's state. In *Blakey v. Continental Airlines*, for example, the court found that New Jersey had jurisdiction because the allegedly libelous statements were posted online, and they caused harm to the plaintiff, who lived in New Jersey.

The problem not only arises between states, but also between countries. Many countries have taken the position that a person may be sued in a foreign nation based on his statements online—even if the statements are perfectly legal in the person's home country. Thus, if an American citizen posts something that would not be considered libel in the United States, but would be considered libel in Australia, he may be sued in Australia. This was exactly the case in *Dow Jones v. Gutnick*, a 2002 case where the High Court of Australia ruled that a U.S. publisher could be sued in Australia over an allegedly libelous article that appeared in *Barron's* magazine. The evidence in court indicated that there were only five copies of the print magazine distributed in Australia, but there were many potential subscribers to the internet version of the article. The court reasoned that if *Barron's* was going to have Australian subscribers, then it must comply with Australian law. Because the plaintiff lived in Australia, the damage was done in Australia, and he could therefore sue there.

In *Bangoura v. Washington Post*, a Canadian court initially came to a similar conclusion and found that the fact that an article could be accessed in Canada was sufficient to give rise of jurisdiction in Canada. However, the Court of Appeals of Ontario later ruled that Ontario did not have jurisdiction. The plaintiff was from Africa and only recently moved to Canada, and his lawyer was the only Canadian that downloaded story from the *Washington Post's* paid archives. Thus, the court found that the connection to Ontario was too tenuous to sustain jurisdiction. Nevertheless, it is possible to be subject to jurisdiction in other countries where there are internet users in that jurisdiction and the plaintiff suffers damages there due to the online statement.

The practical question, of course, is whether that matters. If a person in the United States posts a statement online, and they are sued in another country, can the foreign court effectively enforce the judgment and do anything to the speaker?

Although there are no cases involving the attempted extradition of a U.S. citizen based solely on internet statements, there are some clear practical considerations. First, the American citizen may have trouble if he actually goes to the other country. This is what happened to the American who insulted the Thai king. He was arrested while within Thailand. Or, if the American has assets in the other country, the country could certainly seize those assets.

Second, it is possible that the foreign plaintiff might try to enforce the judgment in the United States, although that would probably be difficult.

It is particularly difficult to enforce foreign libel judgments in America, thanks to a federal libel tourism law—the cleverly named Securing the Protection of our Enduring and Established Constitutional Heritage (SPEECH) Act—that was signed by President Obama on August 10, 2010. Congress realized that plaintiffs were taking advantage of the U.K.'s generous interpretation of jurisdiction and its plaintiff-friendly libel laws by filing suits they could not win in the United States in London instead. To combat this effort to circumvent First Amendment protections, Congress passed the law, which prohibits the enforcement of foreign libel judgments that would be inconsistent with either U.S. constitutional protections or Section 230 of the Communications Decency Act. It should be noted, though, that the law does have certain technical requirements, meaning that not every libel judgment would be invalid. Also, it only applies to libel cases, meaning that plaintiffs may still attempt to enforce foreign judgments in other kinds of cases where First Amendment issues might be raised.

Even if the SPEECH Act protections do not apply, the enforcement of foreign judgments can be procedurally tricky. There was a lawsuit in France against California-based Yahoo! for violating French law by allowing the sale of Nazi memorabilia on the Yahoo! website. The French court ruled against Yahoo!, and the company was concerned that the French plaintiff might attempt to enforce the judgment in the United States. Yahoo! filed suit in California, asking the court to find that the judgment was unenforceable because it violated the First Amendment. While the trial court agreed with Yahoo!, the appellate court reversed—not for First Amendment reasons, but on procedural grounds. In *Yahoo! Inc. v. La Ligue Contre Le Racisme et l'antisémitisme*, the court found that the case was not yet "ripe" because the nonprofit group that sued Yahoo! had not yet tried to enforce the judgment. If it had, it was possible that a court would refuse to enforce it due to First Amendment concerns. The judgment could be enforced against Yahoo! in France, but it's not clear that it would be enforced in the United States.

In any event, a speaker should know the potential consequences of online statements and choose one's options accordingly.

Geo-Filtering and Other Potential Remedies

One option to choose when recognizing the potential for overseas liability is geo-filtering, the attempt to block a story from readers in a certain nation. For example, when *GQ* published a story on a series of Russian bombings, it knew that Russian officials would be upset by it. Rather than deal with liability in Russia, the company chose not to distribute that issue in Russia or post the story online.

At some point in the future, the technology may become available to limit online access from certain countries, although that is currently not a fool-proof option. There are online geo-filtering technologies, but they are also fairly easy to circumvent. Thus, one must consider the possibility of not posting material online if the risks of doing so outweigh the benefits.

Cyberbullying, Cyberharrassment, and Cyberstalking

The term "troll" is internet slang for one who intentionally posts inflammatory or hateful material online. For the most part, users ignore trolls, and the phrase "do not feed the trolls" is sometimes used to convey to other users that they really shouldn't bother to engage in conversation with those who are obviously trolling.

Some states, however, have felt the need to pass laws that target trolling in its most extreme forms, often called cyberbullying, cyberharassment, or cyberstalking. These laws raise some interesting First Amendment issues.

First, it should be noted that harassment and stalking can be legitimate crimes, and thus, whether the conduct occurs in person or online, those who violate such laws can be prosecuted. The fact that the crimes may have speech-related components does not invalidate the law, much like one cannot claim that one has a First Amendment right to engage in fraud, bribery, or extortion merely because the crimes consists primarily of things that are said. The proposed laws, however, are questionable in their breadth.

Arkansas, for example, passed a law making it a crime to post or send any electronic communication "with the purpose to frighten, coerce, intimidate, threaten, abuse, harass, or alarm another person" if it is "in furtherance of severe, repeated, or hostile behavior" toward that person. Although such a law could be used in instances of genuine stalking or harassment, it also seems to cover a lot of communications that might occur between, say, spouses in a hostile divorce, political opponents, or others in a contentious relationship. The language may be a bit overbroad, although it has not yet been challenged, and there are no court opinions interpreting it.

Pennsylvania has a law that makes it a crime to send or post any electronic communication to a minor "with the knowledge or intent" that it would "cause emotional distress" to that minor. As noted constitutional scholar Eugene Volokh pointed out on his website, that would literally prohibit teenagers from breaking up with each other via email, or similar such communications. This law seems overbroad as well, although, again, there is no case interpreting it.

Several states have or are considering similar legislation. While the prevention of cyberbullying is a popular cause, it remains to be seen whether the specific statutory language used can withstand constitutional scrutiny.

Social Media

Social media is a form of communication, and the same legal issues that apply to other forms of communication apply to social media. Thus, you can be sued for libel if you manage to libel someone on Twitter. Courtney Love, for example, has been sued twice for allegedly libelous tweets, and there was a case brought by a NBA referee against an AP reporter who tweeted that the ref was calling fouls to compensate for prior bad calls. You can be sued for copyright infringement if you steal someone's photo from Twitter. In *Agence France-Presse v. Morel*, for example, the court refused to dismiss copyright claims that arose from the use of photos on Twitter finding that there was no implied license to use the photos. In general, anything that might create legal claims in "real life" may also create claims if you do it in social media.

An important thing to keep in mind is that social media sites have Terms of Service just as any site would, and those terms may create a contract, as noted above. Copyright issues are generally the most important aspect of a site's terms, because they will explain how the site will use material you post, and also, how you may use material that is posted by others.

Some of the hottest topics involving social media deal with issues that are addressed in other chapters in this book. For example:

- Is social media use by government officials subject to FOIA? Given the broad definition of "record," it probably is, as long as the use is for official government purposes (as opposed to personal use).

- Does it violate the First Amendment for government agencies to delete or moderate comments on the agency's social media sites? Probably yes! The two cases addressing blocking users on Twitter have found that such blocks violate the First Amendment. Thus, it is likely that a court would similarly rule that deleting comments (in the absence of a compelling government interest that requires it) is a First Amendment violation as well.

- How does social media use affect the determination of whether someone is a public figure for the purposes of libel law? There is some case law suggesting that individuals might be deemed limited purpose public figures if they have injected themselves into the relevant public debate online and have access to social media tools, but the law in this area is not yet fully developed.

- Can courts restrict social media use by journalists covering trials? Some courts have imposed restrictions and others have not. There has not yet been a case brought challenging the constitutionality of such restrictions. But courts are given broad discretion to impose "decorum orders" in high profile trials, and reporters can be held in contempt if they fail to comply.

These questions, and many others, will have to be resolved over time as social media become more integrated into daily life.

Frequently Asked Questions About Social Media and the Law

-An interview with the author, published by The Reporters Committee for Freedom of the Press in *The News Media and The Law*, Summer 2012. Reprinted with permission. All rights reserved.

If someone is under 18, but his/her Twitter and Facebook accounts are public, can I use that information in a story?

Set aside for a moment the issue of the person's age. The first question should be what do you want to use and why? Is it newsworthy? What is the context? Are there libel or privacy issues? Copyright issues? If any potential issues might arise from your use of the material, you might want to consult with your lawyer to evaluate the risk. Now, adding in the fact that the poster is a minor, you might be extra sensitive about any potential privacy issues, and if you need consent for something (for example, to use material that may be copyrightable), you will need to get consent from the parents, because a minor cannot give valid consent. But there is nothing magic about being under 18 that automatically transforms the material into being off-limits.

If someone's Facebook and Twitter accounts are public, do I need to ask him/her for permission to use a photograph or quote a tweet?

Again, the first question should be what you are using and why. Photos, tweets and other materials that might be posted may be copyrightable, and the ordinary rules of copyright law may apply. Your use might qualify as a "fair use," in which case you would not need permission; but on the other hand, your use might be one that requires permission. It would be impossible to say without knowing what the exact use is. The important point, though, is that the fact that the account is "public" is not determinative. You might also look at the terms of service (which change with some regularity, it seems) to see what the terms require of you. Courts have held that a website's terms of service can operate as a contract to which you may be bound. It is also worth noting that other social media sites may offer alternative means of using posted material. Flickr and Wikimedia offer material under Creative Commons licenses, which means you can use the material as long as you adhere to the terms set by the poster (and you should understand what those mean!), and some sites offer material via embed codes.

If someone's Facebook or Twitter is private, but his/her "friend" shows me the content, can I quote from it? Would I get in trouble if that friend offered me access to the private account and I used the information in a story?

The answer to this is a bit tricky, because it would depend a lot on how or why you are "shown" the material, and of course, there is always the question of how you want to use it. But let's start with a simple fact: even "private" Facebook and Twitter accounts aren't truly private: even if the person posting the material makes it available only to certain friends, it is possible for the friend to share, retweet, cut and paste, print, take a screen shot, or do any number of other things with it that may make the material available to others, all of which may be perfectly legal for both the sharer and the recipient. So, again, the question becomes whether your particular use creates issues. You have to separately think about whether your use creates libel, privacy or copyright issues, even if no legal issues are created merely by seeing the material. But back to the question about access to the account: you definitely want to avoid anything that would constitute hacking, fraud or other illegal conduct. The Computer Fraud and Abuse Act potentially applies to improperly accessed material, for example, and other laws may apply, too. You should consult with your lawyer before doing anything that involves using passwords, codes, or otherwise provides access to protected sites.

Who owns my Twitter or Facebook account if I use it for both personal and professional use? Does my employer own that content or have a say in what I write?

That is an excellent question. If you don't already know the answer, then neither do I.

I'm only partly joking in my response. There are a couple of cases on this very topic pending. The opinions so far seem to indicate that the outcomes will be very fact-specific. What representations were made? Does the employee handbook contain relevant terms? Is there an agreement between the parties? What uses were permitted—or required—during employment? Thus, there is no clear-cut answer. Employers or employees who are concerned about this issue should attempt to spell out an agreement clearly at the outset so that problems don't arise later.

Should I have the same Twitter handle for my personal and professional use (as a reporter)?

This really depends on ethical and business considerations more than legal ones. Does your employer want to own your professional account? Then you might want a separate personal one. Do you want to tweet about topics that might seem unprofessional? Keep two accounts. Or rethink the wisdom of those tweets. However, some may find it easier and preferable to maintain one account. Either way. But if you are concerned with ownership of the account, make a clear deal with your employer before you rely on a presumption that you own it.

Can I libel someone on Twitter or Facebook? If I delete it right away, does it count?

Yes. Libel does not depend on the medium used. And, immediate deletion does not take away the libel, although it might make the claim more difficult to prove and would minimize damages.

More of an ethical question, but do I have to be careful who I follow on Twitter in case it shows bias? Likewise, if a source wants to friend me on Facebook and I accept, is that seen as bias?

Whether it is *seen* as bias is a different issue than whether it truly indicates bias. I think that most people who actually use Twitter understand that following someone means only that you have some reason to follow them; it says nothing about approval, disapproval or any other motive or mindset. Similarly, being a "friend" or "connection" on Facebook or LinkedIn doesn't have an inherent meaning. Some people only connect to truly close friends, and others will accept any friend request. If a critic wishes to create a scandal out of nothing more than a social media connection, I would think that effort would reflect more poorly on the critic's lack of critical thinking skills than it does on the reporter. That said, you should still be careful. There are thorny ethical issues involved. It may be wise to avoid connecting with a source if it would reveal the fact that someone was your source. Or, if you are covering a trial, do not friend the judge or a juror during that trial. (You particularly want to avoid any appearance of jury tampering.) And, you might be wary of creating an appearance of a conflict by friending the subject of a story. But all these determinations have to be made on a case by case basis, and you should probably consult with an editor or journalism ethics expert if you find yourself in a delicate situation.

If I contact someone via Twitter for a story, do I have to identify myself as a reporter or is it assumed if my Twitter account makes it clear that I am?

Do not assume that any random person you contact will know that you are a reporter. Even if you think it's obvious. People can be oblivious. The principles of journalism ethics typically require that a reporter identify him/herself as such, and that's a valid principle regardless of the medium in which you are operating.

Legally, how much responsibility do I have in verifying that someone's Twitter or Facebook account is really theirs?

I have to admit, I'm not entirely certain what scenario this question is premised upon. But I guess I would say that you probably would have as much responsibility to verify that as you would any other fact you are reporting.

Is there anything else that you think journalists should understand about Twitter and Facebook and using social media professionally?

The main takeaway should be that social media is not really different from any other method of communication. The same legal issues arise, the same principles apply.

Practical Conclusions

- Most websites have "terms of service" and a "privacy policy" that describe how the site is to be used and how the site will collect and use information about users. It is important that a site actually comply with its own terms because the FTC will sometimes take enforcement action against sites that violate them. Users must also be aware of what terms require so that they do not find themselves in trouble for misusing sites (the most likely scenario would involve the misuse of trademarks or copyrighted material).

- Digital technology is inherently insecure, and thus, as a practical matter, it can be very hard to remain anonymous online. However, the courts are willing to extend some First Amendment protection to online speakers when their identities are subpoenaed. The courts typically require a showing that there is a legitimate legal claim against an anonymous speaker before the speaker can be unmasked. However, this protection is useless against other threats, like hackers, or the potential that one's identity will become known and disclosed by a reporter. Thus, even though there is some First Amendment protection for anonymity online, one must not assume that anonymity and privacy can be preserved at all times.

- The internet is inherently a global tool, but the laws regarding speech vary from country to country. Few countries are as protective of free speech as the United States. Thus, internet users must be aware that their speech could subject them to liability overseas. It is important to be aware of how the laws vary, particularly with respect to libel, privacy, and government regulations of speech, and to figure out whether one could be subject to liability in countries where the laws are not favorable. As a practical matter, this may create problems only for those who travel or have assets overseas. U.S. courts might not enforce a foreign judgment if it would violate First Amendment principles.

- There are a few laws that target online conduct specifically. The Children's Online Privacy Protection Act (COPPA) regulates how sites can collect information from children under 13 and any site that does so must comply with its terms. There are state laws that target "cyberbullying" or "cyberharassment," but the constitutionality of such laws is questionable and will be undetermined until they are challenged in court. Finally, section 230 of the Communications Decency Act provides immunity to Internet Service Providers, so that they will not be liable for content posted on their sites by third parties. As a practical matter that means that plaintiffs must sue the person who actually wrote or posted the offending content rather than the website that allowed the post.

- With respect to social media, the courts have not yet carved out any exceptions for how legal principles would apply to content. Social media is simply one more form of communication, so all the principles of communications law should apply equally to social media.

CHAPTER 21

Practical Issues Related to Media Law

There are certain considerations that aren't purely legal issues but that should be considered in any full and fair evaluation of the issues that arise from communication. This chapter discusses some of these practical concerns, including:

1. The non-legal consequences of speech, such as business consequences, death threats, and the risk of private censorship

2. How risks are assessed and the different ways to approach risk

3. Media liability insurance

4. Principles of journalism ethics

Non-legal Consequences/Considerations

The fact that the First Amendment may protect a speaker's right to say something doesn't mean that there won't be any consequences arising from such speech. In fact, having the right to say something is entirely a separate question from whether it should be said.

A speaker should expect the audience to have a reaction to whatever is said. One might hope that the reaction will be agreement, but there is certainly no guarantee that will be the case. Members of the audience may be offended. The speech may be contrary to their interests or beliefs. They may wish to silence the speaker. Even though the government can't impose a prior restraint or punish a speaker in most cases, the First Amendment applies only to government action and doesn't protect against actions by private parties. Thus, there may be consequences that adversely affect a speaker, even if they aren't imposed by the government.

Business Consequences

Many forms of media are based on an advertising business model: they get their revenue from advertisers who pay to appear in that particular platform. A media outlet that accepts advertising always runs a risk of losing advertisers that are offended by content.

Offending advertisers can happen in two ways: (1) direct criticism of the advertiser, or (2) generally offensive content that the advertiser does not want to be associated with. In either case, the media outlet might lose advertisers, which means losing money, which is usually a bad thing from a business perspective.

An example of direct criticism involves *Village Voice* blogger Foster Kamer, who made a joke about Jimmy Dolan, the CEO of Cablevision, in a blog post. In response, the Independent Film Center, which is owned by Cablevision, withdrew about $20,000 worth of advertising from the *Village Voice*. This is a typical example of how speech can have consequences, aside from First Amendment issues. The First Amendment protected Kamer's right to make the joke (he couldn't be successfully sued or prosecuted for it), but it can't prevent businesses from pulling ads in response.

In an example of generally offensive content resulting in loss of ad support, over three dozen companies pulled ads from Rush Limbaugh's talk show after he referred to a law student as a "slut" in response to her Congressional testimony in support of mandatory health insurance coverage for birth control. Limbaugh's comments should be protected by the First Amendment; no libel claim would likely have been successful because his statements were political hyperbole rather than any kind of believable assertion. Nevertheless, the advertisers were well within their rights to refuse to be associated with Limbaugh's show.

From the standpoint of journalism ethics, news organizations are not supposed to concern themselves with whether advertisers like the news or not. One must report the news independently and without pandering to those in positions of power, including advertisers. Nevertheless, it would be naïve to say that one should never consider whether content will offend the audience, which includes advertisers. This is particularly true with commentary that may be interesting or funny but without public significance. News organizations will often consider whether something will upset the audience, such as graphic displays of violence or gratuitous profanity. In such cases, it is perfectly ethical to decide that material is simply inappropriate and to exercise editorial discretion. What is generally considered unethical is deciding not to use legitimately newsworthy material solely out of fear of losing money. Thus, from a practical standpoint, speakers should weigh the business consequences along with ethical considerations and the degree of newsworthiness of the speech, even in cases where there are unlikely to be legal consequences.

Death Threats

The Committee to Protect Journalists keeps a database of journalists who are killed in the course of duty. It is an astonishing list of over a thousand people across many different parts of the world. Many are intentionally murdered by those who dislike their reporting. Being killed, whether by governments, criminals, zealots, or others, is a real risk of the job, especially when one is reporting on corruption, organized crime, or other abuses of power. Even in the United States where a free press is at least theoretically valued, there have been instances where journalists are threatened or killed.

During the course of the 2016 election cycle, some controversy was raised over a t-shirt worn by a Trump supporter that said "Rope. Tree. Journalist. Some assembly required." While that was not a specific threat to any particular individual, it certainly raised questions about the degree to which reporters are actually safe from harm.

There have been many death threats involving Islamic groups that were offended by content. Iran's Ayatollah famously issued a fatwa for the murder of Salman Rushdie after his book *The Satanic Verses* was published. The Danish newspaper *Jyllands-Posten* was threatened after publishing cartoons depicting the prophet Muhammed with a bomb in his turban. Filmmaker Theo Van Gogh was killed by a Muslim offended by Van Gogh's film *Submission*, concerning the treatment of women in Islam. Gunmen killed 12 people and injured 11 at the office of the French satirical magazine *Charlie Hebdo*; a group affiliated with Al-Qaeda claimed responsibility. And, finally, a cleric issued a fatwa for the murder of a Seattle cartoonist who suggested an "Everybody Draw Muhammed Day" in response to Muslim threats concerning depictions of the prophet Muhammed.

While true threats and any subsequent murders would certainly constitute crimes, victims have to rely on the police and prosecutors to investigate and prosecute these crimes. But law enforcement is often hampered by of lack of leads, lack of resources, or other priorities. In short, death threats are a risk that comes with certain types of commentary or reporting. That risk must be recognized, and private security measures may be required.

Private Censorship

The First Amendment protects citizens from government censorship. It does not provide any rights or remedies with respect to private censorship. Thus, an employer (assuming it is a private employer) can fire an employee if the employer discovers and dislikes an employee's personal blog. Media organizations are not obligated to publish material or ads if they think the content is offensive or problematic. A store can refuse to sell CDs it deems offensive. Apple once famously refused to sell a book by a publisher that wrote an unauthorized biography of Steve Jobs. All of these actions are a form of censorship, but none are prohibited by the First Amendment.

It is a common myth that free speech means that speakers are entitled to be free from consequence. In a high profile example, Dr. Laura Schlessinger, a radio talk show host, used the word "nigger" multiple times in a show. Several sponsors and affiliates dropped their support of her show, so she decided to end the program. She claimed that her "First Amendment rights" had been usurped. In an interview on the *Larry King Show*, she said, "I want to regain my First Amendment rights. I want to be able to say what's on my mind, and in my heart, what I think is helpful and useful without somebody getting angry, some special interest group deciding this is a time to silence a voice of dissent, and attack affiliates and attack sponsors." Her statement expresses a common misunderstanding. Her First Amendment rights were never an issue; the government took no action to prosecute her, nor was she sued in court. Her complaint is about the reaction that private persons or entities had to her speech. The First Amendment does not guarantee that other people will like a person's speech or support it. On the contrary, the First Amendment provides equal protection to those who want to tell Dr. Laura she was wrong. While she is not required to listen to them any more than they are required to listen to her, they are both free to say what they wish and suffer whatever private consequences may accrue as a result.

It is important to understand that the First Amendment applies only to government censorship, and does not provide a free pass from all consequences. There are certainly ethical and cultural concerns with private censorship, and it would be helpful to have more public debate about appropriate ways to respond to speech with which one disagrees; nevertheless, it does not raise constitutional issues.

Assessing Risk

It is almost impossible to prevent all legal threats. Sometimes people sue even when they don't have a good case. But speakers should try to understand the risks they face and their willingness to incur various levels of risk.

Media companies have been dealing with this issue for a long time, and they take different approaches to the problem. Different companies have different risk policies. Some are more risk-averse and prefer to engage in extensive pre-publication review; others are quite risk-tolerant and focus more on managing any lawsuits that arise. Some companies demand high ethical standards, others don't. What's important is that each organization has found a risk-management policy that works for their mission and their budget.

Individuals should make the same kind of assessment. People should consider their own risk tolerance when deciding what to publish, particularly considering the ease of publishing online via blogs, comments, Facebook, Twitter, and other forums. Some kinds of statements are riskier than others, and speakers may wish to edit themselves, or they may decide that the statement is important enough to accept the risk of a claim. But in any case, to be prepared, speakers should strive to be as knowledgeable as possible about what kinds of statements are protected and what are not, so that any risk can be assumed intentionally rather than ignorantly.

Ideally, a journalist would want to work for an organization whose values matched his or her own, and the risk tolerance levels should be about equal. If you find yourself out of sync with your employer's values, you might consider looking for another job. Disputes often arise when journalists feel that their employer won't let them do what they want, or when employers feel that a journalist is too risky. In many cases, neither party is inherently more right or wrong; they simply balance the risks differently. A good fit in terms of risk tolerance is an important part of choosing a job.

Media Liability Insurance

There is such a thing as media liability insurance, and it is exactly what it sounds like—an insurance policy that may provide coverage for the wide range of risks to which media are exposed. It may help to defend against libel or privacy claims, cover claims of infringements on intellectual property, provide defense against subpoenas, or even cover claims arising from the ordinary operation of a website. Several companies sell these kinds of insurance policies, which may help cover defense costs and/or judgments in the event of a lawsuit. Large media companies usually have this kind of coverage. Small companies or bloggers might benefit from having coverage too, although it might be more difficult to absorb the expense of the premiums.

As with any form of insurance, it is important to read the policy carefully and see whether it actually covers what one's risks are likely to be. Some will cover defense costs, others don't, or cover only a portion of defense costs. Policies often also cap limits of exposure. Thus, if the policy has a cap of

$1,000,000, and you are found liable for $2,000,000 in damages, then the insurance may cover only $1,000,000, and you may be personally liable for the other $1,000,000.

Some professional groups, such as the Authors Guild or Online News Association, have offered their members an opportunity to get insurance with group rates. Individuals who want coverage may consider using an insurance broker. In any event, media liability coverage is an option for those who would like some protection in the event of a lawsuit.

Journalism Ethics

What makes a journalist different from any other speaker? This question is hotly debated. On one hand, journalists bristle against the idea that there are some criteria to qualify as a journalist. Anyone who gathers and transmits information for the purpose of informing the public should qualify as a journalist. On the other hand, there is something seemingly inaccurate about claiming that everyone who publishes information online is a journalist.

From a legal perspective, courts have been reluctant to draw distinctions between members of the press and other speakers. Many decisions say that reporters are subject to generally applicable laws like any other citizen and that reporters have whatever First Amendment rights other speakers have.

Professional journalists can distinguish themselves, however, by adhering to certain ethical principles that are designed to enhance the quality of their work and maintain their credibility as messengers of truth. There is a difference between journalism and propaganda, and there is a difference between reporting and commentary, even if those lines can sometimes be difficult to draw. Therefore, this section will discuss:

1. How legal and ethical issues are related

2. What journalism ethics typically require

3. The difference between ethics and self-censorship

The Relationship Between Legal and Ethical Considerations

Journalism ethics are traditionally based in the same philosophy that grounded the First Amendment principles discussed in this book. The ethical principles are a companion to the notion of free speech; the idea is that the press should have great freedom, but accordingly, the press has corresponding responsibilities. These responsibilities aren't imposed to limit speech in the sense of censoring ideas or unpleasant facts. Instead, they are intended to promote credibility. Promoting credibility is the primary goal of journalism ethics. However, as an added benefit, they also help secure First Amendment rights. If news outlets abused their freedoms by regularly publishing false, biased, or unfounded statements, they would lose their credibility and some of the justifications for giving the press substantial freedom from government intervention would erode.

Scholars typically refer to certain principles at the root of free press theory or journalism ethics. John Stuart Mill, David Hume, and John Milton are commonly cited as the leading thinkers who influenced the view that the press should be accorded expansive liberties to serve as a check on government and promote truth via a free marketplace of ideas.

The philosophy of David Hume, particularly his skeptical epistemology, helps to understand some of these legal and ethical principles. Hume examined the concept of truth and how we think we know what we claim to know. In short, he concluded that we rely largely on perception and memory, both of which can be flawed. We form beliefs about what is true, but our beliefs can be correct or incorrect, and it is difficult to discern which is the case.

As a practical matter, we shouldn't simply give up on the concept of knowledge or truth, but the recognition that our beliefs might be incorrect should instill some humility. Both modern First Amendment jurisprudence and codes of journalism ethics are based on this premise. We may have strong beliefs, and there is nothing wrong with that, or with defending one's beliefs. However, it is inappropriate to conflate one's beliefs with objective truth. It is important to leave open the possibility that one might be wrong.

The implications for the First Amendment are obvious: if no one has a monopoly on truth, then we should allow a broad range of speech to be legal so that all ideas and beliefs are heard. If anyone could be wrong, we give persons the ability to sort through competing ideas to discern which assertions seem more truthful than others. This is most famously memorialized in the "marketplace of ideas" theory.

The implications for ethics are perhaps less obvious, but similar: if you believe X, you must accept the possibility that X is not true. You must have the ability to separate beliefs or opinions from an analysis of raw facts or what otherwise forms the basis for a statement. You must recognize that other people might have different beliefs, or come to different conclusions from the same set of facts, and you must not give preference to your beliefs simply because they are yours (unless you are clearly expressing an opinion, rather than engaging in supposedly objective reporting, and then it is incumbent upon you to make clear the distinction between objective reporting and expressions of opinion). You must strive to be independent from influence, including the influence of your own agenda or beliefs. Thus, if you are going to report X, it should be because X is objectively supported by raw facts and not based solely on your own opinion.

Ethical codes that follow this theory require the reporter to remain neutral; report the facts and let the reader draw his/her own conclusions; have multiple sources to justify an assertion; make a clear distinction between fact and opinion; and provide clear attribution to the source of information. Most importantly, these ethical codes require that journalists not offer their own opinions on controversial matters. This is not because journalists don't or can't have opinions. It is because there is an inherent recognition that there is nothing special about a journalist's opinion. Journalists should have as much humility as anyone else about their beliefs. Choosing sides doesn't make one's beliefs any more true than they would be otherwise; it only taints the objectivity of the journalist, calling into question whether he has the intellectual ability to separate the basis for his opinion from demonstrable facts.

This approach has been criticized, however, because there is value in providing analysis, context, and commentary. The audience may be well served by hearing opinions as well as facts. Thus, media companies have taken various approaches to address the question of how to present opinion. The first approach is to report opinion in the same manner one reports facts. The reporter himself does not give his own opinion, but relies on sources (preferably experts, although not always) to provide opinions on the topic. A long as the reporter covers a wide range of divergent opinions from experts/sources without privileging the one he prefers, the reporter has remained neutral and met his ethical obligation. The second approach is to allow opinion or commentary by staff who are referred to as "analysts" or "commentators." This distinction tends to be somewhat artificial because there is often no principled reason why some people are "reporters" and others are "commentators," except that some are allowed to give opinions and others are not. In these cases, the commentators themselves become the so-called "experts," privileging their own opinion, rather than allowing others to speak. The third approach is to provide opinion via op-ed pieces, allowing third parties (not employees) to write commentaries that express opinion. Finally, some companies expressly permit reporters to express opinion as long as they are transparent about their biases.

The conflict between these approaches illustrates an underlying tension about the nature of journalism. The first and third approaches treat the profession of journalism as outside of events, keeping a record of what other people say and do. In the second and fourth approach, reporters become part of the news themselves. They are more active participants, striving to be deemed experts themselves, perhaps even famous for their opinions.

There has been much debate about which approach is superior and produces better results. Advocates for both sides argue that their approach is most likely to promote credibility, the goal of journalism ethics. Advocates of neutrality emphasize that credibility stems from the ability to report all views, privileging none. Advocates of the more involved approach argue that neutrality is a myth: we know everyone has an opinion, so it is better to be transparent about one's opinion so that the audience can better judge the credibility of the reporter's statements. The counter-argument to that is that, when it comes to opinions, people tend to judge as credible those with whom they already agree, regardless of what the facts indicate. Thus, providing a specific viewpoint may actually not serve the public interest because truth will be discredited if it comes from a source with whom the audience disagrees in general, and lies will be adopted as truth if they come from a source with whom the audience thinks it has common beliefs. Of course, there is a counter-argument to that, which is that there is still an ethical obligation to strive for truth in one's opinions or beliefs. Promoting lies is unethical regardless of whether they are served in the form of facts or opinions. And, the counterargument to this is that there is often no way to enforce ethics. One can only attempt to diminish the speaker's credibility by pointing out his lies, but that may be of little consequence if his lies are nevertheless appealing to his audience. Thus, it is important that speakers strive to be accurate and transparent about the sources of their information, and also, that audiences strive to carefully assess the quality of information delivered. The kinds of factors an audience might evaluate to determine whether a speaker is credible may include: how sincere and confident the speaker seemed in the assertion; how well-placed she was to have the knowledge in question; what motives she may have had in speaking; whether the speaker has any motives for insincerity; what pressure the speaker feels to speak responsibly; whether the speaker looked the audience in the eyes or seemed nervous; and whether the assertion made sense or was supported by corroborating known facts.[1]

Even if the relationship between credibility and objectivity is murky, one thing is clear: good ethical practices minimize legal problems (with the possible exception of protecting sources). Most of the principles of journalism ethics correspond nicely with the kinds of practices that are likely to prevent legal liability. The ethical principles to report accurately, verify facts from multiple sources, and ensure that headlines and captions are not misleading will clearly help in minimizing liability for libel. The principle to be sensitive to those affected by news events will help minimize liability for privacy claims. The principle to be sensitive to a defendant's right to a fair trial will help minimize the risk of gag orders or closure orders. Because of the close relationship between ethics and law, adhering to ethical principles will serve as a good guide to what may be protected by law. Straying outside the ethical boundaries can create legal exposure. There are some cases where reporters engaged in arguably unethical conduct and later were subject to adverse court rulings. For example, in *Cantrell v. Forest City Publishing Co.*, the court allowed a case to proceed where a reporter allegedly lied about facts; in *Goldwater v. Ginzburg*, where a magazine allegedly distorted comments to give a false impression; in *Baugh v. CBS*, where a camera crew allegedly misrepresented themselves as being from a camera crew allegedly misrepresented themselves as being from the D.A.'s office and filmed sensitive material from a rape victim; and in *KOVR-TV, Inc. v. Superior Court of Sacramento County*, where a journalist allegedly interviewed young children without parental supervision after a neighbor's murder/suicide.

However, there are also things that are perfectly responsible, ethical things to do that are not legally protected. Figure 21.1 illustrates the relationship between what is ethically appropriate and what is legally permissible.

Most speech falls into the combined area, as it is both legally and ethically permissible. Some speech is legally protected, but could be deemed unethical, such as hate speech, gratuitously cruel statements, publishing unconfirmed rumors about public figures, and otherwise sensationalizing news. Some activities are considered ethically permissible—perhaps even ethically imperative—and yet the law does not protect them. The two most notable examples would be protecting sources in certain cases and neutral reportage in cases where what's newsworthy is the fact that a certain statement is made, even if the facts asserted in the underlying statement are false. In such cases, one may have to choose between legal and ethical obligations or liabilities.

 What is legally protected
 What is ethically acceptable
 What is neither

Things that are legally protected but not necessarily ethical might include hate speech, insults, or gratuitous violence.

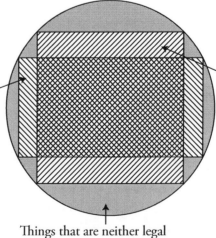

The kinds of things that might not be legally protected but are never the less potentially ethical could include the protection of sources or the neutral reportage of false claims.

Things that are neither legal nor ethical would include child pornography, true threats, fraud, and the dissemination of maliciously fabricated defamatory assertions.

Figure 21.1: The Relationship Between Law and Ethics.

An Overview of the Principles of Journalism Ethics

Many news organizations have their own ethical code or guidelines, and professional groups like the Society for Professional Journalists have model codes as well. There are certain principles that have historically been accepted as ideals to which professional journalists should aspire, as described below.

In Gathering News:

- Be respectful towards those you interview, particularly in tragic breaking news situations.

- Be particularly careful when dealing with minors or those who are incompetent or in difficult situations.

- Be honest about your role as a journalist, who you work for, and what you are doing. Hidden cameras or microphones should rarely be used, and if they are, be aware of the legal considerations.

- Be as thorough as possible in speaking to as many sources as possible and finding as much information as possible.

- You should not have decided what a story will say before you begin (or complete) your research. If you go into the reporting process with your mind already made up, you may miss important details or tell the story unfairly.

- If you are writing about a person (or entity), be sure that you have attempted to interview them or ask for comment. Tell them what you plan to report and give them a reasonable time to respond.

- Be careful about promising anonymity, in part for the ethical reason that you won't be able to attribute the information thoroughly, but also for the legal reason that you might be subject to liability if you are compelled to reveal the source.

- If you decide to use an anonymous source, be sure that the source is credible and be wary of any agendas or biases the source may have. (Actually, that is good to keep in mind with respect to all sources!)

In Publishing:

- What you publish should hew to the truth; avoid misleading or biased statements.

- Use the most accurate word or terminology possible and avoid controversial, "loaded" terms.

- Fairly characterize the people and statements you purport to describe.

- If a topic is complex, strive to capture the complexity rather than minimize it so that nuances are lost.

- Be transparent in describing your sources. Do not plagiarize, and credit sources properly. If you must use third party content, be aware of copyright issues.

- Know what you are writing: is it factual reporting or commentary? Whichever it is, be transparent about your intent. If it is reporting, avoid commentary, speculation, or opinion.

- Many news organizations will not name sexual assault victims as an ethical matter. Many will also refrain from naming others who may not understand the consequences of being named (for example, naming minors who admit to illegal or offensive conduct, not realizing that their name may forever appear in online searches and hampering their future educational or employment prospects).

- News organizations have varying opinions about when profanity or offensive language is permissible, but generally, such terms should be used only when necessary to the editorial context.

- This should go without saying: do not fabricate stories. Reporting is fact, not fiction.

After Publication:

- If errors come to light, correct them right away.

In General:

- Avoid actual or perceived conflicts of interest. This includes maintaining independence, both political and financial. Journalists do not work in politics, endorse candidates, give money to campaigns, sign petitions, volunteer for political causes, or otherwise take positions that would undermine their credibility as an unbiased source of news and information.

- Some reporters will decline to register to vote with a party affiliation, although that option is not available in all states, so one must use judgment. Some go so far as to decline to vote altogether, although most people feel that there is nothing wrong with exercising one's right to vote.

- It is generally not considered a problem for reporters to have a life—to join churches or civic groups, or participate in their children's schools. But one must always be aware of the potential conflicts, real or perceived, and conduct oneself accordingly.

- Reporters should not use information for financial gain. That also means they shouldn't accept gifts. Any freebies should probably be disclosed unless it would be obvious (books and CDs provided for review are generally free, and that needn't be disclosed, but other free opportunities should be disclosed—or in some cases, declined).

- If there is any conflict of interest between yourself and the subject of your reporting, you may need to disclose the conflict or recuse yourself from covering the subject.

Adhering to such principles should enhance credibility and minimize legal risk, as well.

The Difference Between Ethics and Self-Censorship

As noted above, speakers may give thought to considerations other than those that are purely legal in nature. One of the most important factors to consider before speaking is the potential ethical implications.

The question of whether one may legally say something is entirely different from whether one should say it. Think of a simple example: suppose you are shopping with a friend and she tries on a pair of jeans and asks you whether they look good. Perhaps they are terribly unflattering. You probably wouldn't say, "They make you look horrible." You would probably say something more thoughtful, such as "I think the other pair you tried on were more flattering," or "They don't look comfortable; perhaps there's a pair that fit better." When you refrain from saying something hurtful or mean, you do it for ethical reasons, not because a law demands it.

In choosing your words carefully, you might be considering the reaction you will get from your friend. Some statements are going to result in a hostile reaction; other statements will get a more friendly reception. And this applies to other circumstances as well. There are times when you might refrain from saying something because you fear the consequences, whether they are legal consequences, business consequences, potential death threats, concerns about credibility, or simply the hatred of the audience. You are editing yourself—but is this self-censorship?

When one refrains from speaking—or modifies what one intended to say—because of concern for consequences, it is tempting to say that this is a form of self-censorship, and that free speech should prevail. However, there is a fine line between ethics and self-censorship, and the two should not be confused.

Censorship is a word that is vaguely defined. It is often used to refer to unfair restrictions on speech. The most important aspect of the word is its connotation. It connotes something inappropriate. It suggests that the person has restricted speech for improper or invalid reasons.

However, there may be perfectly appropriate and completely valid reasons for being careful about speech. Preserving credibility, being kind, and paying attention to audience sensibilities are the kinds of things that are ethical in nature and may be justifiable reasons for restricting or editing speech.

Thus, the difference between ethics and self-censorship is nothing more than a value judgment about whether a self-imposed restraint is motivated by good or valid reasons as opposed to improper purposes. Speakers should think carefully about what they say and why they say it (or don't say it) and strive to align their speech with their best judgment about what is proper.

Practical Conclusions

- The fact that something is legal doesn't mean there won't be consequences.

- There are many potential consequences to speech that have nothing to do with the law, so think carefully about whether your speech is ethically appropriate and how people might view you. It is also important to remember that the First Amendment applies only to "state action," and thus, private parties, like schools, employers, businesses, and others are free to punish you as a result of your speech.

- It is important to balance legal rights with what is ethically or morally appropriate. There are many things that the law protects your right to say, and yet a speaker may find it morally inappropriate to engage in such speech. You don't have to use pornography or profanity just because the government won't punish you for doing so. And those who exercise their right to speak out against someone else—in any form, ranging from insults to hate speech—can't realistically expect everyone else to approve of or agree with what they say, even if they are free to say it. Although you are free to have your own opinion, you cannot force everyone else to agree with it.

- It is important to assess the risks of your speech, and in some cases, it may be appropriate to seek media liability coverage. If you are in the business of speaking, such insurance can help cover potential liability for the risks you face.

- Journalists will often voluntarily hold themselves to a higher standard than others, adhering to principles of journalism ethics in order to maximize the integrity of their reporting and preserve their credibility with their audience. There are times when ethical principles conflict, and it's not always clear what the right choice is. There are also times when ethical and legal principles conflict. In general, ethical behavior will minimize legal risk; however, there are times when speech may be ethically proper and yet not legally protected. Taking all factors into consideration—legal, ethical, and practical—will help speakers make the most informed decisions.

Note

1.   Sanford C. Goldberg, *Anonymous Assertions*, Episteme, 10 Episteme 135, 142 (2013).

Case Index

#

281 Care Committee v. Arneson, 766 F.3d 774 (8th Cir. 2014), 249, 250

44 Liquormart, Inc. v. Rhode Island, 517 U.S.484 (1996), 254

A

A&M Records v. Napster Inc., 239 F.3d 1004 (9th Cir. 2001), 98

Abbott v. Texas Dept. of Mental Health and Mental Retardation, 212 S.W.3d 648 (Tex. App. 2006), 181

ABC, Inc. v. Powell, 47 M.J. 363 (1997), 172

Abdul-Jabbar v. General Motors Corp., 85 F.3d 407 (9th Cir. 1996), 81

Abrams v. U.S., 250 U.S. 616 (1919), 213

ACLU v. Alvarez, 679 F.3d 583 (7th Cir. 2012), 185, 190

Agence France-Presse v. Morel, 10 Civ. 2730 (WHP) (S.D.N.Y. Dec. 23, 2010), 300

Agency for Int'l Dev. V. Alliance for Open Society, 133 S.Ct. 2321 (2013), 280

A.H. v. State, 949 So.2d 234 (Fla. Dist. Ct. App. 2007), 236

Alpha Therapeutic Corp. v. Nippon Hoso Kyokai (NHK), 199 F.3d 1078 (9th Cir. 1999), 194

American Booksellers Ass'n Inc. v. Hudnut, 771 F.2d 323 (7th Cir. 1985), aff'd mem. 475 U.S. 1001 (1986), 235

Animal Legal Defense Fund v. Herbert, 263 F. Supp. 3d 1193 (D. Utah 2017), 196

Animal Legal Defense Fund v. Reynolds, 4:17-cv-00362-JEG-HCA (S.D. Iowa 2019), 196

Animal Legal Defense Fund v. Wasden, 878 F.3d 1184 (9th Cir. 2018), 195

Anonsen v. Donahue, 857 S.W.2d 700 (Tx. App. 1993), 74

Arkansas Educ. Television Comm'n v. Forbes, 523 U.S. 666 (1998), 271

Ark. Writers' Project v. Ragland, 481 U.S. 221 (1987), 18

Asgeirsson v. Abbott, 773 F. Supp. 2d 684 (W.D. Tex. 2011), 169

Ashcroft v. ACLU, 542 U.S. 656 (2004), 234

Ashcroft v. Free Speech Coalition, 535 U.S. 234 (2002), 137

Austin v. Michigan Chamber of Commerce, 494 U.S. 652 (1990), 245, 246

Authors Guild v. Google, Inc., No. 13-4829 (2nd Cir. 2015), 107

B

Balboa Island Village Inn, Inc. v. Lemen, 156 P.2d 339 (Cal. 2007), 63

Bally Total Fitness Holding Corp. v. Faber, 29 F. Supp. 2d 1161 (C.D. Cal. 1998), 121

Bangoura v. Washington Post, [2005] O.J. No. 3849 (Can.), 298

Barber v. Time, Inc., 159 S.W.2d 291 (Mo. 1942), 71–72, 127, 128

Barclays Capital, Inc. v. TheFlyOnTheWall.com, 650 F.3d 876 (2d Cir. 2011), 111

Barnes v. Yahoo, Inc., 570 F.3d 1096 (9th Cir. 2009), 290

Barr v. Matteo, 360 U.S. 564 (1959), 52

Barrett v. Rosenthal, 146 P.3d 510 (Cal. 2006), 289

Bartnicki v. Vopper, 532 U.S. 514 (2001), 191

Batzel v. Smith, 333 F.3d 1018 (9th Cir. 2003), 289

Baugh v. CBS, Inc, 828 F. Supp. 745 (N.D. Cal. 1993), 199, 312

Beer Nuts, Inc. v. Clover Club Foods Co., 805 F.2d 920 (10th Cir. 1986), 118

Benavidez v. Anheuser-Busch, Inc., 873 F.2d 102 (5th Cir. 1989), 86

Bethel School District v. Fraser, 478 U.S. 675 (1986), 275

Bindrim v. Mitchell, 92 Cal. App. 3d 61 (1979), 40

Birmingham v. Fodor's Travel Publications Inc., 833 P.2d 70 (Haw. 1992), 152

Blakey v. Continental Airlines,Inc., 751 A.2d 538 (N.J. 2000), 298

Blanch v. Koons, 467 F.3d 244 (2d Cir. 2006), 134

Blumenthal v. Drudge, 992 F. Supp. 44 (D.D.C. 1998), 289

BMG Music v. Gonzalez, 430 F. 3d 888 (7th Cir. 2005), 104

Bolger v. Youngs Drug Products Corp., 463 U.S. 60 (1983), 253

Bollea v. Gawker Media LLC, No. 8:2012cv02348 (M.D. Fla.), 76, 237

Bonome v. Kaysen, 32 Media L. Rptr. 1520 (Mass. Super. Ct. 2004), 74

Borreca v. Fasi, 369 F. Supp. 906 (D. Haw. 1974), 182

Boston Herald v. Superior Court, 421 Mass. 502 (1995), 170

Brandenburg v. Ohio, 395 U.S. 444 (1969), 214, 215, 220, 229

Brandt v. Weather Channel Inc., 42 F. Supp. 2d 1344 (S.D. Fla. 1999), 153

Branzburg v. Hayes, 408 U.S. 665 (1972), 206, 207, 208

Braun v. Soldier of Fortune Magazine, 968 F.2d 1110 (11th Cir. 1992), 153, 257

Brinkley v. Casablancas, 438 N.Y.S.2d 1004 (NY App. 1981), 85

Brocklesby v. U.S., 767 F.2d 1288 (9th Cir. 1985), 153

Brown v. Entertainment Merchants Ass'n., 131 S.Ct. 2729 (2011), 238

Brownmark Films, LLC v. Comedy Partners, 800 F. Supp. 2d 991 (E.D. Wisc. 2011), *aff'd* 682 F.3d 687 (2012), 145

Buckley v. Am. Constitutional Law Foundation, 525 U.S. 182 (1999), 247

Buckley v. Valeo, 424 U.S. 1 (1976), 245, 246

Buller v. Pulitzer Publishing Co., 684 S.W.2d 473 (Mo. App. 1985), 75

Burka v. HHS, 87 F.3d 508 (D.C. Cir. 1996), 160

Burnett v. National Enquirer, Inc,, 193 Cal. Rptr. 206 (Cal. App. 1983), 27

Burns v. DOJ, No. 99-3173 (slip op.) (D.D.C. Feb. 5, 2001), 161

Butterworth v. Smith, 494 U.S. 624 (1990), 172

Byers v. Edmonson, 826 So.2d 551 (La. App. 2002), 151

C

Calder v. Jones, 465 U.S. 783 (1984), 298

Campbell v. Acuff Rose Music, Inc., 510 U.S. 569 (1994), 102, 104, 145

Cantrell v. Forest City Publishing Co., 419 U.S. 245 (1974), 45, 312

Carafano v. Metrosplash.com*, Inc.,* 339 F.3d 1119 (9th Cir. 2003), 288

Cardtoons, L.C. v. Major League Baseball Players Ass'n., 838 F. Supp. 1510 (N.D. Okla. 1993), 86

Carlson v. U.S., No. 15-2972 (7th Cir. 2016), 173

Carson v. Here's Johnny Portable Toilets Inc., 698 F.2d 831 (6th Cir. 1983), 82

Carter v. Rand McNally & Co., Case No. 76-1864 (D. Mass. 1980) (unpublished opinion), 153

Carter-Clark v. Random House, Inc., 196 Misc. 2d 1011 (Sup. Ct. NY County 2003), 40

Catsouras v. California Hwy Patrol, 104 Cal. Rptr. 3d 352 (Cal. App. 2010), 130

CBS v. DNC, 412 U.S. 94 (1973), 258

CBS v. FCC, 453 U.S. 367 (1981), 267

CCNV v. Reid, 490 U.S. 730 (1989), 96

Central Hudson Gas & Elec. Corp. v. Public Serv. Comm'n., 447 U.S. 557 (1980), 17, 19, 116, 253, 254, 255

Cerasani v. Sony, 991 F. Supp. 343 (S.D.N.Y. 1998), 51

Challen v. Town & Country Charge, 545 F. Supp. 1014 (N.D. Ill. 1982), 70

Chandler v. Florida, 449 U.S. 560 (1981), 176

Chaplinsky v. New Hampshire, 315 U.S. 568 (1942), 219, 220

Cher v. Forum Int'l Ltd., 692 F.2d 634 (9th Cir. 1982), 88

Chicago Lawyers Committee for Civil Rights v. Craigslist, 519 F.3d 666 (7th Cir. 2008), 258, 289

Chrysler Corp. v. Brown, 441 U.S. 281 (1979), 163

Cincinnati. v. Discovery Network, Inc., 507 U.S. 410 (1993), 217

Cinel v. Connick, 15 F.3d 1338 (5th Cir. 1994), 70

Citizen Publishing Co. v. Miller, 115 P.3d 107 (Ariz. 2005), 233

Citizens United v. FEC, 130 S.Ct. 876 (2010), 245, 246, 247, 251

City of Lakewood v. Plain Dealer Pub. Co., 486 U.S. 750 (1988), 18

City of Renton v. Playtime Theatres, 475 U.S. 41 (1986), 235

Clark v. CCNV, 468 U.S. 288 (1984), 216

Clean Flicks of Colorado, LLC v. Soderbergh, 433 F. Supp. 2d 1236 (D. Colo. 2006), 105

Clift v. Narragansett Television, 688 A.2d 805 (R.I. 1996), 154

Cohen v. California, 403 U.S. 15 (1971), 220

Cohen v. Cowles Media, 501 U.S. 663 (1991), 199, 209

Cohen v. Google, Inc., 887 N.Y.S.2d 424 (N.Y. Sup. Ct. 2009), 35, 292

Comcast Corp. v. FCC, 600 F.3d 642 (D.C. Cir. 2010), 272

Comedy III Productions, Inc. v. Gary Saderup, Inc., 21 P.3d 797 (Cal. 2001), 85

Competitive Enterprise Inst. V. Office of Sci. and Tech. Policy, 241 F. Supp. 3d (D.D.C. 2017), 160

Condit v. USA Today, No. CIV-03-0862 BB/ACT-LFG (D. N.M. 2004), 52

Connell v. Hudson, 733 F. Supp. 465 (D. N.H. 1990), 181, 193

Cox Bct. Corp. v. Cohn, 420 U.S. 469 (1975), 67

Cummins v. Campbell, 44 F.3d 847 (10th Cir. 1994), 276

Curtis Publishing Co. v. Butts, 388 U.S. 130 (1967), 42

D

Dahlstrom v. Sun Times Media, LLC., No. 14-2295 (7th Cir. 2015), 180

Dallas Cowboy Cheerleaders v. Pussycat Cinema, 604 F.2d 200 (2d Cir. 1979), 118

Dambrot v. Central Michigan University, 55 F.3d 1177 (6th Cir. 1995), 231

Dart v. Craigslist, Inc., 665 F. Supp. 2d 961 (N.D. Ill. 2009), 288

Davidson v. Time Warner, 25 Media Law Rep. 1705 (S.D. Tex. 1997), 151

Davis v. Elec. Arts, Inc., 775 F.3d 1172 (9th Cir. 2015), 87

DeFillipo v. NBC, 446 A.2d 1036 (R.I. 1982), 151

DeJohn v. Temple Univ 537 F.3d 301 (3rd Cir. 2008), 229

Dendrite Int'l, Inc. v. Doe No. 3, 775 A.2d 756 (N.J. Super. Ct. App. Div. 2001), 291

Dennis v. US, 341 U.S. 494 (1951), 213

Dept. of Air Force v. Rose, 425 U.S. 352 (1976), 163

Desnick v. ABC, 44 F.3d 1345 (7th Cir. 1995), 194

Detroit Free Press v. Ashcroft, 303 F.3d 681 (6th Cir. 2002), 171

Detroit Free Press v. U.S. Dept. of Justice, 829 F.3d 478 (6th Cir. 2016), 165

Diaz v. Oakland Tribune, 188 Cal. Rptr. 762 (Cal. App. 1983), 73

Dickinson v. Cosby, B271470 (Cal. App. Nov. 21, 2017), 38

Dimas-Martinez v. State of Arkansas, 2011 Ark. 515 (Ark. 2011), 177

Doe v. 2TheMart.com, Inc., 140 F. Supp. 2d 1088 (W.D. Wash. 2001), 291

Doe v. MySpace, 528 F.3d 413 (5th Cir. 2008), 153, 288

Doe v. Oliver, 755 A.2d 1000 (Sup. Ct. Conn. 2000), 288

Doe v. Reed, 130 S.Ct. 2811 (2010), 247

Doe v. TCI Cablevision, 110 S.W.3d 363 (Mo. 2003), 86

Doe v. University of Michigan, 721 F. Supp 852 (E.D. Mich 1989), 9, 228

Donato v. Moldow, 865 A.2d 711 (N.J. Super. Ct. 2005), 289

Doninger v. Niehoff, 527 F.3d 41 (2d Cir. 2008), 275

Dora v. Frontline Video, Inc., 18 Cal.Rptr.2d 790 (Cal. App. 1993), 86

Dow Jones & Co., Inc. v. Gutnick, [2002] HCA 56 (Austrl.), 298

Downing v. Abercrombie & Fitch, 265 F.3d 994 (9th Cir. 2001), 88

DRK Photo v. Houghton Mifflin Harcourt Pub. Co., 2010 U.S. Dist. Lexis 40875 (D. Ariz. 2010), 96

Dr. Seuss Enter. v. Penguin Books, 109 F.3d 1394 (9th Cir. 1997), 104

DTH Media Corp. v. Folt, No. COA17-871 (N.C. App. 2018), 180

Dun & Bradstreet v. Greenmoss Builders, 472 U.S. 749 (1985), 48

Durruthy v. Pastor, 351 F.3d 1080 (11th Cir. 2003), 181, 184, 193

E

Eastwood v. National Enquirer, 123 F.3d 1249 (9th Cir. 1997), 88

Edwards v. National Audubon Society, 556 F.2d 113 (2d Cir. 1977), 53

Eimann v. Soldier of Fortune Magazine, 880 F.2d 830 (5th Cir. 1989), 153

Eldred v. Ashcroft, 537 U.S. 186 (2003), 99

Elonis v. U.S., 135 S. Ct. 2001 (2015), 239

El Vocero de Puerto Rico v. Puerto Rico, 508 U.S. 147 (1993), 170

Embry v. Lewis, 215 F.3d 884 (8th Cir. 2000), 215

Emmett v. Kent School Dist., 92 F. Supp. 2d 1088 (W.D. Wash. 2000), 276

Eramo v. Rolling Stone, LLC, 209 F. Supp. 3d 862 (W.D. Va. 2016), 44

ETW Corp. v. Jireh Publishing Inc., 332 F 3d 915 (6th Cir. 2003), 86

Ex Parte Jones, No. 12-17-00346CR (Tx. App. 2018), 237

F

Fair Housing Council of San Fernando Valley v. Roommate. com, 521 F.3d 1157 (9th Cir. 2008), 258, 289

Fawcett Publications v. Morris, 377 P.2d 42 (Okla. 1962), 39

FCC v. AT&T, 131 S.Ct. 1177 (2011), 164

FCC v. Fox Television Stations, Inc., 132 S.Ct. 2307 (2012), 266

FCC v. League of Women Voters, 468 U.S. 364 (1984), 271

FCC v. Pacifica Foundation, 438 U.S. 726 (1978), 9, 234, 266

FEC v. Beaumont, 539 U.S. 146 (2003), 245

FEC v. Mass. Citizens for Life, 479 U.S. 238 (1986), 245

FEC v. Wisc. Right to Life, 551 U.S. 449 (2007), 246

Feist Publications, Inc. v. Rural Tel. Serv. Co., 499 U.S. 340 (1991), 93

Ficker v. Tuohy, 305 F.Supp.2d 569 (D. Md. 2004), 121

Field v. Google, 412 F. Supp. 2d 1106 (D. Nev. 2006), 107

Fields v. City of Philadelphia, 862 F.3d 353 (3rd Cir. 2017), 185

First National Bank of Boston v. Bellotti, 435 U.S. 765 (1978), 245

Florida Star v. BJF, 491 U.S. 524 (1989), 67

Food Lion, Inc. v. Capital Cities/ABC, Inc., 194 F.3d 505 (4th Cir. 1999), 189

Fordyce v. City of Seattle, 55 F.3d 436 (9th Cir. 1995), 184

Foretich v. Lifetime Cable, 777 F. Supp. 47 (D. DC 1991), 75

Franklin Prescriptions Inc. v. New York Times, 267 F. Supp. 2d 425 (E.D. Pa. 2003), 48

Free Speech Coalition v. Ashcroft, 535 U.S. 234 (2002), 236

FTC v. Accusearch, Inc., 570 F.3d 1187 (10th Cir. 2009), 289

FTC v. Colgate-Palmolive Co., 380 U.S. 374 (1965), 256

G

Galella v. Onassis, 487 F.2d 986 (2d Cir. 1973), 198

Gales v. CBS Broadcasting, 33 Media L. Rep. 1353 (5th Cir. 2005), 39

Gannett Co. v. Delaware, 571 A.2d 735 (Del. 1990), 178

Garcetti v. Ceballos, 547 U.S. 410 (2006), 277, 278

Gentile v. State Bar of Nevada, 501 U.S. 1030 (1991), 175

Gertz v. Robert Welch, Inc., 418 U.S. 323 (1974), 42, 45, 46, 48

Gilbert v. Medical Econ. Co., 665 F.2d 305 (10th Cir. 1981), 72

Gilles v. Davis, 427 F.3d 197 (3 rd Cir. 2005), 184

Ginsberg v. New York, 390 U.S. 629 (1968), 235, 238

Gitlow v. New York, 268 U.S. 652 (1925), 213

Glik v. Cunniff, 655 F.3d 78 (1 st Cir. 2011), 185, 193

Global Relief Foundation v. The New York Times Co., 2003 WL 403135 (N.D. Ill. 2003), 54

Global Royalties Ltd. v. Xcentric Ventures, LLC, 544 F. Supp. 2d 929 (D. Ariz. 2008), 289

Globe Newspaper Co. v. Superior Court, 457 U.S. 596 (1982), 170

Golan v. Holder, 132 S.Ct. 873 (2012), 99

Goldman v. Breitbart News Networks, LLC, No. 17-CV-3144 (KBF) (S.D.N.Y. Feb. 15, 2018), 109

Goldwater v. Ginzburg, 414 F. 2d 324 (2d Cir. 1969), 45, 312

Gonzaga Univ. v. Doe, 536 U.S. 273 (2002), 180

Grand Upright Music v. Warner Bros., 780 F. Supp. 182 (S.D.N.Y. 1991), 145

Granger v. Time, Inc., 568 P.2d 535 (Mont. 1977), 39

Greater New Orleans Bct. Assoc., Inc. v. U.S., 527 U.S. 173 (1999), 255

Green v. Chicago Tribune Co., 675 N.E.2d 249 (Ill. App. 1996), 73

Green v. Cosby, 138 F. Supp. 3d 114 (D. Mass. 2015), 38

Greenbelt Cooperative Publishing Assn., Inc. v. Bresler, 398 U.S. 6 (1970), 33

Greenstein v. The Greif Co., 2009 WL 117368 (Los Angeles Sup. Ct. 2009), 89

Griswold v. Connecticut, 381 U.S. 479 (1965), 65

Grove Fresh Dist., Inc. v. Everfresh Juice Co., 24 F.3d 893 (7th Cir. 1994), 172

Guccione v. Hustler Magazine, 800 F.2d 298 (2d Cir. 1986), 51

Gutter v. Dow Jones, Inc., 490 N.E.2d 898 (Ohio 1986), 152

H

HarperCollins Publishers LLC v. Gawker Media LLC, Case No. 10 CIV 8782 (S.D.N.Y. Nov. 20, 2010), 105

Harper & Row Pub. v. Nation Enter., 471 U.S. 539 (1985), 104-105

Harte Hanks v. Connaughton, 491 U.S. 657 (1989), 44

Hassell v. Bird, 247 Cal. App. 4th 1336 (Cal. 2018), 290

Havalunch v. Mazza, 294 S.E.2d 70 (W. Va. 1981), 34

Hawkins v. Multimedia Inc., 344 S.E.2d 145 (S.C. 1986), 69

Hazelwood School Dist. v. Kuhlmeier, 484 U.S. 260 (1988), 275, 276

Heath v. Playboy Enter. Inc., 732 F. Supp. 1145 (S.D. Fla. 1990), 68

Heffron v. Int'l Soc. Of Krishna Consciousness (ISKON), 452 U.S. 640 (1981), 5, 19, 216

Henley v. DeVore, 733 F. Supp. 2d 1144 (C.D. Cal. 2010), 146

Highfields Capital Management, L.P. v. Doe, 385 F. Supp. 2d 969 (N.D. Cal. 2005), 292

Hill v. Colorado, 530 U.S. 703 (2000), 218

Hill v. Cosby, 665 F. App'x 169 (3d Cir. 2016), 38

Hirsch v. SC Johnson & Son, Inc., 280 N.W.2d 129 (Wisc. 1979), 82

Hoffman v. Capital Cities/ABC, 255 F.3d 1180 (9th Cir. 2001), 87

Holder v. Humanitarian Law Project, 130 S. Ct. 2705 (2010), 214, 224

Hosty v. Carter, 412 F.3d 731 (7th Cir 2005), 276

Houchins v. KQED, 438 U.S. 1 (1978), 184

Housing Opportunities Made Equal v. Cincinnatti Enquirer, 943 F.2d 644 (6th Cir. 1991), 257

Hudgens v. NLRB, 424 U.S. 507 (1976), 215

Huskey v. National Broadcasting Co., 632 F. Supp. 1282 (N.D. Ill. 1986), 68

Hustler v. Falwell, 485 U.S. 46 (1988), 32, 58

Hutchinson v. Proxmire, 443 U.S. 111 (1979), 47

Hutira v. Islamic Republic of Iran, 211 F. Supp. 2d 115 (D. D.C. 2002), 204

Hy Cite Corp. v. badbusinessbureau.com, 418 F. Supp. 2d 1142 (D. Ariz. 2005), 289

I

Iacobucci v. Boulter, 193 F.3d 14 (1st Cir. 1999), 184

Independent Newspapers v. Brodie, 966 A.2d 432 (Md. 2009), 291

In re Geller, No. 2013–1412 (Fed. Cir. 2014), 116

In re Grand Jury Subpoenas, 438 F. Supp. 2d 1111 (N.D. Cal. 2006), 207

In re L.F., 2015 WL 3500616 (Cal. Ct. App. 2015), 241

In re Miller, 397 F.3d 964 (D.C. Cir 2005), 207, 208

In re Subpoena Duces Tecum to AOL, Inc., 2000 WL 1210372 (2000), *rev'd on other grounds, AOL, Inc. v. Anonymous Publicly Traded Co.*, 542 S.E.2d 377 (Va. 2001), 291

International News Service v. Associated Press, 248 U.S. 215 (1918), 111

Iota XI Chapter of Sigma Chi Fraternity v. George Mason University, 993 F.2d 386 (4th Cir. 1993), 231

Italian Book Corp. v. ABC, 458 F. Supp. 65 (S.D.N.Y. 1978), 106, 134, 145

Ivey v. Alabama, 821 So.2d 937 (Ala. 2001), 59

J

James v. Meow Media, 300 F.3d 683 (6th Cir. 2002), 151
   Janklow v. Newsweek, 788 F.2d 1300 (8th Cir. 1986), 29
Jenkins v. Georgia, 418 U.S. 153 (1974), 235
Jessup-Morgan v. AOL, 20 F. Supp. 2d 1105 (E.D. Mich. 1998), 284
Johnson v. Harcourt Brace Jovanovich, 118 Cal. Rptr. 370 (Cal. App. 1974), 70
Joplin Enterprises v. Allen, 795 F. Supp. 349 (W.D. Wash. 1992), 86
Jordache Enters. v. Hogg Wyld, Ltd., 828 F.2d 1482 (10th Cir.1987), 118
Jordan v. Jewell Food Stores, Inc., 743 F.3d 509 (7th Cir. 2014), 84
J.S. v. Bethlehem Area School Dist., 807 A.2d 847 (Pa. 2002), 275

K

Kaelin v. Globe Comm. Corp., 162 F.3d 1036 (9th Cir. 1998), 29
Karantsalis v. U.S. Dept. of Justice, 635 F.3d 497 (11th Cir. 2011), 165
Kearney v. Salomon Smith Barney, Inc., 39 Cal. 4th 95 (2006), 191
Keller v. Elec. Arts, Inc., 724 F.3d 1268 (9th Cir. 2013), 87
Kennedy for President v. FCC, 636 F.2d 432 (D.C. Cir. 1980), 267
Kinsey v. State, No. 11-12-00102-CR, 2014 WL 2459690 (Tex. App. May 22, 2014), 241
Kissinger v. Reporters Committee for Freedom of the Press, 445 U.S. 136 (1980), 160
Knievel v. ESPN, 393 F.3d 1068 (9th Cir. 2005), 32
Knight First Amendment Inst. at Columbia Univ. v. Trump, No. 1:17-cv-05205 (S.D.N.Y. 2018), 183
KOVR-TV, Inc. v. Superior Court of Sacramento County, 37 Cal. Rptr. 2d 431 (Cal. App. 1995), 199, 312
Ku Klux Klan v. Curators of Univ. of Missouri, 203 F.3d 1085 (8th Cir. 2000), *cert. denied,* 121 S. Ct. 49 (2000), 271

L

Lamb v. IRS, 871 F. Supp. 301 (E.D. Mich. 1994), 161
Lamb v. Rizzo, 391 F.3d 1133 (10th Cir. 2004), 51
Lamparello v. Falwell, 420 F.3d 309 (4th Cir. 2005), 121
Lane v. Franks, 134 S. Ct. 2369 (2014), 278
LANS v. KCAL, 108 F.3d 1119 (9th Cir. 1997), 106, 134
Lawrence v. Texas, 539 U.S. 558 (2003), 65
Layshock v. Hermitage School Dist, 593 F.3d 249 (3rd Cir. 2010), 276
Lee v. DOJ, 401 F. Supp. 2d 123 (D.D.C. 2005), 207
Leigh v. Salazar, 677 F.3d 892 (9th Cir. 2012), 181
Lennon v. Premise Media, 556 F. Supp. 2d 310 (S.D.N.Y. 2008), 145
Lenz v. Universal Music Corp., 801 F.3d 1126 (9th Cir. 2015), 107, 145

Letter Carriers v. Austin, 418 U.S. 264 (1974), 33
Leveyfilm Inc. v. Fox Sports Interactive Media LLC, 2014 WL 3368893 (N.D. Ill. 2014), 133
Levin v. McPhee, 119 F.3d 189 (2d Cir. 1997), 32
Lewis v. City of New Orleans, 415 U.S. 130 (1974), 220
Lieberman v. KCOP, 1 Cal. Rptr. 3d 536 (Cal. App. 2003), 194
Lins v. Evening News Ass'n, 342 N.W.2d 573 (Mich. App. 1983), 39
Little Rock Newspapers, Inc. v. Fitzhugh, 954 S.W.2d 914 (Ark. 1997), 40, 126
Live Nation Motor Sports Inc. v. Davis, 2007 U.S. Dist. Lexis 2196 (N.D. Tex. 2007), 108
Lorillard Tobacco Co. v. Reilly, 533 U.S. 525 (2001), 254
Los Angeles Free Press v. City of Los Angeles, 9 Cal.3d 448 (Cal. 1970), 182
Los Angeles Times v. Free Republic, 2000 U.S. Dist. LEXIS 5669 (C.D. Cal. 2000), 104
LSC v. Velasquez, 531 U.S. 533 (2001), 279

M

Madison v. Frazier, 539 F.3d 646 (7th Cir. 2008), 34
Madsen v. Women's Health Center, 512 U.S. 753 (1994), 19, 217
Mahoney v. Doe, 642 F.3d 1112 (D.C. Cir. 2011), 217
Mainstream Marketing Services, Inc. v. FTC, 358 F.3d 1228 (10th Cir. 2004), 255
Major League Baseball Advanced Media v. C.B.C. Distribution and Marketing, Inc., 505 F.3d 818 (8th Cir. 2007), 86
Martin v. Municipal Pub., 510 F. Supp. 255 (E.D. Pa. 1981), 33
Martin v. Parrish, 805 F.2d 583 (5th Cir. 1986), 231
Martin Luther King Jr. Center For Social Change v. American Heritage Products, 296 S.E.2d 697 (Ga. 1982), 85
Massachusetts v. Angiulo, 615 N.E.2d 155 (Mass. 1993), 178
Massachusetts v. HHS, 727 F. Supp. 35 (D. Mass. 1989), 161
Masson v. New Yorker Magazine, Inc., 501 U.S. 496 (1991), 6, 9, 30
Matal v. Tam, 137 S. Ct. 1744 (2017), 116
Mattel, Inc. v. Walking Mountain Productions, 353 F.3d 792 (9th Cir. 2003), 120
Mayhew v. Dunn, No. 580-11-07 Wmcv, Windham (VT) Superior Court (Howard, J., March 18, 2008), 10, 289
MCA, Inc. v. Wilson, 677 F.2d 180 (2d Cir. 1981), 104
McBurney v. Young, 569 U.S. 221 (2013), 169
McCabe v. Village Voice, Inc., 550 F. Supp. 525 (E.D. Pa. 1982), 76, 128
McCall v. Courier-Journal, 623 S.W.2d 882 (Ky. 1981), 43
   McCollum v. CBS Records, 249 Cal. Rptr. 187 (Cal. App. 1988), 151
McConnell v. FEC, 540 U.S. 93 (2003), 246
McCullen v. Coakley, 134 S.Ct. 2518 (2014), 218
McCutcheon v. FEC, 134 S.Ct. 1434 (2014), 246
McIntyre v. Ohio Elections Comm'n, 514 U.S. 334 (1995), 247

McKee v. Cosby, 874 F.3d 54 (1st Cir. 2017), 38

McKevitt v. Pallasch, 339 F.3d 530 (7th Cir. 2003), 207

McMann v. Doe, 460 F. Supp. 2d 259 (D. Mass. 2006), 292

McNamara v. Freedom Newspapers, 802 S.W.2d 901 (Tex. App. 1991), 10, 70, 127

MCW, Inc. v. badbusinessbureau.com, 2004 WL 833595 (N.D. Tx. 2004), 289

Melius v. Keiffer, 980 So. 2d 167 (La. Ct. App. 2008), 56

Memphis Publishing Co. v. Nichols, 569 S.W.2d 412 (Tenn. 1978), 28

M.G. v. Time Warner, 89 Cal. App. 4th 623 (Cal. App. 2001), 72, 127, 128

MGM Studios v. Grokster, 545 U.S. 913 (2005), 98, 144

Miami Herald Pub. Co. v. Tornillo, 418 U.S. 241 (1974), 248 *Michaels v. Internet Entertainment Group, Inc.,* 5 F. Supp. 2d 823 (C.D. Cal. 1998), 71, 77

Midler v. Ford Motor Co., 849 F. 2d 460 (9th Cir. 1988), 82

Milkovich v. Lorain Journal, 497 U.S. 1 (1990), 35, 37, 38

Miller v. California, 413 U.S. 15 (1973), 19, 21, 233, 235, 236, 243

Miller v. Motorola, Inc., 560 N.E.2d 900 (Ill. App. 1990), 69

Miller v. NBC, 187 Cal. App. 3d 1463 (Cal. App. 1986), 188

Milner v. Department of Navy, 131 S.Ct. 1259 (2011), 162 *Mishkin v. New York,* 383 U.S. 502 (1966), 234

Mitchell v. Baltimore Sun Co., 883 A.2d 1008 (Md. App. 2005), 188

Moldea v. New York Times, 22 F.3d 310 (D.C. Cir. 1994), 34

Monge v. Maya Magazines, Inc., 688 F.3d 1164 (9th Cir. 2012), 106

Montana v. San Jose Mercury News, Inc., 40 Cal. Rptr.2d 639 (Cal. App. 1995), 87

Morse v. Frederick, 127 S. Ct. 2618 (2007), 275

Mortgage Specialists v. Implode Explode Heavy Industries, 2010 WL 1791274 (N.H. 2010), 292

Moseley v. V Secret Catalogue, Inc., 537 U.S. 418 (2003), 119

Motschenbacher v. R.J.Reynolds Tobacco, 498 F.2d 821 (9th Cir. 1974), 82

Mr. X v. Google, Inc., et al., Tribunal de Grande Instance de Paris 17eme chamber Jugement du 8 septembre 2010., 294

Multimedia WMAZ, Inc. v. Kubach, 443 S.E.2d 491 (Ga. App. 1994), 68

Municipality of Anchorage v. Anchorage Daily News, 794 P.2d 584 (Alaska 1990), 71

Murphy v. Millennium Radio Group, LLC, 650 F.3d 295 (3 rd Cir. 2011), 106, 133

N

Namath v. Sports Illustrated, 371 N.Y.S. 2d 10 (1975), 89

NARA v. Favish, 124 S. Ct. 1570 (2004), 160, 163

NBA v. Motorola, Inc., 105 F.3d 841 (2d Cir. 1997), 111

NEA v. Finley, 524 U.S. 569 (1998), 279

Near v. Minnesota, 283 U.S. 697 (1931), 223, 224

Nebraska Press Assoc. v. Stuart, 427 U.S. 539 (1976), 175

Nehls v. Hillsdale Coll., 178 F. Supp. 2d 771 (E.D. Mich. 2001), 47

New Kids on the Block v. News America Pub., Inc., 745 F. Supp. 1540 (C.D. Cal. 1990), *aff'd* 971 F.2d 302 (9th Cir. 1992), 118

New Times, Inc. v. Isaaks, 146 S.W.3d 144 (Tex. 2004), 33

New York v. Ferber, 458 U.S. 747 (1982), 236

New York Magazine, Inc. v. MTA, 987 F. Supp. 254 (S.D.N.Y. 1997), 84

New York Times Co. v. NASA, 920 F.2d 1002 (D.C. Cir. 1990), 163

New York Times Co. v. Sullivan, 376 U.S. 254 (1964), 10, 31, 41, 249, 250, 253

New York Times Co. v. Tasini, 533 U.S. 483 (2001), 101

New York Times Co. v. U.S., 403 U.S. 713 (1971), 223, 224

Nichols v. U.S., 325 F. Supp. 130 (D. Kan. 1971), 160

Nieves v. HBO, 2006 WL 516797 (N.Y. Sup. Ct. 2006), 89

Nixon v. Warner Comm., 435 U.S. 589 (1978), 173

Nobles v. Cartwright, 659 N.E.2d 1064 (Ind. App. 1995), 73

No Doubt v. Activision Pub. Inc., 122 Cal. Rptr. 3d 397 (Cal. App. 2011), 87

Noel v. River Hills Wilsons, Inc., 7 Cal. Rptr. 3d 216 (Cal. App. 2003), 56

Noonan v. Staples, 556 F.3d 20 (1 st Cir. 2009), 31

North Jersey Media Group v. Ashcroft, 308 F.3d 198 (3 rd Cir. 2002), 171

Norton v. Glenn, 860 A.2d 48 (Pa. 2004), 54, 64

NPS, LLC v. StubHub, Inc., 25 Mass. L. Rep. 478 (Mass. Sup. Ct. 2009), 290

O

Office of Comm. Of the U.C.C. v. FCC, 359 F.2d 994 (1966), 265

O'Grady v. Superior Court, 139 Cal. App. 4th 1423 (Cal. App. 2006), 78

Oklahoma Pub. Co. v. District Court, 430 U.S. 308 (1977), 172

Olivia N. v. NBC, 126 Cal. App. 3d 488 (Cal. App. 1981), 151

Ollman v. Evans, 750 F.2d 970 (D.C. Cir. 1984), 36

Onassis v. Christian Dior-New York, Inc., 472 N.Y.S.2d 254 (NY 1984), 82

One Wisc. Now v. Kremer, No. 3:17-cv-00820 (W.D. Wisc. Jan. 18, 2019), 183

Oriana House v. Montgomery, 110 Ohio St. 3d 456 (Ohio 2006), 169

Osborne v. Ohio, 495 U.S. 103 (1990), 137, 236

P

Packingham v. N.C., 137 S. Ct. 1730 (2017), 218

Papish v. Bd. Of Curators of the Univ. of Missouri, 410 U.S. 667 (1973), 276

Parks v. LaFace Records, 329 F.3d 437 (6th Cir. 2003), 86

Paulsen v. Personality Posters, Inc., 299 NYS2d 501 (NY 1968), 85

Peavy v. WFAA-TV, 221 F.3d 158 (5th Cir. 2000), 191

Pell v. Procunier, 417 U.S. 817 (1974), 184

Perfect 10, Inc. v. Google Inc., 508 F.3d 1146 (9th Cir. 2007), 107, 109

Perry Educ. Assoc. v. Perry Local Educators' Assoc., 460 U.S. 37 (1983), 215

Phelps-Roper v. Nixon, 545 F.3d 685 (8th Cir. 2007), 217

Phelps-Roper v. Strickland, 539 F.3d 356 (6th Cir. 2008), 217

Philadelphia Newspapers, Inc. v. Hepps, 475 U.S. 767 (1986), 31

Philadelphia Newspapers, Inc. v. Nuclear Regulatory Comm'n, 727 F.2d 1195 (D.C. Cir. 1984), 167

Pickering v. Board of Ed. Of Township High School Dist. 205, Will Cty., 391 U.S. 563 (1968), 277

Planned Parenthood v. Bucci, 42 U.S.P.Q. 2d 1430 (S.D.N.Y. 1997), 120

Planned Parenthood of the Columbia/Willamette Inc. v. American Coalition of Life Activists, 290 F.3d 1058 (9th Cir. 2002), 239

Playboy Enter. Inc. v. Welles, 279 F.3d 796 (9th Cir. 2001), 118

Polygram Records v. Superior Court, 216 Cal. Rptr. 252 (Cal. App. 1985), 33

Pomykacz v. Borough of West Wildwood, 438 F. Supp. 2d 504 (D. N.J. 2006), 184

Pope v. Illinois, 481 U.S. 497 (1987), 234

Press Enterprise Co. v. Superior Court (*Press Enterprise I*), 464 U.S. 501 (1984), 170

Press Enterprise Co. v. Superior Court (*Press Enterprise II*), 478 U.S. 1 (1986), 170, 171, 172, 173, 181

Pring v. Penthouse, 695 F.2d 438 (10th Cir. 1982), 40

Pruneyard Shopping Center v. Robins, 447 U.S. 74 (1980), 215

R

Ragin v. New York Times Co., 923 F.2d 995 (2d Cir. 1991), 257

R.A.V. v. City of St. Paul, 505 U.S. 377 (1992), 230

Red Lion Bct. Co. v. FCC, 395 U.S. 367 (1969), 247, 248, 266

Reed Elsevier, Inc. v. Muchnick, 130 S. Ct. 1237 (2010), 96

Regan v. Time, Inc., 468 U.S. 641 (1984), 137

Reid v. U.S. News & World Report, No. 6828–82 (D.C. Superior Ct. 1983), 125

Reno v. ACLU, 521 U.S. 844 (1997), 234

Rezec v. Sony Pictures, 116 Cal. App. 4th 135 (2004), 255

Rice v. Paladin Enter. Inc., 128 F.3d 233 (4th Cir. 1997), 151

Richmond Newspapers v. Virginia, 448 U.S. 555 (1980), 170, 171, 172

Riley v. Harr, 292 F.3d 282 (1st Cir. 2002), 34

Roe v. Wade, 410 U.S. 113 (1973), 65

Rogers v. Grimaldi, 875 F.2d 994 (2d Cir. 1989), 85–86

Rogers v. Koons, 960 F.2d 301 (2d Cir. 1992), 9, 10, 134

Roy Export Co. Estab. Of Vaduz v. CBS, 672 F.2d 1095 (2d Cir. 1982), 106, 133

Rumsfeld v. FAIR, 547 U.S. 47 (2006), 279

Russell v. Marboro Books, Inc., 183 N.Y.S.2d 8 (Sup. Ct. 1959), 124

Rust v. Sullivan, 500 U.S. 173 (1991), 278, 280

S

Saenz v. Playboy Enterprises, Inc., 841 F.2d 1309 (7th Cir. 1988), 44

Saieg v. City of Dearborn, 641 F.3d 727 (6th Cir. 2011), 217

Sakon v. Pepsi, 553 So.2d 163 (Fla. 1989), 151

Salinger v. Colting, 607 F.3d 68 (2d Cir. 2010), 105

Sandals Resorts Int'l Ltd., v. Google, Inc., 2011 NY Slip Op 4179 (Sup. Ct. NY App. Div. May 19, 2011), 6

Sanders v. ABC, 20 Cal. 4th 907 (Cal. 1999), 194

Sandvig v. Sessions, 315 F. Supp. 3d 1 (D.D.C. 2018), 197

San Diego v. Roe, 543 U.S. 77 (2004), 278

San Francisco Arts & Athletics, Inc. v. U.S. Olympic Committee, 483 U.S. 522 (1987), 115

San Francisco Bay Guardian v. Superior Court, 17 Cal. App. 4th 655 (Cal. App. 1993), 33

Sargent v. New York Daily News, L.P., 840 N.Y.S.2d 101 (2007), 260

Sarver v. Chartier, 813 F.3d 891 (9th Cir. 2016), 86

Saxbe v. Washington Post, 417 U.S. 843 (1974), 184

Schenck v. U.S., 249 U.S. 47 (1919), 213

Schiavone Construction Co. v. Time, Inc., 847 F.2d 1069 (3 rd Cir. 1988), 45

Schneider v. Amazon.com, Inc., 31 P.3d 37 (Wash. Ct. App. 2001), 288

Seattle Times. v. Rhinehart, 467 U.S. 20 (1984), 174

Sedgwick Claims Mgmt Serv. v. Delsman, 2009 WL 2157573(N.D. Cal. 2009), 134

Seelig vs. Infinity Broadcasting, 119 Cal. Rptr. 2d 108 (Cal. App. 2002), 34, 35

Sheppard v. Maxwell, 384 U.S. 333 (1966), 174, 176

Sherrill v. Knight, 569 F.2d 124 (D.C. Cir. 1977), 182, 183

Shoen v. Shoen, 48 F.3d 412 (9th Cir. 1995), 206

Shulman v.Group W. Productions, 955 P.2d 469 (Cal. 1998), 10, 71, 192

Sidis v. F-R Publishing Corp., 113 F.2d 806 (2d Cir. 1940), 71

Silkwood v. Kerr-McGee, 563 F.2d 433 (10th Cir. 1977), 206

Sindi v. El-Moslimany, 896 F.3d 1 (1st Cir. 2018), 63

Sipple v. Chronicle Publishing Co., 201 Cal. Rptr. 665 (Cal. App. 1984), 68, 72

Skilling v. U.S., 130 S.Ct. 2896 (2010), 175

Smith v. Cumming, 212 F.3d 1332 (11th Cir. 2000), 184

Smith v. Daily Mail Pub. Co., 443 U.S. 97 (1979), 172

Smith v. Linn, 563 A.2d 123 (Pa. Super. 1989), 153

Snyder v. Phelps, 131 S. Ct. 1207 (2011), 58, 233

Snyder v. Ringgold, 40 F. Supp. 2d 714 (D. Md. 1999), 182

Solano v. Playgirl, Inc., 292 F.3d 1078 (9th Cir. 2002), 58

Solers, Inc. v. Doe, No. 07-CV-159 (D.C. Cir. 2009), 291

Sony Corp. of America v. Universal City Studios, 464 U.S. 417 (1984), 98

Spears v. US Weekly LLC, Case No. SC087989 Superior Court of California (Los Angeles County Nov. 3, 2006), 27

Specht v. Netscape Communications Corp., 306 F.3d 17 (2d Cir. 2002), 284

Spence v. Washington, 418 U.S. 405 (1974), 220

St. Amant v. Thompson, 390 U.S. 727 (1968), 44

Stanley v. Georgia, 394 U.S. 557 (1969), 235

Stanton v. Metro Corp., 438 F.3d 119 (1st Cir. 2006), 126

Starkey v. U.S. Dept. of the Interior, 238 F. Supp. 2d 1188 (S.D. Cal. 2002), 165

State v. Christensen, 102 P.3d 789 (Wash. 2004), 190

State v. Van Buren, 2018 VT 95, No. 2016–253 (VT 2018), 236

Stern v. Cosby, 645 F. Supp. 2d 258 (S.D.N.Y. 2009), 27

Stewart v. Rolling Stone LLC, 181 Cal. App. 4th 664 (Cal. App. 2010), 87

Susan B. Anthony List v. Ohio Elec. Comm'n, 45 F. Supp. 3d 765 (S.D. Ohio 2014), 249

T

Talley v. California, 362 U.S. 60 (1960), 247

Tambrands, Inc. v. Warner-Lambert Co., 673 F. Supp. 1190 (S.D.N.Y. 1987), 256

Tavoulareas v. Washington Post, 567 F. Supp. 651 (D.D.C. 1983), 31, 64

Texas v. Johnson, 491 U.S. 397 (1989), 18, 221

The Baltimore Sun Co. v. Ehrlich, 437 F.3d 410 (4th Cir. 2006), 182

Ticketmaster Corp. v. Tickets.com, Inc., 2003 U.S.Dist. LEXIS 6483 (C.D. Cal. 2003), 284

Time Inc. v. Petersen Pub. Co., 173 F.3d 113 (2d Cir. 1999), 118

Tinker v. Des Moines Indp. Community School Dist., 393 U.S. 503 (1969), 274, 275

Tipton v. Warshavsky, 32 Fed. App'x. 293 (9th Cir. 2002), 47

Toffoloni v. LFP Publishing Group, LLC (d.b.a.Hustler Magazine), 572 F.3d 1201 (11th Cir. 2009), 77, 87

Too Much Media LLC v. Hale, No. MONL-002736-08 (N.J. Super. 2009), 292

Tory v. Cochran, 544 U.S. 734 (2005), 63

Toyota Motor Sales U.S.A., Inc. v. Tabari, 610 F.3d 1171 (9th Cir. 2010), 119

Turner v. Driver, 848 F.3d 678 (5th Cir. 2017), 185

Turner Broadcasting Sys. v. FCC, 520 U.S. 180 (1997), 265

U

U.S. v. Alvarez, 132 S. Ct. 2537 (2012), 18, 241, 249, 250

U.S. v. American Library Assoc., 539 U.S. 194 (2003), 234, 279

U.S. v. Barnes, 604 F.2d 121 (2d Cir. 1979), 178

U.S. v. Brown, 218 F.3d 415 (5th Cir. 2000), 175

U.S. v. Chin, No. 17–2048 (1st Cir. 2019), 178

U.S. v. Cuthbertson, 630 F.2d 139 (3d Cir. 1980), 206

U.S. v. Dinwiddie, 76 F.3d 913 (8th Cir. 1996), 239

U.S. v. Edge Broadcasting Co., 509 U.S. 418 (1993), 255

U.S. v. Eichman, 496 U.S. 310 (1990), 221

U.S. v. LaRouche Campaign, 841 F.2d 1176 (1st Cir. 1988), 204

U.S. v. Matthews, 209 F.3d 338 (4th Cir. 2000), 137, 198, 236

U.S. v. Morison, 604 F. Supp. 655 (D. Md. 1985), 137, 225

U.S. v. Noriega, 746 F. Supp. 1506 (S.D. Fla. 1990), 175

U.S. v. O'Brien, 391 U.S. 367 (1968), 17, 220, 221

U.S. v. Playboy Entertainment Group, 529 U.S.803 (2000), 265

U.S. v. Sterling, 724 F.3d 482 (4th Cir. July 19, 2013), 207

U.S. v. Stevens, 559 U.S. 460 (2010), 238

U.S. v. The Progressive, 467 F. Supp. 990 (W.D. Wisc. 1979), 224

U.S. Dept. of Justice v. Reporters Committee for Freedom of the Press, 489 U.S. 749 (1989), 164

U.S. Telecom Ass'n v. FCC, 825 F.3d 674 (D.C. Cir. 2016), 272

UWM Post v. Bd. of Regents of the Univ. of Wisc., 774 F. Supp 1163 (E.D. Wisc. 1991), 229

V

Valentine v. Chrestensen, 316 U.S. 52 (1942), 253

Veilleux v. NBC, Inc., 206 F.3d 92 (1 st Cir. 2000), 72

Vera v. O'Keefe, 791 F. Supp. 2d 959 (S.D. Cal. 2011), 192

Video-Cinema Films, Inc. v. CNN, 31 Media L. Rep.1634 (S.D.N.Y. 2003), 106

Video-Cinema Films, Inc. v. Lloyd E. Rigler-Lawrence E. Deutsch Found., 2005 U.S. Dist. LEXIS 26302 (S.D.N.Y. 2005), 134

Vinci v. American Can Co., 591 N.E.2d 793 (Ohio App. 1990), 86

Virgil v. Time, Inc., 527 F.2d 1122 (9th Cir. 1975), 69, 73, 76

Virginia v. Black, 538 U.S. 343 (2003), 230

Virginia Bd. of Pharmacy v. Virginia Citizens Consumer Council, 425 U.S. 748 (1976), 253

W

Waits v. Frito-Lay, Inc., 978 F.2d 1093 (9th Cir. 1992), 82

Walker v. Kiousos, 93 Cal.App. 4th 1432 (2001), 27

Waller v. Georgia, 467 U.S. 39 (1984), 170

Walt Disney Prods. v. Air Pirates, 581 F.2d 751 (9th Cir.1978), 104

Walters v. Seventeen Magazine, 241 Cal. Rptr. 101 (Cal. App. 1987), 153, 257

Watts v. United States, 394 U.S. 705 (1969), 239

Weirum v. RKO General, Inc., 539 P.2d 36 (Cal 1975), 151

Wendt v. Host Int'l., 125 F.3d 806 (9th Cir. 1997), 83

Westinghouse Broadcasting Co. v. Dukakis, 409 F. Supp. 895 (D. Mass. 1976), 182

White v. Samsung Elec. Am. Inc., 971 F.2d 1395 (9th Cir. 1992), 82, 83

Whiteland Woods, LLP v. Township of West Whiteland, 193 F.3d 177 (3rd Cir. 1999), 184

Whitney v. California, 274 U.S. 357 (1927), 213, 214, 229

Wilson v. Layne, 526 U.S. 603 (1999), 188

Winstead v. Sweeney, 205 Mich. App. 664 (1994), 74

Winter v. DC Comics, 69 P.3d 473 (Cal. 2003), 86

Winter v. GP Putnam's Sons, 938 F.2d 1033 (9th Cir. 1991), 152

Wisconsin v. Mitchell, 508 U.S. 476 (1993), 230

Woodhull v. Meinel, 202 P.3d 126 (N.M. App. 2008), 289

World Pub. Co. v. U.S. Dept. of Justice, 672 F.3d 825 (10th Cir. 2012), 165

X

X17, Inc. v. Lavanderia, 563 F. Supp. 2d 1102 (C.D. Cal. 2007), 111

Y

Yahoo! Inc. v. La Ligue Contre Le Racisme et l'antisemitisme, 433 F.3d 1199 (9th Cir. 2006), 299

Yanase v. Auto Club, 260 Cal. Rptr. 513 (Cal. App. 1989), 152

Yates v. U.S., 354 U.S. 298 (1957), 213, 214

Yeager v. DEA, 678 F.2d 315 (D.C. Cir. 1982), 161

Yeagle v. Collegiate Times, 497 S.E.2d 136 (Va. 1998), 32

Young v. New Haven Advocate, 318 F.3d 256 4th Cir. 2002), 297

Youngstown Publishing Co. v. McKelvey, 2005 U.S. Dist. LEXIS 9476 (N.D. Ohio 2005), 182

Z

Zacchini v. Scripps-Howard Bct. Co., 433 U.S. 562 (1977), 88, 89

Zeran v. AOL, 958 F. Supp. 1124 (E.D. Va. 1997), 288

Zerilli v. Smith, 656 F.2d 705 (D.C. Cir. 1981), 206

Zurcher v. Stanford Daily, 436 U.S. 547 (1978), 210

Subject Index

#

2 Milly, 95
911 calls, access to recordings of, 168

A

Abortion protesters, 217–218, 239
Absolute privilege for statements by officials, 52
Access Device Fraud, 196
Access, right of, 157–186, general rules 158, right to use photo/video 184–185, to Congress 167, to educational records 180, to federal agency meetings 166–167, to federal agency records 159–166, to government social media accounts 183–184, to healthcare records 181, to judicial proceedings or records 169–179, to motor vehicle records 180–181, to news scenes 181–182, to press conferences 182–183, to prisons 184, to private materials 158–159, to state records 168–169
ACLA. See American Coalition of Life Activists (ACLA)
ACORN, 192
Acosta, Jim, 183
ACPA. See Anticybersquatting Consumer Protection Act (ACPA), 120
Actual damages, 47–48, 109
Actual malice, 41–47, 48, 59–60, 63, 249–250
Actus reus, 230
Administrative Procedures Act, 163
Advertisements, with respect to publicity cases 83–85, with respect to government regulation 252–259, children's advertising 267–268, endorsements and influencers 256, false or misleading statements 255–256, FCC regulation of advertising 267–268, liability for discriminatory housing advertisement 257, liability for false advertising 257, native advertising 259, refusal of ads 258
Aeropagitica, 14–15
Aesthetic judgments, 34
Ag Gag Laws, 195–196
Agency memoranda, 163
Agency photos, 131–132
AIPAC. See American Israel Public Affairs Committee (AIPAC)
Alito, Samuel, 59
Alternative license, 101–102
American Coalition of Life Activists (ACLA), 239
American Israel Public Affairs Committee (AIPAC), 225
Animal cruelty, portrayal of, 238
Anonymity, of sources 203–211, online 291–293, political materials 247
Anonymous juries, 177–178
Anthony, Casey, 198
Anticybersquatting Consumer Protection Act (ACPA), 120–121
Anti-SLAPP statutes, 56–57
Appeals, 4–5
Appropriation of likeness, 81–83 cartoons, 82 catchphrases, 82 look-alikes, 82 nicknames, 82 sound-alikes, 82
Arbitrary or discriminatory manner, 18, 19, 21
As applied, 18–19
ASCAP, 141, 146

Attorney-client privilege, 203–204
Attribution (BY) tag, 101
Authority, see Precedent
Authors Guild, 107
Autopsy records, access to, 168

B

Backpack Kid, 95
Banking reports, exception to FOIA, 165
Bardot, Brigitte, 295
Benoit, Chris, 87
Benoit, Nancy, 87
Beyond a reasonable doubt, as a standard of proof, 6
Bill of Rights, 13, 15
Bird, Ava, 290
Bipartisan Campaign Reform Act, 245–246
Blackstone, William, 15
Blanch, Andrea, 134
BLM. See Bureau of Land Management (BLM)
BMI, 141, 146
Body camera footage, access to, 168
Bollea, Terry, 76
Bonds, Barry, 207
Bonome, Joseph, 74
Brady, Tom, 81
Brandeis, Louis (Justice), 66, 213
Breyer, Stephen (Justice), 59
Brinkley, Christie, 85
Broadcast indecency 234, 264, 266
Brutsch, Michael, 293
Burden of proof, 6, 31, 150, 206, 224
Bureau of Land Management (BLM), 181
Bureau of Prisons, 184
Burnett, Carol, 27
Bush, George H. W., 40, 48
Bush, George W., 34–35, 48–49
Business consequences, 306

C

Call-out for a contest, 259–261
Cameras and other technology in courtrooms, 176–177
Campaign finance laws, constitutionality of, 243–247
Candidate Access Rule, 267
Carry one, carry all, 265
Carson, Johnny, 82
Carter-Mondale campaign, 267
CARU. See Children's Advertising Review Unit (CARU)
Cases, types of 6–7 civil, 6–7 criminal, 6–7
Caulfield, Holden, 105
CDA. See Communications Decency Act
Censorship, ethics vs. self-, 315 foreign, 294–297
     government, 279 private, 14, 21, 232, 307–308, by
     schools, 274–277
Cerasani, John, 51
Chaplin, Charlie, 106, 133

Chen, Adrian, 293
Cher, 88
Child Online Protection Act (COPA), 234
Child pornography, 137, 210, 236, 243, 312
Child Pornography Prevention Act, 137
Children's Advertising Review Unit (CARU), 268
Children's Internet Protection Act, 225 (CIPA), 279
Children's Online Privacy Protection Act (COPPA), 66,
     260, 287–288
Children's programming, 267–268
Children's Television Act, 267
CIPA. See Children's Internet Protection Act (CIPA)
Circuit court, 4–5. See also Court of Appeals
Citation systems, 7–10 cases, 8–10 constitutions, 8
     executive orders, 8 regulations, 8 statutes, 8
Civil cases, 6–7, burden of proof, 6, media law, 7 parties, 6
     remedies, 6 rules of procedure, 6, subject matter, 6
Clarifications, 61–62
Classics Act, 142
Classified information, as a FOIA exemption, 162
     publication or possession of, 223–227, attempts to stop
     publication, 223–224
Clinton, Bill (President), 137
Cochran, Johnnie, 63
Code of Federal Regulations (CFR), 8
Colting, Fredrik, 105
Commercial Advertisement Loudness Mitigation (CALM)
     Act, 268
Commercial purpose, 83–88
Commercial speech, regulation of, 253–257
Common interest privilege, 56
Communications Act, 263, 265
Communications Decency Act (CDA), 41, 50, 108, 153,
     288
Computer Fraud and Abuse Act, 196, 197, 219, 302
Condit, Carolyn, 52
Condit, Gary, 53
Confidential business information, as a FOIA exemption
     162–163
Confidentiality promises, 199
Consent, 52, 69, 75–76, 79, 126, 128, 132
Consumer & Government Affairs Bureau, 264
Contempt power of judges, 179
Content-based regulations 19, 222, 247
Content-neutral regulation, 19, 216–218, 265
Contests, 259–261
Contributory infringement, 98
Cooper, Matthew, 208
COPA. See Child Online Protection Act (COPA)
COPPA. See Children's Online Privacy Protection Act
     (COPPA)
Copycat cases, 150–151
Copyright 91–112, in music 139–148, in photos 131–136
     alternative license 101–102, Attribution (BY), 96, GNU
     free documentation license, 102, no derivative works
     (ND), 102 non-commercial (NC), 102 share-alike (SA),
     101 copyrightability, 93–95, of facts, 94, of federal

government work, 94–95 of ideas, 94, of names and short phrases, 94, of state works, 95 consequences of infringement, 109–110 contributory infringment, 98 Creative Commons, 101–102, 132, 302 credit, 110–111 damages, 109–110 defenses, 108 derivative works, 97 display of work, 97–98 effect of use upon the market, 103 elements of a claim, 92, 99 embedding, 108–109 fair use, 102–108 first sale doctrine, 97, 142 fixed, as a requirement for copyright 93–94 hot news doctrine, 111 how to obtain, 96–97 incidental uses, 106 linking, 108–109 joint copyright, 96 justification for, 92 license terms, 98, 100–101 moral rights, 110 nature of the original copyrighted work, 102 notice, 96 original, as a requirement for copyright 93 ownership, 96–97 parodies, 104 plagiarism, 110 portion used, 102–103 public display, 97–98 public domain, 98–99 public performance, 97 purpose and character of the use, 102 registration, 96 rights granted by copyright, 97–98 server test, 109 term limits, 98 and trademark, 92 work for hire, 96

Copyright Act, 92, 98, 107–109
Copyright Royalty Board, 142
Copyright Term Extension Act, 98
Corporation for Public Broadcasting (CPB), 270
Corrections, 61–62
Cosby, Bill (actor/comedian), 38
Cosby, William (Governor), 15
Court of Appeals, 4–5
Court systems, 3–6
CPB. See Corporation for Public Broadcasting (CPB)
Creative Commons, 101–102, 132, 302
Criminal cases, 6–7 burden of proof, 6 media law, 7 parties, 6 rules of procedure 6
Criminal libel, 59–60
Cultural values, protection of, 296
Currency, use of images, 137
Cyberbullying or Cyberharrassment, 299–300
Cybersquatting, 120–121
Cyberstalking, 299–300

D

Dangerous ideas, 212–214
Data privacy regulations, 285–288
Death threats, 306–307
Dees, Bill, 140
Defamatory statements, 27–30 changing norms, 27 defamation by omission, 28–29 definition, 26–27 non-obvious, 28 obvious, 28
Defenses, copyright, 108 libel 51–57, privacy, 75–76
Denny, Reginald, 106, 134
Derivative works, 97
Descendibility, 88–89
Digital Millenium Copyright Act (DMCA), 107, 108, 142, 145, 146, 290
Digital Performance Right in Sound Recordings Act, 142
Dilution, trademark, 119–120

Dior, Christian, 82
Discovery documents, 174
District Courts, 3–4
DMCA. See Digital Millenium Copyright Act (DMCA)
DOJ Guidelines, 208
Dolan, Jimmy, 306
Do-not-call registry, 255
Do not track, 286
DPPA. See Driver's Privacy Protection Act (DPPA)
Driver's Privacy Protection Act (DPPA), 180–181
Due Process, 18, 19

E

Eastwood, Clint, 88
Eavesdropping, 189–190
Elonis, Anthony, 239–240
Emergency alert tones, 269
Emoji, 240–241
Enforcement Bureau, 264
Espionage Act, 137, 213, 242
Ethical considerations, of hidden cameras or microphones, 195 of journalism ethics, 309–315 of libel 60 of misrepresenting yourself, 189 of native advertising, 259
European Court of Human Rights, 295
European Union (EU), copyright directive, 109 privacy regulations, 285–287
Executive orders, 8

F

Facial challenge, 18–19
Factual assertion, 32–38 aesthetic judgments, 34 conclusions, 34–35 hyperbole, 33 insults, 33–34 jokes, 32 rhetoric, 33 speculation, 34
Fair Housing Act, 257, 289
Fairness doctrine, 266, 268
Fairness in Music Licensing Act, 142
Fair report privilege, 52–53, 64
Fair use, 92, 102–108 amount used, 102–103 effect on market value, 103 on music, 144–146 nature of the original work, 102 on photos, 132–134 purpose and nature of the use, 102
False advertising, 257
False light, 57–58
False statement laws 248–250
Falwell, Jerry, 32, 58, 121
Family Educational Rights and Privacy Act (FERPA), 66, 180
Fault, as an element of libel, 41–47
FCC regulations, 263–273 advertising, 268 Bureaus, 264 carry one, carry all, 265 children's programming, 267–268 complaints, 269–270 content regulation, 265–269 emergency alert tones, 269 fairness doctrine, 266, 268 indecency, 266 internet, regulation of 271–272 limited spectrum argument, 247, 264–266 must-carry rules, 265 net neutrality, 272 political elections, 267 profanity,

266 public broadcasting, 270–271 right of reply, 266 V-chip, 268

FDA. See Food and Drug Administration

Federal Circuit, 4

Federal Communications Commission(FCC) 8, 107–108, 135, 247–248, 255, 263–273 See also FCC regulation

Federal courts, 3–6 diversity jurisdiction, 5 jurisdiction of, 5 specialty courts, 4

Federal Election Campaign Act, 245–246

Federal Rules of Criminal Procedure, 174

Federal Rules of Evidence, 208

Federal Trade Commission (FTC), 8, 255–256, 268, 285–288

Federal Trademark Dilution Act, 119

Federline, Kevin, 27

FERPA. See Family Educational Rights and Privacy Act (FERPA)

Ficker, Robin, 121

Fighting words, 219–220

Filtering software, 234, 279

FIRE. See Foundation for Individual Rights in Education (FIRE)

First Amendment, generally 12–21 doctrines, 16–19 text of, 12 theories of, 15–16

Flag burning, 18, 221

Flag Protection Act, 221

FOIA. See Freedom of Information Act (FOIA)

Food and Drug Administration (FDA), 268

Ford, Gerald (President), 72, 105

Foreign censorship, 293–299

Fortnite emotes, 95

Forum-shopping, 52

Foster, Vince, 163

Foundation for Individual Rights in Education (FIRE), 277

Fraud, 17, 189, 268, 312

Freedom of press, 13–15

Freedom of Access to Clinic Entrances Act, 239–240

Freedom of Information Act (FOIA), 66, 158, 159–166, 301 agency (definition), 159 agency memoranda, 163 agency rules & practices, 162 appeals, 166 banking reports, 165 confidential business information, 162–163 constructive denial, 166 E-FOIA, 159 fees and fee waiver, 160–161 Glomar response, 166 grand jury proceedings, 172–174 how to request records, 160–161 information about wells, 165 law enforcement investigations, 164–165

Medical information, 163 mug shots, 165 national security, 162 personnel records, 163 practical obscurity, 164 records (definition), 160 reverse foia, 163 statutory exemptions, 162–165

FTC. See Federal Trade Commission (FTC)

Funeral picketing laws, 217

G

Gag orders, 175–176, 179

Gallagher, Michael, 197

Garage Band, 78

Gay Olympics, 115

GDPR. See General Data Privacy Regulation

General Data Privacy Regulation, 286–287

Geo-filtering, 299

Giuliani, Rudy, 84

Glomar response, 166

GNU Free Documentation License, 102

Goldberg, Sanford, 316

Goldman, Justin, 109

Goldwater, Barry, 45

Government employees, regulating speech of, 277–278

Government-funded speech, 278–280

Graber, Anthony, 190

H

Habib, Dan, 126

Hacktivism, 219

Hate speech, 227–233 ethics of, 312 government punishment of, 228–231 lawsuits over, 222–233 private censorship of, 232 punishable crimes, 229–231 university speech codes, 228–229

Hassell, Dawn, 290

Hatfill, Steven, 53, 207

Hauserman, Megan, 154

Health Insurance Portability and Accountability Act (HIPAA), 66, 181 Henley, Don, 146

Hidden cameras or microphones, 194–195

HIPAA. See Health Insurance Portability and Accountability Act (HIPAA)

Hitman Manual, 151

Hoaxes, FCC regulation of, 268 to fool journalists, 60–61

Hoffman, Dustin, 87

Holder, Eric (Attorney General), 208

Holmes, Katie, 29–30

Hot news doctrine, 111

Hulk Hogan. See Bollea, Terry

Hume, David, 15, 309–310

Hussein, Saddam, 84

Hustler parody, 32

Hyperbole, 33

I

IIED. See Intentional Infliction of Emotional Distress (IIED)

Image advertising, 84

Incidental use, 89, 106, 134, 145

Indecency, 234–235, 266

Infringement, see Copyright or Trademark

Injunctions, 19, 62–63, 110

Insults, 33–34, 312

Intellectual Property. See Copyright, Trademark, or Patent

Intelligence Authorization Act, 159

Intentional Infliction of Emotional Distress (IIED), 58–59, 199

International Bureau, 264

International censorship, 293–299

Internet, 283–304 as a public forum, 218–219 cyberbullying, cyberharassment, cyberstalking, 299–300 do not track feature, 286 immunity from claims, 288–290 data privacy regulations, 285–288 foreign censorship, 293–299 GDPR, 286–287 geo-filtering, 299 international aspects, 293–299 jurisdiction, 297–299 privacy policy, 285–286, social media, 300–304 speaking anonymously, 291–293 terms of service(or terms of use), 284–285

Intervention, 179

Intrusion into seclusion, 191–192

Involuntary limited purpose public figure, 45–46

Ivey, Garfield, 59–60

J

Janklow, William, 29

Jewell, Richard, 53

Jobs, Steve, 307

Johnson, Lyndon B., 239

Joint copyright, 96

Jokes, 32

Joplin, Janis, 86

Jordan, Michael, 84

Journalism ethics, 309–315

Jurisdiction, federal courts 5–6, international 297–299

Jurors, access to, 177–179

K

Kaelin, Kato, 29, 44

Kamer, Foster, 306

Kaysen, Susanna, 73

Kelley, Kitty, 48–49

Kennedy, John F. (President), 160

King, Jr., Martin Luther, 85

Knievel, Evel, 32

Koons, Jeff, 134

Kozinski, Alex (Judge), 82–83, 241

L

Lane, Edward, 278

Lanham Act, 117, 121, 146, 255

Leaks, 207–208, 225–227

Lee, Pamela Anderson, 71

Lee, Wen Ho, 207

Leggett, Vanessa, 208

Levy, Chandra, 52

Liar libel, 34–38, 54

Libel, 25–64 -by-implication, 29 criminal libel, 59–60 damages, 47–48 defamatory statement, 26–30 captions, 29–30 defamation by omission, 28–29 headlines, 29–30 from use of photos, 124–127 defenses, 51–57 absolute privilege for statements by officials, 52 anti-SLAPP statutes, 56–57 common interest privilege, 56 consent, 52 fair report privilege, 52–53 libel-proof plaintiff, 51 neutral reportage, 53–55 retraction statutes, 57 SPEECH Act, 57 statute of limitations, 51–52 wire service defense, 55 elements, 26, 48–51 factual assertion, 32–38 falsity, 30 fault, 41–47 involuntary limited purpose public figure, 46

libel tourism, 57 limited purpose public figure (LPPF), 45–47 private person, 46 public figure, 42, 43, 46 public official, 41, 46 valid plaintiff, 38–40

libel per se, 28, 48, 50, 52 libel per quod 28 group libel, 39 injunctions in libel cases, 62–63 republication rule 40–41 substantial truth, 30, 54

Libel tourism, 57

Lies, 241–242

Likelihood of confusion, 117–119

Limbaugh, Rush, 306

Limited purpose public figure (LPPF), 45–47

Limited spectrum argument, 247, 264–266

Locke, John, 15

Locy, Toni, 207

Lohan, Lindsay, 81

Look-alikes, 86

Lotteries, 259–260

Love, Courtney, 300

Lying, allegations of in libel cases, 34–38, constitutional protection for, 241–242

M

Mandatory authority, 11

Marketplace of ideas, 15–16, 213, 310

Massachusetts regulations on ads for tobacco products, 254 on data privacy, 286

Material support to terrorists, regulation of 214

Media Bureau, 264

Media exception, 246

Medico, Charles, 164–165

Mehanna, Tarek, 214

Meiklejohn, Alexander, 16

Mens rea, 230

Merchandise, 85

Michaels, Bret, 71

Midler, Bette, 82

Milkovich, Michael, 35–37

Mill, John Stuart, 309

Miller, Judith, 207–208

Military proceedings, 172

Milton, John, 14, 309

Misappropriation of name and likeness, 80–81. See also Publicity.

Misleading statements, regulation of 255–256

Misrepresenting oneself, 189

Mitchum, Robert, 106

Model releases, 126, 128
Montana, Joe, 87
Moore, Roy, 61
Moore, Tiawanda, 190
Moral rights, 110, 294
Mummers Parade, 33
Murtha, John (Senator), 25
Musical composition rights. See Music rights
Music Licensing Act, fairness in. See Fairness in Music
    Licensing Act
Music Modernization Act, 142
Music, rights and use of, 139–148 blanket license, 141–
    142, 147 composition rights, 140 compulsory license,
    143–144 exclusivity in record contracts, 140 fair use
    of music, 144–146 file-sharing sites, 144 internet radio
    companies, 146 master recordings, 140 mechanical
    license, 143–144 music libraries, 147 parodies, 145
    performing rights organizations (PROs) or performing
    rights societies (PRS), 141–142, 144, 147 podcast, use
    of music in 147 political campaigns, use of music by,
    146 public performance rights, 141, 144 publishers,
    140 sampling, 145 sound recording rights, 140
    synchronization rights, 143–144 videos, use of music
    in 143–144, 147
Must-carry rules, 265

N

Namath, Joe, 89
Narrowly tailored, 17, 216, 245, 247, 250, 254–255
National Endowment for the Arts (NEA), 279
National Park Service's regulation, 96
National security, as a FOIA exception, 162 publication/
    possession of classified information/material, 223–227
NDAs. See Non-disclosure agreements
Negligence, as a standard of fault in libel cases, 43–47
Negligence claims against the media for personal
    injury, 149–154 copycats, 150–151 elements,
    150 encouragement or advice, 151–152 incorrect
    information, 152–153 media-related harm, 153–154
Net neutrality, 272
Neulander, Rabbi, 179
Neutral reportage, 53–55, 312
Newsgathering 187–200 ag gag laws, 195–196 audio
    recordings, 189–191 badges, 196–197 bots,
    197 confidentiality promises, 199 criminal laws
    violation, 198 eavesdropping, 189–191 emails,
    196–197 failure to obey reasonable orders by police,
    192–194 going on property, 188–189 hidden cameras
    and microphones, 194–195 intrusion into seclusion,
    191–192 looking through belongings, 197–198
    misrepresenting oneself, 189 nuclear or military
    facilities, 194 passwords, 196–197 scraping, 197 taking
    photos/video, 191–194 trespass, 188–189 trespass
    to chattels, 197–198 voicemails, 196–197 wiretap,
    189–190

Newsworthiness, definition of, 70–75
Nixon, Richard (President), 105
No derivative works (ND) tag, 102
Non-commercial (NC) tag, 102
Nondisclosure agreements (NDAs), 78
Noriega, Manuel, 175
Norton III, James B., 54

O

Obama, Barack (President), 57, 208, 239, 299
O'Brien, Conan, 269
Obscenity, 233–234, 266
Offensive speech. See Hate Speech.
Office of Government Information Services, 166
Official rules, for contests, 259–261
OGIS. See Office of Government Information
    Services
O'Keefe, James, 192
Olsen, Ashley, 29
Onassis, Jackie, 82, 198
Online publishing. See Internet.
OPEN Government Act, 159, 166
Opinion, 32–38, 64
Orbison, Roy, 140
Osbourne, Sharon, 154
Ottoway, David, 204
Overbroad (or overbreadth), 18–19, 21, 228–229

P

PACER system, 173
Pai, Ajit, 272
Palin, Sarah, 105
Papandrea, Mary-Rose, 226
Parks, Rosa, 86
Parodies, copyright, 104 music, 145 trademark, 118
Passing off, 114
Patents, 92
PATRIOT Act, 227
Payloa, 268–269
Pentagon Papers, 233–234
Performing rights organization (PRO) or Performing rights
    society (PRS), 141–142, 144, 146
Person's name or likeness. See Publicity.
Persuasive authority, 11
Photos usage, 123–138 agency photos, 131–132
    artistic uses, 134 breaking news situations, 133–134
    classified images, 137 creative commons licenses, 132
    currency, use of images, 137 defamatory juxtaposition,
    125–127 ethical issues, 123–124 fair use, 132–134
    handout photos, 132 IIED, 130 image editing software,
    137–138 incidental uses, 134 intentional distortion,
    124–125 libel, 124–127 model release, 126, 128 online
    photos, 132 permission, 135–136 per use license, 131
    pictures of children, 129 privacy, 127–128 publicity

rights, 129–130 sexual images of children, 137 stamps and currency, 137 use of clips, 135

Plagiarism, 110

Plame, Valerie, 207

Plugola, 268–269

Political speech 243–251 anonymity, 247 campaign laws, constitutionality of, 243–247 false statement laws, 248–250 right of reply laws, 247–248

Practical obscurity, 164

Precedent kinds of, 10–11 mandatory authority, 11 persuasive authority, 11, use of, 20

Preponderance of the evidence, 6

Presumed damages, 48

Pretrial publicity, 174–175

Prior restraints, 62–63

Privacy 65–79 constitutional privacy, 65 personal notions of privacy, 66 presumed constitutional privacy, 65 privacy torts, 65–77 statutory privacy, 66

Privacy Act, 179–180, 207

Privacy policy, 285–286

Privacy Protection Act, 210–211, 277

Private censorship, 14, 21, 232, 307–308

Private facts, publication of 66–76 additional defenses, 75–76 celebrity involvement, 71 consent, 69, 75–76, 79 definition of "private," 67–69 elements of a claim, 66–67 highly offensive to a reasonable person, 70 matters of public record, 67 newsworthiness, 70–75

Private figures, in IIED cases, 58–59 in libel cases, 43–47

Privilege, absolute privilege for statements by officials, 52 attorney-client, 203–204 common interest, 56 fair report, 52–53 reporters, 203–209

Privileges and Immunities Clause, 169

Profanity, 219–220, 266

Project Veritas, 61

Promotions. See Contests or Call-outs.

Prosecutorial discretion, 7

Protests, 212–221

Protest zones, 217

Public broadcasting, FCC regulation, 270–271

Public domain, 98–99

Public figure, in IIED cases, 58–59 in libel cases, 41–47, 64

Public forums, 215 limited public forums, 215 non-public forums, 215

Public official, 41–47, 49

Publicity, 80–90 advertisements, 83–85 appropriation of name or likeness, 81–83 commercial purpose, 83–88 descendibility, 88–89 expressive use, 85–87 merchandise, 85 news uses, 87–88

Public performance, 141, 144

Public Safety Bureau, 264

Punitive damages, 48

Purposeful availment test, 297

Q

Quid pro quo corruption, 244, 246

R

Ratzenberger, John, 83

Reasonable expectation of privacy, 192

Reckless disregard. See actual malice.

Refusal of ads, 258

Regulations, as a source of law, 8

Religious hatred, incitement of, 295–296

Remand, 6

Removal, 6

Reported cases, 9

Reporters Committee for Freedom of the Press, 160, 164, 168, 193

Reporters privilege, 203–209

Respondeat superior, 7

Responsible journalism, 294

Restoring Internet Freedom Order, 272

Retractions, 61–62

Retraction statutes, 57

Revenge porn, 130, 236–237

Ribeiro, Alfonso, 95

Ride alongs, 188

Right of access. See Access, right of

Right of publicity. See Publicity

Right of reply, 247–248, 266

Right to be forgotten, 286, 295

Risk-management policy, 308

Rogers, Ginger, 87

Rosen, Steven, 225

Rousseau, Jean Jacques, 15

Rushdie, Salman, 307

S

Saderup, Gary, 85

Salinger, J. D., 105

Schlessinger, Laura, 307

Schmitz, Susan, 278

Schumer, Chuck, 206

Scrutiny, comparison of strict scrutiny and intermediate scrutiny, 17

Sealing orders, 173, 179

Search warrants against journalists, 210–211

Secondary effects, 235

Section 230, 41, 50, 108, 153, 288, 290, 299

Sedition Act, 213

Self-censorship, 315

Self-government theory, 16

SESAC, 141, 146

Service marks, 114

Sexual content, 233–237 child pornography, 236 civil lawsuits, 237 indecency, 234–235 obscenity, 233–234, 266 revenge porn, 236–237 sexting, 236

Sex tapes, 71, 76–77, 79, 127, 130, 237

Share-alike (SA) tag, 101

Shield law, 205–206, 292

Signal (app), 209
Simpson, O. J., 29, 104, 176
Skepticism. See Hume, David.
Skilling, Jeffrey, 175
Smith Act, 213–214
Social media, 300–304, access of government accounts,
    183–184 in courtrooms, 177 threats on, 239–241
Sound-alikes, 82
SoundExchange, 142, 144, 147
Sound recording rights. See Music rights
Spears, Britney, 27
Specialty courts, 4
Speech, commercial, 253–257 government-funded, 278–
    280 student, 274–277 symbolic, 220 unprotected, 17,
    19, 21
SPEECH Act, 57, 299
Spoliation of evidence, 62
Spying on the media, 227
Stare decisis, 11
State action, 13, 21
State courts, 3–5
Statute of limitations, 51–52, 62
Statutes, 8
Stolen Valor Act, 18, 241
Stone, Geoffrey, 226
Stored Communications Act, 78, 196
Strange, Jennifer, 153
Strategic lawsuit against public participation (SLAPP), 56.
    See also Anti-SLAPP statutes
Strict scrutiny, 17, 19, 234, 243, 245, 247
Student Press Law Center (SPLC), 277
Student speech, 274–277
Subpoenas, 199, 203–211
Substantial truth doctrine, 30, 54
Sullivan, L. B., 41
Sunshine Act (1976), 159, 166–167
Supreme Court, 4–5
Swartz, Aaron, 197
Sweepstakes, 259–261
Symbolic speech, 17, 220

T

Taking photos/video, 191–194
Taricani, Jim, 208
Telecommunications Act, 268
Terms of service (or Terms of use), 135, 197, 284–285, 300
Terrorism, speech about, 214
Thompson, Fred, 267
Threat modeling, 209
Threats, 238–241, ethics of, 312 emoji as, 240–241
Time/Place/Manner (TPM) restrictions, 19, 216–218
Tor, 209
Trademark, 113–122 cybersquatting, 120–121
    definition 113–114 dilution, 119–120 duration,
    117 generic terms, 115 immoral, 116 implied

endorsement, 118–119 infringement, 117–119
    likelihood of confusion, 117–119 parodies,
    118 requirements for, 114–115 scandalous,
    116 secondary meaning, 114–115 sufficiently
    distinctive, 115
Trademark Dilution Revision Act, 119
Trade secrets, 77–79
Transformative use, 102. See fair use.
Trespass, 188
Trespass to chattels, 197
Trump, Donald, 94, 183, 272
Twist, Tony, 86
Typosquatting, 120–121

U

United States Code (USC), 8
United States Supreme Court, 4–5
Unprotected speech, 17, 19, 21
U.S. Patent and Trademark Office (USPTO), 114, 116

V

Vague (vagueness), 18–19, 21, 266, 228–229
Valid plaintiff, in libel 38–40
Van Gogh, Theo, 307
V-chip, 268
Video games, publicity claims in, 87 violent
    content, 238
Viewpoint discrimination, 18, 279
Viewpoint neutrality, 18, 215
Violence, incitements to, 214–215
Violent content, 237–238, 312
Visual Artists Rights Act, 110–111
Volokh, Eugene, 300

W

Waits, Tom, 82
Warhol, Andy, 85
Warren, Samuel, 66
Weissman, Keith, 225
Welles, Terri, 118
Wells, information about, as FOIA exemption, 165
Wendt, George, 83
White, Vanna, 82–84
Wikileaks, 206
Williams, Robin, 33
Wire Fraud statute, 196
Wireless Telecom Bureau, 264
Wireline Competition Bureau, 264
Wire service defense, 55
Wiretap, 189–190
Wolf, Josh, 208
Wolfe, Alan M., 54
Woods, Tiger, 86

Work for hire, 96
World Intellectual Property Organization (WIPO), 121
Writ of certiorari, 5
Writ of mandamus, 179

Y

Yates, Andrea, Texas murder trial of, 179

Z

Zenger, John Peter, 15